C. F. Spilman

Yours respectfully
Thomas F. Marshall

SPEECHES AND WRITINGS

OF

Hon. THOMAS F. MARSHALL.

EDITED BY W. L. BARRE.

"His eloquence is classic in its style,
Not brilliant with explosive coruscations
Of heterogenous thought, at random caught
And scattered like a shower of shooting stars
That end in darkness. . . . . .
His earnest and undazzled eye he keeps
Fixed on the sun of Truth, and breathes his words
As easily as eagles cleave the air,
And never pauses till the hight is won,
And all who listen follow where he leads."

CINCINNATI:
APPLEGATE & COMPANY,
43 MAIN STREET,
1858.

CONTENTS.

PAGE

INTRODUCTION, containing a Biographical Sketch of Mr. Marshall, by the Editor........ 3

REPORT ON THE SOUTH CAROLINA ORDINANCE OF NULLIFICATION, made to the Kentucky Legislature, January 9th, 1833........ 13

ADDRESS DELIVERED BEFORE A WHIG CONVENTION, held at Frankfort, Ky., on the 5th of July, 1834........ 26

REPORT ON THE JUDICIARY, made to the Kentucky Legislature, on the 22d of December, 1836........ 47

REPORT ON BANKS, made to the Kentucky Legislature, on the 15th of February, 1840........ 57

SLAVERY LETTERS ADDRESSED TO THE EDITORS OF THE FRANKFORT COMMONWEALTH, containing the argument in favor of the constitutionality of the law of 1833, "Prohibiting the importation of Slaves" into the State of Kentucky, and also defending the propriety and policy of that law, in reply to a pamphlet of Robert Wickliffe, Sen., and to the views taken by other enemies of the law,—published in December, 1840........84–101–113

SPEECH ON THE RESOLUTIONS TO CENSURE JOHN QUINCY ADAMS, delivered in the House of Representatives of the United States, January 25, 26 and 28, 1842........ 142

TO THE PUBLIC, issued to the people of the 10th Congressional District, while Mr. Marshall was a candidate for Congress, in 1845, in reply to certain questions propounded to the several candidates........ 187

PAGE

ADDRESS DELIVERED IN LEXINGTON, KY., ON THE OCCASION OF THE REMOVAL OF C. M. CLAY'S PRESS, August 18th, 1845 196

ADDRESS ON THE LIFE AND CHARACTER OF RICHARD H. MENEFEE, delivered before the Law Society of Transylvania University, in Lexington, Ky., April 12, 1841 211

SPEECH ON THE BILL TO APPROPRIATE THE PROCEEDS OF THE SALES OF THE PUBLIC LANDS, AND GRANT PRE-EMPTION RIGHTS, delivered in the House of Representatives of the United States, on the 6th of July, 1841 232

ADDRESS ON TEMPERANCE, delivered in the Hall of the House of Representatives, before the Congressional Total Abstinence Society, there assembled 255

REPORT OF DEBATE BETWEEN HONS. JOHN J. CRITTENDEN, AND L. W. POWELL, Versailles, Ky., July 10th, 1848 269

ARTICLES FROM THE OLD GUARD, edited by Mr. Marshall, at Frankfort, Ky., in 1850.

NUMBER I.—THE NEW CONSTITUTION 303
NUMBER II.—THE JUDICIARY 320
NUMBER III.—THE JUDICIARY 338
NUMBER IV.—THE JUDICIARY 352
NUMBER V.—THE LEGISLATIVE DEPARTMENT—BEN. HARDIN—PUBLIC DEBT—INTERNAL IMPROVEMENT—THE PUBLIC EXPENDITURE 367
NUMBER VI.—BEN. HARDIN—THE PUBLIC EXPENDITURE—INTERNAL IMPROVEMENT—PUBLIC DEBT—SINKING FUND 385
NUMBER VII.—INTERNAL IMPROVEMENT—JAMES GUTHRIE 402

LETTER TO THE LOUISVILLE JOURNAL, advocating the claims of Mr. Crittenden over those of Mr. Dixon, for a seat in the Senate of the United States, written in November, 1851 409

SPEECH IN OPPOSITION TO THE PRINCIPLES OF THE KNOW-NOTHING ORGANIZATION, delivered at Versailles, Ky., June 25th, 1855 432

INTRODUCTION.

It would seem that a book can not with propriety be ushered into the world without some account of the author, and of the motives which led the editor to its publication. As a Kentuckian born, and many years younger than the author of the following articles, I have from childhood been taught to consider him as one of the sons of my native State, who may justly claim a position in the front ranks of those whom she cherishes as jewels which are destined to form that coronet which is to adorn her historic brow. We of Kentucky, young and old, hold the Hon. Thomas F. Marshall as one of the most effective and gifted of all her popular orators. His reputation, brilliant from his first appearance upon the public stage, has been principally that of a fascinating stump-speaker. For twenty four years, whatever changes his political opinions may have been supposed to have undergone—whatever measures, man, or party, he may have seen occasion to support—he has been the idol of popular assemblies—and, as a speaker, the admiration even of his political opponents.

His success in this way, coupled with other passages, both in his private and public life, and coupled also with the fact, that none of his popular, or forensic speeches have ever been published or reported, save three—which may be considered popular, and which appear in the following pages—has induced the idea with many of his countrymen, who have never heard and do not know him, that he is merely a brilliant declaimer, without depth of learning, solidity of genius, or steadiness of principle. Careless himself of his intellectual progeny, as the bird of the desert, he has chosen to preserve nothing whatever, of all those great efforts at the bar, and very little of those popular addresses which have given him what fame he has; he has left his memory and reputation to oblivion, or to the care of some friend who takes more interest in the matter than he has chosen to do. I have sought, therefore, to collect the scattered evidences of this man's great and profound talents, his stern consistency of principle, and the sturdy courage with which he has sustained it, through all the changes of party for twenty-five years, and to give them in a permanent form to the Public.

Whether we have acted prudently in this matter,—whether it had been better for Mr. MARSHALL, that his writings, few as they are, should have been left in their dispersed condition, the public must and will decide. No criticism that we could pronounce in advance upon our own book could possibly change the case or affect the verdict. Yet we must be allowed to make one remark, as to the peculiar intellectual character of the author. His most distinctive trait is his versatility—not versatility of principle, but of genius and of manner. Let any one read his report on Banking, and the Principles of Paper Currency, and then turn to the oration on the life and character of Richard H. Menefee,—would he conjecture that they were from the same pen, the product of the same mind? Yet there is nothing in the entire series we have collected, which will give the faintest idea of his style as a public speaker—we mean what we call in Kentucky a stump-speaker. Perhaps a few passages from his letter to the Louisville Journal, a very few from his reply to the questions put to him when a candidate for Congress, in 1845, in relation to the slave law, still fewer in reply to Mr. Adams, in 1842, may convey some shadowy notion of it. We have not made this compilation to show what manner of stump-speaker, popular orator, or declaimer he was, but to show that in the intellectual scale, he is something higher, better, purer than all.

Mr. MARSHALL himself has been frequently heard to say, that the world is entirely mistaken in this matter of fine speaking, fine writing, and fine conversation. He thinks that the talents are entirely different,—a speech can not be reported, or an essay spoken. The man who writes speeches that would fire a multitude, will never be read by any body. The man who would attempt to deliver before a crowd, the finest essay ever penned by human genius, as a speech, would inevitably disperse it. Fox wrote speeches, no body ever reads him. Sir James Macintosh spoke essays, no mortal ever listened to him. Yet England crowded to hear Fox, and all England still reads and praises Sir James. Conversation differs from both. He, who in company bursts into splendid declamation, or delivers sage and sustained discourses, though drawn with the power and beauty of Addison, will be shunned by every one. The man who combines all these powers in perfection, is the greatest of human geniuses. We have heard Mr. MARSHALL say that no man ever succeeded in all, save Lord Bolingbroke, the ablest orator in England, the finest writer in Europe, and the most elegant and agreeable drawing-room gentleman in the world. We will attempt no description of Mr. MARSHALL as a public speaker, or the means by which he chains to him for hours and hours the largest crowds, some times composed of all sorts of people, and again purely of the most refined and educated classes.

He is now engaged in delivering what he calls discourses on History. Invitations pour upon him from all parts of the country—villages, towns, and cities. How he is discharging his new vocation, or vindicating his past reputation, will best be seen in the columns of the Louisville Journal, during the twenty consecutive discourses he delivered in that city, without note, memorandum or a scrap of paper before him throughout. He improvises in a style rarely heard out of Italy. Though we have no intention of writing his biography, we must be allowed to give the leading incidents of his life, as throwing some light upon his writings, and offering some evidence and explanation of the character we have ventured to give him.

Thomas Francis Marshall, the eldest son of Doctor Louis Marshall, was born in Frankfort, Kentucky, June seventh, 1801. His father, now aged eighty-five, and who is still living, was the youngest brother of the late John Marshall, Chief Justice of the United States. At the time of the birth of our author, Doctor Marshall resided in the county of Woodford, Kentucky, where he still resides, upon the farm settled by his father, Col. Thomas Marshall, of Virginia, in the year 1783. Our author's early education was conducted by his mother, Mrs. Agatha Marshall, till his twelfth year, when he entered a grammar school, and commenced the study of the dead languages. When he was about fourteen, his father procured an accomplished classical scholar as teacher in his family. By this gentleman were instructed in the Latin and Greek languages some of the finest classical scholars in the Western country, such as Doctor Robert J. Breckenridge, Doctor Louis Green, now President of Danville College, Ky., the Rev. John A. M'Lung, and various others. Our author, under his father's directions, pursued his classical studies till he was twenty years of age, and was never sent to the university, or to any public college. At twenty he was sent to Virginia to study history, as the basis of jurisprudence, and moral and political philosophy. It was not the Chief Justice, but Mr. James Marshall, of Frederic county, Virginia, with whom he studied, a recluse student, and a man of great and varied erudition. He continued his studies there for two years, and returned to his father's at twenty-two years of age, where he pursued the course of reading marked out for him by his uncle till he lost his health, and was utterly prostrated by disease, it was thought, in consequence of his intense application to his books. He was twenty-five years old before he was able to resume his studies, when he commenced the study of law, under the tuition of the Hon. John J. Crittenden, of Kentucky. At twenty-seven he obtained license to practice law in the courts of Kentucky. His proclivities are always said to have been toward politics as a science, and oratory as an art. He had seen little of the world. Educated at home in the country, then sent to Virginia to a secluded country place, then sickening almost to death, and at last having fitted himself in the law, at least far enough to obtain a license, he settled down in the little village of Versailles. In 1829 he went to Virginia, deserting his little village law-office to attend the debates in the Convention then sitting in Richmond. Madison, Monroe, Chief Justice Marshall, Randolph, Leigh, C. Johnson, Tazwell, and a host of others of scarcely less renown were there. He heard them all, for nearly five months, residing for the most part with the Chief Justice. This was the best school he had ever seen.

In February 1830, he went to Washington, and arrived there the day before Col. Hayne spoke on the celebrated Foote's resolutions. He heard Col. Hayne, and afterward Mr. Webster. From that time his mind took a political direction, and he bent himself to the study of the political questions of the day, and entered upon their discussion before the people of his native county with a sweeping enthusiasm, which still characterizes him. Parties at that time in Woodford were nearly equally divided. In 1832, after the veto of the United States Bank, Mr. MARSHALL ran for the Legislature as the friend of Mr. Clay, and was elected in a county polling twelve hundred votes, by a majority of two hundred and sixty-five. During the session which ensued, he was made chairman of the committee on the communication from the State of South Carolina, and made the report which will be found in the following pages. In the spring he settled in Louisville with a sincere purpose, as we have understood, to prosecute his profession, for he was, to use one of his own expressions, "steeped in poverty to the very lips." But his evil genius still followed him, and he again plunged into politics. Twice he represented the city of Louisville in the Legislature of Kentucky, and in 1837 ran for Congress against Mr. Graves, the regular whig nominee. He was beaten of course, and by an immense majority—upward of two thousand—his adopted city casting a majority of four hundred against him. "The iron entered into his soul." "'T were vain to paint to what his feelings grew." He left Louisville instantly and returned to Woodford. The next year he ran for the Legislature from that county, and was elected without opposition. The Legislature rejected him, as being ineligible for want of the full year's residence. He was elected again without opposition, and the next year also. It was at these sessions that he distinguished himself as a debater, on the question of the Charleston, Lexington and Cincinnati railroad, in opposition to the measure, contending for the city of Louisville as the terminus, "heaping coals of fire," as he said, "upon her ungrateful head for the manner in which she had treated him two years before."

During all this time, and at every session, he was the stanch advocate in debate of the slave law of 1832, resisting its repeal. In 1840 he refused to run for the Legislature. That winter the most strenuous efforts were made to repeal his favorite law against the importation of slaves. He had no seat in the Legislature, but at the urgent requests of the friends of the law, presented the arguments he had so often made on the floor of the house, in the form of letters to the Commonwealth, which will be found in the following pages. In the spring of 1841, he was elected to the Congress of the United States, from the Ashland district, without opposition, and commenced his brief career there at the celebrated called session, John Tyler acting President. He spoke often in Congress. There are, however, but two of his Congressional speeches fully reported. Disgusted with the manner in which his first speech was reported, with characteristic irritability, at the close of his second, he insulted the reporters, and ordered them "not to attempt again to pass upon the public their infernal gibberish for his English." They quit reporting him for some time, and took their revenge by squibbing him in their letters written from Washington. At this session Mr. MARSHALL saw proper to separate from the whigs on several very important measures. He voted against Mr. Clay's Bank Bill, and worse than that, he argued against it on the floor of the House, it has been said, with great force. The speech has never been reported, in whole or in part. He was in favor of a Bank of the United States, but objected to the form of the charter. Mr. Adams agreed and voted with him. He voted against the bankrupt law. He was opposed to striking out of the Constitution the veto power. He was sure always to maintain his opinions by his speeches. He contended that he was a whig, and that the whig party had departed from their own long-cherished principles. He ridiculed Mr. Tyler's Administration on the floor, saying that when the history of the country was written, that Administration might be put in a parenthesis, and defined from Lindley Murray, "a parenthesis to be a clause of a sentence enclosed between black lines or brackets, which should be pronounced in a low tone of voice, and might be left out altogether without injuring the sense."

Mr. MARSHALL had offended the leader of his party deeply. Whether he intended to do so or not, it is perfectly evident he was careless about the matter. Upon the expiration of the 27th Congress, he returned home, and declared publicly, in Lexington, that he would not again support Mr. Clay for the Presidency, and declined being a candidate for a second term. This was in 1843. The question of annexation of Texas came up in 1844. Before Mr. Clay wrote his Raleigh letter, Mr. MARSHALL declared himself in favor of annexation, and spoke, upon the invitation of many persons, whigs among others, on that subject in Lexington.

Mr. MARSHALL is known to have declared to a whig friend, that if Mr. Clay would advocate the measure, he would vote for him for the Presidency. Mr. Clay wrote his Raleigh letter, and Mr. MARSHALL voted for Col. Polk.

In 1845, Mr. Marshall ran for Congress against the Hon. Garrett Davis. The district had gone for Mr. Clay, by a majority of 1500, and for Governor Owsley over Butler by 1300. Mr. Marshall was beaten by Mr. Davis 700 votes. In the canvass he gave a full history of the 27th Congress, and vindicated his vote for Mr. Polk on national, not party grounds—declaring that, under similar circumstances, he would have voted against General Washington, and that the territory between the Sabine and the Rio Grande, and stretching from the Gulf of Mexico to the Pacific, was worth more to the United States than four years' administration of the Government by any man who ever had been or ever would be born.

In 1846, he raised a volunteer troop of cavalry, who chose him for their captain, and served in that capacity in Mexico for twelve months. He lost the opportunity of being in the battle of Buena Vista, without fault of his. We know not what he felt; we doubt whether he did himself. A convention was afterward called to revise the Constitution of Kentucky. Mr. Marshall ran for a seat in that body and was beaten, because he was in favor of reviving his old favorite, the slave law, which had been repealed, and he desired to incorporate it into the constitution as part of the fundamental law.

Upon the submission of the new constitution to the people, he edited the "Old Guard" in opposition. The articles which he wrote for that paper will be found in the following pages. He was afterward elected from Woodford for the session in which the contest for the Senate between Mr. Crittenden and Mr. Dixon took place. He stood by his early friend—his master, as he terms him—Mr. Crittenden, and during the session wrote his celebrated letter to the Louisville Journal, defending himself from the charge of hostility to Mr. Clay. He canvassed a large part of the State for General Scott against General Pierce. In 1855, he declared his opposition to the American party, and stated his grounds in a speech which will be found in this work. In 1856 he removed to Chicago, where he still claims his residence. He returned to Kentucky in August of that year, to manage a law suit of great importance, in which he was successful. While in Lexington, his friends literally forced him, understanding that he was opposed to Mr. Buchanan, to take the stump. Again he canvassed considerable portions of the State, and got to Versailles the day of the election. His exertions and exposure, during the most inclement weather, broke down his health. He was attacked by a violent fit of pneumonia, cough, spitting blood, etc., and lay in bed in Frankfort all that winter.

The engraving affixed to this work is an excellent representation of his features. In person he is tall, measuring six feet two inches, very erect and well proportioned. He has passed through a variety of scenes in life, and has been associated intimately with many of the most distinguished men of the nineteenth century. Proud and self relying, his obstinacy has been represented as trimming. The writings of his which we publish, extending from 1832 to 1855, will best explain the character of his understanding, and answer the charge of inconsistency. The fault of the man seems to us to be that he has endeavored to subject the action of parties to the rule of a severe logic, from which he himself never departs. He seems to be a literary politician, a class which has failed, from Rienzi to Guizot and Macauley.

As to Mr. MARSHALL's personal history, were we inclined, we could make a tolerable novel out of it. He has fought four duels; and, amid political pursuits and philosophical studies, has found time to say and do many eccentric things. He has found his way into our leading magazines, and his jokes are considered so very funny, that wretched reporters for newspapers undertake, in their manner and language, to convey the spirit of his immortal wit. We could, from sure information, and with perfect fidelity to the word, communicate some of his jests, but will not. His is that sarcastic levity of tongue, "the stinging of a heart the world hath stung."

Yet those who know him best say that he is kind and gentle, and generous to a fault. His writings show, that although he differed with Mr. Clay, voted against him, and thwarted him as far as he could in his policy, yet, upon the instant that Mr. Clay touched him where they could agree, he sustained that great statesman without the memory of all that the leader had inflicted upon the subordinate. Mr. MARSHALL had been Mr. Clay's friend, when Mr. Clay was in a dead minority. Mr. MARSHALL abandoned Mr. Clay when he was at the head of an overwhelming majority. It has been ascribed to family prejudice. Whether Mr. MARSHALL will ever explain the real cause of the unfriendly relations between Mr. Clay and himself, we know not. What may be his future course of life, we know not; we have already trenched so far upon his private history that we fear to have given offense to him. He may die and give no sign, or he may live to write the history of his country, and to sketch the characters of the great men of the first part of the nineteenth century. He knew many of them, and is a keen observer of events, with a faithful memory; but it is of his mind, not of his manners, his feelings, his peculiarities, personal habits, or the unknown griefs which may have been the cause of his so called eccentricities, that we are the herald, and that through the breathings of that mind itself, in the works we present.

W. L. BARRE.

SPEECHES AND WRITINGS

OF

HON. THOMAS F. MARSHALL.

REPORT ON THE SOUTH CAROLINA ORDINANCE OF NULLIFICATION,

Made to the Kentucky Legislature, January the 9th, 1833.

THE people of South Carolina met in Convention at Columbia, in November 1832. Sustained by the influence of JOHN C. CALHOUN, they denounced the existing revenue laws as unconstitutional, *null* and void. This assumption of a right to sit in judgment upon the acts of the Federal Government, created intense excitement, particularly throughout the Southern States. The Governor of Kentucky, transmitted the proceedings of the Columbia Convention to the State Legislature, with his Message to that body, during its Session of 1832—33. They were referred for consideration to a select Committee, of which Mr. MARSHALL was Chairman. On the 9th of January, 1833, he made the following report: —

THE select committee of the House of Representatives, to whom was referred the message of his Excellency, the Governor, transmitting the documents which contain the proceedings of the Convention, held at Columbia, in South Carolina, in November last, have examined those papers with much care, and beg leave respectfully to report to the house the views they have taken thereon :

The Convention have declared that the existing laws of the United States, imposing duties upon the importation of foreign commodities into the United States, are iniquitous in their principle, and most oppressive and ruinous in their operation; and, moreover, a palpable infraction of the Federal Compact. They have proceeded to decide, authoritatively, that these laws are in violation of the Constitution of the United States, and therefore, null and void; and have directed a course of measures to the Legislature of that State, by which their operation may be obstructed within the territorial limits of South Carolina. In the address to the States, a scheme of general taxation is submitted, with a distinct understanding that it is a concession on the part of South Carolina, which, if promptly met, and in a becoming manner, will be made by her to preserve the Union; and that scheme is, "that the same rate of duty may be imposed upon the protected articles that shall be imposed upon the unprotected, provided that no more revenue be raised than is necessary to meet the demands of the government for constitutional purposes; and provided, also, that a duty, substantially uniform, be imposed upon all foreign articles." It is abundantly obvious, that South Carolina reserves to herself the right of determining what are "constitutional objects;" and should the principle of discrimination in the impost system be abandoned, there is no certainty that the future revenue laws would not be nullified. In the proviso for a substantial uniformity in duties upon all foreign imports, it is impossible not to see a field at once laid open for future disputation and differences. If the intentions of South Carolina be really to prevent future difficulties, she should define, with certainty, what are the "constitutional purposes" for which revenue may be raised. The States should, also, require that the distinction be clearly drawn between an apparent and "substantial uniformity" in the duties imposed upon all foreign imports. The Constitution of the United States declares, that "all duties, imposts and excises shall be uniform throughout the United States:" and your committee are under the impression that the requisition is complied with in the present system. The distinction taken, in the proposition made to the States, would seem to imply, that where a duty was laid upon an article of foreign growth or manufacture, a corresponding tax should be imposed upon similar articles of domestic production. The effect of such a principle is too obvious for commentary, and effectually destroys any hope the friends of American manufactures might derive from the first branch of the proposition, allowing the same rate of duty to be imposed upon protected articles that should be imposed upon unprotected. It would be a great abuse of terms to call any article protected, when loaded with an excise equal to the duty imposed upon its foreign rival. This were not only to forbid the laying a duty, with a view to protection, but to prohibit such incidental protection as would arise from the imposition of duties laid with a sole view to revenue, and adjusted to that standard.

It will not be expected of the committee to enter upon the debated ground of the tariff. They may be permitted, however, to observe, that they can scarcely reconcile the operation of that system, as described in the South Carolina address, with the increase of our navigation, and the extension of our mercantile operations, as communicated by the President of the United States in his message to the present Congress, or the flourishing state of internal trade which we know to exist. The President says, "the returns which have been made out since we last met, will show an increase, during the preceding year, of more than 80,000 tuns in our shipping, and of near forty million dollars in the aggregate of our imports and exports." This picture of growing prosperity, is scarcely compatible with a system which is represented as spreading ruin and desolation over every class of the community, except a few capitalists engaged in manufactures, prematurely begun and artificially sustained. It can not be reconciled with the depression of agriculture, or the idea that that portion of the United States which furnishes almost the whole export upon which foreign trade is based, is ground into poverty and insignificance by an oppressive government.

The committee are unable to perceive that the whole amount of duties falls upon southern productions. They believe that the people of South Carolina pay, like the people every where else, the people of the manufacturing States as well as others, in proportion to their consumption.

The committee believe that the people of this Commonwealth have considered the tariff, so far as it operates to the encouragement of American manufacturers, as a national measure, contributing to our strength and independence, and as a measure decidedly of prospective defense. That its ultimate effect is to develop, to the uttermost, the great natural resources of our country, to enlarge the sphere of our domestic industry and domestic commerce, and to accelerate our advance to that point of opulence and power, which the peculiar advantages of our situation would seem to indicate. Free trade prevails between the States of this Union. The Constitution provides for the unrestrained circulation of commodities, throughout this vast continent. And we can but believe that the permanent residence of the mechanical arts, in any part of it, will be favorable to every branch of industry, in every other part of it. Arts and manufactures require encouragement: they have flourished most in those countries where the government has extended its patronage, and richly have they rewarded, in their matured state, the generous protection which shielded their infancy. In the full perfection in which they exist in other countries, at what conceivable point of time, or under what conceivable state of things, could individual enterprize and capital enter, unaided, into a contest in which the power and resources of foreign governments would certainly be thrown into the scale against them? To deny the principle of protection, is to prohibit manufactures for ever to the United States.

Your committee, without going further into this subject, or without undertaking to decide the extent to which protection ought to be afforded, would remark, that the proposition from South Carolina, should have been made rather in the nature of a remonstrance to Congress, than in the character of an address to the State governments. It is in the style of a proposition for a commercial treaty between sovereign States, in which she lays down her ultimatum, and threatens that, unless it be met speedily, she will dissolve the political connexion already subsisting between the American States. In the view of your committee, that connexion is already dissolved, so far, at least, as the Ordinance of South Carolina can effect so portentous an event. In the view of your committee, the provisions of that Ordinance, and the principles upon which those who framed it have chosen to rest its vindication, are in direct violation of the Constitution of the United States, and if sustained, are immediately subversive of the American Republic. Though, from the tone assumed by Carolina in her address to the States, there is little hope that persuasion or reasoning will produce any effect upon her, your committee have still thought that, in a crisis so momentous, we should spread our constitutional opinions upon the archives of our State.

South Carolina, under the lead of her ablest statesmen in 1832, proclaims a law, laying a duty with a view to protection, and all appropriations for the purposes of international improvement to be plain, palpable violations of the federal compact, and atrocious usurpations upon the part of the general government — a system of legislative plunder, riveted upon her by an irresponsible despotism.

In 1816, this very State, by her champion in Congress, recommends to the general government, the protection of manufactures, with a force of argument not easily resisted.

In 1819, the same talented champion of the South recommends "a judicious system of roads and canals, constructed for the convenience of commerce," "such a system," says Mr. Calhoun, in his report on roads and canals submitted to Congress on the 7th January, 1819, from the department of war, "such a system, by consolidating our union, increasing our wealth and fiscal capacity, would add greatly to our resources in war."

It is of the last importance that judicial decisions should be uniform. If the nation depended for its constitutional law upon South Carolina, it must be confessed that the precedents would be found in irreconcilable conflict. In truth, she led most prominently, in the initiation of that system, to put down which, she would now rend the Union.

The Convention, however, affirm that nullification, or the right of a State to pronounce an authoritative judgment upon the constitutionality of a law, is a right under the Constitution. They deny that this is a revolutionary movement. They disclaim the idea of rebellion. As the Ordinance is the only existing specimen of nullification, it would be well, perhaps, in the solution of this question, to compare its provisions with the Constitution. That instrument declares that the judicial power therein delegated, shall extend to all cases in law and equity arising under the Constitution, the laws of the United States, and treaties made, or which shall be made, under their authority. The Ordinance forbids an appeal to the Supreme Court of the United States, in any case in law or equity, in which the acts of Congress of the 19th of May, 1828, and of the 14th of July, 1832, are, or shall be drawn in question.

The Constitution proclaims itself, and the laws of the United States made in pursuance thereof, and all the treaties made, or which shall be made under the authority of the United States, to be the supreme law of the land, and the judges of every State shall be bound thereby, any thing in the Constitution or laws of any State to the contrary notwithstanding. The Ordinance declares itself paramount and binding upon the citizens of South Carolina, and makes all officers, judicial and others, within the State, swear to observe and execute it.

The Constitution provides that all duties, imposts and excises, shall be uniform throughout the United States. The Ordinance declares that no duties shall be collected within the limits of Carolina, under the existing revenue laws of the Union, although they are in force every where else throughout the United States.

The Constitution gives to Congress the power to provide for calling forth the militia of the Union to execute the laws, suppress insurrections, and repel invasions. The Ordinance declares, that if Congress attempts to execute her laws by force, South Carolina will organize a separate government, and maintain her Ordinance at all hazards.

Your committee conceive the statement of these propositions to render all argument unnecessary.

The extent of the powers of the general government depend most certainly on the Constitution; it is strictly a government of delegated powers, and the powers not delegated to the United States by the Constitution, nor prohibited by it to the States, are reserved to the States respectively, or to the people. But where a power of a sovereign character is expressly granted by that instrument, it would be difficult to maintain that the same power is among the reserved rights of the States. The judicial power in the case under consideration, has been delegated, in express terms, to the general government.

The Convention felt that to maintain their Ordinance, they must abandon the Constitution, and seek elsewhere for argument and illustration. They have accordingly done so, and found the judicial power, not among the reserved rights of the States, but in a theory, partly of their own construction and partly borrowed from certain resolutions of the Virginia Legislature, passed in times of high party excitement. As to the authority of the resolutions in favor of nullification, your committee would remark that the construction given to them by the Convention, has been disavowed in a published letter of Mr. Madison, their venerable author.

Your committee beg leave to give their views of this theory, productive, as it is likely to be, of such important practical results.

It is said that, by our memorable revolution, "the British Colonies in America became, and were declared to be, sovereign and independent States; that as distinct political communities, they entered into a compact, treaty, league or alliance, under the style and title of the Constitution of the United States; but that each remained as absolutely and uncontrolably sovereign as under the articles of confederation, or as any other prince, potentate or sovereign upon earth; that there has not existed at any time such a political body as the people of the United States; that there is not now, nor has there ever been such a relation existing as that of a citizen of New Hampshire and a citizen of South Carolina bound together in the same social compact; that there is not now, nor has there ever been any direct allegiance between the citizens of South Carolina and the Federal Government; the relation between them is through the State; that the general government is in fact a compact between sovereigns, imposing merely a moral obligation upon the States not to exercise certain powers, which still remain in them, and which are in fact unalienable, though we are accustomed to say inaccurately, that they have been surrendered by the States; that the extent of the powers of the general government depends upon the States; in short, that they are as sovereign as Great Britain, France and Russia would be in an alliance, offensive and defensive; that it follows from the nature of their political connexion, and is essential to their preservation, that they, like other sovereigns in the absence of a common arbiter, should be the interpreters of their own agreements, and that in their character of sovereign arbiters, they have the unquestionable right to redress violations and infractions of their compact, and to choose the mode and measure of such redress; that the compact has been violated palpably; that South Carolina has interposed, and by counter legislation, which, from the principles above laid down, is, and must be paramount within her own limits, arrested the operation of the acts, which transcend the charter; "South Carolina can not and will not yield to any department of the federal government, and still less to the Supreme Court of the United States, the creature of a government, which is itself the creature of the States — a right, which enters into the essence of all sovereignty, and without which, it would become a bauble and a name."

Who does not discern in this system, the principles of utter disorganization? It is obvious that the judicial power, in such cases as that under consideration, is as clearly delegated to the government of the United States, as any other power whatever. If South Carolina could not surrender this, as being of the essence of her sovereignty, and therefore unalienable, she could surrender no other sovereign power, legislative or executive; the doctrine denies the validity of the Constitution, and nullifies the whole instrument. It would seem useless in this view of the matter, to appeal to the Constitution: we must drive our inquiries higher and wider — we must explore the foundations upon which that instrument rests its claims to validity, and settle its authority, before we seek to penetrate its meaning. Let us pursue this metaphysical theory (for it seems no less) a little further: They say the powers of the general government are delegated and derivative — the State sovereignties are original and inherent. We would reply, that derivative powers are a trust, and therefore unalienable, but that original and inherent rights can be granted away. The consequence, that flows from this indisputable distinction, is, that if the State governments be primitively, inherently, and of their own right sovereign, and the Constitution was really derived from that source alone, which is assumed as the basis of the argument in the address of the Convention, then the grants contained in the Constitution are valid, and as we have shown the judicial power to be among them, and extending to the very case under consideration, the Ordinance of nullification, from their own showing, is an illegal usurpation of a power, which has been vested in another tribunal.

But we will not place the Constitution upon that ground. It is not a mere treaty of alliance between sovereigns, left to the interpretation of the sword; nor is it dependent, for the execution of its powers, upon the will of twenty-four absolutely sovereign governments. The articles of confederation were the act of the State governments. The old Congress was their creature—and a miserably impotent, dependent creature it was—their acts were mere recommendations, and most frequently disregarded; they were a consulting body merely, and the whole executive authority, or rather entire sovereignty, resided in the States. The fruits of the revolution were likely to be lost in the evils of an inefficient government, and an imperfect union. The great geniuses who achieved the revolution, perceived the defects of their system, and roused the people to a sense of their danger. The Federal Constitution does not derive its authority from the Convention that met at Philadelphia. As the act of that body, it was a mere recommendation of a form of government by which the people of the several States might become united. It was adopted, and made law, by Conventions chosen by the people in each State, in the same manner that their State Constitutions are. The grants of power contained in it are not concessions upon the part of the State governments. They are grants from the people of the States. The State governments did not, and indeed they could not, delegate their authority, which was itself but derivative, but the people, their masters, in adopting the new Constitution, denied them certain powers. The Federal Constitution is the fundamental law of each State, made so by the authority of the people of each State. It is the fundamental law of all the States, made so by the consent of the people of all the States. It created such a body politic as the people of the United States. In the language of Gen. Washington, it consolidated their union.

The science of politics has been thought to have received great improvement from the American revolution, and its soundest principles to have been incorporated in the Federal Constitution. One, and not the least important of these principles is, that all political and governmental power is derivative. The original or *jure divino* right, either in States or princes, is gone. Government is the result of a convention between individuals, deriving its just powers from the consent of the governed. There are no original sovereigns — save each individual man in a state of nature, and his sovereignty extends only to himself. All government is a trust, springing out of the necessities of mankind. It is a conventional method, in every instance, by which the strength and reason of many distinct individuals can be united, in such manner as to give to each the power and protection of the whole. A written Constitution is the deed which creates the trust, and provides a mode of interpretation where difficulties arise. No power, short of that which created, can cancel an instrument so solemn and important; all have an interest in it: nor can it be changed in any other way than by the consent of all, or in such manner as itself provides, or by physical force and revolution. In pursuance of these principles it was made an objection to the articles of confederation, that they had not been ratified by the people, and being dependent upon the State legislatures for their origin, were subject to legislative repeal. The statesmen of that time understood well that a government which was intended to act immediately upon persons and property through its own agents, which was to depend upon itself for the execution of its powers, could not be the result of an international compact; that it could hold no claim of allegiance upon individuals unless it flowed from the people, the pure and only legitimate fountain of power. In the sanctions of the popular authority, therefore, they laid the deep foundations of our social order, and established the relation of citizen and government, with the corresponding duties of allegiance and protection. Your committee can never believe that *government* can justly be created in any other way.

The people of separate and distinct communities are surely competent, voluntarily and upon full deliberation, to unite themselves under one government, with a Constitution containing all the safeguards of liberty, and all the powers necessary for its own preservation: and such a Constitution is perpetually binding upon all. Such a one, and drawn from such a source, the Constitution of the United States purports to be; and such it has been, in its practical operation, for more than forty years, in the constant exercise of those powers which are now denied it. "We, the people," says its caption — "We, the people of the United States, in order to form a more perfect union, establish justice, insure domestic tranquillity, provide for the common defense, promote the general welfare, and secure the blessings of liberty to ourselves and posterity, do ordain and establish this Constitution for the United States of America;" and it has operated these grand results to the full letter of its promise.

South Carolina warns the States against any measure of rashness. Can it be possible that she imagines any State will proceed, in her sovereign capacity, to make war upon her? Does she consider the Constitution so completely at an end, that each State shall seize the sword, which has been committed to our common government? To declare war, is not among the reserved rights. We have no power to enter into alliances, pro or con. Our allegiance to the Constitution requires, that we should obey the call of that power appointed to execute the laws, suppress insurrections, and repel invasions. The people of this commonwealth have obeyed that call, for the latter purpose, whether to the north or to the south. May it please Heaven to spare them the proofs of patriotism, which dangers from domestic sources would compel them to furnish. In the contemplation of an event so calamitous, your committee would forget the terms in which South Carolina announces her lofty resolves, her inflexible determination — terms that would seem to admit neither of answer nor remonstrance. We would remonstrate, we would adjure South Carolina, or those who guide her counsels, by the blood and sufferings of our common ancestors, not to mar their work; not to insult the memory of the dead; not to embitter the last hours of that small remnant of the revolution, who yet linger upon earth, by demonstrating that a republic, that vision of glory which led them on through toil and privation, was a delusion and a cheat. We would adjure them by their own great names — names won in the service of the United States, and hitherto looked upon as a portion of American wealth, — by the talents so gloriously exerted in defense of those very principles which they now denounce — we would adjure them to be satisfied with lawful fame. Let them not dream of a resemblance between their situation and that of the fathers of the revolution. Mankind will not, and can not, recognize it. Should they succeed in goading enthusiasm to madness; should they succeed in infusing their own wild passions into the people of the South, and precipitate the United States into all the horrors and dangers of civil war, the glory which hallows the tomb of the patriot martyr will not be theirs; their past honors will turn to infamy, and they will set in storm and darkness, amid the deep execrations of all mankind.

AN ADDRESS DELIVERED BEFORE A WHIG CONVENTION,

Held at Frankfort, Kentucky, on the 5*th of July*, 1834.

THE Whig party of Kentucky, with great unanimity, opposed the measures of the Jacksonian administration. Denouncing the regal assumptions of power on the part of the Executive, they assembled, in Convention at Frankfort, on the 5th of July, 1834. The following Address was delivered by Mr. MARSHALL, before the Convention. Its effect upon his large and thoroughly aroused auditory was indescribable. The closing reference to the United States Senate, and allusion to HENRY CLAY, are most happily conceived.

MR. PRESIDENT,—During the memorable struggle between Great Britain and her North American Colonies, it was remarked by a great statesman in the British Parliament, that the people of other countries, in estimating the measures of government, decided upon the badness of a principle by the extent of the grievance, but that the Colonists judged the extent of the grievance by the badness of the principle. They looked to remote consequences—"they snuffed the approach of despotism in every tainted breeze." Such was the character of our ancestors. They were not stung into rebellion by long and grinding oppression; they burst no chains, their sensitive ears discerned the clank of fetters at a distance, and they refused to put them on.

Sir, the war of the revolution was a fearful undertaking. Without resources, without allies, without a government, our fathers braved the perils of a contest in which defeat was sure to be followed by confiscation, dishonor and death; a contest in which, according to every probable calculation, defeat was certain. The measure of the English ministry that provoked it, was an "*experiment*," and in its immediate operation, a very gentle one. In a pecuniary point of view, the revenue arising from the obnoxious tax was scarcely worth the powder that was burned at Bunker Hill. In that measure, however, there lurked the germ of political slavery, a seminal principle of future mischief. They resisted it at the threshold. At the period to which I refer, England was at the topmost hight of pride and grandeur. In the language of the great Senator from Massachusetts, "she had dotted over the whole surface of the globe with her possessions and military posts." In the one hand she held the balance of Europe, and with the other she waved in triumph the scepter of the seas. Her vast marine served to consolidate her empire, embracing as it did the opposite extremities of the earth: it gave wings to her power, and to the strength of the lion imparted the speed of the eagle. Under the brilliant administration of Lord Chatham, she had but recently humbled two of the leading powers of Europe, and wrested from France all her American possessions. Nourished "by her salutary neglect," her own colonies had been growing, unheeded, into considerable importance. She now turned her attention to them as a rich source of future revenue. Flushed with victory, gorged with success, she determined to make her provinces contribute to the expenses of her glory. She asserted the right to tax them to be in an assembly where they were not represented. The Colonies were of a different opinion; they quoted Magna Charta upon the Parliament, they appealed to the British constitution, they finally drew the sword and never sheathed it, till they wrung from England such as I have described her, the recognition of that Independence, the declaration of which has made yesterday a day for ever memorable in the history of nations. Pardon me, if I seem to linger upon the recollection of these mighty times. Our fathers fought to establish a system of government under which their posterity might flourish, to the latest ages, in the enjoyment of all that makes men great, and life valuable. With a steadiness and consistency commensurate with the greatness of their object, with a wisdom equal to their courage, with the same firmness and sobriety which had marked their revolutionary career, they proceeded to construct their political constitutions upon the principles for which they had fought.

In their new work they did not permit a rage for novelty, or an ambitious desire of distinguishing themselves by new and brilliant theories of government, to put out the lights of experience, or to draw them from the contemplation of the past. They surveyed their own situation carefully, and adopting the principles best tested by the longest experience, modified and shaped to suit their peculiar condition, they constructed a system of polity under which they and their descendants have advanced in prosperity with a rapidity hitherto unexampled in the history of the human race. It remains to be tested whether, along with their other legacies, they have bequeathed to those descendants their spirit and their foresight.

The principle of representation and the distribution of the powers of government into distinct departments or bodies of magistracy differently constituted, were the great discoveries in political science prior to the American Revolution. For the strict principle that all political authority is delegated, and for the invention of written constitutions, that science is indebted to the founders of our government. The utility of these great principles have been so fully demonstrated by reason and experience, that they have come to be considered as fundamental and indisputable. We may, therefore, safely assume them as true, and consider any new Doctor of Laws, who may assail them, as having obtained his degrees surreptitiously.

Sir, not one or two, but all of these great fundamental truths have been assailed by the present Executive administration of the general government. Independently of the general obligation which the people of this country are under, to watch their public servants and observe any threatened change in their constitution, there is a particular reason for the narrowest scrutiny of every maxim and opinion that emanates from the now President of the United States. That officer has assumed that all his views and opinions, published before his election, were ratified by the people in choosing him as the Chief Magistrate, and that coming from that high authority they are incorporated with and have become the paramount law.

The abuses and corruptions, the falsehoods and delusions which have been practiced by the party now in power, have met with so masterly an exposition in the address upon your table, that I shall confine my remarks to those features in the celebrated "Protest" of the President which have struck me as the most remarkable and appalling.

The subject of that paper may be divided into two great heads, under one of which the President labors to prove that the late resolution of the Senate, in relation to the removal of the public deposits is a violation of the Constitution, inasmuch as it assumes to pass a censure upon a coördinate branch of the government, which is only responsible to the people, or to the Congress, by a regular impeachment and trial in the mode prescribed by the fundamental laws. Under the second, he disputes the fact charged in the resolution, and claims the custody of the public money as a branch of the executive authority.

To the argument of the President, against the right of the Senate to pass such a resolution as the one which elicited the "Protest," there are an hundred answers. It would seem quite sufficient, so far as the "protest" is concerned, to quote from the President and to assert for the Senate, the same right to defend their immunities, and to protest by resolution against what they may deem encroachments upon the legislative power which he claims for himself. It is impossible to perceive any ground for a distinction. But, sir, the whole reasoning of the protest upon this subject is narrow and pedantic, it smells of chicanery, and is based upon a falsehood. The Senate passed no judicial sentence. They did not set as a court to try an impeachment, but as a legislative body, deliberating upon the most important of all the subjects of legislation, the purse of the nation. The resolution had a legislative tendency, and might terminate in an act of Congress replacing the public money in the Bank of the United States. It was so intended. But if it had not been! Why, sir, the Congress is the great inquest of the nation, the two houses are the two eyes of the people. They are authorized "to provide for the common defense and general welfare." They, too, are sworn to support the Constitution. The principle laid down in the protest would annihilate every capacity and function of the Senate, save as a court for the trial of impeachments. The President, it seems, has been so much engaged in superintending the morals of the people, and the press, and the Bank, that he has overlooked those of the Post Office. The Senate have been rummaging there too, although it be an executive department for which the President is only responsible to the people, or by way of regular impeachment and trial. In so doing, according to his notions, they have violated the plainest principles of jurisprudence. They may come to set in judgment upon the Post master General, or, per possibility, upon the President himself, if he will abide by his own doctrines and assume the sole responsibility for the monstrous defalcations of this department. It will be exceedingly difficult, upon the facts disclosed in Mr. Ewing's report, for any Senator to forbear forming an opinion upon the case. The report itself, and any resolution growing out of it, touching the enormous abuses which it unfolds, are unconstitutional assumptions of power. In the language of the President, "if he submit to such censures, the confidence of the people in his ability and virtue, and the character and usefulness of his administration, will soon be at an end." Not only the Senate itself, as a body, but each individual member is bound to shut his eyes against all information upon every subject connected with the departments, lest he might thus prejudge some executive officer. The lower house is within the scope of the President's reasoning. That body can not pass a resolution touching the conduct of any executive officer, unless it amount to an impeachment. What would be thought in England of the doctrine, that neither House of Parliament could debate or resolve upon the conduct of the ministry? Nothing, sir, can be more absurd than to subject the Legislature of a great empire to the rules of the common law, framed for a petit jury.

Although the party now in power have, for the most part, trodden in the worn and vulgar path of usurping factions that have preceded them, yet in one particular they seem to have improved upon their models. Usurpations have generally been gradual. The minds of men have been familiarized to the changes that have been effected by steps so slow and gentle, that they have found themselves in slavery without having been shocked by any one act so violent as to awaken apprehension. Our gentry have reversed this policy. In the space of five years they have achieved what hitherto it has taken generations to accomplish. They have hurried usurpation upon usurpation with a step so rapid, that the people have not had time to view them in one position ere they have found them in another; they can not examine one measure, in all its bearings and aspects, before they are called to the consideration of an other still bolder, and thus have they been hastened over a new road, without time to observe its marks or its course, till by this last gigantic stride they are precipitated into a despotism. Permit me to give one example of this rapid change of position. In the paper read to the cabinet, which contains the President's reasons for the removal of the public moneys from the Bank, we all remember that he derives his right to remove them from the charter itself. He there says that the custody of the public money would seem more naturally to belong to the legislative department, according to the genius of our institutions, but that Congress have parted with it. Here is the argument, sir: The bank charter is a contract between the government and the stockholders, by which, for a valuable consideration, the government has transferred to the bank the custody of the revenue for a limited time; the only reservation to be found in the charter is in that clause which relates to the Secretary of the Treasury. The President proceeds to say, that by this means has devolved upon him, through his subordinate officer, the sole right to remove the deposits should a crisis arise making that measure necessary. Congress have parted with the power and imposed by the charter the duty and responsibility upon the executive department. This was bad enough in all conscience. But in this there was the distinct admission that, under the

Constitution, the purse belonged to the legislature. Although by an "oversight" (that, sir, is the President's phrase, he avails himself of a mistake in the legislature to seize upon this power)—although by an "oversight" they had parted with this flower of all their privileges, still, under that view of the subject, it was but for a limited time. At the expiration of the charter the grant would have terminated, the custody of the funds would have reverted to the original proprietors. But now, sir, what does the President say? Permit me to read the whole passage, and to call the attention of the Convention and the people to what I consider as not the least remarkable feature in this remarkable paper. "Public money," says the protest, "is but a species of public property. It can not be raised by taxation or customs, or brought into the treasury in any other way except by law; but whenever or howsoever obtained, its custody always has been, and always must be, unless the Constitution be changed, intrusted to the executive department. No officer can be created by Congress for the purpose of taking charge of it, whose appointment would not, by the Constitution, at once devolve on the President, and who would not be responsible to him for the faithful performance of his duties." Connect that, sir, with the following: "The act of 1816, establishing the Bank of the United States, directed the deposits of public money to be made in that bank and its branches, in places in which the said bank and branches thereof may be established, 'unless the Secretary of the Treasury should otherwise order and direct,' in which event he was required to give his reasons to Congress. *This was but a continuation of his pre-existing powers, as the head of an executive department to direct where the deposits should be made*, with the superadded obligation of giving his reasons to Congress for making them elsewhere than in the Bank of the United States and its branches. It is not to be considered that this provision in any degree altered the relation between the Secretary of the Treasury and the President, as the responsible head of the executive department, or released the latter from his constitutional obligation to take care that the laws be faithfully executed." Now it appears from this, that although the charter had conferred no power upon the Secretary of the Treasury, the President, as the natural guardian and keeper of the public money, could have removed it from the bank. Here is a change of position, sir, with a vengeance. The "genius of our institutions" seems to have changed since the oracle last spoke. The National Legislature, of which, in the passage of a law, the President is a component part, upon mature deliberation, and after years of discussion, adopt a grave and most important measure of finance, they create a corporation, appoint it their fiscal agent, and establish it as the treasury of the nation. The Senate, the House of Representatives, and the President, in his legislative capacity, approve the bill. A subsequent chief magistrate decides himself to be the original and natural keeper of the public money:—"No officer can be created by Congress for the purpose of taking charge of it, whose appointment would not, by the Constitution, at once devolve on the President, and who would not be responsible to him for the faithful performance of his duties"—"its custody always has been, and always must be, unless the Constitution be changed, intrusted to the executive department." Verily, verily, sir, this furnishes a new argument against the constitutionality of the Bank of the United States. That institution was created by Congress for the purpose of taking charge of the public money; its appointment did not devolve upon the President; it was not made responsible to him for the faithful performance of its duties; it was, therefore, unconstitutional.

The infatuated followers of the President—those who would cling to his skirts till he ascend the imperial throne—still contend that he has not combined, that he does not seek to combine, the purse with the sword. They say that the Protest does not dispute the sole right of the legislature to raise money and to appropriate it—that the President only claims the custody of it when raised, and until appropriated. Sir, what is the meaning of that fundamental maxim in all free governments, that the purse and the sword should be in different hands? Is it a mere theoretical abstraction to round off and preserve the symmetry of a schoolman's system, or is it a great practical truth, essential to the actual enjoyment of liberty, and having its foundations laid deep in the nature of man? It has been thought that whatever accumulation of other powers there might be in the hands of a monarch, that they were harmless so long as the sole and undivided control of the money was possessed by a legislature independent on the crown and representing the nation; and why? Simply because without money no one project of ambition can be carried into effect, either by force or corruption. You may give to the Executive the power of making war, of raising fleets and armies, of appointing ambassadors, of making treaties without the concurrence of either branch of the legislature; but keep from him the purse; place in other hands the means by which fleets and armies are to be sustained, ambassadors paid, and treaties carried into effect; and he can do nothing without the consent of that power. This, sir, is the true and only effectual safeguard against executive encroachments. With this the Commons of England have reigned in a long line of hereditary kings. With this, society is secure beyond the possibility of oppression, unless there take place a corrupt union between the executive and legislative departments. Against that evil our Constitution has aimed to provide by the different modes in which the different bodies of magistracy are appointed. Now, sir, the true power of the purse does not consist altogether either in raising money by taxes and loans, or even in appropriating it by law, but in having the actual custody of it when raised, and the full means of securing its disbursement according to appropriation. Suppose, sir, that you had deposited the annual revenue of your estate in a place selected by yourself as one of perfect safety, one which you had tried long and thoroughly, one which you had constructed for the purpose, one over which you exercised a supervision, into which you could enter for the purpose of examining and counting your money whenever you chose, and a neighbor of yours were to transfer the money into his breeches pocket, or distribute it for safe keeping among a score of friends of his over whom you had no control, and in whom you had no confidence, and were to inform you, that although he could raise no money himself, he was the natural guardian, and entitled to the custody of whatever you raised —is there a man in the world mad enough to say, under these circumstances, that you had the control of your own purse? And yet, this is a parallel case, precisely parallel. Sir, under the doctrines of the protest, the purse is gone from the legislature.

The President can not find the grant of the power which he claims, in the Constitution. Since he has discarded the authority derived to the Secretary of the Treasury from the charter (an authority by far too well qualified and too strictly limited for his purpose, since it reserves the right of legislative revision), he runs up to original executive powers as an inexhaustible fountain upon which he can draw *ad libitum.* Sir, I protest against this. I protest against it as an American citizen; an humble and obscure one, I grant, but still an American citizen, and a descendant of one of those Whigs who poured out their blood like water to secure to their posterity the precious advantage of a written constitution, above and beyond which there is no political power in this country. Sir, the President is heaving at the very foundations of our system—he would strike the key-stone from out the beautiful arch of American liberty. He claims to be the direct representative of the American people, and to be nearer the legitimate source of power than the Senate. The mode of his election places him upon no higher ground than any other department of the government. He derives from that election no other right than to exercise the functions assigned to a President of the United States by the Constitution. Those who framed that instrument foresaw that the chief of a dominant faction might become in this country (as he has in most others claiming to be republics) the most execrable of all tyrants. They, therefore, contrived various bodies of magistracy, some nearer, some more remote, from the people, and they contrived them as a curb upon the executive and upon each other. Against this curb the President is straining hard. God grant that he may not snap it.

But to return to the custody of the public money. If we look into the Constitution of the legislative department, we will find, among others, the following enumerated powers:— "The Congress shall have power to lay and *collect* taxes, duties, imposts, and excises, to pay the debts and provide for the common defense and general welfare of the United States. To borrow money on the credit of the United States." (This last would seem to be an original executive power to be exercised concurrently by the President through the Post Office Department.) "To make all laws which shall be necessary and proper for carrying into execution the foregoing powers, and all the other powers vested by this Constitution in the government of the United States, *or in any department or officer thereof.*" And lastly: "No money shall be drawn from the treasury but in consequence of appropriations made by law." Now I ask if a constitution of government could place the money power more fully in the hands of the legislature? They can not only lay taxes, but collect them—they can borrow money—no money shall be taken from the treasury but in consequence of appropriations made by law. And where, sir, is the treasury? The place where the public money is deposited and kept, most unquestionably. Has the Constitution fixed that place? It has not. Is not such a place necessary in the collection of the revenue and the administration of the finances? Beyond a doubt it is. To whom has the power of collecting the revenue been assigned? To Congress. To whom has the power of passing laws, necessary and proper to the execution of specified powers, been assigned? To Congress: the Constitution, then, has not established a treasury. The establishment of one is essential to the execution of powers vested in the Congress. To Congress alone has been granted the power of making all laws necessary and proper for carrying into execution not only, sir, their own enumerated powers, but all others vested by the Constitution in the government of the United States, or in any department or officer thereof. Sir, the President has thrown us upon the proof of first principles and self-evident truths. He has driven us by his assertions, aye, and his actions too, to the necessity of showing that the Constitution of the United States has separated the purse from the sword.

When we hear the President gravely assert, that no department of the government can inquire into or pass a censure upon the conduct of the Executive without a violation of the Constitution, but that he is bound by his oath of office to protect and preserve the immunities of his department, and to protest and resolve, as loudly as he may choose, against legislative encroachments—that precedents in favor of the executive power, where its action alone is concerned, are binding and not to be disputed, as in the case of removals from office—but that precedents in favor of the legislative power are not at all conclusive upon the President, as in the case of the constitutionality of the Bank of the United States, we are forcibly reminded of the definition given of the royal prerogative in the English law. It is said to be "that special preeminence which the king hath over and above all other persons, and out of the ordinary course of the common law, in right of his royal dignity."

It is evident, indeed, from the whole tenor of the paper, that the President considers himself as invested with authority to amend, to reform, to remodel. He stands somewhat in the attitude of Solon, Lycurgus, or Numa. He claims to be censor of the press, guardian of the morals of the people and of the purity of elections. He speaks of his "fixed determination to return to the people unimpaired the sacred trust they have confided to his charge, to heal the wounds of the Constitution and preserve it from further violation." Who, sir, has inflicted wounds upon the Constitution? Who has conferred upon Andrew Jackson the power to reform it? Who named him to the censorship? Had our State fallen into some mortal distemper? Was our Constitution rotten at the core? Was it necessary to suspend the action of our whole system, to call in a dictator and arm him with plenary powers? And, sir, was this the man?

Mr. President, when we read the professions of puritanical regard for the institutions of this country, with which the protest abounds—when we come to such passages as this, for instance, "It is my fixed determination to persuade my countrymen, so far as I may, that it is not in a splendid government, supported by powerful monopolies and aristocratical establishments, that they will find happiness, or their liberties protection; but in a plain system, void of pomp, *protecting all and granting* favors to none, *dispensing its favors like the dews of heaven, etc.*"—I say, sir, when we read such passages as this, and remember that the present Postmaster General was put into office for the purpose of visiting political opponents with executive vengeance; that under his administration the accumulations of his predecessor have been squandered; that he has borrowed enormous sums without warrant of law; that this fact has been kept from the knowledge of the Congress; that false reports have been made from the department for the purpose of hoodwinking the legislature, and deceiving the nation; that by means of extra allowances a monopoly of the contracts with that department has been secured to political favorites, in fraud of the revenue and the laws—I say, sir, when we remember these things, and are told of a *system protecting all, and granting favors to none*, it requires extraordinary patience to restrain one's self within the bounds of moderate expression.

Sir, to what are we tending? To what have we come? Five years ago such a declaration as we have been considering, from a President of the United States, would of itself have convulsed the world with laughter. If accompanied by any overt act to enforce the claims of power there asserted, an instant impeachment and trial would have been the consequence. What would the people of the United States have said? What would the friends and followers of General Jackson have said, had the younger Adams put forth such a manifesto? If the next five years witness as great a change, "we shall see the diadem sparkling on the President's brow, the imperial purple flowing in his train! We shall learn to tremble at the ferocious visages of murdering Janizaries." We have already had a foretaste of the "seraglio." We have lived to see an American Cabinet dissolved, a great measure of state to turn upon the resentments and intrigues of a "minion and his mistress."

Sir, let us not disguise the truth; let us proclaim it in trumpet tones to our own State, at least. If the principles of the President's protest be acquiesced in—nay, if the seal of popular reprobation be not stamped upon all and sundry the claims of power contained in that portentous paper, then is the Constitution of the United States at an end, and the most remarkable revolution of which there is any record, will have been consummated. Within less than a half century from its foundation, without any pressure from abroad or any known internal disorder, the American republic will have ceased to be, and a despotism the most extensive, the most inexplicable, will have quietly assumed its place without noise, confusion, or bloodshed. Can these things be? They violate the order of nature; they contradict all experience. Other republics have flourished for ages, but they seemed not to rest upon foundations as deep and solid as ours. They have perished, but the seeds of decay are discernible in their original constitution, and can be traced, growing and ripening throughout their history, down to the very crisis of their fate. They have perished from the very necessity of their being; but never, never, sir, did "liberty's great soul depart" from any system into which it had once been infused without a struggle. Rome fell. From "her most high and palmy state" of glory and of power, she bowed her stubborn neck to the yoke of a perpetual dictator. That dictator (mark it well) was a popular idol. He commenced his career of ambition as the champion of popular rights. He came to pull down the proud, the aristocratic, the powerful. He was the enemy of the rich. He proposed and pressed the gratuitous distribution of the public lands among the poorer class of citizens. He ultimately divided them, however, when he came to be the sole guardian of the public property, among his officers and soldiers, as the spoils of victory. Sir, I am describing Cæsar. I am giving a faithful recital of events long since passed. He waged an inexpiable war against a refractory senate—seized upon the public treasure—combined the influence of the purse with the power of the sword—became, in effect, consul, tribune, senate, concentrated in his single hand all the powers of the Constitution, "and bestrode the narrow world like a Colossus." In the possession of absolute power, he still retained the forms of the old republic and feared to take the *name* of king. Under the title of Imperator, he lorded it over his country and mankind. That, sir, was a military title—when rendered literally it means *the general.* We have the word, we have the thing, and the fate of Rome has made that word and that thing ominous to republics. Rome fell, but not before a paper manifesto—not upon a simple summons from the consul elect. The despot came, but not surrounded with scullions and kitchen knights and starveling editors. He came in all the "pride and pomp and circumstance of glorious war." He came with the Gallic legions at his back. He prostrated his country, but he prostrated her by force. That country scorned to yield to the ungrateful citizen upon whom she had heaped honors and offices and command—she summoned around her all that remained of courage and virtue and patriotism. She encountered the usurper, and fell where she had risen, on the field of battle, and bathed in blood. She found some consolation, too, in the character of her conqueror. His noble clemency, his magnanimous forgiveness of personal wrong and hostility to himself, made him at least a generous master. Julius Cæsar was the most accomplished man of his age; inferior to none in eloquence—superior to all in the cabinet, and in the field. His were the "statesman's, soldier's, scholar's eye, tongue, sword," — barring his ambition, he would have been the ornament of his country and his kind.

France, too, in our own times, submitted to a monarch and a master; but France was torn to pieces by the rage of domestic factions. In the tremendous throes of her revolution, in the hour of her travail, and her agony, the neighboring nations combining, rushed upon her and strangled young freedom in its birth. To save herself from dismemberment and conquest, she sought for union and safety under the energetic government of a single ruler. That ruler was Napoleon, and never did the rod of empire fall into hands better fitted to wield it. France bore a terrible front to her enemies, and found glory at least, if not liberty, under his iron sway. France and Rome could plead their necessities; but for us, for us, what apology shall history make to posterity for our abandonment of the rights of mankind? We were at peace with all the world—at home no sedition, no disturbance—our population expanding with an increase unexampled, and employment and the means of subsistence increasing still faster—every class of our citizens happy—every department of industry prosperous—the wages of labor, the profits of capital, the rent of land, all indicating the happiest state of human society. A moneyed institution, one of the finest creations of financial genius, the foundation of which was an era in commerce, had attracted the streams of foreign capital into the great reservoir of American enterprise—had reformed the currency, equalized the exchanges, and placed the domestic trade of the States, and the fiscal operations of the government, upon a footing never before known in an empire so extensive, and utterly impossible between separate and independent communities. American credit was coëxtensive with the fame of the republic, and was supposed to rest upon foundations as durable as the government, as lasting as liberty. The vessel of state rode majestically over the smooth and prosperous ocean that swelled under her in undulations as gentle as the breathings of an infant's slumber. There was no difficulty in the navigation, no storm, no cloud, "not a frown upon the atmosphere." The course of the ship lay straight before her, propitious gales swelled her canvas and fanned her decks. Such was her headway, and so smooth the sea, that she could for a long time have maintained her career without a helmsman—the pilot might have slept without danger. Such, sir, was our condition. The very excess of prosperity begat discontent. To continue the figure, a cry is raised about the expenses of those engaged in working the ship—a silly and delusive cry of retrenchment and reform on board—a new hand is called to the rudder—the veterans who had worked that gallant vessel through many an hour of storm and trial are thrown aside as unfit to hand a sail—"land lubbers,"—men who had never heard the surges of the sea, who knew nothing either of line or compass, are set to work her; and now, sir, under the steerage of folly "sublimed into madness," she is driven, wantonly driven upon a rock that is to shiver her goodly frame to pieces. I have said, sir, that this termination of the American Constitution is out of the harmony of things, and contrary to all the analogies of history. Depend upon it the matter ends not so. The desperate faction which, under cover of the popularity of a favorite chief, has prostrated our policy, spread venality and corruption through every department which they could control—whose reign of terror has been one unbroken series of plunder and usurpations, may destroy the Federal Constitution possibly—they may condense, consolidate into one concrete mass, and place in a single hand all the political powers which that instrument has so wisely separated and distributed among the various organs of the government. But they will never reign over this continent—never, sir. That greatest of all evils has been provided against. There are many wheels in our system. "E. pluribus unum"—it is one State composed of many States. It is not a consolidated empire, but a confederation of republics united upon a national principle—knit together with such exquisite skill as to present one uniform and consistent appearance; the members still retain their separate organization. The machine may be taken to pieces and the parts remain entire. Sir, each rib of that ship of which I spoke, as holding her course at sea so gallantly, is itself a vessel. The cunning architects who constructed her have compounded a whole fleet of frigates into one tremendous man-of-war. If there be among the crew a band of pirates who are resolved to plunder the stores and strand the vessel, dream not, sir, let them not dream that those whose lives, fortunes, liberties and honor are freighted there, will suffer unresistingly. Sooner will they touch the secret springs and separate that stately ship into its original parts. They will do so without a struggle, if possible; if not—if they must founder at sea, they will "incarnadine the deep."

> "The sun that sees their failing day,
> Will mark their sabers' deadly sway,
> And set that night in blood."

Let no man understand me either as a nullifier or revolutionist. I am a National republican of the Webster school. Yet, sir, that great political philosopher, to whom I hold myself more indebted for the very little that I know, than to any living teacher, never taught the doctrine of passive obedience. He well knows that the consolidation of all the powers granted by the Federal Constitution, in a single hand, is a union which he never taught. He knows that it is one of the dangers to which our system is liable, that it is now impending; and, sir, he is resisting it with all the powers of his gigantic genius. A despotism extending over this continent would be the most withering, the most hopeless, the most incurable of any under which the human race has ever groaned. There are no northern barbarians to sweep over it as they did over the despotism established in Europe by the Romans, purging and purifying the political atmosphere, and establishing a new order of things; no Tartar tribes to descend upon us as they do periodically upon the Asiatic empires, sweeping away master and slave in one common wreck. Here, sir, the human intellect would languish and droop in the stagnation of eternal servitude. Sir, I consider the local governments as an essential part of our system. I consider them as the ultimate conservative principle, and as a mean of preserving liberty, for a time at least, even though the central power or general government should terminate in a despotism. This is, indeed, the distinguishing advantage of our system. A revolution in America would not leave the people broken into a disconnected multitude without law or government, and liable to any future forms into which they might be thrown by accident or compressed by force. The choice for them whenever the fearful crisis shall come, will not be between anarchy and slavery. Be these matters as they may, while the members retain their separate organizations, their political capacities and functions, they will never submit to tyranny in the head. A confederation of republics, with a despot at the head of the whole, is a political monster never yet exhibited to the world. But I will not press the subject farther. All good patriots must consider disunion as an evil second only to servitude.

Sir, I have been, I am a devout believer in the reason of mankind. The people at large can certainly have no interest in the overthrow of property, liberty, and law. They are the country. It was to preserve them in safety, freedom and happiness, that this government was instituted. The American people are a generous and a grateful, but they are a sober-minded and a sensible people. They have trusted deeply where they believed they had grounds to trust. Their confidence has been as deeply abused. Look abroad, sir; the frown is gathering on a nation's brow. The thunder cloud is slowly charging, which is to burst upon the heads of those who have deceived, and would have manacled a free people, in a storm of wrath, indignation and reproach, in comparison with which the resolution of the Senate was praise, the roar of artillery at New Orleans but the whisperings of infancy. The President vaunts him of the dangers he has encountered —let him beware of this. The ocean, "when its yeasty war of waves is waging, is not more terrific." His followers delight to call him the "old Roman." Between whom of all that bore that celebrated name and their idol, they may have detected a resemblance, I know not. I recollect one old Roman, however, whose fate might be a beacon. There lived in an early and pure age of that republic, a gallant soldier; there were then many such. When the Gauls had routed the armies and burned the city of the Romans, and all was lost, save the capitol, this man was placed to guard the rock on which it stood. The barbarians came on and found his breast a barrier which they could not pass. With his single arm he made good the defense, and saved the broken remnant of his nation. This man afterward grew presumptuous; he aspired to the sovereignty, and aimed to destroy the Constitution of his country. Has the President, in his late learned researches, since his academic honors have been showered upon him, met with the story of Manlius and the Tarpeian rock? It is an old tale, but not without its moral. That was before the age of the divine Augustus—the god Tiberius had not yet descended upon earth—men were not then worshiped. Patriotism was so common a virtue, that the defense of one's country was considered but as the discharge of an ordinary duty, and conferred no peculiar distinction.

Mr. President, there are in the bosom of every society, bad men and weak men enough to ruin it if they be thrown into power. Providence, however, which is always just to men, and puts before them good and evil, has likewise infused into every community wisdom and virtue to save. Never, sir, did any country produce a greater race of men than are to be found at this instant in the United States. Never in any Senate—no, not even in that which an admiring Gaul mistook for a council of the gods—was there congregated a body of men more eminent for wisdom, eloquence and heroic constancy, than in that which has grappled in desperate conflict with the enraged and reckless head of the executive department. The actors in that scene—"than which no muse of fire that ever ascended the highest heaven of invention, can conceive of aught more swelling and sublime"—the actors in that august scene are fully up to the crisis of the drama. Sir, in that constellation of genius that blazes there, there looms a star of the first magnitude, "its beams unshorn," its brightness undiminished by the proximity of those luminous bodies with which it is now surrounded. It seems rather to have swelled in size and splendor, and still maintains its place at the head of the group, flashing its broad and prophetic light into the far depths of distance. That star arose in the West—it sprang from our own horizon—it has been some times mistaken for a meteor, so brilliant, so rapid was its course—it has proven to be no evanescent exhalation—through cloud, and mist, and vapor, it has struggled on till now "it culminates in the meridian" among the fixed and eternal lights of the skies. Sir, we are forbidden to call names on this floor—it has been deemed invidious to designate individuals. I will not name that star—I need not—I see 't is written in its own bright beams upon the heart of every Whig who hears me.

REPORT ON THE JUCICIARY,

Made to the Kentucky Legislature, on the 22d of December, 1836.

THE Governor of Kentucky, in his Message to the State Legislature, during its session of 1836—37, called attention to the Judiciary. The subject was referred to a committee. On the 22d of December, Mr. MARSHALL, as Chairman of the committee, made the following report. It displays searching investigation, and the closest reasoning. It is an able and vigorous defense of an independent Judiciary, and a correct review of, then, existent defects in that department of State polity: —

THE committee have carefully considered the views taken by the Executive in relation to the Judiciary. The earnestness with which the message presses this subject upon the attention of the Legislature, the recurrence to it at the close of that communication, the evidently lingering anxiety with which he finally quits it, mark the deep interest which the Governor has taken in the subject, and are fully justified in the judgment of the committee by its paramount importance. There is nothing which will engage our deliberations, upon the wise and liberal adjustment of which, depend more eminently the credit and honor of the State, the duration of the most valuable principles in our present constitution, and the liberty, prosperity, and security of the people. It is believed that there is scarcely a dissenting voice in or out of the Legislature as to the propriety of increasing the compensation of the judges. The difficulty lies in settling the precise point to which the salaries should be raised. The committee have thought that this was not altogether arbitrary or capricious, but that there exists some principle, which, when applied to known and existing facts, will guide us to some rationally certain conclusion. In searching for a rule, they have contemplated steadily, in the first place, the public end to be attained. That end is nothing less than a pure, enlightened, and steady administration of justice. The observations of the Governor upon this head, at once profound and practical, comprehensive and brief, have left little for the reasoning or illustration of the committee. In consideration, however, of the incalculable importance of the matter referred to them, they ask the indulgence of the house while they attempt some additional reflections.

Upon the administration of justice among men, depend the security of property, and the enjoyment of liberty. It is the parent of industry by securing its fruits, and as such, is the fountain of revenue and improvement, of civilization, and the arts. In the early stages of society, the executive and judicial authority are generally found united in the same person. The wisest, the bravest, and the strongest man, leads the tribe in war, and settles such disputes as may arise among the members of a simple community in peace. Law is then administered according to the principles of natural equity, and at the discretion of the judge. In an advanced state of society, when the relations of men are infinitely multiplied, that which was so simple in its commencement, becomes the most extensive and complicated of human sciences, embracing every pursuit of man, and every variety of property. The knowledge of it becomes a distinct profession, and requires half a life to attain. The English system of jurisprudence is, perhaps, the most perfect in the world, and the best adapted to a free and commercial people. It is the most perfect, because of the manner in which it has been formed. It is the result, the slow and cautious result, of the joint wisdom of legislators, and judges, through a series of ages, gradually shaping itself, to suit the changes of society in its long march from barbarism to the extreme of commercial refinement. No effort of abstract philosophy can hope to equal a system for the government of men, which has been formed by the experience of men. To master such a system thoroughly, is to have a knowledge of all the relations of human life, and to understand all the business of society.

But this knowledge is not all that is necessary to complete the character or the qualifications of that most important of political functionaries, a great judge. Upon him depend the title to property, the inviolability of contracts, the security of the earnings of labor. He can pass sentence of death, of imprisonment, of infamy. In his hands are placed the life, the liberty, the honor of the citizen. The powers connected with the judicial office, are tremendous; but they spring out of the nature and necessities of human society, and must be deposited somewhere.

To the proper discharge of these duties, learning is necessary; learning, the fruit of long and patient inquiry, and ripened and matured by the mellowing touch of age and experience. But learning is not all; the judge must be impartial. He must be the mouth-piece and organ, merely of the law. At his bar all must be strangers. Acting for the government, he must not stand in awe of power; his decisions bearing upon the rights of individuals, he must not listen to the gentler whispers of affection; settling vast questions of property, he must be above the temptations of want. Understanding the business and the interests of every class, craft and profession, the perfection of his office requires that he should be connected with none. Justice should be his only trade; his time, his talents, and his heart, should be his country's, and his country's alone. Without learning, the best intentioned judge may be misled by the art and subtlety of the bar; without integrity, the most learned will pervert the rules framed for the protection of the weak and the unwary, into the sharpened instruments of fraud and oppression. In the purity and ability of the bench, the poor and the weak have by far the deepest interest; the wealthy and the powerful can speculate upon its corruptions. The salaries which go to sustain its independence are levied upon the rich, for the protection of the indigent; they are the armor taken from the mighty, to shield the impotent.

Human wisdom has not devised, nor philosophy taught, nor experience tested, any check upon power wherever it may be deposited, any preservative to a limited constitution, or any safeguard to personal liberty and the rights of individuals, comparable to this English invention of an independent judiciary.

Antiquity tried all forms of polity, simple and mixed. They threw off the kingly government to obtain liberty; they again fled with terror from the popular, and sought refuge from the bloody fury of proscribing faction in the arms of despotism. Their philosophers taught indeed, that liberty could only be found in a government of fixed laws, but they had discovered no means of controlling the will of men and parties. The history of the ancient democracies, therefore, are brief and bloody, and present, throughout, the picture of the fierce struggles and absolute power of alternate factions, during which the lives, persons, and property of the minority were without protection. Their annals are but the recital of murder and confiscation. The mixed constitution of England, the slow birth of the throes and labor of centuries, springing out of the conflicts between the barons and the king, to which it owes the introduction of the popular principle, boasts of the balanced strength, and security, it derives from the partition of political power among the three orders of the State. The history of England shows, however, that the king, lords, and Commons, are three jarring and eternally contending parties, each aiming at absolute power, and each enjoying it at one period or other of their history. Until the English judiciary became independent, deriving their commissions from one branch of the government, and their salaries from the other, and holding their offices at the pleasure of neither, English liberty had no existence. From the American constitutions we have discarded entirely and for ever the hereditary principle. But though purely and essentially popular in its origin, we have placed limitations upon the sovereign power; we have incorporated certain permanent and eternal principles in written constitutions, and erected an independent judiciary, as the depository and interpreter, the guardian and the priest, of these oracles of freedom. It is in these circumstances, mainly, that we differ from the Republics of antiquity. As a nation, we are great, and free, and prosperous, and happy, and united. Liberty and industry, the twin and giant offspring of our political Union, are the mighty agents which are at work, hand in hand, to achieve for us still further greatness, and deeper glory, than we have as yet enjoyed.

But are we exposed to no dangers? Has faction never exhibited among us its ancient qualities? Have we not seen party in its dominant strength, seeking to overthrow all barriers, and grasping with its wonted rapacity at boundless and uncontrollable authority? And have we not seen our written constitutions, frail and paper checks though they seem, converted into ramparts of adamant, and hurling back into their proper channel the boiling waves of faction, even as the rock repels the raging sea?

The committee feel that they have pressed this view of the subject far enough, the obvious truth and importance of the principles stated with such force and terseness in the message, and which are here only extended, render perhaps all remark from the committee superfluous. The peculiar circumstances of the country must plead their vindication. There seems to be a growing discontent with the present constitution, a spirit of revolution, a restless desire of change. To break up the organic laws and throw society back upon its original elements is always a hazardous operation; to do so from the mere love of experiment is not a proof of wisdom, and is rarely ever productive of good. In searching for the causes of this discontent, among the most prominent seems to be a dissatisfaction with the judicial system. The incapacity of some judges, the frequent fluctuations on the bench and changes among those best calculated for the office, are good grounds of popular discontent. The evil itself, the cause and the remedy, are indicated with equal clearness by the executive. The fault is not in the appointing power. Some of those who seek to change the constitution expect a remedy in an elective judiciary. Without going farther into that subject, the committee will barely remark, that the evils of an unsteady rule of property, resulting from frequent changes on the bench, so happily stated and illustrated in the message, would be increased greatly by this mode. And as to the capacity of the judges, men of the first character and abilities in the profession would be as little inclined to undertake the public business for insufficient salaries, and for a limited time, at the call of the people, as of the executive and senate. The effect of an electioneering court has been anticipated in the previous part of this report. The importance of the object is taken for granted, a pure, enlightened and steady administration of justice. To effect it, the State must be enabled to command to its service the highest qualities which the country affords. Deep learning, strong talents, and spotless integrity, are articles of great value in society, the demand for which is rarely below the supply. The State is by no means without competition in the market; indeed, heretofore, she can scarcely be considered as a rival bidder at all. If she has secured to her use some portion of these costly moral commodities, it is because, connected with them, is for the most part found an enlarged benevolence and a love of honor, which leads the loftiest minds to the service of their country and mankind, at the sacrifice of private interest. The evident rule by which she can command a regular and certain supply, is the measure of reward which the highest abilities in that profession from which the judges must be taken, can command from society. The State price may be some thing below this, though it should approximate it. The permanence and certainty of the salary, the honor connected with the bench, and the more agreeable character of the employment will compensate for some diminution in the pecuniary reward. In treating this subject, the executive has called our attention to the change which has taken place in the value of money since the present salaries were fixed by law. He estimates the value of money, relatively to other commodities at that time, as double what it is now, so that the judges, though nominally they receive the same, in reality are upon half pay.

They are enabled to command for their services but half the necessaries and conveniences of life which they formerly were. As to accumulation, or laying up any thing for their families, that has always been out of the question. If his excellency be right in his estimate, and the committee believe that he is, the State must double the salaries, in order to preserve the spirit of her contract with the judges. If she do not, she has in fact reduced 50 per cent. the pittance which she promised by statute. The Governor thinks, and the committee think with him, that the salaries increased upon this principle will be below the earnings of industrious mediocrity in the profession. In comparing our judicial salaries with those of other countries, where the judiciary is regarded as the main stay of a limited constitution, the committee pass by the judges of England. The great difference in the population, wealth and resources of that country, and in the genius of her institutions, render her example inapplicable. It shows, however, that the people of that country aimed to make their judges really independent, by placing them as far beyond the temptations of want, as they are exempt from the control of power. The land of Hale, and Bacon, and Mansfield, has made the honors of the bench the richest prize in the State; she has secured thereby to the service of justice, and for the improvement of the law, all that was great in science, dignified in learning, and elevated in virtue. She has reared thereby a system of jurisprudence which is the admiration of the world; a system so free as to be adopted by republics; a system in which individual rights are defined with such admirable precision, and protected by remedies so ample, as to preserve in a great degree unimpaired the personal liberty of the subject, when the political constitution tended most to despotism, and private property sacred amid the rage of popular revolution. Passing by England then, the committee beg leave to refer the house to the provision made for their judiciary, by some of the States of this Union. And here, it is to be observed, that the comparison is to be instituted between the present salaries in Kentucky and those cited. The depreciation of money, or the rise in the prices of all articles of consumption, which is the same thing, is general throughout the United States, and will compel the several States to reädjust the government expenditures. At the time, then, when Kentucky gives her supreme court $1,500, and her circuit $1,000, Massachusetts, celebrated for economy and closeness of calculation, gives to the chief justice of her supreme court $3,500, to the associate judges $3,000, and to the chief justice of the court of common pleas $2,100, and to the associate judges of the same court $1,800. Virginia, our mother, gives to the chief justice of her court of appeals $2,720, and to the associate judges $2,500. New York to her supreme court $2,500; Pennsylvania $2,666; Maryland gives to her chancellor $2,600, to her appellate court $2,500. North Carolina gives to her judges of the supreme court each $2,500. South Carolina to her chancellors $3,500, to her other judges, of which she has many more than we, the salaries range from $3,500 to $2,500, according to the different parts of the State where they preside. Georgia gives to her circuit judges $2,100. Alabama to her supreme court $1,750, to her circuit judges $1,500. Mississippi gives her judges $2,000, and Louisiana $5,000.

We have cited enough to show that we are far, far behind the liberality, or rather the policy of other States in the Union. There are, the committee believe, but two, who have imitated our parsimony, and they among the smallest and least important in the Union. The board of internal improvement have made some remarks in their annual report upon the subject of the salaries of the engineers, which are full of sense, and are applicable to every branch of the public expenditure, and contain the true principles of economy.

The committee beg leave to quote them. "The expense of such a work, (say the board,) though conducted with the greatest wisdom, must be considerable, but under the management of ignorance or inexperience can not be estimated. The amount of salary necessary to command the most experienced and skillful engineers vanishes into nothingness, when compared with the vast expense that might be incurred, and altogether lost to the State, by the mistakes and failures of ignorance or inexperience." They have accordingly given to their principal engineer $3,000, and promised him $4,000 for the next year, and to his assistant, a young gentleman, whom they approve for the service, $1,800. Verily this is a strange state of things. A court whose decision is the supreme rule of property for more than half a million of people, and the requisite qualifications for the office costing the labor of half a life, receives from the State $1,500, and a youth, a surveyor of roads and rivers, who may acquire the mathematical principles necessary for him to enter upon his profession in twelve months, receives $1,800. The board of improvement were right. But are we right? Does an able, upright, profound Judiciary save nothing to the public? Can we retain or procure such with the present niggardly salaries which degrade the Judicial office below every other liberal pursuit? The committee believe, that the present number of circuits is not too great, nor the terms too frequent. They believe that the court in the last resort, should have higher salaries than the Circuit Judges. They believe that there are some parts of the State, as Louisville, where the expenses of living, and the amount of labor are so great, that there should be a distinction in their salaries, commensurate with this difference. They venture to recommend that the salaries of the Circuit Judges should be raised to at least $2,000, and of the Judges of the Appellate Court to $2,500. The Chancellor at Louisville, and the Judge of the Circuit Court there, should, to equalize them in fact with the others, receive, the Chancellor $3,000, and the Circuit Judge $2,500.

It is not the business of this committee to provide the ways and means to meet this additional charge upon the treasury. They would feel themselves constrained to propose what they have done, though it led to additional taxation. The increased expense, admitting that there is nothing saved by a modification of the Jury laws, or by some change in the number of the Judicial terms, or in any other way, will be about twenty thousand dollars. The cost of five miles of McAdamized road, to place the Judicial system of a great and growing commonwealth upon a respectable footing, would seem to be no heavy matter. The sum, if collected by a capitation tax, would amount to about four cents a head. If upon our present revenue system, it would be about $1\frac{1}{2}$ cent on the hundred dollars. The proportion between the good to be attained and the instrument is almost ludicrous. Did it cost more, there would be more glory in it, and more importance would probably be attached to it. The insignificance of the means, it would seem, has brought the end, grand as it is, into contempt. The committee have prepared, and beg leave to report a bill for the raising of the salaries of the Judges, leaving the blanks to be filled by the House. In their bill, they have made the salaries prospective. By this means those officers who command the public confidence, and have sufficient reliance upon their own character to risk a resignation, can be reäppointed with a somewhat more adequate provision. Those who fear to trust their pretensions to the ordeal of the appointing power, if there be any such, can linger on the bench upon their present wretched stipend, till death, or the disgrace of such a situation, shall relieve the country and themselves. It is scarcely to be believed that there is any man, however incompetent as a judge, who has not more dignity of mind than to acknowledge such incompetency by continuing in a situation of public trust for half what his brother functionaries receive. And if there be such, it shows into what hands the miserable pittance allowed by law has thrown an office, which, from its nature, should be among the most dignified, as it is, undoubtedly, the most useful and difficult in the Commonwealth.

REPORT ON BANKS,

Made to the Legislature of Kentucky, on the 5th of February, 1840.

THE financial depression of 1837 was succeeded by an universal interest in the condition of the various Banking Institutions throughout the country. The Kentucky Legislature, during its session of 1839—40, appointed a joint committee on Banks, consisting of six members, two from the upper, and four from the lower House,—Mr. MARSHALL being one of the latter. After due investigation, they made a joint report to the Legislature on the 28th of January, 1840. On the 5th of February, Mr. MARSHALL communicated to that body the following additional report. It "was received, read, and three thousand copies ordered to be printed." So highly was it appreciated, that most prudential bankers preserved it in their institutions, as an embodiment of correct banking principles. The financial student may search in vain, the archives of the country, for an abler document upon this subject:—

THE Joint Committee on Banks, in addition to their former report, beg leave respectfully to submit a few suggestions in relation to the dealings of the Banks in Exchange, and the recent suspension of cash payments.

The Exchanges have been the subject of serious complaints in the country, and of frequent and loud denunciations in the Legislature. It seems to be supposed by some persons, that the Banks deal in Bills merely for the purpose of evading the limitations on interest in their charters: that the Exchange is an arbitrary and unnecessary charge, an unjust tax upon the commerce of the country, and a clear and illegal profit to the Banks. Such persons believe that the Banks should be compelled to advance their capital or credit upon the discount of promissory notes alone, and that the Commercial Exchanges should be left to the control and enjoyment of private brokers and individual traders. The reasons mainly for these suspicions among the people, are to be found in the altered state of the Exchanges within a few years. The course of our trade remains unaltered; we deal in the same articles and at the same points. We drive our live stock to Virginia and the Carolinas; we ship our manufactures, and the products of our fields to New Orleans; we import from Philadelphia, Baltimore, and New York. Nature and man and trade are unchanged. Yet a Bill drawn upon the same point, by the same person and upon the same export, has fallen, and the merchant who imports can no longer make his payments abroad upon the same terms as formerly. It is not unnatural that the mass of persons who look not beyond the naked fact, should ascribe it, as they do, to the cupidity and avarice of those to whom the law has allowed, and in whom either the interest of the parties, the law of commerce, habit, or something else, has, in point of fact, vested almost exclusively the management of the business.

Impressed deeply with the opinion that a large participation in the commercial Exchanges is essential to the safety of the Banks and the purity of the currency — that without it they can in no degree fulfill the end of their creation, or discharge the duties which their nature, situation and the circumstances and laws of the country impose upon them — the Committee deem it not impertinent to their duty to state the principles, which, in their judgment, govern the subject and have decided their opinions. The Committee certainly did not conduct their investigations with any disposition to connive at abuses in the Banks. If those institutions lie under heavy obligations, they also enjoy important and valuable privileges. Although, in the legitimate discharge of their appropriate functions, they are inestimable auxiliaries to credit and commerce, still they may be perverted into the most fruitful sources of private ruin and public confusion. The situation of our public affairs is precisely that in which there is the greatest call for steadiness and wisdom upon the part of the Banks, and for candor and firmness, tempered with moderation, upon the part of the Government. It is impossible to treat the conduct of the Banks with any thing like fairness, or at all to explain or reconcile the prejudices and suspicions to which the Committee have heretofore alluded, without extending our view a little back from the present time, and contemplating the great revolution which a few years has brought about in the internal policy and administration of the States of the Union, and their relations with the National Government.

The Committee believe, then, that the Banks can not perform the duties which they were created to perform, without dealing, and that largely, in the exchanges. They can not do that, without which they ought not to exist, to wit, maintain a paper circulation, at all times convertible into gold or silver, without this power. The Committee believe, moreover, from the most thorough scrutiny, that the Bank charges do not exceed the fair rates as determined by commercial circumstances, and that they are far below what private brokers would charge, if free from Bank competition.

Upon the expiration of the charter of the Bank of the United States, and the withdrawal of its capital from our State, a large debt was due to that institution, from our citizens. The total withdrawal of that capital, and the sudden and forced collection of that debt, would have been accompanied by circumstances of distress, the acuteness and force of which, it is not easy to estimate. Kentucky was driven to the necessity of inviting fresh capital, through the agency of Bank charters, conferring upon it important privileges, but regulating and restraining its exercise, and its profits, and thereby saving the country from the sudden collection of its whole debt, and from the unbridled rapacity of private usury and extortion. The Kentucky Banks assumed the debt of the people to the Bank of the United States, and the country passed through a great and total revolution of its currency, without shock or convulsion.

The capital of the Banks consists in stock, subscribed and owned by individuals principally out of the State, and by the State herself. Shortly after the establishment of the Banks, the State went into a liberal and comprehensive system of Internal Improvement — to be conducted by means of foreign loans—the dividends of her Bank stock being pledged for the payment of the interest. It will be perceived, then, that the whole, or nearly the whole, of the dividends of the Bank stock, together with the debt to the Bank of the United States, constituted, at the outset, a charge against our Banks, to be paid abroad. It was, and is, foreign expenditure, to be met by our commerce. In what way could the Banks provide, or can they hereafter provide, for payments of this description, save through the instrumentality of Bills of Exchange? These items are independent of the ordinary commercial debt of the country, growing out of its importations for the annual consumption of the people, or for permanent additions to its capital, in the shape of public works and improvements, which the State is endeavoring to construct in aid of its future industry and production.

There is, also, an other demand against the Banks, growing out of the emigration westward, and the annual investments from this State in the public lands. This differs in its operation from those which we have already enumerated, in as much as it is to be met with specie, not exchange, and thereby imposes upon the Banks the necessity of supplying themselves regularly with an amount of the precious metals equal to it, over and above what the necessities of their circulation would otherwise require. This amount, to be renewed annually, can only be obtained by means of Bills of Exchange, and these importations of specie, to be made merely for the purpose of immediate exportation, are at the entire cost of the Banks. The exportations and investments which are the source of this demand, are a clear and palpable loss of capital to the State of Kentucky, and a loss imposed in the most inconvenient form possible. For these exportations, there is no commercial return of any thing which is to be consumed within our State. They mark the diffusion of the population of the United States, and the rapid settlement, or acquisition, at least, by private individuals, of her vast national domain; a diffusion and settlement, however, which is made at the present expense of capital and people to the older States.

The Banks, in consideration that they are permitted to extend their circulation to twice the amount of their capital, to substitute their credit in the place of coin, and to draw a profit from their Promissory Notes, in which their circulation consists, are under the legal obligation to maintain that circulation at par value with the money of the constitution, by redeeming it always, upon demand, in gold or silver, thereby conferring upon the people an instrument of commerce, of equal value with the precious metals, but of far greater activity, and receiving, as the equivalent for this almost inestimable convenience, the corporate privileges. And how is this to be achieved? The Committee answer, by investing their credit principally in Bills of Exchange; nay, a perfectly sound system of Banking would require that all beyond the original capital of the Banks should be invested in and represent either Bills of Exchange, drawn upon the exports of the country, or Business Paper of short date, and always payable at maturity. The Committee beg leave to explain a position, in their judgment, of the utmost importance, and which they are aware will meet with some opposition. Banks, justly considered among the greatest improvements of modern times, originated among the free and commercial States of the continent of Europe. Genoa, Hamburg, and Amsterdam, struggle for the honor of their invention. Centuries had rolled over the feudal aristocracies, and found them still at tilt and tournament, supporting their warlike pastimes, and barbaric pomp, by exactions and tributes, wrung from the oppressed agriculture of serfs and vassals. Banks were the offspring of liberty and trade—a republican progeny—they have marked or caused the rise of popular industry—the growth of wealth and freedom, among the great body of the people, where ever they have appeared. The first Banks which appeared in Europe, grew out of, and were intended to correct the depreciation of the coin from wearing and clipping. The commercial States to which I have referred, carrying on, at that time, almost the entire trade of Europe, and the balances of payment with the neighboring countries being consequently in their favor, were exposed to an influx of the adulterated, worn and clipped coin of every country in Europe. To protect themselves from the mischiefs of this state, and to rectify commercial exchange, the merchants established Banks of deposit, in which the metallic currency was deposited, according to its actual weight and fineness, and a certificate granted to the depositor, representing the intrinsic value and real amount, by weight, of the metal so deposited. These certificates were called Bank money, and were as much above the value of the currency in common use, as that currency had lost by the wear of the metal. The merchants employed them in all the large transactions of commerce. A Bill drawn upon Amsterdam, payable in these certificates, bore a premium, corresponding to the superiority of the Bank money; and the first idea of a Bank, grew out of the disordered state of the exchanges, and was designed to rectify and to regulate them.

This first plan of a Bank was soon improved upon — suggesting the idea of a paper credit, circulating upon the confidence that it actually represented what it purported upon its face, and that it could be converted, whenever presented at the Bank, into the real amount of the precious metals for which it called, it was perceived that the certificate was preferred to the thing represented, for many reasons. It was more portable. It was easily transmitted to a distant point—any value might be expressed in the small compass of a slip of paper—no time or labor was lost in counting it; and not exceeding in amount the real money of the country which the trade required, it remained in circulation, passed from hand to hand, and never returned to the Bank at all for payment, but only to be renewed when in danger of destruction. It was, also, perceived that in this state of things and in the enjoyment of this most convenient substitute, the metals which it represented were lying idle and unproductive; that so long as the paper certificates completely supplied their place, and performed their functions, this indolence was a dead loss to the country; and, the last improvement, the

Bank of discount and circulation followed, differing somewhat, yet founded upon the original idea of the Bank of deposit. The Committee have traced the principle for which they contend to a great distance, and they fear, after a tedious fashion; but they deem it of the utmost importance, and they wish to explore, and place it firm upon its original, true, and, as they believe, everlasting foundation. And what is the principle? Why, that paper representing coin is preferable, as an instrument of commerce, to coin, and can be circulated within a given country, upon confidence—not authority; upon credit—not force, as a substitute, for an indefinite period of time, provided it do not exceed, in quantity, the amount of coin which the trade and business transactions of the particular country where it is employed, would otherwise absorb and keep in circulation. If the money deposited in the Bank of Amsterdam, which was truly and exactly represented by the Bank certificates of deposit, were greater, at any given time, than the business of Amsterdam required, and she had any relations of foreign trade, there arose at once the temptation to employ this excess abroad. The certificate would be returned to the Bank, the metals drawn and transported, and the circulation, diminished by this amount, go on, without other disturbance, relieved of its excess. What, then, is the great desideratum in modern banking, and what are the means by which the shock of suspensions of cash payments and the consequent destruction of the most delicate of all fabrics, credit, can be warded off and prevented? Are we to be told that the Banks are safe, while they lend upon good and safe securities? That they may advance to any extent, and for any object, and the credit of their paper will be unimpaired—and that confidence will remain unshaken so long as they take substantial guarantees for their debts? If so, a Bank might issue safely to the whole amount of the value of all the real and personal property in the Commonwealth, upon mortgage, which is absurd.

Although confidence in the solvency of a Bank and the soundness of the securities for its debts is all important to the credit of its circulation, yet there are other causes, certain and unavoidable in their operation, which will occasion the return of its circulation upon it to an extent measured by the force of the cause. At this very instant of time our own Banks are unable, in their judgment, to maintain specie payments, although no rational man doubts for an instant the sufficiency of their assets, or their ultimate ability to redeem their circulation and pay their depositors three times over. The circulation of a Bank may return upon it, from distrust of the Bank, from mere panic and alarm, or on account of foreign demand for a subsisting commercial debt, or from an excess of currency. To the two former causes Banks, constituted as ours, are not often liable. To the two latter, all Banks are exposed. To secure the country from an excess of currency, and its consequent depreciation, with the long train of evils which follow, all governments, where the principles of liberty and commercial policy are understood and recognized, require paper, circulating as money and bearing no interest to the holder, to be paid on demand in that which is alone recognized by the laws of this country, and the universal assent of mankind as the standard of value. To protect itself against the constant recurrence of its circulation, and as the best guard over specie payments, the Bank is allowed to deal in exchange. If its whole circulation be invested in funds at the points in favor of which the debt against the country exists, which can only be done by the purchase of bills, is it not at once perceived, that though the whole should return upon it at once, that the foreign demand can be more easily satisfied, by drafts upon funds already at the point where they are required, than in any other way? If our Banks had been supplied with exchange to the extent of their circulation last October, they might have bid defiance to the brokers of Cincinnati. Unless our Banks dealt in exchange, it seems to the Committee that it is scarcely necessary to argue further to show their utter defenselessness. The private dealers, operating upon their currency, would necessarily draw their specie for remittance, and without bills, the Committee know of no way by which the Banks could replenish their vaults.

The Committee have shown, they think, that in a country using a paper currency, and having any foreign commerce, the debt created by its importations, will, without any want of confidence in the issuers of the paper, or any excess of issue, necessarily return their paper upon the Banks, whenever foreign payments are to be made, for the simple reason that the paper will not answer the purpose of remittance, and can not be transmitted to a distant and foreign point without loss. The Banks can have no means of meeting this necessary and regularly recurring demand, unless with specie, or checks upon funds previously provided, at the points where payments are to be made by our merchants. If, with specie, the Banks would be under the necessity of providing it to the extent of the whole commercial debt of the country, the whole business of banking would consist in importing specie to be immediately carried out of the country again, to the great inconvenience and cost of the Banks, in bringing it in, and to the equally great inconvenience and cost of the merchants, in carrying it out. But even this most clumsy and unprofitable of all trades could not be carried on without dealing in bills. A country having no mines can only supply itself with the precious metals by means of bills drawn upon points where the metals can be purchased. To prohibit Banks from dealing in Exchange is the most effectual mode yet devised of breaking down the banking system.

A country having no foreign trade, may, it would seem, extend its paper currency to any conceivable amount. The effect, however, the necessary and unavoidable effect of the great augmentation of a circulating medium, is the depreciation of that medium, in whatever it may consist. In other words, the increase will be absorbed, and exhibit itself in the increased money price of all other commodities, which are the products of labor and the subject of sale or Exchange. This would be the only effect where there was no foreign trade, and a very mischievous and fraudulent effect it would be.

In a country having commercial relations with others, the rise in prices occasioned by a great augmentation in the circulating medium, necessarily increases for the time the importations, and diminishes the exportations, and thereby creates what is called an unfavorable balance of trade against the country having the augmented circulating medium. The balance of commercial debt must be paid, or the trade must cease; neither nations nor individuals give away the productions of their industry. If the debtor country use a metallic circulation, this balance is easily adjusted by the exportation of the metals. This diminishes the circulation in the one country—increases it in the other—relieves the Exchange, and restores the equilibrium of trade. If the debtor country use a paper money, convertible into coin, the same effects will be produced by excess, and the same thing will happen, but in a different way. The paper can not be exported, as it will not satisfy the foreign demand for money. To the extent of that demand it will be thrown back upon the Banks, and the specie drawn for exportation. If the excess of circulation equal the whole specie of the Banks, it will all be drawn. If it exceed it, suspension is the necessary consequence—the paper will depreciate; that depreciation will exhibit itself in the Exchange, and will fall, as a dead loss, upon the mercantile class engaged in importation.

It seems obvious, from these principles, that where the great portion of Bank circulation is based upon the exports of a country, and is represented by bills drawn upon those exports, so far as the Banks are concerned, no improper or unhealthy stimulus can be given to importations. If they be excessive, it can not be ascribed to the currency, nor will such excess affect the stability or the purity of it. The Committee will not extend their views farther on this head, but will pass to the charge of extortion against the Banks in the rates of exchange which they charge. There is one fact developed upon this subject, which, in the judgment of the Committee, settles the question as to whether the Banks exceed, in their charges, the natural rates of exchange as determined by commercial circumstances, or do the business upon better terms than private brokers would do it. It is this: the rates of discount charged by the Banks upon bills drawn on those points against which the balance of trade exists with this country, is always less, from two to three per cent., than the discount charged by brokers upon the Bank paper payable at the same points. The note of a specie-paying Bank ought to be a good Bill of Exchange upon the place where it is payable, and its price elsewhere ought to be regulated by those circumstances which determine the rates of exchange. Those circumstances are, the relative state of the currencies, and the balance of trade. If the paper of two countries be convertible at home into specie, at home, respectively, the currencies are equal to each other, because when measured in the metals, which are the common standard of value throughout the commercial world, they represent equal quantities. A twenty dollar Bank note convertible into specie at Charleston, is worth as much at Charleston as a twenty dollar bank bill convertible into specie at Lexington, is at Lexington. The currencies are, therefore, equal in this state of things, and the only cause operating upon the exchange is the balance of trade. If the debts and credits of two countries are precisely equal, they balance each other, and exchange is even, or the bills drawn in either country upon the other are at par. If the debts of either country exceed what is due to it from the other, exchange is said to be against the debtor country, and bills drawn upon it are at a discount, and bills or checks purchased in it upon the creditor country command a premium. As thus: if one class of merchants at Lexington are indebted to the city of Charleston in any sum, say $10,000, and the city of Charleston is indebted to another class of merchants at Lexington in the same sum, there is at once the foundation of an equal exchange of debts. The Lexington debtor wants funds at Charleston. The Lexington creditor has funds there to an equal amount, which he wants at Lexington. The debtor merchant advances the money to the creditor at Lexington, and receives a bill upon Charleston payable there in specie—he remits the bill, without cost, and pays his debt without the loss of time, or the risk and expense of transmitting the metals. In this state of things, it is evident that there can be no difference, whether the creditor merchant at Lexington give to the debtor a Bill of Exchange, or the note of a specie-paying Bank, at Charleston; they are of equal value. But vary this statement. Suppose that Charleston is indebted to Lexington, and Lexington not indebted to Charleston, which in the course of our trade is always the fact, then the balance of trade is against Charleston, and the man in Lexington who holds a note on Charleston holds a security perfectly good, and worth, at the place of payment, exactly what it purports on its face to be worth; but not payable where it is, and no person there wanting money at Charleston, no person will give for it its par value, and saddle himself with the trouble and loss of time of sending it home, drawing the money, and bringing it to Lexington: the bill or note falls, and it should seem they ought to fall in an equal degree. What should be the natural rate of this fall, or what, in other words, the exchange? Why, evidently, the time lost in remitting the note, and in bringing home the money, the insurance or risk and a profit upon the capital advanced for the bill or note equal to what the person advancing it could make out of it in any other way at home, are the circumstances which determine it. The Banks deal in Bills of Exchange. The brokers in Bank paper. The discount upon bills bought by the Banks is always less than the discount upon notes bought by the brokers, though payable at the same place. There can be no good reason assigned for the difference, but that Banks are enabled to conduct the operations of exchange, by means of their capital, their credit, their agencies, and their connection with the various commercial points with which our industry has any relations, upon better terms and with more certainty than private dealers.

When a Bank buys a bill, having four months to run, it sometimes charges a greater rate of exchange than for a bill upon the same point at a shorter date. The attention of the

Committee was especially directed to this particular. The reasons assigned by the Banks, and which appear satisfactory to the Committee, are, that they purchase bills upon the points at which the great exportations are made from this country, for the purpose of reinvesting their proceeds in exchange upon those points where the balance of payments are against this country. That the facility of obtaining this exchange is greater at some seasons of the year than others. That after a bill which they purchase is paid, it yields them no profit, and is, in fact, dead capital till reinvested. That, in the disturbed state, and unsettled condition of the banking system in the United States, there can be no absolutely certain calculations upon the currency in which the bills are to be paid. That the Banks consider they have a right to an adequate compensation for these circumstances. With regard to the last, they remark that, upon the bills purchased upon the South, before the suspension in October, the Banks have actually lost.

That the Bank of the United States dealt in exchange upon much better terms than the present Banks, is admitted on all hands, we believe. Remittances were made and balances settled, during the existence of that institution, at much less cost to commerce than now. But is it just or fair to ascribe the change to the injustice and extortion of our Banks? We have already glanced at the principles which regulate, and the circumstances which determine, ordinarily, the rates of exchange; let us examine and apply them to the Bank of the United States. The circumstances which mainly influence the commercial exchanges between countries, or States, which trade with each other, are, the relative state of the currencies, and the balance of trade. These causes may be counteracted, or aggravated, in their operation, by the power or weakness of the instruments employed in the commerce. The Bank of the United States was one body, but occupying, with its various branches or members, every point of business in the whole Union. Its dividends were the result of the combined profits of all its branches. It was immaterial to the

Bank whether its funds were in New York or New Orleans, in Lexington or in Charleston, wherever commerce bore or required them, they were for ever active. Whether employed by the parent, or the branch, the profit was still the Bank's, and went to swell the dividends of the stockholders. When the Northern Bank of Kentucky buys a bill upon New Orleans, payable at a season of the year when exchange upon Philadelphia or New York can not be procured, the funds of the Northern Bank, so invested, lie idle in New Orleans, as a deposit, in some Bank there which pays no interest for it, and the Northern Bank compensates, and has a right to compensate, herself for this loss, in the enhanced rate of exchange upon New Orleans. When the Bank of the United States threw funds there, by the same means, she was exposed to no such risk. Until she required them in New York or Philadelphia they were actively employed by her branch at New Orleans, the profits of which were a portion of her own. Here, then, is an item in the rates of exchange which did not enter into the operation of the Bank of the United States. The difference in the machinery of that institution enabled it to save this cost to commerce without loss to itself. If two States trade with each other, and the currency of the one is depreciated below the specie standard, and the other not, this depreciation will be exhibited in the exchange against the country whose currency is depreciated. As thus: a bill drawn upon Mississippi, when Mississippi currency is worth fifteen per cent. less than silver, and sold in Kentucky for a currency equal to silver, the bill would be fifteen per cent. below par, although the balance of trade was even between the two countries. This cause could never operate upon the exchanges between the States during the existence of the Bank of the United States. Its circulation was common to all the States, and was always at par with specie. But even if the Bank of the United States had suspended, its circulation was equal to itself, and any depreciation in it would have been uniform throughout all the States whose currency it composed: so that this cause of fluctuation and disturbance in the exchanges could not happen during the existence of that institution. The balance of trade itself, which among nations having no common currency but the metals, is considered as the great index and regulator of exchanges, had none or scarcely a perceptible influence over the domestic trade of the States. The Bank of the United States equalized the exchanges between the States. And how? The currency of South Carolina, was the currency of Kentucky and the currency of New York, receivable and payable there. The cost of transmitting the metals was saved, by the substitution of a medium which was of par value with them, not only in the debtor State, but at every other point. The stock drover who sold his mules or horses at Charleston, received a paper which lost nothing of its value by being brought to Lexington. The merchant at Lexington, who received it from the drover, need not convert it into a Bill of Exchange upon New York or draw the specie for it. It was itself a Bill of Exchange. It was not South Carolina or Kentucky paper, payable only at those points; it was American money, equal to specie every where, flowing without restraint or depreciation throughout the whole commercial body of which it was the blood. Nothing but the precious metals ever enjoyed so extensive a credit as the paper of that Bank. It was, in relation to the whole Union, what the precious metals are in relation to the whole world, a universal equivalent. Commerce distributed it with just so much more facility and at so much less cost, than it does the precious metals, as is the difference between the physical properties of paper and bullion. That difference is the true measure and the cause of the improved rates of exchange under the operation of that Bank. It would be felt and exhibited though the whole banking system should be disused, and a circulation exclusively metallic adopted in its stead.

This universal credit of the paper of the Bank of the United States had a broader foundation even than its capital. It was the depository of the national revenue, and its paper was received in payment of that revenue. During the existence of the Bank, that revenue was annually equal to the whole capital of the Bank. It was a fund in the hands of the Bank for commercial purposes, up to the very instant when the Government required its disbursement, and the disbursement was then made through means of that very credit which the Bank derived from the revenue. Wherever revenue was payable, there, of course, the paper was in demand. The debts of the interior States were due principally at the great points of importation on the seaboard, and at those points the revenue was mainly collected. Thus, who ever held a note on the Bank of the United States, held a certificate, which, if transmitted to New York, Philadelphia, Boston, Charleston, New Orleans, or to the extremest Western Land Office, was received at its full value, in the payment of a debt to the Government, which debt annually exceeded the whole amount of the circulation of the Bank at any one time. Thus the credit of the Bank was as diffusive as the revenue. When idle to the Government, the revenue was busy in commerce; and when needed by the Government, it was present at the very spot where it was required. It gave to the Bank, strength, and derived from the Bank, activity. To illustrate this connexion, let us put a case: The Government of the United States has its means on deposit with the Bank of the United States in Philadelphia —means which are then actively employed in the commerce of that city; the Government of the United States owes an installment of the public debt, payable in London; she calls upon the Bank for that much of the revenue which the Bank has on deposit; at Charleston and New Orleans the Bank has purchased Bills upon London, drawn upon the cotton exported from those points; the proceeds of those Bills are lying in London, to the credit of the Bank; the Bank gives the Government a draft on London, and the debt is paid. Thus the revenue at Charleston or New Orleans is advanced to commerce in the purchase of English Bills, and the revenue at Philadelphia is thrown to London by the scrape of a pen; and in both cases the circulation is undisturbed; not a dollar changes its place. Let us suppose another case: Two millions of the surplus revenue are due to Kentucky from the

Government of the United States; she directs the Bank at New York or Philadelphia to pay it out of the public deposits there; the commercial debt from Kentucky is due at New York, and it is there that she wants the money; the Bank gives to Kentucky a credit at New York; Kentucky checks on it in favor of her merchants; and thus, by this simple operation, the Bank pays the Government of the United States, the Government pays the State of Kentucky, the commercial debt of Kentucky is paid at New York, and by this general settlement, the State of Kentucky realizes at home the two millions of dollars; and this without the transmission of a cent. Thus did the Bank, the revenue, and the commerce of the country, assist each other. Never were the foundations of credit dug so deep as those of the Bank of the United States, and never did foundations better sustain a superstructure. With a capital of thirty-five millions, the Government deposits thirty-five millions more, and a credit of thirty-five millions more, derived from its receivability in payment of the revenue, it is not to be wondered at, that the credit of a circulation of twenty-one millions was equal to gold and silver.

The committee have referred to this subject, from a desire simply to rescue our present Banks, in the eyes of the people, from an odium, on account of evils and disorders, with which they are not justly chargeable. It is the hight of cruelty to exact duties from agents upon whom there is not conferred the power to perform them. The clamor against the Banks upon the subject of Exchange, has, we have no doubt, had its influence upon their management, and may force them into a line of dealing which will convert a sound circulating credit into a wretched system of paper money. By a circulating credit, we mean a Bank paper based upon confidence, and convertible into cash at the will of the holder: by paper money, a medium forced upon the people by the authority of government, inconvertible, and not intrinsically worth what it affects to represent, and circulating either by a direct exertion of the power of the State, or submitted to from the force of circumstances induced by vicious legislation. An illustration of the first may be found in the paper of the Bank of the United States; the Assignats of France or the Commonwealth's Bank of Kentucky may serve as examples of the latter. The committee place a high estimate upon a well regulated banking system, and have stated some of the advantages flowing from it; but paper credit has its dangers, and they are terrific. That a currency consisting of Bank notes can be kept permanently sound with the check of cash payments thrown off, is at war with all experience. The Committee mean not to deny that there are occasions when a temporary suspension of cash payments is to be justified. In the commercial system of the world, there occur some times convulsions against which no foresight can provide, and which baffle and render inefficient all the calculations of prudence; but the rules and maxims of wisdom and experience, though wisdom herself may dispense with them on occasions which know no law, are never to be lost sight of, nor thrown away. The suspension of 1837 may be justified, not as an example, but as an exception to all rules. That case stands upon its own reasons. It was indeed the regular consequence of a series of commercial and political events over which our Banks had no control, and for which they are not responsible, but which should afford to them and to us, matter for deep reflection. If that case is relied upon to prove the propriety of habitual suspensions, and to establish as a general rule, that our Banks are at liberty to suspend whenever the Banks at New Orleans and Philadelphia suspend, and are then only to resume when they resume, we deny its authority. This were to place our currency, nay more, our law, at the foot, not of an other government, but of the private corporations of other governments, and they recreant from the obligations of their own laws. Great changes have come over the United States in a few years; but the principles of credit and the nature of sovereignty can not be so utterly revolutionized, or fallen, rather, as to require so monstrous a sacrifice as this. The commercial system we know is a sensitive one; the shock of 1837 vibrated through every nerve and fiber of its whole frame. Kentucky was affected sympathetically. The present condition of her Banks shows that she has nearly recovered from the effects of that event.

Great changes have come over the United States. The payment of the national debt, the expiration of the charter of the Bank of the United States, the reduction of the tariff, the stupendous system of debt, internal improvement and banking, adopted by the States, were events, any one of which must have been followed by important consequences; but when combined, and all operating in the same direction, they afford a spectacle at which those who are intrusted with the management of public affairs may pause and ponder. Are we to search for new rules of political conduct, or to apply old ones to a new state of political circumstances? Shall we rush upon expedients, or resort to the steady guidance of tried principles? Shall we pay debts by the destruction of credit, and out of prostrate credit wring the means of supplying boundless exertion, with inexhaustible finance? Shall we vail from the people the true condition of our public affairs; impose upon the Banks the necessity, or at least afford the pretext and apology, for an indefinite suspension of their legal obligations, by large government loans upon time, and hide our own improvident timidity, beneath the ample folds of a depreciated currency, that mantle which, like charity, "covereth a multitude of sins?" The facility with which the Legislature passed over the suspension of 1837 without rebuke, the recurrence of a similiar event in 1839, are fast familiarizing the public mind with what ought justly to be regarded as the most threatening and portentous omen of the times. In a period of suspension every temptation to error allures the Banks, the Government, and the people. The Banks, the very law of whose being is profit, are directly interested in the continuance of a suspension, provided it does not work a forfeiture of their charters. Mark the advantages; they are authorized to extend their credit to twice the amount of their capital, exclusive of their deposits.

We have already shown that the check of cash payments limits their circulation to the real demand, or if an excess be committed, such excess, by the necessary operation of the thing and the conservative principle in commerce, is thrown back upon the Bank. Take off this check, and there is no limit to their issues or circulation, except the limitation in their charters to twice the amount of their capital, if indeed their charters can be considered as any longer binding. In this state of things the dealings in exchange or in real transactions is no longer a guarantee against excess, but becomes each a means of increasing it. The proceeds of the bill purchased are not, and need not be, employed in the redemption of the circulation thrown out in purchasing it. That remains in the channel, and the exchange is loaned upon accommodation paper. Business notes, based upon real transactions, may also become the means of extending the circulation indefinitely. A single piece of property may change owners an hundred times, and upon each transfer a business note be given and negotiated at the Bank. Thus A may sell to B and take his note, B to C, and so on, till the value of a single article may be represented an hundred times by as many notes in Bank, and a corresponding amount of their circulation be thrown out. Without cash payments the circulation will, of itself, never return.

But is this increased circulation of debt an increase of capital to the country? Is there actually that much more money in the world? If so, an irredeemable paper, and an irresponsible Bank, are the most glorious inventions of the mind of man. Where slumbers the conservative principle which we have spoken of and described as limiting the circulation of a specie paying Bank? It never slumbers, it is in active operation, but in a different way. It formerly limited the amount of the paper, it now limits its value. Increase the amount as you will, you can not increase thereby your wealth, and the changeless law of equality cuts down the currency by depreciation to the specie standard. This depreciation exhibits itself in the increased prices of every thing, including the precious metals, if indeed they make their appearance at all in such company. But chiefly and most clearly it is made manifest in the commercial exchanges with other countries. We can not palm off the product of our labor in exchange for that of other countries, at the price affixed by our altered standard. The exchange must be settled by an other rule. A yard of cloth will have laid on it, by way of exchange, the full amount of depreciation, though it be an hundred per cent. A mule sold in Carolina will have the full amount of depreciation taken off his price there. Thus, whether we buy or sell, we lose it. This will alter the exchange with Carolina, an event which some persons seem so anxiously to desire. Bills drawn upon her will not be at a discount then. But the most iniquitous effect of depreciating money is that upon contracts previously made, and here the law interposes: "No State shall make any thing but gold and silver a legal tender for debts." This is the eternal recognition of the principles of this report. Here is established, by constitutional consecration a principle equally dear to commerce and to freedom. And here, too, is the point of greatest danger. Practically, the metals are banished from circulation when, legally, they are demandable. Practically, says the creditor, if I take this money I lose my debt, or a portion of it at least. Legally, says the debtor, if you require specie you sacrifice my property and require what the course of the laws have rendered it impossible for me to furnish. The country must have *relief*. All confidence between man and man, all faith in the laws, is gone. Every man wishes to get what he can before worse times come on. Creditor is precipitated upon debtor, and a long catalogue of evils, fresh in the memory of men yet alive, follow in the rear. One of the distinguishing features in depreciation is, that the farther you go in it the more difficult to return. It is easy, very easy to pause upon the threshold. We have not crossed it, and we need not.

The Committee do not charge the Banks with a design to perpetuate the suspension; but we know that the career of depreciation would not check their profits. The power to increase their debts to twice the amount of their capital, without the obligation to pay, but on the contrary drawing an interest from their own excesses, is a stupendous privilege, and a fierce temptation. What, then, do the Committee recommend? The effect of the suspension, if the Banks continue to act prudently, and with an eye to resume, will be to enable them gradually to rectify the errors which they may have heretofore committed. The proportions of Exchange and specie to circulation and deposits, the limitation of their direct loans to their original capital, or to an amount below it, are circumstances which the Banks themselves say indicate a sound course of business. The process of resumption is not very profitable to the Banks, and not very agreeable for the time to the country. It does not, however, involve necessarily, any great or violent reduction of the circulating medium. It need not be reduced below the point to which specie payments must and does limit it, and that is the true and healthy point. It, most probably, is not above that point at this instant. The Bank officers understand the steps which they should take, better than the Legislature can dictate them. Perhaps the most prudent course for the government to pursue, is simply to speak to their interest, by prohibiting the possibility of any profit to be made out of the suspension, leaving the precise steps by which resumption is to be effected, to the experience and discretion of the directory themselves; retain the penalties, and prohibit any dividend over six per cent. upon the capital during suspension, and the State, perhaps, would hold a more effectual guarantee than would be furnished by any statute attempting to fix the limit of their circulation, or to mark out the precise course of their dealing in detail. No man, who will attentively examine their reports, can doubt the sufficiency of their assets or their entire solvency. The great demand for specie, which they say occasioned the suspension in October, a demand which they had no means available to satisfy, was not brought about, at least not entirely, by their mismanagement. The Banks had a right to calculate on the loan of a million authorized by the last General Assembly as a means of satisfying the commercial debt of the country. That loan failed, and their exchange was diminished to that extent, the commercial debt remaining nearly the same with what it would have been had the loan succeeded.

We wish to do these institutions entire justice, and will endeavor to explain the operation of the State loan and the consequence of its failure. The State, when she negotiates a loan abroad, does not realize it by introducing that much money from abroad. She has a credit at the place where the loan is made. Upon this she draws, and the Banks advance the money here upon these drafts, which are then in the hands of the Banks as so much eastern Exchange. It will be at once perceived that this necessarily occasions an expansion of the Bank circulation — an expansion, however, which does not threaten its purity, as the Banks hold in their hands the certain means of its absorption, and as it is sure to return upon them so soon as it has performed the function for which it was destined by the State. Now the failure to negotiate this loan was followed by two important consequences. The Banks relying upon this, did not supply themselves with exchange from other sources as abundantly as they otherwise would have done; and yet made large advances to the Board of Internal Improvement upon direct loan. It was perhaps their duty to do so in the then condition of the State; but the effect was certainly to swell the currency, with no other means in the hands of the Bank to meet such extension, save the obligation of the Board of Internal Improvement. It is not the duty of this Committee to indicate the policy in relation to the system of Internal Improvement, and they have only alluded to it as connected with the currency. It must be evident, however that under a permanent system of suspension, Government loans from the Banks, exhibited in the increased circulation of Bank paper, may become a pregnant and most aggravated cause of depreciation.

The committee, in conclusion, beg leave again to reiterate

the principles with which they set out. Bank paper is not capital, but credit — a credit equal to cash only so long as it is convertible into cash. A currency, so composed, is pure only so long as it is intrinsically worth what it purports to be worth. A sound paper currency can only be permanently maintained by the check of cash payments. A sound paper currency and a sound Banking system, may be maintained within any given country, without reference to the policy or unsoundness of any other country. No country can permanently maintain a greater currency, in value, whatever may be its nominal amount, than the extent of its industry and production, its trade and business, will support with reference to the common standard of value among commercial nations. The laws of trade and the operations of exchange will cut it down, by depreciation, to the common measure of mankind. Every effort to achieve what is, in nature, impossible, will be followed by mischief and injustice. Bank paper being credit, the purity of which depends upon its always being met upon demand, is, from its nature, designed to circulate and exchange the annual and marketable products of industry, and is, therefore, an unfit subject for long loans and permanent investments. As an advance upon real transactions, an advance to be returned when the transaction is terminated, Bank credit is the fruitful source of activity and punctuality in business, and of inestimable value to labor and production. Beyond this point it is always dangerous. In illustration of this principle, the committee have heretofore laid it down as a test of sound banking, "that all beyond the original capital of the Banks, being the whole of its credit, should be invested in and represent either Bills of Exchange, drawn upon the exports of the country, or business paper of short date, and always payable at maturity." The operation of this principle limits the circulation at any given time to the actual business of the time. But that circulation by no means represents the total of the operations of the Bank, or the extent of its accommodations to the people. A different course of dealing will swell the circulation by permitting it to lie in and clog the channels of industry, without extending any additional accommodation to the people, or increasing the sum of commercial transactions. As thus: the total exports of Kentucky, represented by bills drawn on it, is exchanged with the Bank for its paper here, and at this time measures its circulation. That circulation is distributed in the first instance among the people, in proportion to the amount of the exports which each one produced and sold. The exchange into which those Bills were converted, is intended to pay the commercial debt of the country, and is advanced to the merchants, on business paper, due from the people in whose hands the circulation is, and payable at such time as the new supply of Bills drawn upon the exports comes round. The Banks then draw in their circulation, by the collection of the notes, and immediately throw it out again in the purchase of new Bills, drawn on the second production of the country's labor. Here we see that there is advanced to the people, through the exporting merchants in the first instance, a credit in Bank paper equivalent to cash, to the whole extent of the surplus and vendible products of their labor; and an other credit to the same people, through their importing merchants for what they have purchased; and this credit is extended till the very period when the exporting merchants again purchase the annual product, when it is collected, but immediately reïssued in the purchase of new Bills, and again thrown back by the trader upon the people in the purchase of the products of labor, and this without increasing circulation, but limiting it, and accommodating it exactly to the prices which the laws of supply and demand affix to the productions of industry. This, in the judgment of the committee, is sound banking, and is evidently exposed to no dangers in the ordinary course of human transactions.

Let us examine the other mode and see whether it affords really any increased facilities to industry. The circulation is thrown out in the same way, the proceeds of the bills are invested in accommodation paper, yielding an interest to the Bank, and including the premiums upon exchange. The season of the year comes round for a new sale of Bills; the Bank again purchases, but not having drawn in her former issues, which are represented by the accommodation paper at interest, the next issue is a clear addition to the circulation without adding to the amount of property circulated, (which is the only real capital in the matter,) or affording any additional aid to the business of the country. Let this operation be repeated several times, and what is its effect. The increased circulation exhibits itself in the high prices of every thing; prices, however, which are not favorable to production, (for exportation diminishes under them,) but which necessarily swell the importations. The debts are increased, the means diminished. The Bank has not exchange, it rises, the commercial debt presses. The Banks can not relieve the community, nor the community the Banks. They are both in debt. The whole pressure both of the commercial and Bank debt falls, with combined and horrid force, upon the community. Suspension is of course the consequence. Money was never known so scarce, though we have just seen that the amount was excessive. How is this paradox to be explained? It was not money, it was credit. The debt to be paid represents its amount, but the value is altered and cut down just in proportion to the excess committed. A Bank note for $100 will not pay a foreign debt of $100. The excess has caused depreciation, and the power of the money to pay debts is diminished in proportion. Quantity is squared to value, and nominal abundance is the cause of real scarcity. And this the Committee call unsound banking.

In illustration of their idea, that the business may be large and the circulation small, the Committee beg leave to refer to one undoubted but pregnant fact. The Bank of the United States conducted the whole foreign and domestic Exchanges of the Union, dealt largely in discounts, collected and disbursed the whole National Revenue, paid the annual interest and gradually sank the principal of the public debt, and upon a circulation of twenty-one millions of dollars, with a capital of thirty-five millions. Just before the last suspension of specie payments, the Bank circulation in the United States amounted to nearly two hundred millions. Whatever inference may be drawn from them, the facts are undoubted. The Committee believe that they demonstrate that circulation is efficient in proportion to its activity, and that its bulk is diminished in the same proportion. The Banks in Kentucky have not, the Committee know they have not, committed such wild excesses as have been here described. The disastrous failures in the South bore heavily on the Bill line, particularly in the Bank of Kentucky in 1837. The apparent increase of her Discount line was produced in this way. She forbore to press her customers to instant bankruptcy, but gave them breathing time. A strong constitution,—and our Banks are strong—may bear occasional excesses and recover, but beware of repetitions. Their frequent recurrence entails disease, prostration, madness and death. With these suggestions the Committee quit the subject, hoping that the Banks, guided by their own good sense and integrity, may, in pursuance of principles which they well understand, lend their whole policy and means to bring about the earliest possible resumption, consistent with the steady maintenance, in future, of cash payment.

LETTERS TO THE EDITORS OF THF FRANKFORT COMMON-WEALTH,

CONTAINING THE ARGUMENT IN FAVOR OF THE CONSTITUTIONALITY OF THE LAW OF 1833, "PROHIBITING THE IMPORTATION OF SLAVES INTO THIS COMMONWEALTH," AND ALSO DEFENDING THE PROPRIETY AND POLICY OF THAT LAW, IN REPLY TO A PAMPHLET OF ROBERT WICKLIFFE, SEN., AND TO THE VIEWS TAKEN BY OTHER ENEMIES OF THE LAW.

NO. I.

The objections to the law of 1833, "prohibiting the importation of Slaves into this State," considered with reference to the Constitution of Kentucky.

ROBERT WICKLIFFE delivered a speech in Lexington, Kentucky, on the 10th of August, 1840, in opposition to the law of 1833. The speech was soon after issued in a pamphlet, and extensively circulated. Mr. MARSHALL was one of the ablest and most determined advocates of the law, and consequently came in for a large share of the animadversions to its friends contained in Mr. Wickliffe's pamphlet. On the convention of the ensuing State Legislature, strong efforts were made for the repeal of the law, and Mr. Wickliffe's statements influentially used by its enemies to consummate that end. As a friend to the law, and to counteract any influences prejudicial to it contained in the arguments of Mr. Wickliffe, and to set himself right, Mr. MARSHALL, in December, published in some letters to the Frankfort Commonwealth, the following triumphant vindication. They are written with a diamond pen, and show, in every line, the research, analysis and genius of the author. No abler arguments have ever been adduced, in the whole range of excited controversy, upon the slavery question.

A PAMPHLET containing thirty-six pages, and purporting to be a speech delivered by Robert Wickliffe in the courthouse, in Lexington, on the 10th August, in reference to what is termed in the title page the "Negro Law," made its appearance some time ago. It has provoked replies from two gentlemen, who were particularly implicated by the speech, and produced very considerable excitement in the county of Fayette. The debate which took place in Lexington between one of the gentlemen referred to, and the author of the pamphlet, has been widely circulated, and has attracted and continues to attract general attention. The effort now making in the Legislature to repeal what Mr. Wickliffe is pleased to term the "Negro Law," is calculated to deepen and extend the interest occasioned by the dispute. No connection which I may have had with the passage of the obnoxious law, and no resistance which I may have afforded to its repeal, when I was honored with a seat in the Legislative councils of the State, would have induced me to enter upon the argument in this form. But the very extraordinary view taken by Mr. Wickliffe of the law which he assails, the charges hurled upon the original authors, and present friends, of the measure, and the repeated allusions to myself personally, and the connection sought to be established between those upon whose motives and principles he is severe almost to rancor, and myself, coupled with the rank, authority, influence and position of the Senator from Fayette, have determined me to present my own reasons for the course which I have pursued in relation to the law of 1832–3, prohibiting the importation of slaves into this State. I was a member of the House of Representatives the session in which it passed, I have uniformly voted against its repeal, and last year, for the first time, pending its discussion, took occasion to present the argument which had long since satisfied my own mind. Nothing which Mr. Wickliffe has brought forward has wrought any change in my opinions, though with all deference and without the slightest intended disrespect, I am constrained to say, he has, in my judgment, misconstrued the law as widely as he has mistaken the motives of its friends. It is a misfortune, that a question of such grave importance as the one under discussion, should be mixed up with feelings of personal bitterness, and treated with reference to prejudices past or present, local or political. That it has been so treated, any man will be satisfied who will take the trouble to read Mr. W.'s speech. It is too long to quote at large, but that my position in relation to it may be understood, I will attempt a synopsis in brief. Mr. W. thinks that the British government, from motives of policy, and to break down the growth and culture of cotton in the United States, have determined upon the abolition of slavery in America; that a fanatical sect, known technically as "Abolitionists" in the Northern States, are connected with the British government in this design, and are employed as the agents to effect it. The reasoning which establishes this charge upon the British government, is curious enough—see p. 21–2—but the consideration of it is aside from my present purpose. The law of 1832–3, is part and parcel of the system of the Abolitionists, which is to find its consummation in the severance of Kentucky from the Southern slave States by diminishing the number of slaves here, increasing the proportion of non-slaveholders and free laborers, forcing the entire slave population upon the "southern angle," and, finally, terminating slavery there by the murder of the whole white race. As part, and a very necessary part, of this most iniquitous scheme, planned by domestic traitors and a foreign rival and enemy, the first great step in Kentucky is to prostrate Mr. Wickliffe and his family, from his known hostility to Abolitionists, and his quick discernment of their "traps" and plans, rendered peculiarly odious, — that a *gentleman from Woodford* had shown himself as an auxiliary of this plan and an abettor of the conspiracy. Mr. W. then denounces the law as a flagrant and palpable violation of the organic law of the Commonwealth, and a disgrace to the statute book—recommends its instant repeal—a convention of the slave States, the mutual removal of all impediments to the free circulation of slave property, and the equal diffusion of that class of population throughout; and furthermore, that all and sundry persons who look to the extinction of slavery in any way, or at any time, are Abolitionists, and should be treated as public enemies. To find myself thus connected will, I hope, be a sufficient apology for the course I pursue. I mean not to be implicated upon this subject with the opinions of any man living or dead; nor do I mean to be involved in charges wild as these, without responding in my own proper person at the bar of public opinion; I say that I mean not to be implicated in any man's opinions. How far the charges which Mr. W. has piled upon others are just, it is not for me to determine. The chief personages upon whom he rests the origination of this law, are the Rev. Robert J. Breckinridge and John Green. The former gentleman has answered for himself; the voice of the latter has been silenced by death. With the personal altercation between Messrs. Breckinridge and Wickliffe, I have nothing to do. Whatever may be the merits of that controversy in other respects, Mr. B. has at least acquitted, not only himself, but his deceased friend of the guilt, if guilt there be, in the authorship of this law. So far from Green's having originated the bill in the lower house, so far from its having been urged through the Senate late in the session, without the Senate being apprised of its contents, as charged by Mr. W. in his pamphlet, page 20, the Journal of the Senate shows that the bill originated in that body; that it was reported by three of the best lawyers in the State, Owsley, Thornton and Guthrie. That four days intervened between the reference of the leave to those gentlemen and the report of the bill. Four days more elapsed, and the bill was read a second time and referred to a committee of the whole. Three days after, it was acted on in committee of the whole, reported to the House, engrossed, and read a third time. The day after, being the 15th January, the bill was passed by a vote of 23 to 12, Mr. Wickliffe himself present, and voting for it. It would seem, too, from the Journals, that the Senator from Fayette was present at every session of the Senate at which this bill was acted on, save one. Thus it appears, that in the Senate where this bill originated, it went through its regular course, was acted upon with great deliberation, was referred first to the ablest lawyers, and afterward to a committee of the whole, and passed, not at the end, but about the middle of the session. I refer to these things not for the purpose of involving Mr. Wickliffe in contradiction or inconsistency; whether his memory was at fault, or in what way his statements are found to be so utterly at war with the record, is a matter of no importance to me, to the question, or to the country. I do it that I may divest the law of that odium which is attempted to be thrown upon it in advance of any examination, by charging it upon those whose opinions are supposed, or at least represented, as leaning to modern abolitionism. I do it to acquit the Senate of 1833 of the gross negligence of passing a law of this consequence, without examination, a law revolutionizing, or at least determining the policy of the State upon one of the most deeply important and agitating of all the subjects of legislation. I do it that this law may be discussed upon its own provisions and merits, as a question of State, and in its relations to the public interest, and to the Constitution of the country, without reference to persons or prejudices with whom and which it has in truth not the most remote connection.

Pending the effort to repeal the statute under consideration, during the last session of the General Assembly, it was argued that the law was against the Constitution of Kentucky, and against the Constitution of the United States. I propose to state the argument then used on both points and to give the answer. The objections urged by Mr. Wickliffe were not presented in the debate in the House of Representatives; they appear to me, however, to present no difficulty, and shall be considered in their turn. The statute imposes a penalty of six hundred dollars, recoverable by indictment or an action of debt, in the name of the Commonwealth, in any circuit court of the county where the offender may be found, upon any person who shall thereafter import into the Commonwealth any slave or slaves, or who shall buy or sell, or shall contract for the sale or purchase, for a longer term than one year, of any such slave, knowing the same to be imported; the penalty to accrue upon each slave, so imported, sold or bought, etc. That emigrants to this State, bringing with them any persons deemed slaves by the laws of any one of the United States, are exempted from the penalties of the statute, as to such persons so brought; provided that, within sixty days after their arrival, such emigrant, before some justice of the peace, shall have taken the following oath or affirmation: "I do solemnly swear, or affirm, that my removal to the State of Kentucky was with intention of becoming a citizen thereof, and that I have brought with me no slave or slaves, with the intention of selling them: so help me God." And provided that, within thirty days thereafter, such person shall have had the oath recorded in the office of the court of the county where it was taken. Travelers, sojourners, and transient persons, bringing slaves for the purpose of necessary attendance, are also exempted. Residents of the State, importing slaves to which they derive title, by will, descent, distribution or marriage, or gift in consideration of marriage, and such citizens of the State as may (having slaves in their possession, at the time of the hiring) have hired their slaves to any person out of the State, are also exempted. Before I proceed to consider the main question of constitutional power in the government to enact this law, I beg leave to notice a construction given to it by Mr. Wickliffe, which, to say the least, is most extraordinary. He argues, that every bringing in of a slave is an importation within the meaning of the act, save only in the cases enumerated; and hence, citizens who may have gone out of the State on business, without a change of residence, members of Congress, etc., who may have taken a slave or slaves with them, for the purpose of attendance, upon their return with their servants, are exposed to the penalties of the statute. (See p. 10.) It would be as rational to treat the citizen, so returning, as an emigrant, and to consider his temporary absence as depriving him of his residence and his franchises, as to consider the slave who accompanied him as an importation from abroad. When a citizen hires his slave abroad, the residence of the slave is changed, a temporary ownership is established in him out of the State, and it was therefore necessary for the laws to provide for this case. A provision to meet the cases put by Mr. W. would have been superfluous and idle. In all those cases, the "Domicil," as it is termed in law, is not changed, and the domicil of the slave follows that of the master. "If a person go on a voyage to sea, or to a foreign country for health or pleasure, or business of a temporary nature, with an intention to return, such transitory residence does not constitute a new domicil, or amount to an abandonment of the old one." Story (Conflict of Laws, p. 42, and p. 45), after remarking that infants and married women follow the domicil of the father or husband, the same author adds: "This results from the general principle that a person, who is under the power and authority of an other, possesses no right to choose a domicil." A fugitive slave, therefore, brought back into the country, or slaves in attendance upon their master in a temporary absence, can not, in law, be said to be *imported* into a country from which, in law, as to all the purposes of domicil or residence, they were never absent. It is thus seen, that the rights of masters of slaves within the Commonwealth, are either by direct provision or undeniable construction completely guarded, so long as the ownership continues. But the constitutional question recurs. Has this government the power to prohibit the importation of slaves from other States or countries into this Commonwealth, under the exceptions contained in this statute? I will consider this question first in reference to the Constitution of Kentucky. The first section, article seventh of that instrument, contains all that relates to this subject, and is as follows: "The General Assembly shall have no power to pass laws for the emancipation of slaves, without the consent of their owners, or without paying their owners, previous to such emancipation, a full equivalent in money, for the slaves so emancipated. They shall have no power to prevent emigrants to this State from bringing with them such persons as are deemed slaves by the laws of any one of the United States, so long as any person of the same age or description shall be continued in slavery by the laws of this State. They shall pass laws to permit the owners of slaves to emancipate them, saving the rights of creditors, and preventing them from becoming a charge to any county in this Commonwealth.

They shall have full power to prevent slaves being brought into this State as merchandize. They shall have full power to prevent any slaves being brought into this State from a foreign country, and to prevent those from being brought into this State, who have been, since the first day of January, one thousand seven hundred and eighty-nine, or may hereafter be imported into any of the United States from a foreign country." The residue of the section is not material to the question. It was argued in the House of Representatives, that this Constitution recognized the relation of slavery as it existed at the time of its adoption. That by such recognition, the rights of individuals, as then secured by law, are rendered inviolable by the government, save in those cases where there is an express grant of power to the Legislature, and that the power is limited by the precise terms of the grant. That when this Constitution was adopted, every individual had the right to import slaves from other States for their own use, and that the same class or description of persons held to slavery in other States, as were held in slavery by the laws of this State, were thus far recognized as slaves by our laws. That the only powers granted to the government to interfere with these preexisting rights of the citizen are: "They shall have full power to prevent the importation of slaves as merchandize, and they may prevent the importation of slaves from a foreign country, or of those who have been brought into the United States since 1789, or of those who may hereafter be brought into the United States."

That these express grants of power, of themselves, prove that, in the view of the framers of the constitution, the power would not have existed without the grant, otherwise they are nugatory and superfluous. That the same article existed in the first Constitution of Kentucky, and that the practice of the government under that, and under the present, down to the passage of the act of 1833, demonstrates that this was the construction put upon it by the government. That the act of 1794, under the former constitution, and the act of 1815, under the present, prohibiting the importation of slaves, are both confined to the cases specified in the article quoted, to wit: the case of merchandize, and the importation from foreign countries. I state the argument to the best of my recollection, and my attention was very particularly directed to it. It is, in my judgment, radically defective in every particular. In the first place, the nature and office of the State Constitution are misconceived. It did not create a government of enumerated powers. "The legislative power of this Commonwealth shall be vested in two distinct branches; the one to be styled the House of Representatives, and the other the Senate, and both together the General Assembly of the Commonwealth of Kentucky," — article 2d, section 1st. Here is a general grant of the power to make laws, and there follows no specification either of particular laws, or of the general subjects upon which the power may be exercised. The General Assembly represent the community, and are armed with the whole force which that community certainly possessed for its own government, unless there be exceptions and reservations found in the charter itself.

In our mixed system of government, this distinction exists between the State and National Governments. The former possesses all power which is not expressly denied. The latter is strictly a government of enumerated powers, and can claim or exercise none which are not expressly granted. It is paramount, however, and contains not only specific grants to the general government, but prohibitions to the States. With reference to an act of Congress, therefore, the question is, has the power been granted? With reference to an act of the State Legislature, the question is, has the power been denied, either by the State Constitution, or that of the Union? I have already quoted the grant of legislative power from the State Constitution, and shown it to be general and unlimited: the article under consideration, and the 10th article, are exceptions out of the general power so granted. That we may comprehend the distinction clearly, let us examine the grant of power in the Federal Constitution. "All legislative powers *herein granted*, shall be vested in a Congress of the United

States, which shall consist," etc.—article 1, section 1, Constitution of the United States; and in the 8th section of the same article, "the Congress shall have power to lay and collect taxes, borrow money, regulate commerce," etc., with a long list of specifications of the subjects upon which the power so granted may be exercised. When we examine the 1st section of the 7th article of the State Constitution, in relation to slaves, altogether, it is perfectly apparent, that the principles I have laid down, and the distinction I have taken, are entirely applicable to it, and were understood perfectly by the framers. And first, it is prohibitory and restrains the legislative power, which would have been unnecessary, unless the framers had understood that the power prohibited, would have existed without the prohibition, and if it would, it must have been under the general grant of legislative power, for I have shown that there is no enumeration of specified powers in the instrument. "The General Assembly shall have no power to pass laws for the emancipation of slaves," etc. "They shall have no power to prevent emigrants to this State from bringing with them, such persons as are deemed slaves, by the laws of any one of the United States, so long as any person of the same age," etc. Now these are prohibitions, and so far as I have quoted them, are absolute and without exception. They show, however, that, but for this article, the General Assembly would have had the power both to pass laws for the emancipation of slaves without the consent of the owner, and to prohibit their introduction by emigrants. Then follow the grants of power which are assumed in the argument I am answering, as containing all the authority which the Legislature has over the subject. I have already shown the prohibitions so far as quoted, to be absolute. Now what is the effect, and what the true design of the positive grants? "They shall pass laws to permit the owners of slaves to emancipate them." What is this, but an exception, or modification, or limitation upon the first prohibitory clause, in which the General Assembly are forbidden to pass laws emancipating, etc.? Now take them together, and it is to be remarked, that as the subject of emancipation is the first in the order of prohibitions, so this authority to pass laws for emancipating is the first in the order of express grants. Now take them together, as they are connected, both by the order in which they stand, and the subject matter to which they relate, and what is the fair and obvious construction? Not that the Legislature would not have had the power to authorize masters to emancipate their slaves, if the whole section had been wanting to the constitution, most certainly not. But that notwithstanding the foregoing clause prohibiting them from passing laws for the emancipation of slaves, without consent of the owners, they may, nay they *shall* (the clause is imperative), pass laws to *permit* the *owners* of slaves to emancipate them. The second prohibition is, "they shall have no power to prevent emigrants," etc., and standing alone, as I have before observed, it is absolute, and without some exception or modification, emigrants to the State might bring as many slaves as they chose, and for any purpose; and this power in the emigrant is most clearly derived from the prohibition to the government in the clause just cited. Now the second grant of power, most clearly relates to this prohibition, and modifies it. "They shall have full power to prevent slaves being brought to this State as merchandize." This grant by no means limits the power of the Legislature over importation, to the case of merchandize, but extends their power even over emigrants upon this subject, notwithstanding the foregoing prohibition in their favor. And so with all the rest. The Legislature have power to prevent even emigrants from bringing in slaves from foreign countries, or such as have been brought from foreign countries since 1789, or as merchandize. They have this power over all others, without the specific grant, because it comes under the general idea of legislative authority, they would not have had it over emigrants without the specific grant, because of the absolute prohibition in the foregoing clause. They can not prohibit emigrants from bringing slaves for their own use, and with no intention to sell, because upon this point they are expressly restrained. They can prohibit all others from importing for any purpose or on any account, because, as to all others, the constitution is silent. This is the plain and natural construction of the section, and squares with and preserves the true, well known and acknowledged theory of our government. If the provisions of the act of 1833, fall naturally under the head of legislative power, and they are not expressly prohibited by the Constitution of Kentucky, so far as that is concerned, they are constitutional. We have seen that they are not expressly prohibited, and it will scarcely be contended that the prohibition of the migration of persons or importation of property into any particular country, belong either to the Judicial or Executive authority, and if not, and there be any such political power known to government at all, it must be legislative, there being but the three departments.

The argument which I have already noticed, limits the power of the government, simply to the prohibition of the importation of slaves as merchandize, but admits that that power extends to emigrants, claiming for the citizen the constitutional right to import slaves for his own use. That portion of the law which relates to emigrants, it admits to be constitutional, but rejects that portion which relates to importation in any other way. Mr. Wickliffe rests his constitutional objections to the act, most especially upon that portion of it which applies to emigrants. I will take the liberty to quote the passage. The high professional standing of that gentleman, and the intimate acquaintance which he is supposed to have with all subjects connected with jurisprudence, render it proper that he should receive a detailed and particular answer. In the ninth page of his printed speech, he employs the following language after quoting the law, and the section of the constitution in relation to emigrants:

"And here I might defy any lawyer or sensible man living, to put his hand on his heart and say that the constitution is not plainly, obviously and palpably violated. The constitution says the Legislature shall have no power to prevent emigrants from bringing slaves with them. It does not merely restrain or abridge the power of legislation over the subject, but declares that the Legislature shall have no power over the rights of the emigrants to come freely with their slaves, whether he intends to be a citizen or not—whether he be an alien or denizen. Our constitution opens the bosom of our country to him, and invites him to come freely, and at his will and pleasure settle among us, bringing with him his slaves. And yet this act requires an odious test oath. It requires the emigrant to swear that he does not intend to sell any one of his slaves—it requires him to swear that he intends to become a citizen although he may be an alien, and may never intend to abjure the allegiance he owes the sovereign he was born under. He may be a citizen of an other State, and not wish to forfeit or abjure his citizenship in such State, and still desire to live among us to educate his children, or for the health of his family, or for agricultural, mercantile or other purposes, and the free right to settle thus among us, is guaranteed by the constitution, but by this act is utterly subverted: thousands of aliens that never intended to be any thing else but aliens, are settled in every portion of the United States." "These frequently change their residence, and are invited by the constitution to settle among us, to improve the arts and sciences, or the face of the country by the application of their talents and capital. Such are for ever driven from the country if this act is suffered to exist." This last passage contrasts singularly enough with an other, on the 15th page, where we are told that the effect of this law will be to diminish the number of slaves in the country; and, as a natural consequence, the country will be overrun with "mechanics from Europe and the free States," as assuredly as ever Goths and Vandals overran Rome. This strange man argues on one page that the effect of the law is to exclude the talents, skill, and capital of aliens wishing to engage in agriculture, commerce, or other pursuits, and then, that unless repealed, the country will be overrun with such. The passage which I have just quoted at large, remains, however, to be considered. It may be remarked first, that as to persons who are really emigrants to this State, Mr. Wickliffe has either misunderstood or misrepresents the Constitution of the State, when he says, the "Legislature have no power to prevent emigrants from bringing slaves with them." The constitution, as has been before shown, contains this grant. "They (the General Assembly) shall have full power to prevent slaves being brought into the State as merchandize." There is no exception to this; the expression is plenary and unreserved. In considering the oath as applicable either to aliens or citizens of other States, coming to this, without any view to settle, he has certainly mistaken both the legal and popular idea of emigrant.

None but *emigrants* to this State *who bring slaves with them* are required to take this oath. None but emigrants to this State are protected by the constitution.

In what sense can a foreigner, or the citizen of an other State, coming to Kentucky with no view to settle or become a citizen thereof, be said to be an emigrant to this State? In what sense can persons so situated be said to be protected by the constitution? An emigrant from one country to an other is a person, who removes himself, his property and family, from the jurisdiction, the government, the rights and franchises of one country or State to an other, with a view to permanent settlement and citizenship. Story, Conflict of Laws, page 39, thus defines domicil: "In a strict and legal sense, that is properly the domicil of a person, where he has his true, fixed, and permanent home, and principal establishment, and to which, when ever he is absent, he has the intention of returning, (animus revertendi.)" Can an American gentlemen, residing temporarily in Great Britain, with the fixed purpose of returning to his own country at some period, and with no intention whatever, of becoming a British subject, be said with any propriety, either in a legal or popular sense, to be an emigrant to Great Britain? Can "the thousands of aliens in the United States, who never intend to be any thing else than aliens," claim the benefit of any law in any State, which, from its clear letter, and even clearer spirit, was intended to swell the number of citizens, and to invite emigration, by conferring upon emigrants constitutional exemptions from the legislative power which is not conferred upon the existing citizens of the State? Can it be conceived that the Constitution of Kentucky, intended to confer upon a foreigner, always intending to remain a foreigner, who comes into the State, a privilege which is not reserved to a citizen of the State?

The Constitution most clearly intended to permit citizens from the slave States, desiring to remove to Kentucky, to bring their slaves along with them for their own use; and the clause was evidently inserted, that *bona fide* emigration, especially from the parent State, might not be checked. But the Constitution as clearly authorized the Legislature to prohibit any one under cover of the privilege granted to "emigrants to this State" from bringing in slaves as merchandize, or with the intent to sell, which is the same thing. If, then, the Legislature have the power to prohibit any one to assume the character of an emigrant, who is not so in reality, and under this cover to introduce slaves into the Commonwealth from abroad, and to prohibit even emigrants from introducing them as merchandize, who shall limit the government in its choice of the means by which this constitutional end is to be effected? Is there any thing unconstitutional, in ascertaining the true character and intent of the party, by his own oath or affirmation? Is it not the easiest and most liberal course toward the party himself? If the party be no emigrant to the State, the Constitution does not protect him. If he bring slaves with intent to sell, it does not protect him; the law refers the extent of his protection to his own affirmation. Is there any right more sacred than the right of suffrage under the Constitution? Will any man contend that the oath administered at the polls, as to the party's qualification, and without which, if demanded, the right can not be exercised, whether the qualification exist or not—will any man contend that this is unconstitutional? Is there any thing of more importance to genius and ambition than the right to pursue the honorable and lucrative profession of the law, the broadest and most open path known in our country to extended fame and political distinction? Will any man contend that it is unconstitutional to ascertain the legal qualification by the oath of the party? Is a government bound in every or in any instance where a right either constitutional or legal exists, coupled with a qualification, to permit the exercise of the right, without ascertaining the qualification in any manner in the first instance? Most clearly we think not. In relation to this "odious and unconstitutional test oath," a word or two more and I am done for the present. Mr. Wickliffe seems not to be aware of its antiquity and its pedigree. In 1778, there was an act passed by Virginia, "To prevent the farther importation of slaves." The first, second, and third sections of that act, prohibit the importation of slaves by sea or land, or the sale or purchase of slaves, so imported, under the penalty of one thousand pounds upon the importer, and five hundred pounds upon the purchaser, and moreover, *that every slave imported contrary to the act shall be free.* Mr. W. would surely pronounce Virginia the very mother of abolitionism. But the fourth section I will give entire.

Section 4. "Provided, always, that this act shall not be construed to extend to those who may incline to remove from any of the United States and become citizens of this, provided that, within ten days after their removal into the same, they take the following oath before some magistrate of the Commonwealth: I, A B, do swear, that my removal to the State of Virginia was with no intention to evade the act for preventing the further importation of slaves within this Commonwealth, *nor have I brought with me,* or will cause to be brought, any slaves, with an intent of selling them, nor have any of the slaves now in my possession been imported from Africa or any of the West India islands, since the first day of November, 1778: so help me God." See Litt. Laws of Ky., vol. 1, p. 241.

Virginia perceiving too late the fatal error of that colonial system, which declared, "that all persons imported into Virginia, not being *christians* in their native country, except Turks and Moors, in amity with his Majesty, should be accounted slaves." See Littell, same page—almost immediately upon her becoming an independent State, and long before that independence was acknowledged, she endeavored to arrest this tremendous evil. It will be perceived that she went a long cast beyond the law of 1833: one thousand pounds penalty, and freedom to the slave. In 1815, the Legislature of Kentucky passed a law upon the subject of the importation of slaves. By the third section of this act, it is provided, "That no defendant, or defendants, who have been a resident or residents of any other State or territory of the United States, and shall remove to this State, *to reside therein*, and bring with him, her, or them, any slave or slaves, shall be discharged or acquitted from the pains and penalties inflicted by this act, unless he, she, or they, can satisfactorily prove, by competent legal evidence, that within sixty days after his, her or their arrival in the Commonwealth, he, she, or they, have taken the following oath or affirmation, before some justice of the peace, to wit: I, A B, do swear, or affirm, *that my removal* to the State of Kentucky was with an *intention to become a citizen thereof*, and that I have brought with me no slave or slaves, and will bring no slave or slaves to this State with intent of selling them."

This oath is identical with the one prescribed by the law of 1833, except that it compels the emigrant to swear, prospectively, which the latter law does not. Thus am I fortified by the Virginia and Kentucky Legislatures, long prior to 1833, in the opinion that this oath does not abridge or affect the emigrants' rights.

In an other number, if the public will bear with me so far, I will consider the objections to this law, growing out of the Constitution of the United States, and review some of the grounds which, in my judgment, render it peculiarly unwise to change the policy of the State upon this subject, in the present circumstances of the country.

NO. II.

Farther objections considered in reference to the Constitution of the United States.

Before I proceed to notice the objection to the law drawn from the Constitution of the United States, as urged with great force last winter in the House of Representatives, there is one made by Mr. Wickliffe, p. 23, which, from its singularity, requires a moment's attention. That gentleman imagines that the statute is in conflict with the second section, first clause, article fourth, of the Constitution. The clause is this: "The citizens of each State shall be entitled to all privileges and immunities of citizens in the several States." The statute prohibits all persons from importing slaves into this Commonwealth, under a certain penalty. So far every human being stands upon the same footing. But there is an exception in favor of emigrants from other States, who are permitted to do what our own citizens are not; so that, instead of the law excluding citizens from other States from a privilege enjoyed by our own, in this instance it allows a privilege and immunity to them which is denied to our own. This, among a thousand others, is given, not as an argument to be answered, but as a specimen of the unfairness with which the whole subject is treated in the pamphlet referred to. Here are Mr. W.'s own words: "This act, and your laws, allow to the citizens of Kentucky the power of working their own lands with their slaves, while it refuses the same privileges to the citizens of other States—a right to work their lands in Kentucky with their own slaves." Has a citizen of Kentucky a right to import slaves with which to work his lands? Has not a citizen of any other State the right to employ his slaves which are legally within the Commonwealth in the cultivation of his land? Where is the difference between them? Neither can import slaves, unless in the case of emigration, in which the stranger has the advantage. Either can employ slave labor already within the Commonwealth. "By this clause" (the first section of the fourth article of the Federal Constitution), says Mr. Wickliffe, p. 23, "no State can grant a privilege to its own citizens that is "not immediately common to the citizens of all the States." I have already shown that this law makes no distinction. The citizens of Kentucky have the privilege of voting for members of the House of Representatives, the Senate, and Governor of the Commonwealth of Kentucky. Quære, Mr. Wickliffe—Have the citizens of all the States in the Union the right, under this clause, to pour in upon us and decide our elections, and rule our councils? But enough of this.

The question made last winter, under the Federal Constitution, and pressed with great ingenuity by the gentleman who introduced the bill to repeal, is one of the most momentous which can possibly arise under that instrument. I understand that it will be relied upon again by the friends of repeal, at the present session. It was originally stirred and is vehemently pressed by a sect in this Union, with which, of all others, the enemies of this law would choose last to be connected in opinion or in effort. I will state the argument fully: it demands the most profound consideration; and if it be found not susceptible of an answer, and if Mr. Wickliffe be correct as to the views of the free States and the British cabinet, then wo betide the South. The practical exertion of the power claimed by the argument, must rend this Union in twain, and, in very deed, wrap the entire South in the flames of civil and of servile war.

The argument is this: Slaves are property, and the subject of commerce. The third clause of the eighth section of the first article of the Federal Constitution, gives to *Congress* "the power to regulate commerce with foreign nations, and among the several States, and with the Indian tribes." The first clause of the ninth section of the same article contains the following prohibition: "The migration or importation of such persons as any of the States now existing shall think proper to admit, shall not be prohibited by the Congress, prior to the year one thousand eight hundred and eight; but a tax or duty may be imposed on such importation not exceeding ten dollars for each person." The latter clause does not confer a power; it prohibits or rather postpones the exercise of one already granted. It recognizes the power to prohibit the importation of persons from abroad. Since the period to which it was postponed, it has been actually exercised. The importation of slaves has been prohibited under the highest of all possible penalties. The African slave trade has been declared piracy. So far as the foreign traffic in human flesh is concerned, it is repudiated by the National Government; and, as to that trade, man is considered as incapable of becoming the property of man; and by the laws of the United States, is not and can not be the subject of barter, or an article of commerce, among the citizens—the laws of any State in this Union, or of any nation upon earth to the contrary notwithstanding. And whence, proceeds the argument, did Congress derive this power? Not from the section last quoted—that does not confer the power, but suspends its exercise. It is derived from the power to regulate foreign commerce; and, but for the foregoing section, might have been exercised upon the first formation of the Government. But the power to regulate commerce between the States is conferred in the same clause, and in the same language, with that to regulate commerce with foreign nations. The power, then, by unavoidable inference, over the domestic slave trade, is as complete as that over the foreign. The penalties of this law are in the nature of a duty laid upon an article imported, and, as such, is a regulation of commerce. The second section of the tenth article provides, among other things, that "no State shall, without the consent of Congress, lay any imposts or duties on imports or exports, except what may be absolutely necessary for executing its inspection laws; and the net produce of all duties and imposts, laid by any State on imports or exports, shall be for the use of the Treasury of the United States; and all such laws shall be subject to the revision and control of the Congress." And thus they show that the law is an usurpation of a power which belongs to Congress, and is in direct conflict with every provision of the section just quoted.

It will be at once perceived, I think, that this view of the subject comprehends the whole scheme of the sect called Abolitionists. They press the argument one step further than those who urge it against the law of 1833, and invest Congress with the power not only to regulate, to the exclusion of the State authorities, the traffic among the States in slaves, but to declare that the thing itself is not the subject of property, and to abolish the relation of slavery in toto. Admit the premises to be true, and the analogy to the power over the foreign trade which has been exercised, and is acknowledged to exist, to be complete, and it seems logically impossible to resist the additional inference drawn by them. Under the power to regulate commerce with foreign nations, the Congress can make it piracy, punishable with death, in any citizen of the United States, to traffic in human beings. They can send armed vessels to the coast of Africa to seize and confiscate the vessels of American citizens engaged in it. They can declare the person seized or captured, or however acquired by the trader, being an American citizen, as not being the subject of property, to be free. In other words, as to American citizens in the foreign trade, they can *abolish* slavery. Who can stop the argument? Who can say that the legislative power of the American Congress over its own citizens, in regard to the trade they shall carry on, or as to what in law is susceptible of ownership, is not as complete within as without the United States, when the same power over the same subject is conferred in the same clause, and in the same language over the interior as the exterior relations of the citizens? Who can say that the Congress can not, with the same penalties, and under the same tremendous sanctions, destroy the relation of master and slave, within their territorial limits, as upon the coast of Africa, or the high seas? It would seem sufficient, in Kentucky, or at least with the enemies of the law, to indicate the necessary consequences flowing from what has been deemed the most unanswerable of their arguments. Were the proposition reduced to the form of a resolution, and submitted to the Legislature, surely there would be found no one hardy enough to vote for it. And it would seem scarcely consistent with candor, to urge in argument what is in fact and practice not admitted to be true. The proposition itself is not a mere abstraction to be played with; it is not a logical predicament to be taken up at pleasure, and employed for purposes of wordy victory, and then thrown aside. It is a vast practical question, pregnant with the most stupendous mischiefs, and threatening to rend the frame of the most gigantic empire on earth. Whatever, in other respects, may be the merits of the law of 1833, Kentucky should look well to the principles upon which she decides the question of power. Believing, as I do, that, upon this subject of domestic slavery, each State is supreme within its own limits; knowing, as I do, that the free States, at the last enumeration, were, in point of numbers, as eight to five, to the slave States, and, of the five, two were slaves, leaving the proportion between the free population as eight to three; having every reason to believe that the next census will exhibit an increased disproportion, I view with horror the surrender of a principle, even in argument, which will arm a Legislature in which there is so vast a preponderance against us with the power to sweep from existence the peculiar institutions of the South. Kentucky statesmen should look well to the concessions they make, their very words are noted.

Having stated the argument, as I believe, in its utmost force, I will not evade it by an appeal to our peculiar position, or to our fears. In the first place it is to be observed, that the power here claimed for Congress, if it exist at all, extends over the free States as well as the slave. If they can interfere with the subject as between Virginia and Kentucky, they can between Virginia and New York, and between Kentucky and Ohio. The Constitution is universal, and the national authority is the same over all the States. If a law of Kentucky, prohibiting a slave to be introduced from Virginia or South Carolina, be an invasion of the national authority, most certainly a law of New York or Ohio, prohibiting the introduction of slaves from Maryland or Kentucky, is equally so. The power claimed for Congress is general; if they can prohibit, they can permit. If they allow one portion of American citizens to hold this species of property, or to pursue this traffic, they can, nay, are bound to extend the privilege to all. The power claimed is exclusive, and the States can not intermeddle with it. Hence, it follows, that the laws of New York and Pennsylvania, abolishing slavery, and prohibiting persons to be introduced into their territory, as a subject of sale or of property, are unconstitutional. Until Congress abolishes slavery within the United States, every American citizen, whether of Ohio or Kentucky, Virginia or New York, has an equal right to purchase and hold this species as he has every other species of property, and to introduce it, duty free, into every State in the Union. The argument is as fatal to the institutions of the free as of the slave States. Slaves, they say, are property, and pass under the general power to regulate commerce. Grant it for the moment. Beeves, and horses and mules are property, and no duty, impost or tax of any kind shall be levied upon them, whether imported or exported, by the authority of any State. Would not a law of Ohio, declaring that any Kentuckian importing a beef into Ohio should lose the ownership, or that any citizen of Ohio purchasing a beef in Kentucky and importing him into Ohio should forfeit his property, would not such a law be unconstitutional? Are not, then, the laws of Ohio in relation to slaves just as much so? The fallacy of the argument consists in this—that the distinction taken in the Constitution between persons and things is not observed. No human being doubts, or has ever doubted, that the laws of Pennsylvania and New York, in relation to slavery, are strictly and properly within the power of those States, so far as the Federal Constitution is concerned. And yet they would not be so but for this distinction. And most clearly within their own limits, so far as the Federal Constitution is concerned, they have no greater authority over this or any other subject than every other State in the Union. Slavery existed within the United States at the time of the adoption of the Federal Constitution. It existed by force of the laws of the several States within whose limits it did exist. It is recognized by the Constitution as an existing institution, within the States, and the power of the States over the subject, each State, within its own limits, is, I think, most distinctly admitted. Nay, more: the power is treated in the constitution as so completely and exclusively with the State governments, that an exception is made to its exercise upon the part of any particular State, in behalf of the citizens of other States; which, according to all reason, would not have been done if the whole control of the subject was considered as vested in the Congress. In this case, if ever, the exception proves the rule. I have said that slavery within the States is recognized by the constitution as an existing State institution, at the time of its adoption. In the third clause of the second section of the first article, we have the following: "Representatives and direct taxes shall be apportioned among the several States which may be included within this Union, according to their respective numbers, which shall be determined by adding to the whole number of *free* persons, including those bound to service for a term of years, and excluding Indians not taxed, three-fifths of all other persons." The constitution seems cautiously to have avoided the use of the word slave in every section which relates to the subject. But who could persons, other than free persons, and persons bound to service for a term of years—who, I say, could such persons be but slaves? I have also said, the power of the State, over the subject within the limits of each, is distinctly recognized by the Federal Constitution. In the third clause of the second section of the fourth article, are the following provisions: "No person, held to labor in one State, under the laws thereof, escaping into an other, shall, in consequence of any law or regulation therein, be discharged from such service or labor, but shall be delivered up on claim of the party to whom such service or labor may be due." Again the same delicacy in avoiding the use of the word slave. And in the clause heretofore quoted, "the *migration* or *importation* of such *persons*, as any of the States may choose to admit, shall not be prohibited," etc. The framers seem to have thought that, although they treated of the *thing*, the *word* SLAVE would stain an instrument formed to establish and transmit the blessings of *justice*, *tranquillity*, and *liberty*, to the remotest American generation. The clause above quoted proves, beyond disputation, that the condition and obligation of persons held to service or labor, both as to kind and duration, is dependent entirely upon the laws of the particular State; and that persons, slaves by the laws of one State may not be so by those of an other: and that the only authority over the subject conferred upon the general government, or rather excepted from the general power of each State, is, that fugitives into one State, even though persons of the same description be free by the laws of that State, shall still be surrendered, if slaves by the law of the state whence they have escaped. Here, then, is not only recognized the relation of master and slave, but it is referred entirely to the authority of the State laws, as to whether it shall exist; and a perpetual protection is extended over it where it does exist, from all interference upon the part of those States where it does not exist. Admitting, then, which I do, that the power of Congress to abolish the African slave trade, is derived from the power granted, "to regulate commerce with foreign nations," still, as it respects this article of commerce, the analogy between the foreign trade, and that between the States, is destroyed by the constitution itself. In the foreign trade, there is no distinction made between persons and things, only that the power of Congress over the importation of *persons*, is postponed till 1808. Over persons out of the limits of the United States, no State could claim any jurisdiction; there could not arise any conflict between the National and State authorities upon this subject. The authority of each State is confined to its own limits, and it is only as to what is property within these limits, that any question could arise. The difference in the internal policy of the States in relation to this subject, presented a very serious obstacle to the formation of a national government, which should embrace them all. It was felt more particularly in the apportionment of representation. The free States, believing that, in the adjustment of political power, slaves could not be weighed with freemen and citizens: the slave States, contending that this class of persons, constituting a large part of their population, and being also a subject of taxation, formed a proper foundation for political power, the article I have quoted, adding three-fifths in the enumeration of the people, was adopted as a compromise between these opposite claims. In the apportionment of taxes and of representation, the same principle prevails; and, as no more slaves can be included for taxation than representation, the slave States were satisfied with this indemnity against any oppressive levies upon that species of property which was peculiar to them, the whole of it which was liable to taxation, being represented in the government. But, at that day, the same reasons existed with the Southern States, in all their force, which exist at present, for resisting any power which should attempt to destroy a relation established by their laws, and to place large masses of men, in whom those laws had invested them with the absolute ownership, between whom and themselves the past relation must plant an eternal hostility—eternal, because heaven had stamped a mark on the one; an everlasting badge of disgrace and servitude; an all-enduring memorandum of past wrong and sufferance and oppression, which no time could obliterate, nor all the waters of the multitudinous ocean wash out — I say, the spirit of the Southern chivalry would have revolted at the establishment of a power then, as certainly as it would at its exercise now, that could place these masses of degraded slaves upon a level with their former masters. The free States, too, had as deep an interest in this question as the others. It has been already shown, that if the control of slaves had passed to the general government, under the power to regulate commerce among the States, coupled with the prohibition upon the States to lay any tax or duty upon export or import, from or into any State, slavery must have been universal, so long as it existed at all; and no State in this Union could have prohibited the introduction of a slave within its borders, by any citizen, so long as it was recognized by the general government as property within the territorial limits of the United States. The parties being equally interested in retaining the full power over the subject within their respective limits, have done exactly what it was natural for them to do. The authority of the laws of those States, where servitude existed when the constitution was adopted, is acknowledged by it. The power in other States to repel it, is as clearly recognized; and, to prevent a conflict between the members of a confederacy, whose variant policy and complete independence upon this subject is so clearly admitted, the general government only interposes, to protect the slave States, by preventing the operation of the laws of a free State upon their fugitives. "No person held to service or labor in one State, *under the laws thereof*, escaping into an other, shall, in consequence of any *law* or *regulation therein*, be discharged from such service or labor, but shall be delivered up on claim of the party to whom such service for labor may be due."

I deem it unnecessary to press the argument further. It is useless to inquire how far Congress could have legislated upon the subject of slavery within the United States, had the constitution not taken the distinction which nature has taken between *persons* and things, and recognizing the variant municipal institutions of the several States upon the subject, left slavery where it was found—under the control of the State governments. One thing is certain, however, that any legislation must have been uniform, and that slavery must have been abolished, or universal. I have said, at the outset, that I meant not to be implicated in the opinions of any man. In closing this number I beg leave to give the result of my reasoning, as to the power of the government over this subject.

1st. The government of Kentucky has full legislative powers within the limits of the State.

2d. The plenary grant of these powers, is unrestrained, unless by express prohibition in the Federal Constitution, or the Constitution of Kentucky.

3d. That but for the 7th article "concerning slaves," the power of the Legislature over the whole subject would have been absolute and uncontrolled, and Kentucky might have legislated as Pennsylvania and New York have done.

4th. That there are no prohibitions in that article, save only as to the emancipation of slaves without the consent of their owners, and the preventing emigrants from bringing slaves with them, so long, etc.; consequently, that the legislative power over the subject, as to all other persons, and in all other cases, remains untouched.

5th. That the doctrine, "that the expression of the one is the exclusion of the other," does not apply to that clause which gives to the Legislature full power to prevent "slaves being brought into this State as merchandize." That power would have existed, independently of any grant, unless expressly prohibited; or we are driven to the absurd conclusion, that the State Legislature has no power not expressly granted —a principle which would nullify every act of the General Assembly since its creation, except the law prohibiting the importation of slaves as merchandize, or from any foreign country, or the introduction of such as may have been imported into the United States since 1789, etc.—the grants of power in this article being the only specific grants in the instrument.

6th. The reason for the introduction of this specific grant is easily explained, and perfectly reconcilable with the true theory of the State Constitution, on the following grounds: From the foregoing clause in relation to emigrants, it is evident, if there had been nothing else added, that they could have imported slaves either for their own use or as an article

8

of merchandize. The constitution never intended that slaves should be a subject of traffic with other States. It was therefore necessary, under the full privilege of importation given to emigrants in the first clause, to insert the latter, otherwise it would have been as Mr. Wickliffe has stated — "The Legislature have no power to prevent emigrants from bringing slaves with them." "They shall have *full* power to prevent slaves being brought into this State as merchandize," adds the constitution, and thereby extends the power of the government over emigrants, as to the traffic, most certainly without abridging it, as to other persons, from that complete state in which we have shown it to exist, independent of express prohibition.

7th. It follows, then, that the Legislature have the power to prohibit emigrants from importing slaves as merchandize, because the constitution has limited the general privilege conferred upon the emigrant in one clause, by the express grant of this power to the Legislature in an other, without which the privilege of the emigrant would have been unlimited. It follows, equally, that the Legislature can prevent, by such means as to their wisdom may seem good, their own citizens, and all other persons, save emigrants, from importing slaves at all into the State, because the constitution has no where prohibited the power, save in the case of emigrants. This is what the law has done, and it is therefore within the just scope of the powers of the government.

8th. The Federal Constitution has expressly recognized the subject of domestic slavery within the limits of the several States, as originating with, and appertaining to, the State governments and laws exclusively; nay, has interposed its own authority to protect the institution, where it exists, from the interference of the legislation of other States. The doctrine of the Abolitionists is as false in theory, as it would be destructive in practice. Slaves are not treated in the Federal Constitution as an article of domestic commerce, appertaining to the national authority, under the grant to regulate it, but are considered as persons standing in a certain relation to other persons, by force of peculiar municipal laws, whose authority is recognized and established. The six hundred dollars, imposed by the law of 1833, is not therefore a tax, duty, or impost laid upon an article of commerce, within the meaning of the Federal Constitution, but is a pecuniary penalty for an indictable offense, imposed by a government with which none other on earth conflicts, or can conflict, upon this particular subject.

I feel that I have sacrificed brevity to perspicuity. I have the strongest personal reasons for desiring to be clearly understood upon this branch of the subject, and offer this as my apology for what might otherwise be regarded as unpardonable prolixity. Having established the authority of the government, (as I am persuaded,) to pass this law, I will, in my next, consider it in the more interesting aspect of its practical effects, its propriety and wisdom.

NO. III.

Vindication of the law of 1833, *upon the score of policy and the public interest.*

I HAVE proven, I think, that the Government of Kentucky had full power to enact the law of 1833, and upon the subject of slavery within her limits is absolutely sovereign, except in the cases expressly prohibited by the State Constitution. In defending the policy of that law at the time of its passage, and in maintaining that the reasons for its continuance are far stronger even than for its establishment, I shall not discuss the abstract question of slavery. Those who choose to search for its foundation among the original and natural rights of men may do so. I take slavery as I find it, a positive institution, recognized by the constitution of my country. The right of the master to such persons as were slaves, within the Commonwealth at the time of the adoption of that constitution, by the laws then in force, and to such persons as the laws since have permitted to be introduced into the country, being slaves by the laws of other States, and being of the same description with persons held in bondage here, is as complete and as entirely protected by law from the power of the government as any other right of property whatever; and this, whether the legislation be present or prospective, whether it relate to slaves in existence at the passage of the law, or grasp at future and unborn generations. The doctrine of the emancipating power of the government over the "*post-nati*" I have ever denied. The reasoning which seeks to distinguish between the constitutional right of the master over his slave in existence, and over the unborn issue of the females, has no foundation either in law or nature. The law of servitude is express; it places the descendants of the females, without limitation, upon the same footing with the ancestors. The issue follows the condition of the parent, "*Partus sequitur ventrem.*" It is no answer to say that a person not in being can not be a slave. It is just as true that a person not in being can not be free. The unborn can neither be the subject of the law of servitude or the statute of emancipation. Neither can attach till birth, and then the constitution takes the precedence.

By the Constitution of Kentucky, the Legislature can not pass a law emancipating the issue of female slaves born thereafter, in any other manner than they can slaves then in existence—they are upon the same footing, and the rights of the master are equally protected in both cases. But although the constitution recognized the existing laws and shielded the rights of the master, it very clearly does not embrace the principles or the policy advocated by Mr. Wickliffe. Under that gentleman's reasoning and definitions, the instrument itself may be considered as an abolition document. "But what is an abolitionist," asks Mr. Wickliffe, p. 17—"One who intends to abolish negro slavery by an immediate or a slow process—by a direct attack upon the tenure of slavery, or by an indirect mode." That the constitution contemplated the extinction of negro slavery as a possible event, is obvious from the language employed in the article heretofore quoted.

It declares that the right of emigrants to bring slaves with them into this State shall only continue "so long as any persons of the same age or description "*shall be continued in slavery by the laws of this State.*" And it leaves it in the power of the Legislature to bring about the event here alluded to, by conferring the power to emancipate slaves, with the consent of the owners, or by paying a full equivalent, and to prevent their importation by emigrants as merchandize, and leaving the power to prohibit their importation by all other persons for any purpose, untouched. The framers of the constitution would be astounded, one would suppose, at the doctrines of Mr. W.'s pamphlet.

The policy of the law of 1833 was especially aimed at the traffic in slaves, and the introduction of them as merchandize from other States.

The laws of 1794 and 1815 prohibiting their introduction as merchandize only, but leaving the right in the citizens to import for their own use, had failed in the effect which they were intended to produce. They prohibited, to be sure, the introduction of slaves with the intent to sell, or for the purposes of merchandize, within the Commonwealth, but they established no test by which the intent was to be ascertained; and they did not and could not prohibit the sale of a slave once brought in. The crime did not consist in selling a man's own slaves after they were imported. His necessities, his debts, his convenience, a thousand things might induce the sale, and, above all, the right to dispose of his own property within the country could not be reached or questioned. It was the intent with which they were introduced, to which, and to which alone, the penalty attached. Every body knows that between 1815 and 1833, nothing was more common than to see whole droves of human beings driven in chains, like wild beasts, along the highways. Slaves were driven into the Commonwealth, and hired out for long terms, in some instances for 99 years, in evasion of the laws. Feeling that the past Legislation was entirely inefficient, the Legislature of 1833 struck at the root of the evil, by prohibiting all importation, except in the cases authorized by the constitution, and some other cases in favor of citizens, as to slaves already within the Commonwealth, and others heretofore noticed. As a farther and scarcely less important object, the law was designed to prevent the increase of this species of property, by the introduction of the desperate, and vicious, and outcast portion of this outcast race from Maryland, Virginia, and the Carolinas. At the time of the passage of this law, the sect now known by the title of "Abolitionists" had not made their appearance. And, as I was sworn then upon the constitution of my country, by all the obligations of that oath, I affirm now, that I do not believe, that the principles and designs, ascribed to that party, were in the contemplation of any human being who voted for the law. I was myself not only never an abolitionist, but never an emancipationist upon any plan which I ever heard proposed. I was not an emancipationist, because I believed that the power did not exist. I would not have been, even though it had existed, unless coupled with the means for the deportation of the race. No plan of that sort had occurred to me which seemed feasible. I have uniformly voted against the Convention Bill. The year it passed, I voted against it in the Legislature, and opposed it warmly before the people, the summer the question was submitted to them.

But holding every opinion heretofore advanced in these papers, I still regard negro slavery as a political misfortune.

That the laws enacted before 1833, had failed of any beneficial effect, and that the evil was increasing upon us fearfully, a reference to the statistics of the respective periods will demonstrate. A comparison of the state of the population before the passage of the law, and at present, will show that since that period there has been none, or a very trifling increase. In 1820, the total population of Kentucky, according to the census then taken, was 564,317, of which 126,732 were slaves, leaving the white population 437,585. In 1830, by the same authority, the total population was 687,917, of which 165,213 were slaves, leaving 522,704—which exhibits an increase, within ten years, of 85,119, in the white population, upon a basis of 437,585; and an increase of 38,481, in slaves, upon a basis of 126,732. If this number of slaves gave an increase of 38,481, in the same proportion 437,585 whites should have given an increase of 134,209, whereas it only exhibits an increase of 85,119—so that, in the ten years immediately preceding the passage of the law under consideration, the white population did not increase in the ratio or the same proportion with the black, upon the data given, by something like fifty thousand souls, a difference of something like 12 per cent.—11 per cent. and a fraction. The present amount of the black population, according to the Auditor's report of slaves listed for taxation, is 166,616, exhibiting an increase of 1400 slaves in ten years, including two years before the passage of the law. Until the census of 1840 is known, we have no certain means of determining the increase of the white population within the same period. Any statement upon the subject would be conjectural. There is no doubt, however, that, notwithstanding the immense emigration from the State, the white population has increased steadily, and in a ratio nearly equal to what it was within the former period. The total valuation of the taxable property within the Commonwealth, in 1833, as taken from the Auditor's books, was $126,601,004. The total valuation in 1840, excluding that taken under the equalizing law, which was not taken in 1833, is $240,551,187—exhibiting an increase in the capital of the State, since the passage of this horrible law, of $113,950,183, being very near one hundred per cent. These are indisputable facts. Let us cast our eyes within the period of ten years before the passage of this law upon South Carolina, whose principles and institutions are an object of such peculiar admiration with the Senator from Fayette. Between 1820 and 1830, the increase of slaves in that State was 56,926; of the whites, 21,518—a difference of more than one hundred per cent. in the increase of the black over the white population. Again let us compare Ohio with Kentucky and South Carolina, within the same period—the three States being nearly equal in population in 1820. Ohio had, at that period, 581,434; Kentucky, 564,317; and South Carolina, 502,741—total population. Starting from these nearly equal bases, Ohio, within ten years, exhibits an increase of 356,469 souls; Carolina, 78,444, and Kentucky, 123,600, including slaves in the latter States. The same astounding facts will present themselves by a comparison of all and each of the slave States with the free. I put it to the people of Kentucky, whether the operation of this law has been mischievous. I ask them to weigh well their present position, and consider the consequences of its repeal. The avowed object of the repeal of the law, is to satisfy the demand for labor in Kentucky by the introduction of slaves. There is no difference between the friends and enemies of the law as to the effect of its repeal. Let us trace it: Virginia, the Carolinas, and Georgia, contain one million two hundred and forty-eight thousand two hundred and ninety slaves. In our commercial relations with these States, the balance is always against them. Repeal this law, and who does not perceive, that while slaves are cheaper there than here, this balance will be settled annually, by the introduction of slaves to the whole extent of the balance. I have no means within my reach of ascertaining what this is in amount. Every one knows, however, that it is immense. The laws of trade will indisputably cause the flow of this property into Kentucky, until the price is equalized between the two countries. While a trader can obtain a larger price for his horses and mules in the South, than they cost him here, he will export horses and mules; while he can, in exchange for them, receive slaves at a less price than he can obtain for them here, he will import slaves. I am of course understood to mean that the difference in price must be sufficient to defray the charges of transportation, and reimburse the capital with a fair profit. In the present state of the market, no branch of traffic would be so profitable as the slave trade between Kentucky and the South. The effect of the law upon the trade has been similiar to that of a dam across a stream. Had it been permitted to flow, it would have been of equal depth above and below. Tear away the dam, and all the accumulated waters, the whole dark flood, will pour upon us with the force of a sudden inundation, overwhelming or sweeping away every vestige of improvement below. The torrent will only lose its violence when it finds its level. The current of the trade will continue till the channel here is filled up even with the precious fountains whence it is derived. The Senator from Fayette may fairly be considered as the great champion of repeal. His own position, which he has very clearly defined, may, with propriety, be considered as that of the party which he claims to lead. That I may not be suspected of misrepresentation, I will take from his own book the scheme of policy which he suggests, and the consequences which he anticipates from the pursuit of it. That the consequences will happen, I feel morally certain; and that the policy is therefore ruinous, I am equally convinced.

I have already shown the effects of the law, from a comparison between the present condition of the Commonwealth in capital and population, and what it was at the date of its passage. This comparison fills Mr. Wickliffe with horror. He admits that the increase of slaves in Kentucky has ceased under the operation of this law. Their price has risen, and, along with it, there has been a general rise in the wages of labor. That the proportion of non-slaveholders to slaveholders has increased. That under the operation of the law it will continue to increase. The increase of our slaves is our only defense against the influx of mechanics from Europe and the free States. "No, fellow-citizens," says the Senator from Fayette, "our slaves, upon this point, are our only defense; for so soon as they disappear, a new race will overrun the State of Kentucky, as assuredly as ever Goths and Vandals overran Rome." The slaveholder and non-slaveholder are represented as of necessity enemies. "Mr. Green's plan," says Mr. W. "was to drain the slaves from the State until none but the wealthy shall own them, and then to set the non-slaveholder upon the slaveholder, and through the ballot-box, by the mere force of numbers, to set the negroes free."

The wise and experienced mind of the Senator from Fayette has reached the conclusion that States claiming to be free, are in reality not so; that in all countries there must be slaves, and the difference between himself and the gentleman from Madison (against whom he is reasoning) is, that he (Mr. W.) wishes black slaves, and that gentleman white ones. That the great body of the people in England, who support themselves by their labor, are, in very truth, the slaves of the landholders and capitalists who employ them, and that the free States of this Union are tending rapidly to this necessary consummation of all social existence — see p. 14. As a cure for all these evils, to wit, the decrease of the black race, the increase of white population, the influx of mechanics, the appreciation of the slave property remaining, the high wages of labor, all of which horrors, it seems, are brought about by the machinations of England, Mr. Wickliffe recommends the repeal of this law, and of all laws restricting the free circulation of slave property throughout the States which hold it. After painting the horrors of abolitionism, Mr. W. closes with these remarkable words: "Is this a time for slaveholding States to make statutory wars upon one another? I think not." He afterward adds: "But on the contrary, conventions should be held by delegates from all the slave States, and rules adopted for their general safety. Nothing would contribute so much to defeat the machinations of England against them, as to break down all restrictions made by particular States, and thereby to extend the slave population over the whole face of the territory of each and every State where slavery exists." The old humbug of the South Carolina Railroad is held *in terrorem* over us too. On page 11, of this ever remarkable pamphlet, we have the following precious threat: "I well recollect seeing published in the South Carolina papers a series of numbers warning the people of the South, against expending their substance in making the South Carolina Railroad to Lexington: and one of the strongest arguments used was, that the State of Kentucky had made war with the Southerners, in not permitting them to send or use their slaves in Kentucky." "Sirs," says Mr. W., indignantly, "do you expect that Carolina will ever make the road while this abolition tinder-box disgraces your statute book? If you do, you greatly deceive yourselves."

Would any man imagine, that after Mr. Wickliffe's defense of slavery, his definition and denunciations of abolitionists, and his plan for defeating their schemes, by banishing all non-slaveholders from the country, and flooding it with slaves from the South, to the everlasting exclusion of those "Goths and Vandals," the free mechanics from other countries — would any man imagine that he himself looked to the extinction of slavery? And yet he says after his proposition "to extend the slave population over the whole face of the territory of each and every State where slavery exists" — "This plan will give time and space for prudential legislation on the subject, and will wear out rather than break the chain of slavery." Was he shocked by the enormity of his own opinions, and did he put this in as a salvo; or are we really to understand that he proposes to increase the evil as a mean of finally getting rid of it? If Mr. Wickliffe be really desirous of a prudential course of legislation, by which, without violating the right of property, or, to use his own phrase, "breaking the chain of slavery," we may ultimately and gradually "wear it out;" I put it to his reason and to his conscience, whether the policy of 1833 is not better adapted to that end, than the plan he proposes? If Mr. Wickliffe really believes that the British Government and the abolitionists mean forcibly to interfere with this property, and "to break the chain," I again put it to his common sense, whether Kentucky is not better prepared to protect herself from insurrection in her present situation than in that to which he would reduce her? Kentucky now contains about 600,000 whites to 166,000 blacks — a majority in numerical strength of 434,000 in favor of the white race. Divide the blacks equally, give one slave round as far as they will go, and you will have 166,000 slaveholders and 434,000 non-slaveholders. Here there is no danger. Here we are spared that last horrible curse of domestic slavery, the constant terror of a domestic foe. Unless, indeed, we are to believe that the free white population, holding none of this property, is the natural ally of the negro—a supposition, by-the-by, upon which Mr. Wickliffe's whole reasoning seems to be based. The consequences of the repeal of this law, to which Mr. Wickliffe looks as a blessing, in all candor, I avow, that I regard as the most unmitigated curse which the avenging hand of God could inflict upon my country. As to what those consequences will be, he and I do not differ. The wages of labor will be lower—the price of slaves will be reduced—the influx of free mechanics and artisans will be effectually prevented—those who are not able to purchase slaves, or are not willing to hold them, will be driven out — a check, effectual and eternal will be given to the increase of white population, and the black encouraged and stimulated to its utmost capacity of expansion. And are these blessings? If so, upon whom are they to fall? Not upon the present race of slaveholders, surely. Will Mr. Wickliffe's fortune be improved by a general reduction of the value of slaves? Will the non-slaveholder consider it as a blessing? The avowed ground of the policy is jealousy of him. Hear Mr. Wickliffe: The scheme of the abolitionists for Kentucky is "to drain the slaves from the State until none but the wealthy shall own them, and to set the non-slaveholder upon the slaveholder, and, through the ballot-box, by the mere force of numbers, to set the negroes free. To effect this object the law was passed," etc.

The law is tending to this result by diminishing the number of slaves, and it is to alter, and for ever prevent, this state of things that its repeal is sought. And what is the "*modus operandi*" of Mr. Wickliffe's policy? To open the doors wide to the importation of slaves, and thereby so to reduce the wages of labor as for ever to exclude "the free mechanics" from Europe and the North, who can, in the proposed state of things, find no means of employment within our country.

And yet Mr. Wickliffe denies that the repeal of this law will drive free labor from the State. In proof of this, I will make one more, and the last, quotation from his pamphlet: "A *gentleman from Woodford*, I am informed, stated to you the other night, that every negro that is brought into the State drives a mechanic from it. Had the gentleman told you that every negro that comes into the State keeps a mechanic from being driven from it, he would have come nearer the truth." Is there a man in the world who does not perceive, that the same causes which would exclude, would also expel. If the wages of labor, from the number of slaves, be reduced so low that a mechanic, or free laborer from abroad, can not come into the country, because he will find no means of supporting himself and family, or improving his fortune—must not the same circumstances induce the mechanic, already in the country, to seek a more congenial market for his industry? Has not the operation of slavery been precisely similar in the Southern Atlantic States? Has it not banished manufactures and the mechanical arts from Virginia and the Carolinas? Has not Mr. Wickliffe told us that his leading object is to keep out head mechanics and head manufacturers, and to confine the population to landholders and slaves, to liken us to Virginia and South Carolina—to link us in for ever with their policy and their fate. The effect and policy of the law is to diminish the number of slaves and to increase the white population—this, the Senator from Fayette admits, and dreads, and opposes. The repeal of the law is to increase the number of slaves and to diminish the white population, and thereby to defeat the influence of non-slaveholders in elections. The people of Kentucky should consider of this policy. There are now in Kentucky about 600,000 white souls and about 166,000 black. The proportion between slaveholders and non-slaveholders is not known accurately, but the great preponderance of the latter is obvious from the foregoing statement. Were we to distribute the black population equally, giving one to each man, there would be 434,000 non-slaveholders to 166,000 slaveholders. But they are not equally distributed.

It is said that the Senator from Fayette owns some three hundred himself, and, consequently, the preponderance is greater than what is represented above. What must this class of voters think of a policy which is aimed at their very existence, and that, too, upon a supposition that they are of necessity abolitionists, and the enemies of the slaveholders? Is it wise, or is it humane, in any man to endeavor to draw a party line of this description within the Commonwealth, and to represent these classes of citizens, as naturally and necessarily hostile upon a subject, of all others, the most exasperating?

Have the non-slaveholders in Kentucky deserved the charge made against them? The Legislature of Kentucky, a short time back, passed a law authorizing the people to vote upon the call of a Convention. Mr. Wickliffe says that this was an abolition scheme. Kentucky was to be the battleground, and the tenure of slavery was to be destroyed by a new constitution. What said a people in which there were at least five non-slaveholders to one slaveholder? They voted down the convention bill, and refused to change a constitution which recognized slavery, and placed the right of the master beyond the reach of the government. They were far more liberal to Mr. Wickliffe and his class, than we have every reason to believe he would be to their rights, if he had the power. He is afraid of their influence at the ballot-box—he is afraid of the exercise of their suffrages. These opinions are not peculiar to Mr. Wickliffe—the principles upon which they are founded, are incorporated in the Constitutions of Virginia and South Carolina. The slaveholders in those States have not left their cherished rights, and the perpetuation of slavery, to a mere constitutional provision. They have taken more substantial guarantees in the composition of their Legislature and in the distribution of their representation. The representation in Kentucky is apportioned among the several counties, according to the ratio of voting freemen in each—a ratio equal and uniform throughout the Commonwealth. The representation in Virginia and South Carolina is distributed among the several districts into which the States are respectively laid off, not according to the number of free white men in each district—no such thing. In fixing the districts, the negro population is considered as the basis of political power, and the preponderance of representation is given to those districts in which there is a preponderance, not of freemen, but of slave property. In some instances, a dozen freemen, in respect to the slaves which they hold, may have as large a representation in the General Assembly as five hundred in an other district where there are fewer slaves. I heard the question discussed long and keenly in the Virginia Convention. The Lowlanders contended that the principle was essential to the security of that description of property, and they carried the day. According to the present Constitution of Virginia, no change in the state of the white population can affect the distribution of the representation, or shake the power of the large slaveholding districts in the constitution. The House of Representatives consists of one hundred and thirty-four members—of which, fifty-six are chosen by the counties west of the Blue Ridge mountain, and seventy-eight by the counties east of the Blue Ridge. The Senate consists of thirty-two-members—of whom thirteen are assigned to the counties west, and nineteen to those east of the Blue Ridge, giving to the country below the ridge, upon joint ballot, a majority of twenty-eight in the General Assembly. The constitution further provides, that every ten years the Legislature shall apportion the representation among the several counties and towns, within the districts, but that the number of delegates assigned by the constitution, as above shown, to each of the great sectional divisions of the Commonwealth, shall not be altered or affected. So that, in the progress of time, should there be left in the lower counties only enough freemen to complete the representation to which they are entitled—to wit, ninety-seven—and the white population in the West should increase an hundredfold, still those ninety-seven would wield a greater political power in the State, by twenty-eight votes, than the million of men who might be found in Western

Virginia. The constitutions of these States seem to be based upon the idea that the non-slaveholders are not to be trusted, and have no doubt furnished Mr. Wickliffe the argument he has employed. In the present state of our population, an attempt to make our free constitution conform to those of these States would be hopeless, and the next best thing to be done is, to sweep off the non-slaveholders, by the introduction of such masses of slaves, as working for their masters free of wages, and absorbing all the capital destined for the employment of labor, will soon banish all competitors, and limit the population to that most desirable state in which there will be found none but the large landed capitalist and his grubbing slave. The non-slaveholders have, then, surely no interest in the repeal of this law. Will it advance our commerce? Will it extend mercantile operations and enterprize? The object of commerce is to supply those articles from abroad, for the consumption of the people, which are not produced at home. Its very definition proves that its extent must depend upon the number of consumers, and their ability to purchase. Do the four hundred and sixty-nine thousand slaves in Virginia, or the three hundred and fifteen thousand in South Carolina, afford the same effectual demand for the importation of merchandize, which the same number of free and independent citizens would do? The answer is obvious: their consumption of whatever is to be purchased by the master is limited to what is absolutely necessary, and their means of purchase for themselves are nothing. Will having the whole returns of our Southern trade, made in the most degraded, the most vicious of Southern slaves, the very vomit of Virginia and South Carolina jails, instead of money or bills upon the East, better enable us to meet our foreign balances at the points whence we import? Every merchant, every banker, will answer, no. But to do Mr. Wickliffe justice upon this branch of the subject, he has taught for years that our commerce with the East and North is ruinous; that it has drained us constantly of all our specie, and is grinding us into absolute poverty. The Mississippi trade has been equally unfortunate, and, according to him, Georgia and the Carolinas are the only source of wealth to us—to them we sell, from them we ought to buy. Commerce has mistaken its own interests, and the merchants do not know their true market. Be it observed, however, that, as those States have nothing which, in the present condition of our industry and of theirs, we could possibly import but negroes, the whole and entire commerce of Kentucky would be reduced to the slave trade. Will it advance agriculture more than it will manufactures or commerce? Ask the ruined fields—the waste and depopulated districts of lower Virginia. Will it improve the condition, the morals, or the character of our present race of slaves? They are at present a sort of inferior rural population—a degraded cast, to be sure, but intelligent and virtuous when compared with the brutal and savage masses in the Atlantic States. From the smallness of their number they are rendered more valuable as servants, but perfectly insignificant as enemies. Neither the government nor their masters feel any terror from them. Their very weakness improves their condition, and is the source, to them, of kindness and indulgence. In many instances, they are a sort of household dependents and humble friends, and are often found in the same field laboring in company with their master. With us, resistance or insurrection is impossible. The husband can leave his wife, the mother her child, without apprehension from this source. Phantoms of conflagration and massacre haunt not our slumbers—the terrors of St. Domingo, or of Northampton, vex not our waking thoughts. Will it strengthen us politically? Look at the state of the representation in Congress between the free and slave States, and the question is answered. Shall the government of Kentucky let go the check-rein which they now hold in this law, upon the growth of the most threatening evil in the constitution of American Society?

I have said that I considered negro slavery as a political misfortune. The phrase was too mild. It is a cancer—a slow, consuming cancer—a withering pestilence—an unmitigated curse. I speak not in the spirit of a puling and false philanthropy. I was born in a slave State—I was nursed by a slave—my life has been saved by a slave. To me, custom has made the relation familiar, and I see nothing horrible in it. I am a Virginian by descent—every cross in my blood, so far as I can trace it, in the paternal or maternal line, is Virginian. It is the only State in the Union in which I ever resided, save Kentucky. I was never north of the Chesapeake Bay. My friends, my family, my sympathies, my habits, my education, are Virginian. Yet I consider negro slavery as a political cancer and a curse. And she taught me so to consider it. Hear her own early declarations—ponder on her history—look at her present condition.

The delegates and representatives of the good people of Virginia, in convention assembled, on the 29th June, 1776, in the preamble to their first constitution, containing the memorable declaration against the government of *George III, of England*, and setting forth their grievances, among others, present the following as cause of rebellion and dismemberment from the British empire, that the aforesaid George had endeavored to pervert his kingly office "into a *detestable* and *insupportable tyranny*," "by prompting our negroes to rise in arms against us—those very negroes whom, *by an inhuman use of his negative*, he had refused us permission to exclude by law"—see preamble to amended Constitution of Virginia. One of the causes, then, of the American revolution, at least in Virginia, was the "*inhuman*" refusal of the British crown, to ratify a law prohibiting the importation of slaves. I have shown in my first number, that almost the first use made by that venerable and renowned Commonwealth of her newly acquired liberty, was an effort to arrest, by legislation, the increase of that tremendous evil of which she complains so bitterly against the king. In 1790, just after the adoption of the Federal Constitution, that point of time which forms the true starting post of these States, in the race of nations, what was the situation of Virginia? Occupying the most central position upon the American seaboard—having the greatest extent of coast in the Union—stretching from the

Chesapeake bay to the line of North Carolina, and from the Atlantic ocean to the Ohio river—covering a surface of 70,000 square miles—embracing under the mildest latitudes the greatest varieties of soil—prolific of the richest and most dissimilar products—intersected in every direction by the noblest navigable streams, connecting her mountains on the one side with the ocean, on the other with the bright waters of the Ohio—she seemed to comprehend within herself all the elements of empire. Nature never spread out a fairer, a nobler theatre for the enterprising genius of liberty and industry, than the State of Virginia. In the diversified productions of the different portions of her extended territory, there were laid the foundations of the largest domestic trade of any State in the world. Abounding in minerals of every species, from gold to lead, with the finest salt-wells on the continent, her valley teeming with grass and grain, and her lowlands giving her a monopoly in the then richest staple of the planting States, what more could she ask at the hand of Heaven? Did she want manufactures? She had the finest water power, the most abundant materials, and the easiest communications. Did she desire foreign commerce? The ocean lay before her, and the inlet of the Chesapeake, meeting the waters of her own Potomac, washed her entire eastern border. Behind, and touching her, lay the great valley of the west—the fairest portion of it once her own—that valley which was competent to sustain countless millions of men—which was destined to comprehend within its capacious bosom many States—States whose consumption is even now incalculable, and whose powers of purchase and of payment far exceed even their vast demand. This trade which sustains the commerce of Pennsylvania and New York, and the manufactures of New England—this enormous trade, which is still in its infancy, but which, even in its cradle, is competent to absorb and digest the capital—to keep in full and profitable employment the commercial industry of cities containing more free people than are to be found in all the broad territories of the old Dominion—might, and should have been all her own. It seems, indeed, to have been designed for her by nature, and to have tempted her by every inducement of circumstance and position. She had but to extend her arm and grasp it with all its treasures in full monopoly. Through the Ohio river, and her western streams, it was brought home, to the very foot of her mountains—that barrier passed, and it was poured through various channels, dividing and watering her whole eastern territory, into the bosom of the Atlantic. No State lay so convenient—to none were presented so many facilities, and so few difficulties, in the acquisition and entire command of the trade of the West. Did she lack the intellect to perceive—the genius to comprehend her position and her interest? Oh, no! *Magna mater virum*, she had produced a race of men "with minds to comprehend the Universe"—men whose names and actions placed Virginia first in fame, as she was in power and position, among the States, and threw a splendor over her early history, which still shines in lingering and melancholy radiance round her worn and faded brow—"a gilded halo, hovering o'er decay." They saw, and would have seized, all her advantages. George Washington, great in all things, and having stretched before his prophetic vision in long perspective, the future fortunes of the empire he had founded, warned Virginia of the importance of the West. He first projected the connection of the Chesapeake with the Ohio river, through means of the waters of the Potomac and Monongahela. They lacked not the intelligence. Had other States the start of her in population? Let us compare Virginia with New York, the only State which could challenge a comparison with her.

In 1790, Virginia, with 70,000 square miles of territory and internal resources such as I have described, contained a population of 748,308. New York, upon a surface of 45,658 square miles, contained a population of 340,120. This statement exhibits in favor of Virginia a difference of 24,342 square miles of territory, and 408,188 in population, which is the double of New York, and 68,000 more. In 1830, after a race of forty years, Virginia is found to contain 1,211,405 souls, and New York 1,918,608, which exhibits a difference in favor of New York of 707,203. The increase upon the part of Virginia will be perceived to be 463,197, starting from a basis more than double as large as that of New York. The increase of New York, upon a basis of 340,120 has been 1,578,588. This exhibits a positive difference in increase of 1,115,391 human beings. Virginia has increased in a ratio of 61 per cent., and New York in that of five hundred and sixty-six per cent. What the next census will show we can not tell. The total amount of property in Virginia, under the assessment of 1838, was $211,930,508 08½. The aggregate valuation of real and personal property, in New York, in 1839, was $654,000,000, exhibiting an excess in New York over Virginia, of capital, of $442,069,492. Statesmen may differ about policy, or the means to be employed in the promotion of the public good, but surely they ought to be agreed as to what prosperity means. I think there can be no dispute that New York is a greater, a richer, a more thriving, prosperous, and powerful State than Virginia. What has occasioned the difference? We have already seen that, as to advantages merely physical—as to all the original elements of grandeur, wealth, and power—Virginia was unsurpassed. Has accident or misfortune operated in this case? Has a despotic government bowed the spirit and cramped the efforts of Virginia? Has she suffered under the desolations of war or scourge of pestilence? Over this fair land, a balmy atmosphere and purest skies, smile health and cheerfulness. Healing fountains of mineral and medicinal waters burst from her mountains. The most delicious baths, the most salubrious springs, tempt from every land the pilgrims of affliction and disease. With war she has nothing to do; against its dangers, its horrors, or its burdens, she has no provision to make. Her government and people are not charged with the care or expenses incident to defense. The broad shield of the Union is spread before her. The potent arm of that government which combines the strength and revenues of twenty-six States, and wields the whole for the protection of each, is pledged to maintain her rights and her safety against all the world. There is but one explanation of the facts I have shown. There is but one cause commensurate with the effects produced. The clog which has staid the march of her people, the incubus which has weighed down her enterprize, strangled her commerce, kept sealed her exhaustless fountains of mineral wealth, and paralyzed her arts, manufactures, and improvement, is negro slavery. This is the cancer which has corroded her revenues, laid waste her lowlands, banished her citizens, and swallowed up her productions. This is the magazine, the least approach to which fills her with terror. This is the slumbering volcano which will bear no handling. The smallest breath to fan, the slightest threat to stir its sleeping but unextinguished fires, drives her to madness. Oh! well might she curse the tyrant who planted this dark plague-spot upon her virgin bosom.

I have given the total population of Virginia, at the two periods, and shown the total increase. Let us examine the relative fortunes of the two races as to their numerical progress. In 1790, there were of whites 544,881, in 1830, 741,648, showing an increase in forty years, of 196,767, or about 36 per cent., a little over one-third. In 1790, the slave population amounted to 203,427—in 1830, to 469,757, showing an increase within the same period, of 266,330 blacks, being one hundred and thirty-three per cent. increase on the original number.

If we examine the other slave States, we will perceive the same principle at work. In North Carolina, the black population has increased in a ratio of one hundred and forty-five per cent.; and in South Carolina, about three hundred per cent. In the former State, the whites have increased in a ratio of about thirty per cent. In the latter a little over eighty per cent. Throughout, it will be found on examination, that within the period embraced by the census, being forty years, the black population has increased within the slave States, faster than the white, and comparing the slave States with the free, that the total population increases in the latter with far more rapidity than the former. The slave States of this Union, at the last census, contained five millions of people, of which two were black. The free States contained eight millions of whites. Eight to three, is the proportion between the whites, in these two sections of the United States.

It is in vain to say, that the tremendous difference already indicated in the growth of Virginia and New York, was the result of the soil of Virginia. That her lowlands are poor and exhausted. They were not always so. One hundred years ago, and Virginia below the mountains, was the most desirable portion of America. Her condition in 1790, proves how much she had been preferred, and how vastly she had gotten the start of all the colonies. Her present poverty and exhaustion, are the result of the system of slave cultivation—the most slovenly and the least productive of any. The skillful and prudent husbandry which has made the rocky and inhospitable regions of New England, adequate to the support of two millions of people, would have preserved the plains of Old Virginia in their original fertility. But the reason, such as it is, can not apply to Kentucky. Compare her with Ohio or Indiana. She, too, has her mineral mountains—her sealed up fountains of wealth—her thousand sources of capital unopened—but who shall say that her soil is exhausted. "Here grain, and flower, and fruit, gush from the earth until the land runs o'er." Yet compare her, all lovely as she is, with Ohio, in all the elements of social strength and political power, and tell me the result and the reason? Whether, then, we compare the planting with the grain-growing States, or the grain-growing States with each other; throw but this ingredient of slavery into the one, and I care not whether they be equal in all other respects, or whether the slave State has every other advantage, the fatal influence of this poison is immediately perceived. In 1790, Ohio was a wilderness. In 1840, if her population bear the same proportion to ours that her votes do, she triples us in people, and numbers two millions. The tolls from her canals amount to $504,306—about double our whole revenue. Her representation in Congress will be in proportion to her people. But why compare her with Kentucky? With the restless and unpausing energy which belongs to a community entirely free, she has passed us long since. She will now take her station, third in the Union, and Virginia, who twenty years ago stood first in power and place—Virginia, the nursery of Presidents, the mother of States, the proud, the chivalric, must yield up her honors, and quietly fall in the rear of this creation of yesterday. Verily, these same "Goths and Vandals"—the free mechanics and artisans, the object of Mr. Wickliffe's classic horror—are the most renowned of conquerors. "No dangers daunt them, and no labors tire." They cut through mountains—they hew down forests—they build up cities—they connect the ocean with the lakes, the lakes with the rivers—they conquer time and space—they subject nature, throughout all her kingdoms and in all her elements, to the uses of men, and men multiply and population bounds forward, to meet and enjoy the supplies thus furnished by "their victorious industry." A comparison of the history and progress of the States of this Union, leaves no doubt of the fact that, in all that constitutes greatness and power in a community—in wealth, in population, in industry, in fiscal resources to the government, in multiplied employments, and extended and diffused comforts and intelligence among the great mass of the people—I say, there is no doubt that, in all these particulars, the advance of the free States has been wonderfully the most rapid, and the distance is widening at every observation that is taken. I have ascribed it to negro slavery. What other circumstance is there that is peculiar to the one section of the Union, to which this remarkable difference in progressive power can be ascribed? If we would examine philosophically into the process of production, the sources of wealth, and the principles of population, we would doubtless, find the principle here, as in every thing else, to correspond with and explain the fact.

I have run out these papers to such unreasonable length, that I have not room to trace the *modus operandi* of slavery through all its details. That the law of 1833, combined with other circumstances, has had a tendency to check its advance in Kentucky, and to keep it stationary for the last ten years, is admitted by the enemies of the law, and proven by the statistics of the country. That the repeal of that law would give a stupendous impulse to its increase, is equally admitted and desired, by those who seek its repeal, and is too obvious for argument. Between these opposite views of policy the country must decide. There are persons who say they desire a modification of the law, so as to permit citizens of the State to introduce slaves for their own use, but still to prohibit their importation as merchandize. This appears to me to be trifling with the subject. If it be the policy of Kentucky, to prevent, so far as she may, by legislation, the increase of slaves within her borders, without violating the constitutional rights of masters and emigrants, then the law, as it stands, is adapted to the policy. If that be not her policy, why then repeal it altogether. Where is the difference between permitting every body that wants slaves to introduce them for their own use, and permitting traders to bring them in for sale? The traders would bring them in for the use of the citizens, and would bring in no more than would be purchased for such use. Prohibit the trader from selling, but allow the citizen who desires it to import, and he will appoint the trader his agent to import for him, and pay him a commission, instead of buying from him. We will be thrown back upon the law of 1815, which had no effect at all. If the law of 1833 had been passed in 1800, and enforced, Kentucky, without violating the vested rights of any body, would have so reduced the evil, that it would have terminated of itself, or could have been easily done by the act of the masters, or the purchase by the Commonwealth. But Mr. Wickliffe styles me an abolitionist. He calls slavery a blessing. Will the slaveholders in Kentucky answer his appeal, and fall in with his reasoning? Will they repeal this statute —call a convention of the slave States — break down all restrictions on the free importation of slaves from every point of the compass, where slavery lies? Mississippi has overtraded herself in slaves — shall she throw back her excess upon us? And will the slaveholders do this — not to advance their wealth—not to improve the face of their country—not to introduce new branches of industry—not to invite skill, intelligence, and capital, and improvement, social, moral, or physical—but to keep out manufacturers, and mechanics, and artisans? Will they bring in the vicious, degraded, brutal, unproductive, and unimprovable African slave, from Virginia and Carolina?—a race which has brought down upon those States the double curses of weakness and danger—a race from which Virginia would have extricated herself while it was yet possible, if she had been permitted—a race which was inflicted and riveted upon her by a foreign tyrant ere she was yet free?—will they bring them here as an ally and an instrument, by which to lower the wages of labor, when those very wages are the highest indication of an advancing society and an improving condition, and the surest means in the power of the State of retaining her citizens within her bosom, of stopping the tide of emigration, and alluring back its current? Will they enlist the African race to keep out and to drive out their own? And for what are they persuaded to do this unnatural thing? To render themselves and their property more secure against the attacks of the abolitionists. Is South Carolina more secure with her 315,000 slaves to 265,000 citizens? If, as Mr. Wickliffe charges, the British Government is leagued with the Abolitionists to destroy the tenure of slavery by force, is it a wise measure of defense to increase the number of that domestic foe, till it exceeds your own? The idea and the argument appear to me to border on madness. Abolitionist I am none, and Mr. Wickliffe knows it. On the only occasion when that subject was ever fairly before the Government of Kentucky, I was in the Legislature and Mr. Wickliffe knows well the part I played then. The trial of Mahon disclosed the fact that there was a regular plan of operations, and band of agents, in Ohio, for the abduction of our slaves from the river counties. When that fact was laid before the Kentucky Legislature, no man there pressed more earnestly for the sending a special commission to Ohio, with a demand that she should legislate in such manner as to protect our property, and punish her citizens for its violation. The commission was sent, and she did legislate to our entire satisfaction. No power on earth, with my consent, should interfere with the internal regulations or policy of my native State.

The session of 1833 was the first of my service in the councils of the State. I had occasion that winter to observe with some attention the principles and the policy of the Senator from Fayette. How he came to vote for the law prohibiting the importation of slaves, I am at a loss to conjecture. It certainly was not of a piece with the rest of his policy then, or with his course and his objects since. The situation of the dominant party in the Legislature, the party to which I belonged, was very peculiar. General Jackson had just been elected, for his second term, to the Presidency of the United States. The majority in Kentucky was decidedly against him. The quarrel of South Carolina with the General Government had reached its crisis. The convention of that State, at Columbia, had passed its ordinance. The Executive had transmitted a copy to our Government, with an address to the States, which was laid before our Legislature. The principles set forth in that ordinance and that address, are familiar to the world. The doctrines that the Constitution of the United States was not a form of government founded by, and operating immediately upon, the people themselves—that there was no direct relation of government and citizens, of allegiance and protection, between the individuals in the several States and the Federal authorities—that, in truth, there was no such people as the people of the United States, but that the Constitution of the Union was a compact between the States in their political capacity—a treaty between independent sovereigns—of which each, of course, was to be the judge as to the extent of the obligations it imposed, and as to the cases of its infraction, formed the groundwork which supported the right to nullify. The States were informed that if the tariff was not modified to suit the views of South Carolina, or if any attempt should be made to force it upon her, she would secede, and that would be a signal of general dissolution. Kentucky, it was stated, would, of course, go with her, since she would surely not "continue to pay a tribute of fifty per cent. upon her consumption, to the northern States, for the privilege of being united to them; when she could receive all her supplies through the ports of South Carolina without paying a single cent. of tribute." The Legislature of Kentucky responded, in a report and resolutions, in which are repudiated the power of nullifying an act of Congress by any State, together with all the reasoning upon which it was claimed. The very comfortable invitation to cheapen our consumption by dissolving the Union, and receiving our supplies through the port of Charleston, was declined, for various reasons.

The Senator from Fayette, in a speech, which occupied seventeen close printed columns of the Commonwealth, assailed the principles of the Kentucky report and resolutions—abused General Jackson like a good whig, but maintained the construction given by South Carolina to the Constitution—in short, showed himself opposed to any expression on our part of disapprobation of her course, and voted against the report and resolutions. Notwithstanding the Senator's kindness, or at least indulgence, to the nullifiers, and his argument to show that the eastern trade, and our commercial connection with the north were a ruinous business to us, and that our true market was the south, he still was a most devoted friend to the tariff. The next proposition from South Carolina, on which Mr. Wickliffe and myself were called to act, as members of the same Legislature, was to create a Bank, common to four States, and as many more as could be brought into the arrangement—the controlling power to be at Charleston, and a branch in each of the States parties to the charter. I regarded this as part and parcel of a system of policy, which was to prevent the reëstablishment of the national authority over the currency, by enlisting as many States as possible in a sort of banking confederacy, with which the establishment of a truly national institution would, of course, interfere. That, indeed, was the avowed object in a report made by Col. Memminger to the South Carolina Legislature just before he started to Kentucky. The Senator from Fayette argued that this branch would have the same beneficial effect upon the exchange, which the Bank of the United States had. That there was no longer any hope of seeing that institution revived, and that we ought to adopt the best substitute we could. While I am writing these papers, a resolution has been before the Senate of Kentucky requesting, upon the part of Kentucky, the establishment of a United States Bank. The Senator from Fayette takes the ground that all the confusion and disasters which befell our currency and banks, from 1816 to 1820, was attributable to the old United States Bank—that the same results would occur again, etc. So intimately are the several parts of his system connected in his own mind, that in speaking upon this resolution, he recurs to the nullifying ordinance of 1833, re-denounces the report of the Legislature, which he had then opposed, intimates that the author was a federalist, although every body in both Houses adopted the report, but himself and two others, and assails Mr. Clay for compromising the tariff. Some persons consider all this as inconsistent and unintelligible. It does not strike me in this light. I have been a close observer of Mr. Wickliffe for a length of time, and upon a series of measures. His mind and his policy are indeed "a mighty maze, but not without a plan." To defend the ordinance of South Carolina nullifying the tariff, and at the same time to be a warm protective tariff man, looks a little odd. To abuse General Jackson's proclamation at the top of his speed and with the most unmeasured violence, and to defend the ordinance, may not seem so strange; but, at the same time, to denounce Mr. Clay for his compromise, by which South Carolina was appeased, and General Jackson robbed, as Mr. Wickliffe thought, of his prey, seems to some persons utterly unaccountable. I have put it altogether, and added thereto the argument on the "negro law."

South Carolina vowed, in the face of men and Heaven, that, unless the tariff was modified, she would secede, and that Kentucky would go along with her. Well, Mr. Wickliffe vindicates her right to do so, and proves, or at least tries to prove, that Kentucky's interest lies with the south, and that her eastern connections are ruinous; but, at the same time, is for screwing up the tariff to the highest notch, and is in a perfect fury with Mr. Clay for letting it down to the Carolina standard. Now this either means that Mr. Wickliffe wishes Carolina to be driven out of the Union, and Kentucky to go along with her, or it is the arrantest nonsense that ever fell under my observation. Mr. Wickliffe thinks that a branch of the Charleston Bank, located in Kentucky, would bring more capital into the country—not injure our stocks in the least—have the most beneficial influence upon our commerce and currency—but that a Bank of the United States would play the wild with every thing, as it did once before. If this does mean that the authority of the General Government over the currency, at least so far as the south and southwestern States are concerned, should be transferred to South Carolina, then I confess it is utterly inexplicable. Lastly, Mr. Wickliffe thinks that the slaves should be equalized between Kentucky and South Carolina; and those everlasting objects of his hate and execration—the free mechanics and manufacturers of the north—kept out of Kentucky; that a *convention* of the slave States should be called to concert measures, etc. Now what does this mean?

To each and all of the Senator's plans I have been opposed. For years I have looked to the restoration and exercise of the just powers of the General Government over the subjects, peculiarly committed to its charge by the Constitution, with anxious hope. I have anticipated therefrom order in the finances, and stability in the currency. Such a system of duties, or tariff, if you please, as will wipe off the present debt of the national treasury, and furnish an abundant revenue for national objects independent of the proceeds of the sales of public lands, will enable the latter fund to be distributed among the States, to which I think they are in all justice entitled. Pending the rage of parties and the suspension of all beneficial action upon the part of the General Government upon the currency, I have struggled hard against excessive banking in Kentucky, though I have sustained, so far as my humble abilities and limited influence would go, the character and the credit of the institutions of that kind which we were in some measure forced to establish. While in the councils of my native State, through a very remarkable and difficult political era, I have kept my eye fixed steadily upon the national authority as the only point of political contact between the States of this Union. I have resisted every thing that looked like interference from any quarter, with our internal policy, and every effort to entangle us in alliances with other States. I have seen Kentucky, through a period of eight years, maintain a just and wise moderation upon subjects which seemed to have run other States mad. Her currency is sound, her credit unimpaired, I hope, her public debt not at all alarming, and her taxes insignificant. Poised on her own brave center, she has beaten off both abolitionists and nullifiers. She fears neither, and abhors both. May she pursue and maintain her own internal and settled policy, without reference to any judgment, opinions, or interest, save her own, is the prayer of one who loves her well, and has tried to serve her faithfully.

SPEECH ON THE RESOLUTIONS TO CENSURE JOHN QUINCY ADAMS,

Delivered in the House of Representatives of the United States, January 25, 26, and 28, 1842

THE question being on the proposition of Mr. GILMER, of Virginia, which was in these words:

"*Resolved*, That, in presenting to the consideration of this House a petition for the dissolution of the Union, the member from Massachusetts, Mr. Adams, has justly incurred the censure of this House."

Mr. MARSHALL, of Kentucky, rose and addressed the Speaker as follows:

Mr. SPEAKER: I have prepared resolutions with a very short premable, but going somewhat more at large into the subject than is done in the proposition of the gentleman from Virginia. I wish to propose them as a substitute for that gentleman's resolution, and I hope that he will assent to it. As the resolutions are drawn in my own handwriting, and as there are alterations and interlineations in the manuscript, with the permission of the House, in order that the gentleman may judge whether he will accept what I offer in lieu of his own, I will read it in my place, rather than send it to the clerk's table.

Mr. MARSHALL then read the following:

"WHEREAS, the Federal Constitution is a permanent form of government and of perpetual obligation, until altered or modified in the mode pointed out by that instrument; and the members of this House, deriving their political character and powers from the same, are sworn to support it; and the dissolution of the Union necessarily implies the destruction of that instrument, the overthrow of the American Republic, and the extinction of our national existence: A proposition, therefore, to the representatives of the people, to dissolve the organic law framed by their constituents, and to support which they are commanded by those constituents to be sworn, before they can enter upon the execution of the political powers created by it, and intrusted to them, is a high breach of privilege; a contempt offered to this House; a direct proposition to the Legislature, and each member of it, to commit perjury; and involves, necessarily, in its execution and its consequences, the destruction of our country and the crime of high treason.

Resolved, therefore, That the Hon. John Q. Adams, a member from Massachusetts, in presenting for the consideration of the House of Representatives of the United States, a petition praying the dissolution of the Union, has offered the deepest indignity to the House of which he is a member; an insult to the people of the United States, of which that House is the legislative organ; and will, if this outrage be permitted to pass unrebuked and unpunished, have disgraced his country, through their representatives, in the eyes of the whole world.

Resolved, farther, That the aforesaid John Q. Adams, for this insult, the first of the kind ever offered to the government, and for the wound which he has permitted to be aimed, through his instrumentality, at the Constitution and existence of his country, the peace, the security, and liberty of the people of these States, might well be held to merit expulsion from the national councils; and the House deem it an act of grace and mercy, when they only inflict upon him their severest censure for conduct so utterly unworthy of his past relations to the State, and his present position. This they hereby do, for the maintenance of their own purity and dignity; for the rest, they turn him over to his own conscience and the indignation of all true *American* citizens."

Mr. Marshall resumed: I am very well aware, sir, and had, before I drew these resolutions, maturely considered of all I should expose myself to by submitting them; and if I am at all acquainted with my own temper, or with the movements of my own mind and heart, I have been induced to take a position of this kind by no personal feeling toward the gentleman upon whom it is proposed to inflict the censure of this House, still less by any sectional feeling against that portion of the United States which he represents on this floor; and, sir, it is of the last importance to the course I am now pursuing, a course which involves heavy responsibilities, that I should be free from all such motives. From the short time I have had a place on this floor, it can scarcely be charged against me that I have ever manifested any hostility to the northern portion of our fellow-citizens. The policy which I have advocated here—in advance, too, of the question—has looked to the protection and promotion of their peculiar industry. Toward the gentleman himself, the history of the past, and my personal bearing to him here, will absolve me from the suspicion of being actuated by personal hostility. His name and the name of his family have been connected in political history and administration with that which I bear; and I devoted the first warm years of my manhood in earnest endeavors to support the gentleman himself for the first office within the gift of this great people—an office which, if the proposition I am now animadverting upon be carried into effect, will be terminated with the existence of the nation, over whom the gentleman and the gentleman's father have been heretofore called to preside. Whatever feelings of personal bitterness may exist in the gentleman's bosom toward other portions of the slave States,—however deep the cause he may have for that determined spirit of hate and vengeance toward them, which seems to actuate him on this floor,—he should entertain no such feelings against me, or at least there is nothing in my past conduct to warrant them.

Within the last few days, scenes have been enacted in this hall, which have presented the American Congress to the world in a point of view equally discreditable to themselves and to the country, and which bring crowds to the galleries to witness the termination of what I have heard denominated by the crowd in the streets, "the row in the House of Representatives." Even in such scenes, in which the gentleman from Massachusetts has been the prime actor, my conduct toward him has been marked by courtesy and kindness. Sir, I moved to give him the opportunity of defending himself against the charges contained in a petition which he presented, praying his removal from the chair of the Committee on Foreign Relations. I repeat it, sir, that courtesy, personal courtesy and kindness toward that gentleman, have distinguished me, from the commencement of my services in Congress to this hour. But, sir, when a proposition so monstrous as this is made, and that too in the midst of the difficulties, embarrassments, and confusion, in which our public affairs are involved, and all the sources of popular discontent we see around us—a proposition calling upon the members of this House to betray the trust solemnly confided to them by the people, violate their oaths, and destroy a constitution which they are bound by every consideration of honor, conscience, and patriotism, to support and defend,—it strikes me with horror, and exhausts my patience. That there may exist out of this House men under the influence of a fanaticism, wild enough and mad enough to nourish such a project, or urge such a petition, I do believe, and did hope they were few and contemptible; but that there was a member on this floor who could be willing to assume the responsibility, through all coming time, of presenting to the government of the United States a proposition to terminate its own existence, I had not believed. I had indeed heard it whispered that such a memorial would be presented, but I rejected the idea with utter incredulity and perfect scorn.

Now, it may be said, and perhaps has been said, that the petition is worthy only of contempt; and that the Congress of the United States should pass over this insult without notice. To this view of the matter I can not give my assent. Holding this Union, as I do, to be the only pledge for, and the only means of, perpetuating the liberties of the people,—holding this Union, as I do, in a most especial manner, as the only means under high heaven by which that State in which I live, and that people whom I represent, can be preserved in safety and independence,—there is, in my judgment, sacrilege in approaching it in this manner. Coming from any quarter, it is sacrilege. Coming from the quarter it does, it assumes a political importance which it would not otherwise possess. He, sir, through whom the proposition is made to pull down the temple of liberty, was once its high priest, and ministered at its altar. It is no obscure hand, and no obscure name which is connected with this procedure. That name has gone abroad, and must go down to posterity in permanent connection with our country's history. The enemies of freedom, who have so fondly predicted the dismemberment of this confederacy, have now their eyes turned to the movements of this hall, and to the movements of this gentleman, in relation to a question which, of all others, presents the greatest danger to our institutions. And this question, regarded by our rivals and enemies abroad as the thorn in the side of the giant republic—a thorn which is to rankle and fester till, in their judgment, it will ultimately divide and destroy—this is the very question which that gentleman has been fonder of stirring than all others; which he nurses, indeed, to the exclusion of all others. This subject, however, does not enter, in the remotest degree, into the paper I have offered. God forbid that I should draw a line which is to array the southern men on one side, and the northern on the other. Surely, surely, the north is bound by love of country to oppose the memorial presented by the gentleman from Massachusetts, as strenuously as the south. Are northern men prepared to say that, under any law or right, petitions of this sort shall be laid before the Congress of the United States without censure or rebuke?—that a member shall be allowed to present a question here, and start it as a subject of legislative consideration in this House, which looks to the dissolution of the Union? But I am told here, that, at the time this proposition was presented, there was connected with it another—that the committee to which it was proposed to refer it, should report the reasons why the prayer of the petitioners should not be granted. In my humble judgment, this does not affect the question; or, if it does, it makes the case worse. If, under some fancied right of petition, extending to subjects over which the party petitioned has neither jurisdiction nor control, and to which, though they can be neither granted nor acted upon, so much importance seems to be attached in one portion of the Union, the gentleman had barely presented the petition, in fulfillment of what he believed to be a solemn duty, it might alter the case: but here it was proposed to be made the subject of legislative consideration, and that a report should be prepared and presented to the House in accordance with the views of the mover. It was to become a precedent, as far as it went, amounting to this: that the dissolution of the Union was a fair subject of legislative consideration, and could be brought up in this House, in the shape of a report, for discussion. It was to be a debatable question here—it was a matter to be regarded by the legislator as within the scope of his ordinary functions; and this position I would meet at the threshold, with the sternest possible rebuke. I know that the action of this House, on this subject, will go abroad to the nations of the world; and I wish it to be shown that, whatever of mischief, and misery, and confusion, may come upon us in after years, at this time of day the Congress of the United States will not permit one of its members to become the vehicle of a proposition so monstrous, that it can not be acted on without dishonor to themselves, or carried into effect without ruin and crime. Thus much I have thought proper to say in presenting the resolutions. If there be wrong, or injustice, or falsehood in them, let the responsibility fall, without shield or mitigation, on my bare head. That mischief can follow what truth and justice and our own dignity most clearly indicate, I can not believe. I do not harbor the idea that the general sentiment of the north can approve the movement which I have asked you to censure with so much severity. What! Massachusetts—of all the lands o'er which heaven's free sun flings his radiant smile — Massachusetts to come forward, and, through a man bearing the name which this gentleman does, make a proposition to dissolve the Union!

Mr. Adams, after having spoken at some length in reply to the foregoing, the next day made a question of order, "whether the House has the right to entertain this resolution, because it charges him with crimes of which this House has no jurisdiction; and because, if the House entertain the jurisdiction, they deprive him of rights secured to him by the Constitution of the United States." Mr. Adams relied mainly on the sixth article of the amended constitution, securing, in criminal prosecutions, the right of trial by jury. In reply, Mr. MARSHALL spoke as follows:

Mr. SPEAKER: The gentleman charges me with entire ignorance of law. I confess, sir, that I am not so profound a jurist as I could desire, or as I ought to be. I can inform the gentleman, however, that were I inclined to hold him to strict law, it is too late for him to file his dilatory plea to the jurisdiction, after having entered his defense to the merits and proceeded at some length in his argument. I waive, however, all technical objections, and give him the full benefit of his plea in abatement. In the question now made, there are two points to be considered: one a matter of fact, the other of law. The gentleman has assumed, in the first place, that the resolutions charge him with subornation of perjury and high treason, and that he is on trial here for those offenses. A very superficial examination of the resolutions, I think, will satisfy any one that the gentleman is mistaken in point of fact. He is not charged with either of those offenses. It is charged, in the preamble, that a proposition "to the representatives of the people, to dissolve the organic law framed by their constituents, and to support which they are commanded by those constituents to be sworn, before they can enter upon the execution of the political powers created by it, and intrusted to them, is a high breach of privilege; a contempt offered to this House; a direct proposition to the Legislature, and each member of it, to commit perjury; and involves, necessarily, in its execution and its consequences, the destruction of our country and the crime of high treason."

Now this petition was not drawn by the gentleman, nor is he charged with drawing it.

Mr. ADAMS here asked, Why am I to be punished for it?

Mr. MARSHALL resumed: Because, as a member of this House, the gentleman has permitted himself to be used as a vehicle by which a petition, involving within itself the proposition here set forth, was offered to the representative body of the nation; and the charge against the gentleman, of offense against the privileges of this body, for which I have ventured to arraign him, was not that he had petitioned for this object, or sanctioned the prayer of the petition; because the journal showed that he had, at the same time, moved that the committee report the reasons why the prayer of the petition should not be granted. The gist of the charge was, that the petition was offered; the ground of the contempt to the House is, that the gentleman, knowing its contents, has laid before them from others a proposition offensive and insulting, as inviting the House to do that which amounts to a violation of their official oaths. It is not charged, even, that the petitioners are guilty of treason; nor that the act of Congress which they seek would amount to treason; but that the execution of that act, and the consequences, to wit: the overthrow of the constitution, must needs be attended by the commission of treason some where. Now, sir, this is the only fair interpretation of the preamble. Indeed, sir, the gentleman's name does not appear in it; nor is it found any where in connection with perjury or treason.

Mr. ADAMS again interrupted: The charge is involved in the resolution.

Mr. MARSHALL: God knows in what crimes the gentleman may involve himself before he gets through this matter. He is, however, only charged by me with the presentation of a petition, the nature and consequences of which are set forth in the preamble. Here is the resolution, and the charge against the gentleman:

"*Resolved, therefore*, That the Hon. JOHN QUINCY ADAMS, a member from Massachusetts, in presenting, for the consideration of the House of Representatives of the United States, a petition praying the dissolution of the Union, has offered the deepest indignity to the House of which he is a member; an insult to the people of the United States, of which that House is the legislative organ; and will, if this outrage be permitted to pass unrebuked and unpunished, have disgraced his country, through their representatives, in the eyes of the whole world.

"*Resolved, farther*, That the aforesaid JOHN Q. ADAMS, for this insult, the first of the kind ever offered to the government, and for the wound which he has permitted to be aimed, through his instrumentality, at the constitution and existence of his country, the peace, the security, and liberty of the people of these States, might well be held to merit expulsion from the national councils; and the House deem it an act of grace and mercy, when they only inflict upon him their severest censure for conduct so utterly unworthy of his past relations to the state, and his present position. This they hereby do, for the maintenance of their own purity and dignity; for the rest, they turn him over to his own conscience and the indignation of all true *American* citizens.'

But were it otherwise, and were the gentleman really charged, and really guilty of subornation of perjury and high treason, it is in no sense true that this House is usurping the province of a jury. Nor is this a criminal prosecution, within the meaning of the article quoted and relied on by the gentleman. The consequences of the trial here had, and the nature of the judgment to be rendered by this House, are not, on the one hand, an acquittal from the crime, so as to bar indictment and trial before the proper tribunals; nor, on the other, to inflict the legal penalties appointed for the crimes supposed to be charged. This House tries only the offense against itself, and punishes under its own law—the law of parliament. Does the gentleman contend, or will any one believe, that the contempt merges in the felony; or that this House must summon a jury to find the facts, or turn the party over to the courts of law, before they can proceed to inquire into violations of their own privileges? Should one member maim or slay another on this floor, without excuse or justification, he would be indictable: does it therefore follow that we could neither censure nor expel? And if we could do either, does it not follow that we can inquire into the facts upon which our judgment is to be rendered? And does that inquiry, or that judgment, in the slightest degree encroach upon the party's right to a trial by jury, when the penalties affixed to his offense by the municipal law are to be inflicted? If it were so, a member need only commit a felony, to be exempt from the censure of this House. I deny the gentleman's law as well as his fact. Treason against the United States is not only an offense against the constitution, punishable in the federal courts; but it is a contempt, and the very highest contempt which a member could commit, against this House. The House can punish, and must of course have the right to inquire into the fact, with a view to punishment under the law of parliament; of which they are the judges, and the sole judges; of which courts and juries have no cognizance. The gentleman has sneeringly told me that I never learned my law from my uncle. From whatever source I may have derived it, I must have read utterly in vain, if there be any thing in the article to which the gentleman has referred which can protect him, even if the charges were made, from the parliamentary inquiry; and, secondly, the gentleman must himself, by this time, perceive that neither in the preamble nor resolution is a charge of either kind made against him. There are but two matters involved in the charge against him as subjects of inquiry: 1st. Did he present a petition to dissolve the Union? and, 2d. Does that presentation amount to a contempt? The preamble is simply a description of the petition itself, and a declaration that it does invite the House to perjury. And does it not? Where, forsooth, did the gentleman from Massachusetts learn his law? Not from his father, I am sure. A petition to the Congress of the United States to dissolve the Union, to repeal the constitution by statute, and they sworn to support it! This law would cut a figure in the Supreme Court, when the court itself, the constitution by which its validity must be tested, nay, the legislature which passed it, would, by its operation, be all annihilated. I see no mode of executing such a statute, in the absence of all judicial authority, save by force of arms; and the overthrow of the constitution by force of arms, is high, nay, the highest conceivable treason. If John Marshall, or the elder Adams, ever thought the Union could be dissolved by act of Congress, I have found no trace of it in their writings; and if I had, I confess my respect for both gentlemen would have essentially diminished. But more of this hereafter.

The House decided against Mr. Adams. The debate upon the resolutions was resumed. Mr. Adams was defended by Mr. Underwood of Kentucky, Mr. Botts of Virginia, and Mr. Arnold of Tennessee. Mr. Marshall, after great difficulty, obtained the floor on Friday, January 28, the resolutions being offered the Tuesday preceding, and made the following reply to Messrs. Adams, Botts, Underwood, and Wise.

Mr. Speaker: I have risen for the purpose of endeavoring at least to extricate the proposition I have offered to the House from all those matters extraneous, which have been so assiduously attempted to be connected with it, as well by those who are its avowed enemies, as by those who have professed in argument to be its friends. The gentleman from Massachusetts, and those who have addressed the House in his defense, have pressed on its consideration the situation in which he is placed here, by the charges said to be contained in the resolutions I have had the honor to propose. But it ought to be remembered that there is another trial yet to come, in which I must stand as the accused party, at the bar of public opinion. I have been well aware of the past services, of the weight of character, of the dignity, of the learning, and of the important position of the honorable member from Massachusetts, in this House and before the world. I well know that that gentleman is placed at an almost infinite distance from myself in personal importance and standing before this country, from his age, his past reputation, and the thousand memories that cling around his name. In this contest between the vigor of manhood and the trembling nerves and hoary locks of an advanced, venerable, and honored old age, the chivalrous sentiments and sympathies of this House and of mankind will naturally lean to him. And I am precisely the more anxious, on that account, to place in its true light before the country the course which, notwithstanding all the circumstances which surround it, I have, from motives which I deem adequate, deliberately chosen to pursue. And here, sir, permit me to express my astonishment that, after the debate which occurred here the other day upon the point of order raised by the gentleman from Massachusetts, and which, after full argument, had been decided against him by the House, my colleague (Mr. UNDERWOOD) should have again brought it forward, and in the manner which he did. How is it possible that, with the preamble and resolutions before him, my colleague could have contended that the member from Massachusetts stood here charged by me with subornation of perjury and high treason; or that those resolutions any where intimate that the bare *presentation* of a petition to dissolve the Union constitutes either of those crimes. I had, indeed, been a worse lawyer than the gentleman from Massachusetts has been pleased to represent me, could I have been guilty of such absurdity. Before I sit down, I shall take an opportunity to discuss the truth and propriety of the principles contained in the preamble, in which alone it can be pretended that I have involved the gentleman from Massachusetts in the crimes which he alleges I have charged.

I mean not to abuse the patience of the House, by introducing or enlarging upon what is irrelevant to the subject; but, before I come to what is the real question, I must be permitted to take a brief survey of what yesterday fell from my friend from Virginia over the way (Mr. WISE). Of all men on this floor—of all men living—I should be the last to let the grounds on which that gentleman has placed the subject go before the country, as containing my views in relation to it. Entertaining toward him—and I say this, not with the view of screening what I now advance from the freest course of animadversion by him or others, but in all seriousness and sincerity — entertaining toward the gentleman the most perfect respect, and being, moreover, in our private and personal relations and intercourse, not only on the most friendly terms, but holding myself under personal obligations to him for acts of kindness and courtesy extended to me out of this House, whatever I shall say in regard to the gentleman's course here will be, in its bearings, purely political.

While, then, I sever myself utterly from that gentleman's political views, and from what I believe to be his political objects, and without expressing any censure upon him for those views—none whatever—the gentleman may be right, or I may be right; the one is perhaps as likely as the other; the country must judge between us—I mean here only to say, that we are wide apart as the poles, and I fear shall remain so.

Mr. WISE here explained. He had never meant to advocate Mr. MARSHALL'S resolutions: he had spoken on the motion to print; and had risen to explain the reason why he would not vote on Mr. ADAMS' case. The gentleman from Kentucky need not premise his speech by disavowing his willingness to have his proposition to rest on any grounds taken by Mr. W.; for he had not intended that what he said on that occasion should be understood to have any thing to do with it whatever.

Mr. MARSHALL resumed: I am very glad to hear this disavowal upon the part of the gentleman, and am very thankful that the fact stands as it does; for, had the gentleman indeed intended his speech as friendly to my proposition, I should have been tempted to exclaim with the Spanish proverb, "God, deliver me from my friends, and I will take care of my enemies." I have read the report of the gentleman's speech with great attention, (for it was impossible, from the confusion during a part of its delivery, to hear all that he had said,) and I find it will still be necessary for me take a very cursory review of what the gentleman advanced; in doing which, I shall take the liberty of condensing the speech a little, which, as reported to the public, occupied, in all, some seven columns of the National Intelligencer. Should I, in this process of condensation, reduce the speech of the gentleman to the form of distinct resolutions, they would amount to about these:

1. *Resolved*, That the existence of slavery, as a political institution, is essential to liberty and equality.

2. *Resolved*, That there has been, from the very foundation of this government, an English anti-American party in this country, led and headed by the house of Braintree, changing its name at different periods, but steadily pursuing its object, which is to bring back this country under the dominion of England; and that this is the grand principle of the northern policy.

3. *Resolved*, That this faction was first crushed by Mr. Jefferson; that having afterward somewhat revived, it was prostrated a second time by General Jackson; but that, still retaining the principle of vitality, and now again appearing with a new name, and the avowal of new objects, it will be extinguished finally, if the whole South will unite and rally under John Tyler against the entire North, supported as they are by England, in this attack upon liberty and equality.

4. *Resolved*, That one of the schemes of this English party to destroy this confederacy, is to establish a tariff, by which English commerce is to be curtailed, a threatening rival raised up in the North, the right arm of England (viz: her manufacturing industry and the power of her machinery) to be palsied, and the northern States to be put up in her room as the great customer, not only of our own country, but of the rest of the world.

And this is the notable plan by which Great Britain is to be conciliated, and, with her consequent aid, this Union is to be dissolved! Now, against the reasoning, at least, raised upon this last statement of fact, I beg leave to enter my dissent.

Mr. Speaker, of all the objects I may have had in view in offering the resolutions under discussion, certainly the very last which could have entered into my imagination would have been to revive here, and at a time like this, the bitter and envenomed animosities of 1801. Those unhappy enmities grew out of a state of the world, and of the politics of this country, which exist no longer, and which never can exist again. I can, of course, have no personal remembrance of those days, since the year 1801 happened to be the very year in which I was born, and the troubles of that stormy era had terminated before I was old enough to bear arms or to take any active interest in politics. I hold myself accountable for my own sins only, and not for those of a generation gone by. All these matters are with me matters of history merely; but, for one, come weal come wo to me from the resolutions I have offered, or the opinions I here express, I now enter my most solemn disclaimer and unqualified denial of the proposition that northern men, or that the party termed federalists—whatever might have been their mistakes—ever were, as a party, traitors to their country, or a banded faction conspiring to bring us back to those very chains which they themselves—ay, they were the very men—which they themselves had cut in two; to rend which, they had pledged their lives, their fortunes, and their sacred honor; had girded on their swords, and never had sheathed them till they saw their country in liberty and peace. They might in some things have been mistaken; the system of government which they had constructed, and whence they derived their party designation, *federalist*, was as yet a sheer experiment. It went into operation under an accumulation of disastrous circumstances in our own internal condition: prostrate credit, ruined commerce, disordered finance, and a heavy public debt;—these were the elements whence the federal constitution emerged, and with which it had to contend in its first administration. It was precisely coeval, too, with the birth of a revolution in the other hemisphere, which shook, in its earthquake progress, the whole frame of human society to its deepest foundations. They might in some things have been mistaken; but on the leading points of domestic policy especially, the whig party are the very last persons in this world who ought to charge those men with having been political traitors. Friends of England, to the injury or dishonor of their own country, they never were. In the then existing state of the world, when the balance of power in Europe was utterly overthrown—when one vast military dynasty had risen over the subjected and affrighted kingdoms around—when one gigantic and commanding mind was wielding the entire military force of the continent, and with as much ease as though it were a willow wand—those men believed, devoutly and sincerely believed, that the safety and independence of our young republic were involved in the issue of the fierce struggle going on in Europe. With the example of Switzerland and Holland before their eyes, they shrunk from the imperial embrace of France. They maintained that it was not the true policy of the United States to abandon her neutral position, and aid in the destruction of that power whose navy at that time formed the only counterpoise to the colossal strength of Napoleon,—the only bar to the establishment of a universal despotism in Europe, in comparison with which that of the Cæsars shrinks into insignificance. This had been their honest belief. Their policy was condemned; and the question has long been settled in the public judgment. The war which ensued was popular; it raised our national character; it served to develop the real arm of our national defense; and in its glorious termination were realized none of the fears of the federal party. The success of the war accomplished their fall. The overthrow of the French empire, and the restoration of the political equilibrium in Europe, and the return of universal peace, were events which they most earnestly desired. The reverse was what they feared and deprecated. Had Russia and England fallen under the blow, and their resources, naval and military, passed into the hands of the greatest genius and the most daring and ambitious soldier the world had yet seen, the result to our infant institutions is matter of conjecture, thank God, and not of history. The result of the war, although precisely what they desired, accomplished their fall, and stamped the seal of popular odium upon the name of that man whom the democratic party and their great leader dreaded more than all the world. The interpretation and defense of the constitution under which we now live, as embodied in the Federalist, were mainly the production of his mind, and still form the text-book for American statesmen, lawyers, and judges. The measures recommended and the principles maintained by him in relation to the foreign and domestic policy of the government he had so signally aided to establish—the assumption and funding of the revolutionary debts of the States; the full and faithful payment of the public securities; the administration of the national finances, and the supply of a national currency and commercial medium for the people, combining the solid credit of the metals, with the lightness, facility of transmission, and cheapness of paper, through the agency of a Bank of the United States; a strict neutrality, and the encouragement of a navy, with a view to its maintenance and the protection of our commerce; the fostering care of American manufactures; and, above all, the indissoluble union of these States under a common government, having complete, national, and paramount authority over all, touching those things which are common to all:—these are among the opinions he has left recorded in his immortal works; and there is abundant evidence that they were formed in the school and ratified by the judgment of that *slaveholder* whose sacred dust now reposes within a few miles from this spot, in the soil of his native Virginia, and on the banks of his own once loved Potomac. Against the hated head of this great statesman and illustrious man were hurled the whole thunders of a victorious and triumphant party; nor did they cease till the hand of one, now branded in his country's history as a traitor, in an evil hour had laid him low. Whatever may have been his errors, it would be hard to convince me that one who had entered the family of George Washington at the age of nineteen—who had served with him for seven years, through all the soul-trying scenes of the Revolution—who enjoyed his entire confidence then, and continued so to enjoy it, that afterward, when the leader of the Revolution became the civil head of the republic he had founded, this same traitor was called by him to preside over that department, the most embarrassed, the most difficult, the most responsible; and his genius was invoked and his judgment trusted to devise the means of establishing credit, creating revenue, and reforming the most debased currency ever employed in the transactions of mankind; and well did the first Secretary of the Treasury vindicate the opinion his old leader had formed of him. And, sir, when George Washington, after his retirement from civil office, was again, and I believe in the last year of his life, called on by his country to head her armies in a war then expected with France, he stipulated, as the condition of his acceptance, the right to name his officers; and he appointed this same traitor-federalist, Alexander Hamilton, his second in command;—I repeat it: it would be most difficult to convince me, with all my confidence in the sagacity, judgment, acute discrimination of character, and untarnished honor of George Washington, that there was treason in the heart of one whom he reared, loved, and trusted throughout his glorious life. If admiration of this man's genius, sorrow for his faults, and pity and regret for his untimely fate, be federalism —I stand convicted.

That I may pursue the views of the gentleman from Virginia a little farther, I must here also declare, most explicitly, that these resolutions were not offered with the most remote intention or desire of rallying the southern portion of this House, as a party, under any lead, or any administration, present or prospective. Entirely the reverse; such a design, indeed, would be as fatal to their passage, as it is foreign to their tone and character, and subversive of their object. There is—at least, I trust there is—nothing sectional about them. There is incorporated with them no dogma of any particular school of politicians. They are guarded, carefully and purposely guarded, from all connection with the questions of agitation and strife, which so unhappily divide, and so readily inflame, the sectional parties on this floor. They were brought forward as purely American in their character, as a test of how much American feeling exists in this body, and as affording to all who are actuated by it an opportunity of subscribing here to what I conceive to be the indisputable principle of our social fabric. Whatever may be their fate, I fondly hope that agitators, whether from the North or South, may not be able to drag the question down to a fierce party or personal quarrel, which is to be decided by geographical lines, without reference to the principle, and the only principle, involved in the resolutions themselves.

Having said thus much as to what may be considered in some sort foreign to the subject immediately before the House, I proceed now to the matter in hand. And first, sir, as to the nature of the defense here set up. The House has had four speeches addressed to it in behalf of the gentleman from Massachusetts, some of which were most able and interesting. After a touching description of the venerable age, the long and important services, the weight of character, the talent, the influence and power of the gentleman from Massachusetts, and comments on the severity of the censure proposed to be inflicted, it was argued that his real object had been to obtain an opportunity of replying to the petitioners; of producing a State paper, the effect of which should be to stay these incendiary measures of discontent; and with all the power of his eloquent pen, and all the vast resources of his mighty mind, to repress, by the force of unanswerable argument, the wild projects and headstrong purposes of those who desire to strike at the Union; that the true design of the whole movement has been a triumphant defense and vindication of the American Union, and such a reproof to those who have asked its destruction, as will for ever seal their lips in silence; the production of an argument which will satisfy all the world, rectify the sentiments, and put down, at once and for ever, the designs and purposes which have given birth to the memorial. This has, in substance, been the defense set up, not by the gentleman from Massachusetts, but by the most eloquent of his champions, (Mr. Botts.) Now, if this defense had been urged before this House by the accused himself,—if he had so much as breathed such a wish as has been ascribed to him by his zealous and able advocate from Virginia—though by no means convinced that even his motive could justify the deed, or that this House should receive and tolerate such propositions, for any purpose or on any considerations, I might possibly have been tempted to withdraw the resolutions. But, sir, I can not consent to overlook the defense set up by the gentleman himself, and be thus turned over to what has been advanced for him by others, upon their own authority.

What has the gentleman said? As to what he may have uttered in the irritation of the moment, against myself personally, it has gone by; my understanding and temper are fixed upon things so much higher than aught which concerns me individually, that matters of this sort make but slight impression upon either. Although the gentleman from Massachusetts has pronounced me not possessed of mind enough to judge of the meaning of the constitution, or to comprehend the definition of treason, (and the judgment of the gentleman on such subjects is held by this House as entitled to great weight;) and although he has taunted me with being a member of the temperance society, and kindly and humanely ventured the hope that I would persevere in the pledge, coupled with the suggestion that, in three years, I might so far recover the understanding which God had conferred, as to be fit to enter a law school; and although the gentleman has further said that I have admitted to him in private conversation that his complaints of oppression under a refusal to receive petitions of this sort were just; still, sir,—

Mr. ADAMS here interposed; and the floor being yielded for explanation, corrected the statement of Mr. MARSHALL, by observing that what he had said was, that the gentleman from Kentucky had admitted to him, in private conversation, that he was a friend to the right of petition, and believed abolition petitions ought to be received.

Mr. MARSHALL resumed: I am happy in being corrected. But, sir, I have said nothing to the gentleman in private, touching the reception of abolition petitions, or the repeal of the twenty-first rule, which I have not said in argument upon this floor. It is true, and the House know it to be so, that I have taken the ground that the twenty-first rule should be repealed, and the abolition memorials received and referred to a committee composed exclusively of northern men, with the gentleman himself at their head; not as matter of right—never; but for the purpose of quieting this eternal agitation of the subject by the gentleman himself, by extracting a report from northern statesmen, which should inform the House and the South whether they meant to sustain here the views, objects, and opinions of these fanatical incendiaries. But to proceed. If the gentleman thinks, by these irritating taunts, which no man better understands than himself, to sting me from my propriety in this hall, or to provoke me into unseemly and passionate retort, he little understands the character of the man with whom he has to do, intemperate as he may take him to be. He may in future, therefore, spare himself the shame of indecorums unworthy of himself, if not unjust to me.

Mr. Speaker, the petition which has given rise to this proceeding is now on the table of the House. It prays the national legislature to take the preliminary steps to a dissolution of this Union. What is the defense which the gentleman has offered in bar of the censure for presenting such a document here? Two points have been made by the gentleman in his reply to my remarks upon introducing the resolutions. First, the gentleman insisted upon the right of the petitioners to do this thing. They have a natural right to dissolve this government, and to sever the union of these States, whenever that union shall, in their opinion, be injurious or inconvenient to themselves. And here he fortifies himself by the declaration of American independence, in which the right of the people to alter or abolish their form of government is enumerated among the self-evident truths in politics, and as one of the original and indestructible rights of mankind. And, in the second place, that this right is nugatory, and of no value, unless they can petition Congress to effect such dissolution. What does this argument prove? That the American Government can not be abolished by the gentleman's constituents, without their asking Congress to do it. This is the body which must destroy the Union, if it is to be destroyed at all. So much as to the matter of right.

And then the gentleman, as the next step of his argument in defense, went on to enumerate the grievances which lead these people to desire a dissolution of the Union; and the grievances are many and terrible. I will go over a few of the heads of complaint, by way of contrast to the statement made by the gentleman from Virginia, (Mr. BOTTS,) as to the object and motive of the gentleman in bringing that petition into this House. The gentleman from Massachusetts has stated upon this floor that the portion of the Union whence I come are trying, with all the influence they can exert, to effect a repeal of the habeas corpus, and the right of trial by jury; that they are industriously endeavoring to extend the institution of slavery over the free States; that they seek to involve this country in a war with Great Britain, with a view to restore the African slave trade, and to fix it upon these States for ever; and that the project of the Secretary of the Navy for the establishment of a home squadron had for its real object, not the defense of the country, but was designed as a convoy for the slave trade. And then, sir, after enumerating all these different grounds of grievance, the gentleman has warned the House that he will go home to his people, and say to them that it is time to take the alarm; that he will give them the alarm; and that he has introduced this petition for the very purpose of exciting alarm.

Mr. ADAMS denied this, and declared that what he had said was, that he had presented the petition because he considered it his duty.

Mr. MARSHALL. I appeal to the report of the gentleman's speech in the National Intelligencer, given by one of the regular reporters of that establishment in this House. Mr. M. then read from the report:

"And when he (Mr. A.) came to that in the defense which he should make, if called on, he should consider other matters of oppression, not only actual but intended. He would come and state before this House how that portion of the country whence that gentleman came was endeavoring to destroy the right of habeas corpus and the trial by jury, and all the rights in which the liberties of this country consist.

"He would show how, in that portion of the country, there was a systematic attempt even to carry it to the dissolution of the Union, now carrying on between different States. He would look into the controversy between Virginia and New York, between Georgia and New York, and between Georgia and Maine, in order to prove the continual system and purpose to destroy all the principles of civil liberty among the free States; and by power to force the detested principles of slavery on the free States of this Union. He would show it by documents and by reference to arguments which had been used, in such a manner that every man in this House should be convinced of the truth of it. He had seen, and he was now seeing, that among those measures so constantly and so perseveringly pursued, was the project of smuggling this country into a war with Great Britain, for the purpose of protecting the slave trade, African and American. He had seen that that was the deliberate purpose. And one of his reasons for presenting this petition was to give the alarm to the people of that portion of the country whence he came. It was time for them to take the alarm, or they would find themselves smuggled into a war for the protection of the slave trade; and that the most absurd and false principles of the laws of nations had been asserted by our minister in England, all for the purpose of smuggling this country into a war with that government, under pretense of defense against her aggressions. He would show all this in the utmost detail, if he was called on to defend himself against this charge."

Thus, sir, the gentleman's language has gone forth to the world. And after he stated these heads of grievances, he pledged himself that, if the House forced him to answer the charge I had made, he would show the truth of all this.

Mr. Adams. And I will show it.

Mr. Marshall. I mean not to discuss their truth with the gentleman. Neither shall I discuss here, and now, the right of Great Britain to search American vessels on the coast of Africa, or elsewhere, under the pretense of suppressing the slave trade; for engaging in which, even were the fact so, our ships and citizens are only amenable to the laws and jurisdiction of their own country.

Mr. Adams. You had better not.

Mr. MARSHALL. Neither shall I discuss the necessity or propriety of the home squadron, for the defense of our exposed coast against the strongest maritime power in the world, with whom we have many delicate and unsettled questions involving our territorial rights; or enter upon the question whether such defensive measures are a grievance to the North. I have adverted to this list of grievances merely to show what ground has been actually taken by the gentleman himself, in his defense. He has undertaken to make out a case of such grievous oppression and tyranny exercised by this government upon him and his, that, if aught can justify an outraged people in going into a revolution, and bursting the bands of society, this is the very case; and the gentleman insists that he has done it. And, sir, he contends that the action of Congress in preparing for a dissolution of the Union is the only means by which the sacred and eternal right of his constituents to abolish an oppressive and tyrannical government can be carried into effect. The gentleman has avowed that he has brought this petition forward in order to give those constituents the alarm, and to afford them needed information and proof in the documents and arguments he means to adduce in the progress of his defense. Still, however, the gentleman says that he has guarded himself in his proposition for a reference; and that he would not, if permitted to report on the subject, advise an instant dissolution of the Union. No; not yet, not yet; but the time is coming —is approaching.

Now, let any gentleman compare all this with the ground of defense taken in behalf of the gentleman from Massachusetts by his friend from Virginia, (Mr. BOTTS,) and where will the gentleman stand? The gentleman only wished an opportunity to prepare a report which should allay agitation, and quiet the minds of his constituents! Oh, yes; and a precious foretaste the House has enjoyed of the nature of that document, which the chairman of the Committee of Foreign Relations may be expected to send forth to the world, should his own instructions to the committee be adopted. This is allaying agitation, with a vengeance! This is soothing irritation; this is a healing persuasive to convince men that the Union of these States must be maintained! The gentleman from Virginia longed that the opportunity should be given to the gentleman from Massachusetts, that he might, by his eloquent pen, by the force of his luminous understanding, and the whole weight of his personal influence, put down for ever the unhappy spirit of northern discontent, and make his constituents ashamed that they had ever harbored a thought of so dire a sacrilege as the dissolution of this Union! What! trust this task of an angel of peace to the man who openly avows that he has introduced the memorial for the purpose of bringing forward, in its discussion, fresh subjects of alarm! Assign this duty of healing, to the man who fortifies the right to abolish the constitution through the agency of Congress, by an appeal to the Declaration of Independence; and who stimulates men to the exercise of this right, by presenting an accumulation of grievances such as never had been endured on earth before, and for which, in the judgment of these men, there is no remedy, other than the total destruction of our system of government? And an American House of Representatives, themselves the embodied image of this great nation, are to leave to hands like these the task of soothing the irritations and quieting the alarms of a discontented people!

I confess that I heard the gentleman from Virginia (Mr. BOTTS) with astonishment; but if I wondered at the ground taken by that gentleman, how was it increased when I listened to the gentleman's (Mr. ADAMS') own immediate friend. A gentleman from Massachusetts (Mr. SALTONSTALL) has appealed not only to the age and past services, but to the blood, and lineage, and remote ancestors of his friend. He has dwelt on his talents, his learning, his high standing, his influence, his weight of character, and, above all, his indomitable, persevering courage. The gentleman has advised the House not to take him in hand, for he was a descendant of one of that stubborn crew who, beginning with a petition of right, had gone forward with untiring and undeviating footsteps, till they had ended in overturning the English monarchy, and bringing the head of Charles Stuart to the block;—men who had cast themselves on the bosom of the wild ocean, and had sought a home upon the bleak and desolate shores of an unknown wilderness, rather than yield an inch of what they deemed their rights at home;—who had warred, and warred, and warred to the death, without one thought of submission. Finding in this House a descendant of one of those sturdy commons of England, who were pilgrims or regicides as their fortunes fluctuated, but who yielded never — a man whose imagination seems thoroughly possessed with the idea that he and his associates are as grievously and intolerably oppressed on this side the Atlantic as his ancestors had been on their native shores, and who, remembering that the race from whom he springs had prostrated the British throne, seems equally confident that he can upheave the foundations of the American republic;—upon such a one it is vain to think of laying the hand of authority. It would seem that duty and policy alike require that we should fold our arms and let him run. And why? Because, by attempting to control him, we shall only provoke his people the more; and they will but come upon us the more fiercely, should they see a finger laid, however lightly, upon their indomitable leader. For one, so help me Heaven, it is an argument to which I will never yield. If, standing as I do under my oath to the Constitution and my obligation to the American people, I could be brought to legislate under terror, these are the circumstances—these the very considerations — which should induce me to vote for a deeper and sorer punishment than that now proposed.

The gentleman from Massachusetts told me that I was not able to comprehend the rights of the citizen; that I knew nothing of the Constitution of my own country, or of the liberties and franchises which that instrument was designed to protect; and that the resolutions I have offered here indicate such ignorance.

I listened, too, to what my colleague (Mr. UNDERWOOD) said about the charge of treason which these resolutions involved.

Will the House bear with me while I read once more the passage with which it was my desire to preface the resolutions I have offered? [Here Mr. MARSHALL again read the preamble.]

Now, sir, can it be necessary again to reiterate that neither the drawing nor presentation of the petition, nor the enacting of the statute prayed for, is charged as treason; but that its execution and consequences, in the destruction of the country, the government, the body politic of the United States, necessarily involve treason. Human language, as it seems to me, can not be more explicit.

Mr. ADAMS. You beg the question.

Mr. MARSHALL. I beg nothing of you, sir; nothing. But I am told that I must correct the position here taken, because the memorial asks for a peaceable dissolution of the Union. A peaceable dissolution of the Union! It can not be. Before the bonds are broken, war must be made. It will be made for the Union on one side, and against it on the other; and making war on the United States, by any portion of the same, is treason in all concerned.

A peaceable dissolution! How will you go about it? The petition implies, and the gentleman maintains, that it can be done only by Congress. I put it, then, to my colleagues to say if we have it in our power to do any such thing. I lay it down, as a philosophical and political truth, that a Union like ours never can be dissolved, save by universal assent, or by force of arms. I lay it down, that the government of this country is a government essentially, and that the United States is a body politic. I, as a citizen, am a component part and member of that body; I am a party to this government. My relations and my allegiance are direct and immediate. It operates upon me, not through any other sovereign interposed, to whom alone I am responsible, and who represents me, as in the case of a league or treaty; but directly, by its own laws and officers. The United States is my country; and her Constitution, and my share of protection under it, constitute my birthright. It is seldom worth while to discuss an abstract proposition; but when you come to the right to dissolve this Union as the basis of legislative action, it is abstract no longer; it becomes fearfully and momentously practical. The gentleman can not find it in the constitution or laws. He traces it to the declaration of American independence, itself a revolutionary paper, sustained by the pledge of blood, and carried out by the sword. That was no peaceable dissolution, at least. And the right claimed then for the people does not sustain the gentleman nor the petitioners in their application to those who are the sworn servants of the people, under an authority which none but their masters can abolish. But, sir, does the gentleman contend that a simple majority of the people can of right peaceably abolish the Constitution of the United States, against the will of the minority? I say of the people, far less of the Congress. I speak not now of revolution by physical force, but of peaceable dissolution of the social Union by a majority of its members, against the voice of the minority, as matter of right, either natural or acquired under our constitution. It is plain that no such right is recognized by grant, reservation, or implication, in the constitution itself. It must then be inferred by right reason from the nature of things. Whence do a majority of men derive the right to control by law the will and the action of a minority? From positive agreement, certainly. The right is conventional, not natural. Ten men are thrown together, between whom there subsists no previous agreement, who will say that the will of six can control the remaining four? In such a state of things, each man is master of his own actions, and independent of the other nine. The rightful power of a majority is the result of contract in every instance;—a contract in which the minority have originally agreed to be so governed. The right to make such a contract is a natural right, and, when once entered into, is binding upon all. Such contract and consent are laid down by the Declaration of Independence as the only just foundation of government. In all true theory, then, political constitutions repose upon the original contract to which each individual upon whom they operate, and whom they can bind, is a party. This agreement, according to the reasoning of our own *declaration*, must be presumed, or the principles of that declaration can not be sustained; and, in point of fact, it is in every instance made either expressly or by tacit consent. The foreigner who wishes to bind himself to our constitution, to take upon him its obligations, and to entitle himself to its protection, makes his declaration and swears his allegiance. He thus becomes individually a party to the government, and by the most solemn of all contracts. But as men, in the absence of agreement, are entirely independent of each other, so are they competent and strongly impelled by the laws and necessities of their common nature to form agreements. When formed, they are binding upon all who are parties, according to their terms, and can not be cancelled but by the consent of all, or by force. Government, then, the highest of all contracts, by means of which all others are enforced, partakes still of the nature of all others. Founded in agreement, it binds men together in one body, or community, or society; and can not be dissolved without the same authority by which it was formed—to wit, the consent of all the members, or by some original stipulation in the constitution or contract, or by force. There is no stipulation in our national contract by which a part of the people, be it great or small, can throw the residue out of their social union, and from under the protection of the national laws and the national strength. There remain but the other two modes. What prospect is there that a government including seventeen millions of people is to be dissolved by universal assent? You may sever the Union. God in his infinite mercy forbid that you ever should; but you will never do it, save by force. Never, never.

I have said that the execution of an act of Congress providing for such an event does involve treason, because it could only be executed by force of arms; and that this very passage of the act does involve perjury, because we have sworn to support the constitution. Suppose we do so much violence to our imaginations as to conceive that such an act has been passed: how will it work? It will go to Kentucky, and it will tell the people of that State that there is no United States—no American constitution; that there is no federal government and no State governments; that society is resolved into its original elements; that the people, the sovereign people, are a people no longer, but a mere disconnected multitude, dependent upon accident or force for any form of polity into which they may afterward be thrown. I say there would be no State government; because, if the federal constitution be overthrown, there would remain no government armed with the attributes of sovereignty. The State governments can not make war, enter into alliances, own a navy, coin money, lay duties, or collect revenue from commerce: and therefore I say the dissolution of the Union is, for the time, the dissolution of society. The State governments must be recast and invested with new power, before there would be any political organization in America at all competent to achieve the ends of society. And will any gentleman tell me that, in a juncture like this, under an attempt to cast to the winds all civil and social ties, that I, who have sworn again and again to support the federal constitution, will have no right to draw the sword in its defense? Dissolve the Union! Yes, throw Kentucky back upon herself, buried in the interior, a dependent and tributary province of some new empire established on the Atlantic coast; levy taxes on her consumption to fill the treasuries of New York, or Virginia, or South Carolina; taxes imposed by legislatures in which she is not represented, if we are to be broken into as many independent communities as there are States. Or rend the empire in twain, and convert her, from the center of the American Union, into the frontier State of a slave confederacy—the very Belgium on which the battles of abolitionism are to be fought. Heavens! that a scheme so fraught with ruin, so pregnant with unutterable horrors to mankind, should become familiar to the minds of Christian men! But think you, sir, that this could be effected without force? That it is all to be done under the mild, the bland, the pacific, the amiable reasoning of the most sage and learned member from Massachusetts? When has a government, however bad, been overthrown, without finding some to fight in its defense—some brave spirits, who, if from no motive but a selfish interest in its abuses, have still drawn the sword, and died for what had at least protected them? When has a free people been denationalized, without convulsions, war, and bloodshed? And think you that a constitution, the freest in its spirit, the most magnificent in its conception, the most fortunate in its origin, the most felicitous in its execution and its results, binding together the greatest extent of territory and the largest mass of interest ever yet found united upon earth on principles of freedom,—think you, sir, that it is destined to fall without a struggle? Come that day when it will, it must be bloody. It would be so at any time, and under any circumstances; but at a period like this, and under a state of society like ours, with a people of such characteristics and such means, the convulsion under the motives now at work must be followed by horrors for which history has no parallel. Sir, if we can not live in peace while we are united by all manner of ties, obligations, oaths, and interests, most assuredly we never shall when all these ties are broken, State sundered from State, and all left to the fierce collisions engendered by mutual rivalry, jealousy, and selfishness—the theatre of foreign intrigue, and the prey of foreign ambition.

Mr. Speaker, when I wander from the subject, I wander in pursuit of the gentleman from Massachusetts, who has led the way. That gentleman objects to his triers. He tells us that gentlemen from the South are not competent to try him on the charge of bringing forward a proposition to dissolve this Union. The South may well thank the gentleman from Massachusetts. It is a glorious compliment he has paid her; and this testimony alone, coming from such high authority, ought to be sufficient, in itself, to wipe from her escutcheon any shade of past restlessness or rashness that may bedim its brightness. The day of those errors has now gone by; and the gentleman from Massachusetts himself being judge, the men of the South in this hall are so deeply, so irrevocably attached to this Union, that they are not fit to try a man on the charge of bringing forward a proposal to dissolve it. According to the gentleman, northern men are fit; they can judge, having no such bias in their way. Will northern gentlemen here acquiesce in that statement? Will they answer their colleague's appeals? Will they endorse this petition, and the reasoning by which it is sustained? When the question comes, is such a course worthy of censure? will northern statesmen here declare, upon their oaths and their honor as American legislators, that it is not censurable? Are they prepared to tell the American people that the people of Massachusetts have a right to dissolve this Government? That to attempt it through her representatives in Congress, is justifiable; and that they are ready to connive, at least, at the movement. Oh, sir, if they do, how a few years must have changed them! how must Massachusetts herself have changed since the memorable era of 1798, when the South spoke of obstructing or nullifying, not the constitution, but acts of Congress. Do gentlemen recollect the short and pithy answer given by her to the Virginia resolutions, an answer which extorted, by its dagger-like pungency, the famous report of James Madison? On all the great points of our glorious constitution, she was then sound as granite. How has she changed! When the question to be decided shall be, has a portion of the people of the United States a right to abolish the constitution of the United States; and is Congress a necessary organ to effect that purpose, so that without its action the right is nugatory; will Massachusetts be found voting *aye*, while the south votes *no?* Ah! but there is a cause adequate to the phenomenon, here to be explained. It is the detestation of the South to abolitionism that makes her a Unionist, and renders her unfit to try the gentleman. He insists on the connection between the questions. And has the love of the North for abolition brought her in favor of dissolution? Has she vowed that slavery shall cease; and does she resort to dissolution as the mean to effect it? Frightful, indeed, are the omens with which we are surrounded. My colleague over the way (Mr. UNDERWOOD) declares that if the Union is dissolved, slavery will be abolished. So far, he and the gentleman from Massachusetts perfectly agree. All know, or may know, who can read, that the institution of slavery is guaranteed by the constitution, and placed exclusively under the control of the States. And all who know the facts of the case, know that the people of the South are falsely charged when they are accused of attempting to introduce slavery into the free States; although the power to do this, follows necessarily the power to touch the subject by the general government. If slaves come within the power of Congress to regulate commerce between the States, then the States can not obstruct their free circulation as property throughout the Union; and so long as slavery exists at all, it must be universal. But if the governments of New York and Pennsylvania can abolish, then surely the governments of Virginia and South Carolina can retain it. If the argument from the commercial power (which I have seen urged by pretty high authority about Boston) be sound, then the Kentuckian has as much right to sell, and the Pennsylvanian to buy his slave, as his beef in the Philadelphia market. But it is ridiculous to reason the point. No man doubts that slavery is guarded by the present constitution from federal interference. And it was wisely and rightly guarded. Without it, the States could not and ought not to have united. Slavery being peculiar, and confined to a portion of the confederacy, could never, upon the original principles of the social union, be subject to the action of a legislature, a large part of which has nothing of community in the subject-matter. Massachusetts does not doubt it. I do not understand the gentleman himself (Mr. ADAMS) to doubt it, except in the case of insurrection. Do they, therefore, (the gentleman and his State,) stumble upon dissolution in quest of abolition? And does my colleague, agreeing with them that such dissolution is the surest means of abolishing slavery, therefore vote that a presentation here of a petition from that quarter to dissolve, is not censurable?

Mr. Speaker, I do in my soul believe that if the gentleman from Massachusetts himself, instead of looking into books, could travel among us, and look at facts as they exist,—if he would see with his own eyes, instead of his learning,—he would at once be induced to depart from his plan.

Mr. ADAMS. They would lynch me.

Mr. MARSHALL. If you endeavored to kindle the flame there which you do here, I must admit that, in all probability, they would.

Mr. ADAMS. You are doing them that service now, as much as you can.

Mr. MARSHALL resumed. It is the gentleman's privilege to interrupt and to insult every man on this floor; it is his privilege, and I accord it to him freely. But slavery, it seems, is to be abolished, if the Union is dissolved. Abolish slavery! —and how? Why, according to my colleague, it is to be done by all the negroes running away to Ohio, and through Ohio into Canada. Well, sir, this may do very well for Kentucky; but how is it to work in South Carolina and Georgia? Are they to come into Ohio, too, and make a regular march into Canada? And is no hand to be lifted to prevent or interrupt this grand migration—this modern exodus of two millions of people—a migration equal to that of the Goths and Vandals upon the Roman empire? The blacks are to come forth as the Israelites did out of Egypt. I wonder who is to be their Moses? Is it the venerable gentleman from Massachusetts? A magnificent conception this, truly! Abolish slavery!—and how? Never in that way.

But the gentleman from Massachusetts does not look to this mode of doing the thing; he is not quite so monomaniac as that. He is not so little read in the past history of the world, or so unacquainted with the practical affairs of mankind, or so unable to look into the causes and springs of national revolutions, as to believe a fond tale like this. How, then, is it to be done? The Constitution—the American

Constitution — that sacred bond of liberty and peace, whose potent arm, eternal voice, and covering shield have hitherto been our safety and our pride—the constitution, with all the oaths of the North to support it, must first be broken down. And then—ay, then—the descendants of the puritan and the regicide, who were driven from England by the persecutions and oppressions of the English nobility; and of the cavalier, expelled by the equally relentless persecutions of the puritan, after both had united on this side the water against a government which had alternately oppressed them both, buried their differences, and, with their common hands, constructed a new government, united, strengthened, cemented by the shedding of their common blood, are once more to be driven asunder; and a more fearful strife than that which convulsed Europe two hundred years ago, is to affront the sun, and pollute the blessed light of heaven, on the soil of these once free and happy States. The fierce and vengeful fanatic, true to the principles of his fathers, and the sworn champion of universal emancipation, holding in one hand his proclamation of freedom and alliance to the slave, and a firebrand in the other—elated, too, with the consciousness of numerical superiority—is to invade the South, and avenge the wrongs of Africa, in massacre and conflagration. He will be met. The haughty slaveholder will greet the new crusader with bloodiest welcome. The cavalier's sword will leap from its scabbard, in vindication of a broken covenant, a violated national compact, to which he had vainly trusted as a shield to his property and his rights. Surrounded by his household gods, in defense of his hearthstone, the honor of his wife, the purity of his daughter, *pro aris et focis*, he will incarnadine his weapon to the hilt.

> "To patriot vengeance ne'er hath sword
> More terrible libations poured."

And should he fall, "outnumbered, not outbraved," it will be amid the ashes of all he holds dear—his home, his family, his country, and his race. Glorious consummation! worthy only of the philanthropic genius and all-grasping benevolence of the gentleman from Massachusetts, to rear a black republic, a sister and ally for that of Hayti, upon the ruins of the social fabric, constructed by Europe's best and purest chivalry.

Sir, there is in that region a state of society which the gentleman and his allies can not alter, without involving consequences more horrible than he can now conceive. The gentleman will have gone far when he obtains the preparatory legislative act; but that which must follow will give him, in more terrible fruition, the almost boundless consequences of the crime which his petitioners meditate. That for which they ask involves the utter destruction, the obliteration of that race to which he should be allied by color, by a common blood, by education, by association, by descent, by friendship, by a near and blessed alliance, by a common glory, by every indissoluble ligament that can bind a human heart; or the as certain destruction of that very race toward whose liberation all his efforts are given, and in consummating whose deliverance he hopes to close a long and illustrious life in a blaze of glory, which is to rival the pure eternal light which encircles and haloes the name of Wilberforce. If that be his hope, it can never be fulfilled. There is no parallel between the cases. There is nothing in the enterprise of Wilberforce, the manner in which it was conducted, or the consequences which were to follow it, which can for a moment be likened to that achievement which seems to be the object of the gentleman's ambition. But, sir, I quit this branch of the subject.

Mr. Speaker, the gentleman from Massachusetts told me the other day that it did not become me to complain of him for presenting this petition, inasmuch as the Senator from Kentucky, (Mr. CLAY,) who is my immediate constituent, as well as the representative of my State, was now urging a proposition which, in effect, amounts to a dissolution of the Union. Sir, it is vain to liken a proposition to dissolve the Union, which involves the destruction of the government and the termination of the republic, to a proposition to amend the constitution, such as is now under consideration in the other end of the Capitol. That proposition seeks to preserve the instrument, and does not touch the unity of our government; if adopted finally, it leaves the American people entire. It suggests, indeed, a modification of the national charter—a specific modification, and in one particular. The suggestion is a legitimate subject of legislative action, authorized by the instrument it seeks to amend. In the distribution of the powers of government, you may give more, or give less, to the legislative or to the executive department, and still the Union will remain; the bonds which hold us together as one people will be unbroken. There will still be such a thing as the United States. There will be such a thing as the people of the United States, and there will remain a Constitution of the United States. That instrument itself has pointed out the only peaceful and legitimate mode of its own amendment; and that is the mode in which the Senator from Kentucky proposes to effect his object. That proposition is said to be a whig measure—at least it was put forward in what has been termed the "whig manifesto" at the close of the extra session. If what the gentleman (who, I understand, claims to be a whig) says is true, whiggery must have wonderfully changed its physiognomy since the days when this illustrious gentleman was President of the United States, and the distinguished Senator, who is urging that measure, was his Secretary of State. I am, myself, a whig. I am not a very old man; yet, if this be true, I have lived longer than I expected—long enough to see one of these two eminent individuals introduce a proposition to dissolve the Union at one end of the Capitol, and the other at the other end. "Tell it not in Gath, publish it not in the streets of Askalon," that these two great political leaders, combined once more, are now in consultation to overthrow the constitution of their common country. And I suppose that all good whigs are bound by party allegiance to track full and fair in the path of these patriarchs of our tribe.

The voting in favor of a censure upon the man who has had the hardihood to bring before this august body, for the first time, a proposition such as that upon your table, is—at least it has been so hinted by the gentleman from Massachusetts—so far as northern votes are concerned, to be confined to the democracy. And he sneered at the thought. For whom the sneer was intended, or whom it may best fit, it may be difficult to determine. And has it come indeed to this—that when the question of dissolution shall come up, the democracy alone will be found base enough to desert their northern brethren, to brave with bold defiance the influence and the threats of fanatics and incendiaries, and stand videts in the front of the outworks of that good old constitution which their fathers helped to frame, and under which they have lived and enjoyed so much social happiness and prosperity? Am I indeed to understand that it is a part of the whig policy to sustain the gentleman from Massachusetts in his course upon this subject, and to back him in the defense upon which he has chosen to throw himself? Now, I have been, and am, politically opposed to the democratic party; but not quite so much opposed as that they can drive me, from a spirit of opposition, into doing wrong, because they have chosen to do right. I was opposed to many, almost all, of the measures of the man who was once their great leader; but when he swore that the Union must and should be preserved, my heart swelled high under the sentiment, and, had all his public acts conformed to this, I might have been his man too. Strange indeed is the argument, and strange the positions we have seen taken on this occasion; and well and truly may it be said, we are fallen on evil times.

What a singular spectacle is exhibited by this House at this moment! Instead of exerting the legislative powers conferred upon us, and making the necessary provision for the public service, an exhausted treasury, and a suffering people, we have been disputing of abolition petitions, till at last those disputes are merged in a question of dissolving the Union. But who is to blame? The gentleman from Massachusetts taunts me with having voted for the repeal of the twenty-first rule, and then against the reception of the petitions he has offered here. I did indeed vote for the repeal of the twenty-first rule; but it was not repealed, it remains in force, and I refused to aid the gentleman in getting surreptitiously into the House petitions forbidden by one of its standing rules. I should still be in favor of the repeal of the twenty-first rule; though, upon the subject of referring these petitions to him, I may have changed, since I have seen what is, as I sincerely believe, his real object. After he has avowed himself an alarmist, and described the operations and designs of this government against the liberties of his constituents, as he has, I can not consent to trust him with any thing in which its existence is involved; nor shall I act inconsistently.

The gentleman has charged me individually, and particularly, with being an enemy to the North, and with a settled purpose to oppress her. So far is this from being true, that I am ready to do all that a man in my condition can do, to remove all causes of discontent; and, in addition to their political connection, which I will never see broken without resistance, to bind together the North and the South by the strongest ties of a mutual commercial interest. I would to-morrow, if I could, render this American continent of ours wholly independent of other countries, for the supply of every thing which her own rich and varied soil, and equally diversified population and industry, are naturally capable of producing. To the jealous legislation of other countries, excluding from their markets, and from competition with their domestic productions, all similar articles of ours, I would oppose counter-legislation. I would interpose strong commercial regulations, with a view the more promptly to develop our mighty sources of manufacturing production. I would guard our infant establishments, as they arose, from the powerful rivalry of foreign governments, and the jealous combinations of foreign capitalists; well assured that the agriculture of the planting, and grain-growing, and grazing States, could never languish under the fullest expansion of northern labor, and capital, and machinery. Our country has all the elements of a world within herself; and elements exactly so distributed by nature, as to make the several parts necessary to, and dependent upon, each other. Could my will prevail, the products of southern agriculture should be exchanged against the manufactures of the North, if possible, to the full extent of the demands of each; and the valley of the Mississippi—a greater than that of the Nile—should be the granary and the pasture for them both. The perfect freedom of our domestic trade is an article of our political liberty. Its enlargement, by the opening of every channel of industry possible to our situation, is the darling passion of my mind. I would do this, not so much to increase our wealth and power, as to show the various sections of this mighty empire —an empire destined, if propitious fortune and human virtue shield it from dismemberment, to include within its embrace the largest number of prosperous human beings ever yet comprehended under one political system—that the distinctive peculiarities between them, properly understood, are blessings from the munificent hand of Heaven, and constitute the best and strongest bonds of their union, meant to be everlasting. I am no enemy of the North; nor will she ever find me so, unless the new principles and new opinions, which seem to be springing up there, shall precipitate her into the effort which some of her children so madly urge.

But I have been told, sir, on this floor, and by a northern member, that I must not press my resolutions, because that is the surest way to bring about such a result; and I am to avow a fear, lest such a thing should actually be done. The North can dissolve the Union, and will, if we question her right to solicit our coöperation! If they can and will, why let them do it in their own way; but, for Heaven's sake, and in the name of all that is decent, let them not ask us to do it. We may well say to them, what Hazael said when his treason was prophesied to him: "Is thy servant a dog, that he should do this thing?" But we are warned not to breathe the slightest censure on one of our own members for bringing here a proposition which may well be characterized as atrocious—the first, the very first of the kind that mortal impudence has ever laid before this body. Sir, we heard the southern gentlemen taunted yesterday—jeered, for arraying themselves against this petition. It goes a whole stone's cast beyond any thing which the southern nullifiers ever dreamed of. The gentleman has gone beyond them far away. It seems that the New England brain, in this department as in all others, needs but a hint straightway to improve on it. The convention that sat at Columbia never took the ground that Congress had power to dissolve the Union; nor did they so much as pretend that they were themselves overthrowing the constitution. I know what they said, though I differed from them then, and shall for ever differ. They said they were maintaining the constitution. They insisted they had a right, a constitutional right, (I confess I never knew where they got it from,) to arrest within their own limits, by State authority, the execution of what they deemed an unconstitutional law, until there was time for a convention of the other States; which is, according to their theory, a sort of fourth department of our government, constitutional in itself, and to be resorted to on extraordinary occasions, to settle a constitutional dispute between a sovereign State and the decision of the entire federal government.

But we are told that it is an ungracious act to inflict so severe a censure on one so venerable; to brand with parliamentary disgrace the name of one who has passed a long life in the public service, and stands connected with the entire history of his country, from Washington to Tyler. He has taken up in his old age, to be sure, some peculiar notions, (and very peculiar they are, I acknowledge;) and, though we do not quite approve them, he is to be allowed to proceed and carry them out, even to the extent of overturning the government; and we must not stir a finger, lest we precipitate the very doom we dread; and that those who urge this censure are responsible for the waste of time and sacrifice of public interest. Waste of time, forsooth! Does the gentleman from Virginia (Mr. Botts) remember that the gentleman from Massachusetts, whose cause he now so strenuously and so ably—I will not say artfully—advocates, the other day offered a petition praying his own removal from the head of the Committee of Foreign Relations, and asked the permission of the House to defend himself from the charges contained therein? Does the gentleman also remember that his friend and client then was assured, by the representative of the district whence the petition purported to come, that it was fictitious and a hoax; and, from the peculiar stamp of the paper, the memorial was evidently manufactured here? In good faith, sir, and with the hope that the gentleman would place himself right before the country, and vindicate himself from the strong suspicions growing out of his course here, I moved that he should be heard. How did he requite the indulgence of the House. Why, sir, he turned upon southern gentlemen and southern institutions, in words of fire and tones of fury, such as he alone could ever utter; with all the passions of his passionate nature blazing out, as they are always ready to do when one hated word, the word *south*, strikes upon his ear. Sir, on that occasion—an occasion of indulgence, procured for him by the motion of a member from a slave state—with the floodgates of his wrath and bitterness flung wide, he poured forth a torrent of invective, in terms so outrageous and offensive, as threw the House into an uproar, and compelled his friend and champion (Mr. Botts) to vote against permitting him to proceed. On that occasion he was silenced, and by the assistance of the gentleman from Virginia. Well, sir, his next step is to offer this proposition to dissolve the Union; and then such a defense as I have been examining. And this is to be passed over, out of pity or contempt! We are to treat him as a superannuated imbecile, beneath parliamentary inquiry or notice. Sir, his friends and advocates have arrayed him in every quality which can make a man at once great and terrible. They have conceded to his hand every instrument of mighty mischief: gifts of understanding, of eloquence, of knowledge, of dignity, of power to move the public mind;—and yet, after painting him thus, the same gentlemen turn round and tell us that he is no fit subject for the action of this House. I have placed myself near his seat, and listened with profound attention to all he has said upon the subject of these petitions. I wanted to understand distinctly his object, in the extraordinary course he seems determined to pursue; and, for one, I am convinced. If the gentleman's combined declarations and actions are to be trusted as true exponents of his purpose, then his purpose is, ultimately, that which is expressed in the petition he has offered. Not yet—not yet, perhaps. Things are not ripe; agitation, deep agitation for the present;—such agitation as he has promised, if he be indeed called on for further defense—and execution hereafter.

Now, sir, I call upon the North to say whether these are their serious purposes or not. I ask of the able and honorable men who represent northern interests on this floor, whether these be indeed their views. Do they really mean revolution; and do they put this gentleman forward, by way of feeler, because his age, and dignity, and past services, and venerable appearance, are calculated to suspend the vindictive action of this House? Do they thus seek to escape personal responsibility?

Mr. Speaker, when that most touching and tearful scene between the gentleman from Ohio (Mr. Giddings) and my colleague (Mr. Underwood) was enacting before our wondering eyes the other day, the gentleman from Ohio expressed himself as coinciding perfectly with the views of my colleague; he returned thanks to my colleague for having expressed them. He assured my colleague, and all southern gentlemen, that he had no thought of such a thing as interfering with slavery within the States where it existed; but he and his friends—mark that, sir—he and his friends wanted to be freed from the expense of maintaining it. One word more, sir, and he would have developed his plan; but southern members rose and stopped him. I entreated them not to do so; I implored them to let him talk on. The gentleman is a neighbor of mine; we are coterminous, with but a river flowing between. The views of himself and *friends* are matters of mighty interest to my section of the country. Never lover longed for the whispered consent about to be wrung from his reluctant mistress, as I to hear the disclosure he was about to make under this newborn alliance between himself and my colleague.

Mr. Speaker, this is the first time in our history that any man has been bold enough to introduce on this floor a paper proposing a dissolution of the Union. He ought to be boldly met. If, sir, we meet him and the petition with as decided a temper as he himself exhibits,—if we rebuke the infamous proposal to us to break our oaths, in tones of indignation such as it justly merits,—it will have a healthful effect throughout the whole extent of the land. The action of government has, and ought to have, a powerful influence over public opinion; the people and their representatives, like opposite mirrors, are mutually reflectors of each others' sentiments. It will gladden the heart and strengthen the hands of every loyal, true-hearted American, of whom I well know there are millions in the North as violently opposed to the incendiary schemes at work among them as am I; and this, if any thing, will have the effect of checking this gentleman and his associates in any farther proceedings they may meditate in this line of policy.

Sir, for all the bitter and envenomed things he has said against me, in the progress of this debate, I forgive him. He said that I boasted to him of my aristocratic blood. The rules of this House forbid my characterizing that assertion as it deserves. I forgive him that, too; and were it in my power to exorcise from out his heart the demon of mischief which threatens all that is dear to me; if it were possible that he could be brought in any good degree to recant what he has here declared; if I could see any gleaming of that spirit of pacification, that love for the constitution, and that zeal for the Union, which has here been accorded to him by others;—I would instantly and joyfully retract all that I have said. I am the last man on this earth who would strike wantonly at that venerable head, around which there rally so many associations to intercept even a merited blow.

I now, sir, in redemption of my pledge to the gentleman from Indiana, renew the motion to lay the whole subject on the table; trusting, however, that the House will not thus evade a direct vote on a question which, I must think, their own dignity, its own intrinsic importance, and the public expectation, require us to meet full in the face.

TO THE PUBLIC.

IN the summer of 1845, Mr. MARSHALL was a candidate for Congress in the 10th Congressional District of Kentucky. In the midst of an excited political canvass, those opposed to his election alleged that he favored the sentiments of the North upon the slavery question. In support of these allegations, garbled extracts of his letters upon Slavery, published in 1840, in the Commonwealth—the same before referred to—were freely circulated, and commented upon throughout the district. Finally certain questions relative to the subject were propounded to the Congressional candidates. In answer to these interrogatories, and to set himself right in the public mind, Mr. MARSHALL issued the following Circular, under the caption of, "To the Public." It was written at night in Lexington, after his return from a laborious tour through portions of the district, before he had taken the slightest repose: it shows evidently an energy that never tired, a genius that never failed him.

ON my way to Jessamine week before last, the "Inquirer," of this city, of the date June 27th, 1845, was placed in my hands, and my attention drawn to a series of questions propounded therein, the original paper being said to have been signed by one hundred and twenty citizens of Fayette county. The questions are directed to the candidates for Congress in this district, as well as to the county candidates for both branches of the State Legislature. When I saw the paper I was hastening to fulfill a succession of appointments I had made to address the people of Jessamine, running through seven successive days. I have stated the questions, and answered them orally, in every address which I have made since their appearance. On my arrival in this city last night, I was informed by various persons that an answer was expected through the press. Till now I have had no time to prepare a response in writing. There are five questions in the series.

The four first may be embodied in one, and amount briefly to this: Whether the candidate is in favor of the abolition of slavery in Kentucky, or of emancipation, either gradual or immediate; if in the affirmative, what is the mode in which it is to be effected, and what disposition is proposed to be made of the enfranchised negroes? Is the candidate in favor of a change of the Constitution of Kentucky, and what change does he desire? The fifth and last question relates to the law of 1833, prohibiting the importation of slaves, and interrogates the candidate whether he is in favor of the entire repeal of the law?

It has been the fashion for some time past to charge me with political apostacy, and with an entire and radical change of opinion and principle in relation to the laws and policy of my country. To the several interrogatories referred to, I should feel neither hesitation nor difficulty in giving a direct response, without discussion or explanation, and would do so as most convenient to myself, but for the frequent reference in the public prints to certain letters of mine, written in 1840, in defense of "the law of 1833, prohibiting the importation of slaves," and published in pamphlet form.

These letters were written, that the ground I occupied in relation to the question in all its bearings might be defined by the clearest boundaries, and that I might not be implicated or confounded in any wise with men with whom I had neither sympathy nor communion, and with opinions and objects between which and my own there was neither affinity nor resemblance. Clear as I thought I had made myself in relation to the abolition of slavery in Kentucky, the power of the Government to pass laws of protective emancipation, or the policy of changing the constitution with a view to enlarge the powers of the Legislature on this head, still, I am informed by my friends, that garbled extracts from these letters have misled many persons as to the positions I really occupied and the views I entertained. I refer now to these letters, and the misapprehensions in relation to them, as an apology for giving my answers to the questions in the "Inquirer," in the very language I then employed.

On page 20 of the pamphlet will be found the following paragraph:

"At the time of the passage of this law, the sect now known by the title of "Abolitionists," had not made their appearance, and as I was sworn then upon the constitution of my country, by all the obligations of that oath, I affirm now, that I do not believe that the principles and designs ascribed to that party were in the contemplation of any human being who voted for that law. *I was myself not only never an abolitionist, but never an emancipationist, upon any plan which I ever heard proposed.* I was not an emancipationist, because I believed that the power did not exist. I would not have been even though it had existed, unless coupled with the means for the deportation of the race. No plan of that sort had occurred to me which seemed feasible. I have uniformly voted against a Convention Bill. The year it passed I voted against it in the Legislature, and opposed it warmly before the people the summer the question was submitted to them."

These were my published opinions then. I answer now, I am not in favor of the abolition of slavery in Kentucky. I believe, in the first place, that there is no government on earth armed with the constitutional power to effect this object, and if there was I would resist its exercise. With those who look to the abolition of slavery in the United States, the enfranchised race remaining among us, as a measure either lawful, practicable or desirable in the present state of things, I hold no communion of opinion. What changes may come over the face of the world, or what revolutions over the human understanding, lie hid in the deep bosom of the future. That which shall mold the European and the African races, however, into one harmonious community of freemen and fellow citizens, will confound varieties which nature has made distinct, and obliterate the lines by which Heaven has bounded and separated different classes of its creatures. The abolition of slavery in the United States involves more than a civil, or political, or social revolution. It is not a mere prejudice of rank or caste, a despotic prejudice, founded in injustice and upheld by power, which the abolitionist seeks to destroy. He aims at a revolution in nature and the moral structure of the species, unauthorized alike by physical or intellectual laws. I might wish to see it effected when it shall please the Creator to wash out the marks he has branded on the African's brow, to obliterate the all-enduring monument of past wrong, the pledge of eternal hate, the badge of physical inferiority and past servitude, that dooms the African and his descendants, while among us, to be a slave, protected by the benevolence or the interest of his master, or an outcast, shielded by no laws, linked with no sympathy, the miserable victim of a prejudice incurable, because founded in the nature of things; or a stern, desperate domestic foe, burning with hate, panting for revenge—armed with the power of freedom, yet stripped of all its most precious blessings and advantages. The idea of citizenship and equality, social and political equality, a domestic society in Kentucky or Virginia compounded of liberated African negroes and the descendants of the European chivalry, the races kept, too, for ever distinct, is an absurdity too monstrous for abolitionism itself. Eternal war, war to extermination, slavery, or amalgamation of the races, are the three alternatives. Shield me and mine from that philanthropy which would blend the crystal eye, the elevated feature, the ambrosial and waving curl, the rosy skin, all the striking and glorious attributes that mark the favorites of nature, exhaling fragrance, and redolent of beauty and of bloom, with the disgusting peculiarities, the wool and grease and fœtor of the blackened savage of the Southern deserts. The Saxon and the Celt, the Norman and the Dane, even the Tartar and the Hun, the Turk and the Saracen—the races of Japhet and of Shem may compound and melt and mingle into one people when met upon the same soil—but the race of Ham must serve or separate.

The opinion has been maintained by ingenious men in favor of emancipation, that although the Constitution of Kentucky declares that no law shall be passed for the emancipation of slaves without the consent of their owners, still the Legislature may pass laws declaring that negro children born after the passage of the law should be free. The argument upon which this opinion rested was subtle. It was contended that the Constitution referred only to persons in being. That a child not yet born was not a slave, and that a law declaring prospectively a being free that as yet could not have been a slave, did not emancipate a slave without the consent of the owner, but by anticipation prevented or prohibited an unborn creature from ever becoming a slave.

This opinion is reviewed and answered in the third letter to the Commonwealth.

On page 18 of the pamphlet will be found the following:

"In defending the policy of that law at the time of its passage, and in maintaining that the reasons for its continuance are far stronger than for its establishment, I shall not discuss the abstract question of slavery. Those who choose to search for its foundation among the original and natural rights of men may do so. I take slavery as I find it, a positive institution, recognized by the Constitution of my country. The right of the master to such persons as were slaves, within the Commonwealth at the time of the adoption of that constitution, by the laws then in force, and to such persons as the laws since have permitted to be introduced into the country, being slaves by the laws of other States, and being of the same description with persons held in bondage here, is as complete and as entirely protected by law from the power of the government as any other right of property whatever; and this *whether the legislation be present or prospective, whether it relate to slaves in existence at the passage of the law, or grasp at future and unborn generations.* The doctrine of the emancipating power of the government over the '*post nati*' I have ever denied.

"The reasoning which seeks to distinguish between the constitutional right of the master over his slave in existence, and over the unborn issue of the females, has no foundation either in law or nature. The law of servitude is express; it places the descendants of the females, without limitation, upon the same footing with the ancestors. The issue follows the condition of the parent, *partus sequitur ventrem.* It is no answer to say that a person not in being can not be a slave, it is just as true that a person not in being can not be free. The unborn can neither be the subject of the laws of servitude or the statute of emancipation; neither can attach till birth, and then the Constitution takes the precedence."

If any one has the curiosity or will take the trouble to examine the pamphlet, he will find in the second letter, the most elaborate argument I have seen, against the proposition that the general Government has any control in any way over the institution within the States, or of the trade in slaves between the States. It is too long to cite here, nor is it necessary to my purpose to do so. There is one view, however, and one argument in favor of the power of Congress over the subject of slavery, which is not noticed in those letters. I had not known at that time that any man would plant the abolition power of the general Government upon such a ground.

It is maintained by Mr. Adams, and after him by others of lesser note, that so long as slavery is confined in its consequences and its burdens to the States where it exists, the Government of the United States has no power to interfere with its regulation; but that when it becomes a source of national expenditure, or the occasion of national exertion, it is at once subjected to the national jurisdiction, and can be regulated or abolished by the authority of Congress. The case put, upon which this formidable jurisdiction attaches, is that of a servile insurrection. And the clause in the Federal Constitution, from which the argument is drawn, is that which authorizes the employment of the national force "to suppress insurrections," etc. It was the assertion of this principle by Mr. Adams that induced me first to assail that singular man in the House of Representatives. Coupled with the principle of the Abolitionists of the right of resistance in the slaves, the ferocious appeals of these incendiaries upon this very subject, the overpowering weight of the free States in the

National Legislature, the possibility of such an event under the incumbent pressure of all the circumstances in some of the Atlantic States, where the number of slaves exceed the white population, the declaration of such a power arising on such a contingency, smote me, I confess, with horror. The clause in the constitution is evidently a guarantee, taken by the slave States. It is the pledge of the whole Union to protect the weaker States against a domestic danger. That it should be wrested into an occasion, and an instrument by which the very right to be secured, should be taken away, is a commentary upon that fairness with which power ever reasons to its object. The abortive effort which was made to censure Mr. Adams for offering a petition to dissolve the Union, and the part I bore in that transaction, have been fully before the people of this county. I refer to it now, and to the argument I made in the House of Representatives upon the resolution of censure, merely to show that I maintained in Congress the same principles on this subject that I did in 1840, and that I do now.

In answer to the fifth and last question in the "Inquirer," I say briefly, I should be opposed, were I in the Legislature of Kentucky, to the repeal of the law of 1833. I have reviewed my opinions on that subject with great care, and am unable to perceive any advantage which Kentucky could derive from its repeal. I do not perceive how she would be rendered safer or stronger, or slave property made more secure, or the character or value of that property improved by the introduction of such slaves, and in such masses as it would seem to me would inevitably follow the repeal of the law. I can not, as yet, understand how the repeal of that law, and the change in the relative proportion of the black and white population, that would ensue, taken especially in connection with our geographical position, would better enable us to meet the tremendous question which the Abolitionists seek to force upon us.

Had I changed my opinions upon the subject of this paper, I should not have hesitated to avow the fact. I have written to correct misrepresentation, and I hope I am understood. Since 1840 my acquaintance with some of the principal actors in American affairs has been much enlarged, important events have transpired, and important questions connected with this very subject of slavery have arisen.

That I have suffered some alteration in my estimate of the character, principles and objects of leading public men, may be, nay, is true enough. That I have changed or abandoned any of the great and general principles by which I steered my political course, particularly on the subject of slavery, is utterly false. My action, mainly in Congress, and particularly since I left it, has been influenced by these very principles, and on this very subject.

That the importance of the Abolitionists as a party in the United States is infinitely greater than I had imagined—that the institution of slavery, and the views and projects of this sect in regard to it, excites the keenest interest in foreign countries, particularly in England—that they are hostile to the continuance of the Union upon principle, and will be found the ready ally of a foreign power in any scheme to curb the southern extension of our empire, or to break in twain the frame of the Republic, in pursuit of what they call human emancipation, are facts which the events of the last four years have forced upon me. The determined fanaticism of this sect alone would make them formidable. Their number is so great that they already aspire to hold the balance in the great national elections. They claim to be heard, and consume much of the time of the National Legislature, in the fierce agitation of the question of the power of the Government to execute their scheme of liberating two millions and a half of African slaves. They rave at the National Constitution for the guarantees it contains, and the protection it affords to this detested institution. They have presented petitions at the bar of the House for the dissolution of the Union. They have selected and secured as their agent and their organ in the House of Representatives the most learned, the most persevering, the most eloquent, the most distinguished, and decidedly the ablest and most efficient member of that body. What is to be the future course and termination of this question — what the final solution of this terrible problem in American History, is beyond my ken, and is scarcely a fit subject for present speculation. Great men in England thought or said that it turned upon the question of Texas and annexation. Great men on this side of the water, opposed to the acquisition of that territory, said the same thing. The action of the Government of the United States, and the determination of the people of Texas, have postponed the date of Abolition in America. If the predictions at least of that "ominous conjunction" of political seers were to be trusted, British philanthropy must pause for a season. "The pledge of the power and the will given by the greatest nation on earth for the ultimate emancipation of the human race," as Mr. Adams termed the British act of Parliament emancipating the slaves in the West Indies, can not yet be redeemed. But I must not extend these remarks, as I shall continue to respond to these questions on the stump.

REMOVAL OF C. M. CLAY'S PRESS.

ADDRESS,

Delivered in Lexington, on the occasion of the removal of C. M. CLAY'S *press, and the suppression of the "True American," the 18th of August,* 1845.

NEVER, perhaps, was there a period of greater local excitement, than at that time prevailed in the vicinity of Lexington. C. M. CLAY, an able and avowed antagonist to the institution of slavery, was then publishing the "True American" in Lexington, his main object being to disseminate his own peculiar views. He departed, however, from the reasonable, conciliatory course, essential to the success of his sheet, and penned inflammatory appeals, as editorial, well calculated to arouse a community of slaveholders to a protection of their rights, homes, and families. Remonstrance and rebuke did not in the least suppress a repetition of these appeals. On the 12th of August, 1845, his paper contained the following as editorial:

"Slavery, the most unmitigated, the lowest, basest that the world has ever seen, is to be substituted for ever for our better, more glorious, holier aspirations. The Constitution is torn and trampled under foot; justice and good faith in a nation are derided; brute force is substituted in the place of high moral tone: all the great principles of national liberty which we inherited from our British ancestry are yielded up, and we are left without God or hope in the world. When the great-hearted of our land weep, and the man of reflection maddens in the contemplation of our national apostacy, there are men pursuing gain and pleasure, who smile with contempt and indifference at their appeals. But, remember, you who dwell in marble palaces, *that there are strong arms and fiery hearts and iron pikes in the streets, and panes of glass only between them and the silver plate on the board, and the smooth-skinned woman on the ottoman.* When you have mocked at virtue, denied the agency of God in the affairs of men, and made rapine your honied faith, tremble, for the day of retribution is at hand, *and the masses* will be avenged."

On the appearance of the above, the citizens resolved to adopt a more vigorous and decisive course than persuasion. A note was sent to Mr. CLAY, assuring him that such publications would no longer be countenanced in their midst, advising him of a public meeting to be held the next evening, and requesting an answer by that time. This note elicited a reply in perfect keeping with the editorial before named. It closed with—"Go tell your secret conclave of cowardly assassins that C. M. CLAY knows his rights, and how to defend them." On the same day this reply was written, Mr. CLAY published the following extraordinary appeal:

"KENTUCKIANS: You see this attempt of these tyrants, worse than the *thirty despots* who lorded it over the once free Athens, now to enslave you. Men who regard law—men who regard all their liberties as not to be sacrificed to a single pecuniary interest, to say the least, of doubtful value—lovers of justice—enemies of blood—laborers of all classes—you for whom I have sacrificed so much, where will you be found when the battle between liberty and slavery is to be fought? I can not, I will not, I dare not question on which side you will be found. If you stand by me like men, our country shall yet be free, but if you falter now, I perish with less regret when I remember that the people of my native State, of whom I have been so proud, and whom I have loved so much, are already slaves."

On the 18th a large and excited meeting was held at the court-house yard. After reading a communication from C. M. CLAY, somewhat modified from his former imperious tone, Mr. MARSHALL delivered the following address. Its effect was powerful and instantaneous. Several thousand excited men were immediately quieted. The press and type of the "True American" were subsequently carefully taken from the office, by action of the meeting, boxed up and shipped to Cincinnati, to the care of January & Taylor, subject to Mr. CLAY's order.

MR. CHAIRMAN AND FELLOW-CITIZENS OF FAYETTE: The vast concourse of men around me, independent of every thing else, gives ample proof of some deep and powerful excitement of the public mind.

You know, you all know, that this assemblage of the people has been convened upon a published notice, to take into consideration the safety of this community, and to adopt such measures as may secure your peace, and guard from the threatened danger your homes and families. I rise not as upon other occasions, to make you a speech. I seek not to inflame your passions, and will not hazard by one word of extemporaneous appeal upon the subject of this day's action, the terrible responsibility of precipitating this already excited assembly. It is in keeping, however, with the order, decorum, and dignity, which have characterised all the previous steps in this great popular movement, and which mark the aspect of this crowd, that some one should formally explain what has gone before, and state the circumstances which have led to this extraordinary call of the people. I can but achieve this object, by reading to you the proceedings of a smaller body of citizens, the correspondence opened by them with the editor of the "True American," and their address to the public, and the resolutions which accompanied it. (Here Mr. MARSHALL read the documents referred to, which had been agreed upon, and then proceeded.) It had occurred to several gentlemen who had been active in the proceedings of last week, that the transactions of this day would extend, probably, in their influence, far beyond this immediate neighborhood. That they would become the subject of severe examination and the most rigid and scrutinizing censure, throughout the United States. That the character of our people, and the good name of our Commonwealth, would be involved in the resolutions we adopt, and the temper and the mode in which they may be executed.

Liable as all these may become to misrepresentation, it was thought best for your honor and your interests, and it was hoped, that it would not be deemed by you presumptuous, to prepare such a statement of the facts and the principles upon which your action this day is based, as forms in their judgment a complete defense in morals and in laws for this great exertion of the original power of society. Such a statement, these gentlemen had instructed me to prepare and offer for your acceptance, not without the hope, that though imperfect in its execution, you may not deem it altogether unworthy to be sent forth to the world, as your declaration of the ground upon which you rest your justification at the bar of that public opinion, to which communities as well as individuals are amenable for their action. As such, and under their instructions, I tender it, and beg leave to read it in lieu of all other remark or argument. (Here Mr. MARSHALL read the address and resolutions, which when the question was taken upon them at the close of the reading, were adopted without a dissenting voice.)

The people of the city of Lexington and county of Fayette, together with many hundreds from the adjoining counties, assembled in the city of Lexington on the 18th August, in pursuance of a general notice made by the authority of a body of the citizens of Lexington, calling a general assembly of the people, to concert measures for the suppression of the farther publication of the "Abolition paper," called the "True American," having heard the proceedings, correspondence, and address of the meeting which called this assembly, approve the same, and now make and publish to the world this declaration, to vindicate their resolutions and their action.

To have *prevented* the establishment of this press by legal means would have been impossible. There is no regular judicial process by which it could have been achieved. To have resorted to means like the present would have been premature, and perhaps indefensible. The liberty of the press and the freedom of political discussion, are essential elements of our social system. An effort to establish a press in Kentucky devoted to the discussion of the question of domestic slavery and the propriety and practicability of emancipation by law, as an individual enterprise, might, in this simple view of the proposition, have been tolerated by the people, as it is in all probability not prohibited by our laws. The precise purpose and principles of the editor of the "True American," and the position he meant to assume here in relation to the subject, together with the effect he, his principles, and his paper, were to produce upon our peace and our property, were of course, at the outset, matters of speculation. After an experiment of some months, however, there can be no doubt remaining in this community in relation to any of these particulars.

The institution of slavery existed in a portion of the States of this Union before the adoption of the Federal Constitution, by force of the municipal constitution of the particular States. The institution itself is clearly recognized and guaranteed by the articles of the Union, and left where it was found, under the exclusive control of State governments and laws. In the enumeration of the people three-fifths of the slaves are included as the basis of federal representation, and direct taxation upon the several states is subjected to the same apportionment. Fugitive slaves must be rendered up upon claim of the master, nothwithstanding the law of the State into which they escape may not recognize the relation.

The United States shall guarantee every state against domestic violation upon application of the Legislature or the Executive, and shall provide for calling forth the militia to suppress insurrections.

These are among the securities taken by the slave States in the National Constitution; not only that they were not to be disturbed but that they were to be protected in this property by the national arm and authority.

A formidable party has arisen within a few years in the United States, who seek actively and practically to disturb these guarantees, to change the constitution in relation to some of them, and who deny its palpable import, or wrest to fearful purposes its powers in relation to others.

They aim at the Abolition of Slavery in America and halt not at the means. They are organized, active, united in pursuit of this object, and desperately fanatical. They have found their way into the National Legislature, and already exercise a threatening influence there. They command a powerful press in the United States. They have among them a burning zeal, commanding talent, and a large amount of political influence and monied capital. They scout the idea of gradual emancipation or colonization. They treat the institution as equally opposed to religion, morals and law. They maintain that the negro slave here is an American born, entitled to the full benefits and blessings of republican freedom, under the Declaration of Independence, which freed all of American birth. They maintain for him the right of insurrection and exhort him to its exercise, and with an infernal subtlety claim, that the power conferred upon Congress to "suppress insurrections" gives to that body in which the free States have now so overwhelming a preponderance, the right to remove the cause by abolishing slavery. That a servile war becomes by force of this clause a national affair, and can be settled upon any terms under the national discretion. With this party, we believe, from the fullest evidence of which the nature of the case is susceptible, the Editor of the "True American" to be connected by sympathy of opinion, burning and fanatical zeal, and concert of effort. With his speculative opinions we presume not to interfere; with his practical exertions, in our midst, to disturb the settled order of our domestic life, to inflame to discontent and rebellion our household slaves, we have the most direct and incontestible connection. In proceeding by force and without judicial process, to arrest the action of a free citizen, to interfere in any degree with his private property, and if the necessity of the case and the desperation of the man require it, to proceed to extremities against his person, we owe it to our own fame, and the good name of our community, to set forth the facts, upon which arises in our justification the highest of all laws, the law of self-defense and preservation from great and manifest danger and injury.

Before the Editor of the "True American" had established his press in Lexington, or made his celebrated visit to the North, he had corresponded with the New York Tribune, a leading Abolition paper. In certain letters over his signature some of the leading and most dangerous principles of the sect were avowed and defended. The Abolition of Slavery in the District of Columbia—the exclusion of the three-fifths of the slave population in the apportionment of representation by a change in the constitution, thereby weakening still farther the slave States upon the floor of Congress—the exclusion of Texas from the Union, in pursuit of which object he avowed himself ready to take up arms—the enlisting the whole force of the non-slaveholders in Kentucky against slave property, and thus forcing a change in the constitution of the State, were among the means and instruments relied upon by him for effecting the entire abolition of slavery in America. In one of his letters, he anticipates from the abolition of slavery in Kentucky and some other of the western States by the means above noticed, and the exclusion of Texas, that the slave population will be crowded upon the planting States to such an extent, that abolition, if not voluntarily achieved by law, will be forced by a war of colors exterminating one or the other of the races, in either event, (and the editor seemed to contemplate either with equal serenity) terminating in that universal liberty so fiercely sought. Holding these opinions, and after visiting northern cities and being received there in full communion by the abolition party, caressed and flattered and feasted, hailed in the stages of his triumphal progress by discharges of cannon, and heralded in the papers devoted to the cause as the boldest, the most intrepid, the most devoted of its champions, he returned to his native State, the organ and the agent of an incendiary sect, to force upon her principles fatal to her domestic repose, at the risk of his own life and the peace of the community. In the preparation and establishment of his office in Lexington, Mr. Cassius M. Clay acted as though he were in an enemy's country. He has employed scientific engineers in fortifying against attack, and prepared the means of destroying the lives of his fellow citizens, it is said, in mines of gunpowder, stands of muskets, and pieces of cannon. The whole course of the man bears evidence incontestable that he was entering upon a career fatal to the peace of the community of which he was a member. The citizen has a right to arm in his own defense, and to protect his house and his person from unlawful assaults; but why should a peaceful citizen engaged in a lawful calling, make preparations suited to repel an invading army? It is needless to our purpose, to notice the editor's ruthless attacks upon individuals, and his threats to terrify resistance of his course. We proceed at once to the last number of the "True American" and the publications since put forth by its editor, as conclusive evidence of his temper toward the community, and of the character, purpose, and inevitable tendency of the paper. In this paper of the 12th of August there is a leading article, for which, although not from the pen of the editor, the print is responsible to the public, and which at all events is evidence of the purpose of the print and the character and objects of those who support it. We make from this article a few extracts of the most ominous character. The fundamental proposition with this writer is as follows: "Our Legislatures, State and *General*, should raise the platform upon which our free colored people stand. They should give to them full political rights to hold office, to vote, to set on juries, to give their testimony, and to make no distinction between them and ourselves." After tracing the delightful effects of this equality, the article proceeds: "Our national character, our best consciences, our duty, all weigh nothing in the scales of slavery, *against the pride and selfishness of the master. The instrument called the Constitution, after pronouncing all men equal and having equal rights, suffers slavery to exist, a free colored person to be denied all political rights*, and after declaring that all *free persons shall enjoy a free intercourse with the States, suffers the free negro to be driven out of all and excluded from such rights. Deliver me from an instrument thus partial, thus unjust, that can be thus perverted and made to sanction prejudices and party feelings, and note the accidental distinction of color.*" We think nothing from the North can beat this. The western apostle transcends, if possible, his mission. But again as to the necessity of our being civil and submissive to our friends, the abolitionists, and the danger of restiveness on our part:

"The slaveholders must calm themselves into just thinkers, *and cease to provoke the northern free States by putting them at defiance in Congress* and out of it.

"They must look upon abolitionists as enthusiasts if they will, but also as in earnest, and in design, at least, as real patriots. *The Abolitionist is becoming as reckless as the slaveholder when thus provoked, and may add violence and injustice to his course that was intended to be mild and conciliatory.*" Very rational and prudent advice. Submit quietly or the matter will be forced upon you. But we quote farther the following pregnant sentences: "It is in vain for the master to try to fence his dear slaves in from all intercourse with the great world, to create his little petty and tyrannical kingdom on his own plantation, and keep it for his exclusive reign. He can not shut out the light of information any more than the light of heaven. It will penetrate all disguises, and shine upon the dark night of slavery. *He must recollect that he is surrounded.* The North, the East, the West and the South border on him, the free Mexican, the free Yankee, *the more than free Abolitionists of his own country. Every thing trenches upon his infected district, and the Wolf looks calmly in upon his fold.*" We were mad not to listen to warnings like these. We have quoted these passages to prove the thorough identity between the doctrines and objects of this paper, and the worst principles of the ultra Abolitionists of the North. Here is the assertion of the equality of the African race under the constitution, and the repudiation of the practical working of the instrument: "Deliver me from an instrument thus partial, thus unjust —— that can be thus perverted." Here, too, is the threat to the master of the consequences of the light and information, "*that the more than free Abolitionist*" of his country is pouring upon the negro mind.

When we contemplate the mild form of negro slavery in this district, the happy and peaceful and contented relations of the master and the slave, where such a thing as cruelty was scarcely known, where the master was without fear or distrust, and the well-fed, well-clothed, intelligent slave bent to his lot of labor, the lot by the way of all mankind, without repining, regarding his master rather in the light of parent, and himself as a necessary and no mean portion of the family, we could pour curses on the fiends who would break up the intimate, and not the least endearing relation of domestic life, and when all was peace and mildness, plant discord and fury, and fiery hate, and render cruelty a necessary policy on the one side, by inculcating disobedience as a principle on the other. But we must hasten with our proof. In the same day's paper, an editorial appeared, backing the reasoning of the article to which we have referred, and by a brief recapitulation of violated law, a trampled constitution, the triumph of brute force over moral right, the falsification of the great principles of the revolution, all illustrated by "slavery the most unmitigated, the lowest, basest that the world has seen;" and winding up with the following extraordinary threat: "When the great-hearted of our land weep, and the man of reflection maddens in the contemplation of our national apostacy; there are men pursuing gain and pleasure, who smile with contempt and indifference at their appeals. "*But remember you who dwell in marble palaces—that there are strony arms and fiery hearts, and iron pikes in the streets, and panes of glass only between them and the silver plate on the board, and the smooth-skinned woman on the ottoman.* When you have mocked at virtue, denied the agency of God in the affairs of men, and made rapine your honied faith, tremble, for the day of retribution is at hand—and the masses will be avenged." Here is more light and knowledge thrown upon the negro's mind, and horrible fires kindled in his already "fiery heart" by the hand of the daring incendiary, the audacious emissary of the "more than free Abolitionist." Roused and alarmed by these atrocities, and determined no longer to endure the presence of an armed Abolitionist, hurling his firebrands of murder and of lust into the bosom of a peaceful and polished city, a number of the citizens of Lexington undertook the task of remonstrance. To a mild—a wonderfully mild request—to discontinue the paper, the haughty and infatuated fanatic responded in terms of outrage, unparalleled, to the committee of gentlemen who waited on him, denying the right of the citizens to consult together on such a subject, and denouncing the meeting which had opened a correspondence with him, as a cowardly conclave of pirates, robbers, and assassins, and assigning as the ground of their excitement, the apprehension, that their power was about to be taken away from them. The editor himself has published this correspondence, appended to a handbill, which appeared before the call of this meeting of the people, and before his answer was laid before the first meeting referred to. The whole together proves either that C. M. Clay is a madman, or that he meditated, and has prepared himself for a civil war, in which he expected the non-slaveholding laborers along with the slaves, to flock to his standard, and the war of abolition to begin in Kentucky. That we may not be suspected of that extravagance which we charge on him, we quote from his letter the closing sentence. "Go tell your secret conclave of cowardly assassins, that C. M. Clay knows his rights and how to defend them." To this he appends an appeal addressed to the Kentuckians. That we may not be suspected of garbling, we insert this extraordinary summons:

"KENTUCKIANS:—You see this attempt of these tyrants, worse than the thirty despots who lorded it over the once free Athens, now to enslave you. Men who regard laws—men who regard all their liberties as not to be sacrificed to a single pecuniary interest, to say the least of doubtful value—lovers of justice—enemies of blood—*laborers of all classes—you for whom I have sacrificed so much, where will you be found when this battle between Liberty and Slavery is to be fought?* I can not, I will not, I dare not question on which side you will be found. If you stand by me like men, our country shall yet be free; but if you falter now, I perish with less regret when I remember that the people of my native State, of whom I have been so proud, and whom I have loved so much, are already slaves."

That this infatuated man believed that the non-slaveholders of Kentucky would feel and act as a party against the tenure of slavery, and that through them he expected to change the Constitution of Kentucky, and finally overthrow the institution, is evident from one of his letters to the Tribune. That he should have calculated on kindling the flames of civil and servile war, and rallying free laborers and negro slaves under his standard, would seem incredible, yet his acts and his words can bear no other construction: "laborers of all classes—you for whom I have sacrificed so much, where will you be found when this battle between Liberty and Slavery is to be fought? If you stand by me like men, our country shall yet be free; but if you falter, I perish, etc."

Such a man and such a course is no longer tolerable or consistent with the character or safety of this community. With the power of a press, with education, fortune, talent, sustained by a powerful party, at least abroad, who have made this bold experiment in Kentucky through him, the negroes might well, as we have strong reason to believe they do, look to him as a deliverer. On the frontier of Slavery, with three free states fronting and touching us along a border of seven hundred miles, we are peculiarly exposed to the assaults of Abolition. The plunder of our property, the kidnapping, stealing and abduction of our slaves, is a light evil in comparison with planting a seminary of their infernal doctrines in the very heart of our densest slave population. Communities may be endangered as well as single individuals. A great and impending danger over the life or personal safety of a single man, justifies the employment of his own force immediately in his own defense, and to any extent that may be necessary to his protection. He whose aim it is, or the inevitable tendency of whose conduct is to bring about intestine convulsions and servile war, threatens to inflict upon society the greatest horror it can endure. Our laws may punish when the offense shall have been consummated; but they have provided no remedial process by which it can be prevented. To war with an Organ of Abolition by action or indictment for libel, would make that powerful party smile. To injoin the publication of the "True American" would only change its name. A perpetual injunction against the publication of any paper whatever by Mr. C. M. Clay, were beyond the power of the chancellor. The danger continues. An Abolition paper in a slave State is a nuisance of the most formidable character—a public nuisance—not a mere inconvenience, which may occasion delay in business or prove hurtful to health or comfort, but a blazing brand in the hand of an incendiary or madman, which may scatter ruin, confla-

14

gration, revolution, crime unnameable, over every thing dear in domestic life, sacred in religion, or respectable in modesty. Who shall say that the safety of a single individual is more important in the eye of the law than that of a whole people? Who shall say that when the case of danger—real danger, of great and irreparable injury to a whole community, really occurs—that it is not armed legally with the right of self-defense? In either case the circumstances must be left to the judgment of the world, or the decisions of justice. An unauthorized crowd, who inflict death upon persons or destruction upon property, for the gratification of passion or even for the punishment of crime, is a mob, and is the most fatal enemy to security and to freedom. But as in case of sudden invasion, or insurrection itself, the people have at once, independent of the magistrates, the right of defense, so when there be a well-grounded apprehension of great, and, it may be, irreparable injury, the use of force in the community is lawful and safe. We hold the Abolitionists traitors to the Constitution of the country, and enemies to the terms upon which the Union was originally formed, and the only terms upon which it can continue to subsist. When they bring their doctrines and their principles into the bosom of a slave State, they bring fire into a magazine. The "True American" is an Abolition paper of the worst stamp! As such, the peace and safety of this community demand its instant and entire suppression.

In some countries, Mr. Clay might have dreaded summary popular vengeance on his person, or secret murder. He is among a people who abhor mobs, who know no lynch law, and where assassination is unheard of. He has pressed the patience of his countrymen to its utmost capacity of sufferance—they can bear no more, without being traitors to all the trusts reposed in brave and patriot men. Though he has bearded and defied them—attacked the tenure of their property, and outraged decency by the terms in which he has characterized them, they are too conscious of their strength to chafe at insult. They thirst not for his blood, and they would not injure his property. He is a trespasser upon them, they have requested him mildly to desist. He is contumacious, and they will remove him by force. Mr. Clay has complained in his recent handbills of his indisposition, and charged the people as deficient in courage and magnanimity in moving upon him when he is incapable of defense. If all that be said of him, his purpose, and his means, be true, his indisposition is fortunate. He may rest assured that they will not be deterred by one nor 10,000 such men as he. He can not bully his countrymen. A Kentuckian himself, he should have known Kentuckians better. His weakness is his security. We are armed and resolved—if resistance be attempted, the consequence be on his own head. For our vindication under the circumstances, we appeal to Kentucky and to the world.

It is therefore *resolved* by this assembly:—

1st. That no Abolition press ought to be tolerated in Kentucky, and none shall be in this city or its vicinity.

2d. That if the office of the "True American" be surrendered peaceably, no injury shall be done to the building or other property. The presses and printing apparatus shall be carefully packed up and sent out of the State, subject then to Mr. C. M. Clay's order.

3d. That if resistance be offered, we will force the office at all hazards, and destroy the nuisance.

4th. That if an attempt be made to revive the paper here, we will again assemble.

5th. That we hope C. M. Clay will be advised. For by our regard to our wives, our children, our homes, our property, our country, our honor, wear what name he may, be connected with whom he may, whatever arm or party here or elsewhere may sustain him, he shall not publish an Abolition paper here, and this we affirm at the risk, be it of his blood, or our own, or both, or of all he may bring, of bond or free, to aid his murderous hand.

6th. That the chairman be, and he is hereby, authorized to appoint a committee of sixty of our body who shall be authorized to repair to the office of the "True American," take possession of the press and printing apparatus, pack up the same, and place it at the railroad office for transportation to Cincinnati, and report forthwith to this body.

AN ADDRESS ON THE LIFE AND CHARACTER OF RICHARD H. MENEFEE,

Delivered before the Law Society of Transylvania University, in Lexington, Kentucky, April 12, 1841.

In the month of September, 1840, Kentucky was called to mourn the death of Richard H. Menefee. A champion in her Legislature, and a star of the first magnitude in the national councils, he stood in the front ranks with those on the list of fame. Though he had not attained his thirty-second year, he already stood upon the apex of an immortal pyramid of his own erection. Of generous impulses, possessing talents of the highest order, and an ardent thirst for that glory he acquired, and having "died ere he reached his prime," the universal sorrow at the time was but natural. On the 12th of the ensuing April, the members of the Law Society of Transylvania University met in the chapel of Morrison College, in Lexington, for the purpose of paying a tribute to their lamented associate. Before a large audience, that felt deeply the solemnity of the occasion, Mr. Marshall arose and delivered the following address. The annals of eulogy and panegyric may be sought in vain for a happier piece of composition. Rich in feeling, copious in thought, and glowing with the eloquence of a soul gushing its fervor at the grave of a departed friend, it is a monument to the genius and talents of the dead and the living,—equally imperishable to both.

Gentlemen of the Law Society:—I am not here to recount in set phrase, and with that courtesy which the living always pay to the dead, the virtues, real or supposed, of one around whose fate, youth and interesting private relations alone have cast a transient interest. I come not merely to acquit me of a duty to one whom I personally loved and admired, to weave a fading garland for his tomb, or scatter affection's incense over his ashes. Mine is a severer task, a more important duty. I stand here, gentlemen, as a member of a great commonwealth, amid assembled thousands of her citizens, to mourn with them the blow sudden and overwhelming, which has fallen upon the country. He about whose young brows there clustered most of honor—he, around whose name and character, there gathered most of public hope—the flower of our Kentucky youth, "the rose and expectancy of the fair state," lies uprooted. He, who by the unaided strength of his own great mind, had spurned from his path each obstacle that impeded and rolled back the clouds which darkened his morning march—who in his fresh youth had reached an eminence of fame and of influence, which, to a soul less ardent, might have seemed the topmost pinnacle, but which to him, was only a momentary resting-place, whence, with an undazzled eye and elastic limb, he was preparing to spring still upward and nearer to the sun of glory which glowed above him; while the admiring crowd below were watching with intensest interest each movement of his towering step, each wave of his eagle wing.

"Why sudden droops his crest?
The shaft is sped, the arrow's in his breast."

Death canonizes a great name and the seal of the sepulcher excludes from its slumbering tenant the breath of envy. I might fling the reins to fancy and indulge in the utmost latitude of panegyric without offense; the praises of the dead fret not the living. But I am not here upon an ordinary occasion to pronounce a pompous eulogy in set terms of vague and general praise. You have directed me to draw the life and character, to delineate the very form and figure of the mind of one, whose moral likeness you wish to inscribe in enduring and faithful colors upon your archives, not only as a memorial of one loved and lost, but as an example and model for the study and imitation of yourselves and successors. It is not a sample of rhetoric, but a perpetuation of his image, that you seek, as the monument best suited to the subject, as a real and historic standard by which the youth of after times may measure and elevate the idea and the stature of excellence. And surely, if ever there were mirror in which young genius could glass and fashion itself; if ever there were mold in which the forming intellect could be cast in the just and full proportions of graceful energy and perfect strength; he, of whom we are to speak this day, was that mirror and that mold. Would that the artist were equal to his work, would that his mind were fully up to the dignity of his subject; then indeed would I gladly obey your high command, and give to posterity embodied in my land's language, the very form and lineament, the breathing attitude, the intrepid port, the beaming hope, the dauntless energy of a genius which "poverty and disease could not impair, and which death itself destroyed, rather than subdued." Ah, had he but have lived! on that broad pedestal laid already, he would himself have raised a statue colossal and historic, an individual likeness, but a national monument, than which never did the Grecian chisel, from out the sleeping marble, awake a form of grander proportions or of more enduring beauty. He meditated such a work, and was fast gathering round him the eternal materials. Type of his country, he sought to mingle himself with her existence and her fame, and to transmit his name to remote generations as an epitome of her early genius and her history, and as the most signal example of the power of her institutions, not only for the production, but for the most perfect development of the greatest talents and the most exalted virtue.

Richard H. Menefee, whose death clothed this immediate community with mourning, threw a shade over Kentucky, and awakened the sympathies of the whole American public, was born in the town of Owingsville, and county of Bath, 4th December, 1809. His father, Richard Menefee, was an early emigrant from Virginia. He was a man by trade a potter, and exercised his calling for many years in Bath. Although of exceedingly limited education and originally of very humble fortune, the native strength of his mind and the love of information raised him to very repectable attainments in knowledge, while the integrity of his character, no less than his sagacity, commanded the confidence as well as the respect of all who knew him. He was repeatedly elected to the legislature of Kentucky, and served one term in the Senate. The characters and the careers of distinguished men have sometimes been traced to circumstances apparently trifling, which even in infancy have been thought to have settled the bent of the mind. The biographer of Napoleon has noted among the earliest and most prominent incidents of his infancy, that his first plaything was a miniature cannon, with its mimic equipments. From this first impression, or early predilection, the indelible image of war may have been stamped upon the mind and decided for ever the genius and the passions of the conqueror of Europe. In 1809, Kentucky's great Senator was fast drawing upon himself the gaze of men. The saffron tints of morning had already announced the coming of that orb which has since shone forth with such splendor in the eyes of the civilized world. The father of our Richard had at one time determined to call his son Henry Clay, and indeed the infant statesman and orator wore the name for the first two or three months of his existence. It was subsequently altered to Richard Hickman, from respect to a warm personal and family friend, but the boy was apprised of the prœnomen of his infancy and fired even in childhood by the fame of his great countryman, breathed often to heaven his fervent orison, that he might one day equal the eloquence, the greatness and the reputation of Mr. Clay. That the love of glory was the master-passion of his nature, and that sooner or later some event or circumstance must have roused it into life and action we can not doubt, and yet it may be, that the simple circumstance we have cited, may have marked out the path and determined the object of his ambition. That it made a deep impression upon his childish imagination, is a veritable and very interesting fact in his boyish biography. He was left by his father an orphan at about four years of age, and an estate never large was almost entirely wrecked by mismanagement and that bane of widows and orphans, a law suit—in which it had been left involved. Richard's utmost inheritance of worldly goods did not exceed a few hundred dollars. He seems, till he was about twelve years of age, to have been indebted almost exclusively to his mother's instructions for the rudiments of knowledge he received. For her he cherished to his latest hour the fondest veneration. He was her champion in boyhood, for sorrow and misfortune fell fast upon her. It was in his mother's defense that the lion of his nature first broke out. Incidents might here be related, exhibiting in rare perfection the depth of filial piety and dauntless heroism in a boy of fifteen, but they involve circumstances and feelings too delicate for a stranger's touch. In proof of the strength and tenderness of his private affections, it may here be stated, that after he commenced the practice of law, though pressed by the claims of his own family, he devoted a portion of his own slender means to the support of a brother overwhelmed with personal misfortunes and an orphan sister, and continued it till his death. At twelve years of age, so far as I have been able to learn, he first entered a public school. Like steel from flint, the collision of other minds struck instant fire from his own. The first competition brought into full play the passion for distinction, which formed the master principle of his nature. His teacher was astonished at the intense application, surpassing progress and precocious genius of the boy. He predicted to his pupil his future greatness, exhorted him to perseverance and furnished him every facility in his power. With this gentleman, whose name was TOMPKINS, (it should be written in letters of gold,) he seems to have remained without interruption for two years, at which period his mother married a second time, and he was removed from school. Clouds and thick darkness gathered now, over his fortunes and his darling hopes. At fourteen, he was summoned to attend at a tavern bar in Owingsville. But the omen of his first name still cheered him on, and the fire which had been first kindled within him, could not be extinguished. He compromised the matter at home and served at the bar or labored in the field during the summer, for the privilege of school during the winter months. Even this did not last, for want of means, (mark that, ye of more prosperous fortunes;) for want of means to defray his tuition fees, this unconquerable boy exchanged the character of pupil for preceptor at fifteen years of age, and taught what he had learned to others for hire during the winter months, that he might accumulate a fund with which to prosecute his own education thereafter. He continued thus till about his sixteenth year; when, in consequence of unpleasant difficulties with his step-father, he was taken to Mount Sterling by Mr. STOCKTON, an intimate friend of his deceased father. From this time he seems to have been left to his own guidance, and wrestled alone with his fortune. Upon the division of the wreck of the paternal estate, a negro was assigned to Richard about the period of his removal from home. He sold this slave to his friend, and with the proceeds, together with what he had earned as a preceptor, maintained himself at the public school in Mount Sterling till his eighteenth year, when he entered Transylvania as an *irregular* Junior. The rules of college would have excluded him from the privilege of examination, and debarred him even from a trial for the honors of his class. But that discipline which fixes a given time for given accomplishments and deems their attainment impossible, save within the limits and in the mode prescribed, was not framed for such as he. The hardy orphan who had been tutor and instructor of others at fifteen, and absolute and unheeded master of himself at sixteen, was not likely to be damped or daunted from his not having passed through a technical routine of studies, based upon ordinary calculations and framed for ordinary minds. He had already trampled upon the legal maxim which fixes one-and-twenty as the age for self-government, already "had his daring boyhood governed men." He gazed in scorn upon the artificial impediment which would have barred him from academic honors, and cleared it at a bound. His intrepid genius, his intense application, and the bold and extra-collegiate range of his information had attracted the eye and the admiration of the celebrated President HOLLEY. Through his intercession and influence the strict canon of the University was dispensed with in Richard's behalf; he was admitted to an examination with his class, and bore away the palm. Upon his return to Mount Sterling his funds were exhausted, and he again became a private tutor, while he prosecuted the study of law with Judge JAMES TRIMBLE. He persevered in his labors and his studies till the year 1830, when upon the death of his friend STOCKTON, whose affairs required the superintendence of a lawyer, and to whom he held himself bound by a debt of gratitude, in his twenty-first year he obtained a license to practice, and undertook as his first professional act, without charge, to settle and arrange the complicated and embarrassed affairs of his friend. In the fall of 1831 he was enabled to attend the law lectures here, when he became a distinguished member of your society. In the spring of 1832 he received the appointment of commonwealth's attorney, and in August before he had attained his twenty-third year he was married to the eldest daughter of the late MATTHEW JOUITT. It is not among the least interesting circumstances which concentrate in the union of these two orphans, that the dowerless daughter of Kentucky's most gifted artist should have found a tutor in her childhood every way adequate to form her taste and fashion her understanding, and that in the dawning graces of her first womanhood, reflecting back upon its source the light she had borrowed, should have drawn and fastened to her side as friend and protector through life, that same boy preceptor from whose precocious mind her own had drawn its nutriment and its strength. JOUITT and MENEFEE! what an union of names, what a nucleus for the public hopes and sympathies to grow and cluster round, to cling and cleave to. And they are united in the person of a boy, a glorious, beauteous boy—upon whose young brow and every feature is stamped the seal of his inheritance. I have seen this scion of a double stock, through whose young veins is poured in blending currents the double tide of genius and of art. Bless thee JOUITT MENEFEE, and may heaven which has imparted the broad brow of the statesman orator along with the painter's ambrosial head and glowing eye, may heaven shield and preserve thee boy, from the misfortunes of thy house.

Mr. Menefee retained his appointment, and located at Mount Sterling, continued the practice of law with extraordinary success in the various counties of that mountainous district till August, 1836, when he was returned the member from Montgomery to the House of Representatives of Kentucky. It was the fortune of your speaker to-day, to have served in the same body during that session, and it was at this period that he first saw and became acquainted with the illustrious subject of this discourse. The impression which Mr. Menefee then made was instantaneous and ineffaceable. He was in his twenty-seventh year, but the lightness of his hair, his delicate complexion and almost beardless face, and a certain juvenile outline of person, made him look to a transient observer some years younger than he really was. I knew nothing then, nor till long after, of his private history. He stood among his colleagues in legislation, almost an entire stranger. He was surrounded by no peculiar circumstances or associations of influence or of interest. No pomp of heraldry blazoned his hitherto obscure name; no hereditary honors glittered around his pale brow; no troop of influential connexions or family partisans stood ready to puff him into prompt notice, or to force him upon fame. Even the incidents of his young life, which would have won for his chivalric spirit an admiring and generous sympathy, were unknown. The storms through which his star had waded in its ascent, the strife perpetual which he had waged from infancy with evil circumstance and most malignant fortune, had rolled over him unknown or unheeded by that world to whose service and applause he had been fighting his way. He came into the lists unattended, without device, armorial bearing, squire, pursuivant, or herald. Entertaining the views which Mr. Menefee did, it can not be doubted that he regarded the Legislature of Kentucky as an important theatre to him. It was the entrance into that temple upon whose loftiest turret his eye had been fastened from childhood. The scene was, practically at least, an entirely new one to him. He was well aware, no man more so, of the importance of first impressions upon a body constituted as that of which he was a member. One would naturally have expected, from a person situated as he was, great anxiety, not unmixed with bashfulness and timidity in his debut. You might have anticipated, too, the selection of some question of great and general interest, and the careful and elaborate preparation, by so young and aspiring a member, of a *speech* duly laden with flowers, and studded with all the rhetorical gems of trope and figure. No such thing. He threw himself easily and naturally, and with apparent carelessness into debate for the first time, upon a bill entirely private in its character and of not the smallest interest to the house. No sooner had he risen, however, and his bell-tones vibrated through the hall, than every eye and ear were riveted into attention. There was about him an air of practiced ease, a self-possession, a deliberation, as utterly remote from affectation or impudence, as it was entirely free from confusion or timidity. He wore the cheek of a boy, and moved with the tread of a veteran. There was no impatience for display, no ambitious finery, no straining after effect about him, but there was a precision and clearness in his statement, an acuteness, a strength and clearness in his argument, which bespoke a mind not only of the greatest original power, but trained in the severest school of investigation, and to which the closest reasoning was habitual and easy. He seemed to move, too, in his natural element, as though he had so long and so carefully revolved in his own mind the theatre of public affairs as being the true stage for him, that he stood there, albeit for the first time, without surprise or anxiety. It was upon a motion of his own to reverse a report from the committee of courts of justice upon a bill authorizing the sale of some infant's real estate, that he was first heard to speak. The present governor of the Commonwealth was at the head of the committee, and some of the most experienced members of the house, and of the ablest professional men in the country were members of it. The member from Montgomery attacked their report with so much vivacity and such remarkable ability, that they felt themselves compelled to make a regular and formal defense, which they did seriatim, and it is no reflection upon their talent to state now, what all felt then to be true, that their young antagonist was a match for the whole. This debate and the occasion of it would have passed from my memory long since, but that they served to develop to my view, for the first time, the character and the powers of a man evidently marked out for greatness, whose subsequent career was one unbroken series of splendid successes, whose genius then first fairly risen upon the public, within three years from that date, shot into the zenith with an horizon stretching to the utmost boundary of the American States. After this first effort, trifling as would seem the occasion, Mr. Menefee was no longer considered in the light of a promising young man. He did not climb gradually into favor and influence with the house, but sprang at once, and with an elastic ease truly surprising, into the position not only of a debater of the highest order, but of a leading mind, whose ripened judgment and matured thought rendered his counsels as valuable as the eloquence in which they were conveyed was striking and delightful. He was a member of the committee of finance, and reported and carried in the face of the most violent opposition, what is usually termed the "equalizing law," by which the ordinary revenue, without an increase of taxation, but by including new subjects, has gained upward of thirty thousand dollars per annum. The debates in the Kentucky Legislature are not reported, and little attention is paid, and little interest manifested throughout the country in what is passing at the capitol in Frankfort. Yet upon the narrower and more obscure theatre which he then trod, did Mr. Menefee display during that winter, powers and qualities which in Washington would, as they afterward did, have covered him with glory and fixed his name. Compelled, by the particular interest which I then represented, (being a member from the city of Louisville,) to be thrown into frequent collision with Mr. Menefee in the debates of the House, I had ample opportunity both to know and to feel his intense power as a disputant. Attracted powerfully by the whole structure and style of the man, I studiously sought occasions for a close and critical observation of him. To men curious in such things he was a subject altogether worthy of study. Accident threw me somewhat into his personal confidence, which furnished better opportunities of ascertaining the distinctive traits of his character and the habitual complexion of his mind, than the mere contests of argument and public discussion would have afforded. In the course of the session, he was heard upon every question of State policy and always with an attention which showed how deep he was in the confidence of the House. Upon a proposition to reduce the salaries of the State engineers, to which he was opposed, he took occasion to discuss the system of internal improvement, as it is called, in which he showed that lawyer as he was, he had found time to study deeply the sources of national wealth, and the principles of public economy. Upon a proposition of his own which he lost, to place the salaries of the judges at Louisville upon the same footing with the other judges of the Commonwealth, he displayed, in the most eminent degree, the peculiar traits of his genius. It was not the discrimination in the amount of the salaries to which he objected. It was that principle in the law, which virtually made the Commonwealth's judges at Louisville to be paid by, and of course to be dependent, to a certain extent, upon that corporation, which he resisted and exposed. But the master effort of his mind that winter was on the bill to repeal the law of 1833, prohibiting the importation of slaves. Never yet have I heard or read among all the discussions to which that law has given rise, an argument so masterly, so statesmanlike, so triumphant as that of Mr. Menefee. Profoundly practical, and standing utterly aloof from the extremes of fanaticism, he displayed the deepest knowledge of the natural foundations of social prosperity, and the most cautious regard for existing institutions. Equally exempt from the rash spirit of political empiricism which would tear the subsisting frame of society to pieces, in search of that which is abstractly good, and from that worse than cowardice, which, shutting its eyes upon what is absolutely and demonstrably evil, would deepen and extend it, for the wise reason that it is not perfectly curable, that desperate quackery, which would spread a cancer over the whole body, because it could not be safely extirpated, he neither lauded slavery as a blessing, nor dreamed with crazy philanthropists, or murderous incendiaries, of its sudden and violent extinction. He adhered to the law of 1833 as a mean of checking the increase of an evil which could not now be prevented. It is a public misfortune, and a drawback upon Mr. Menefee's fame, brilliant as it is, that his speeches in the legislature of Kentucky were not preserved. Regarding him, as I have already said, with the deepest interest, and under circumstances very favorable for observation, I describe him as he impressed himself upon me. The great characteristic of his mind was strength, his predominant faculty was reason, the aim of his eloquence was to convince. With an imagination rich, but severe and chaste, of an elocution clear, nervous and perfectly ready, he employed the one as the minister, and the other as the vehicle of demonstration. He dealt not in gaudy ornament or florid exhibition; no gilded shower of metaphors drowned the sense of his discourse. He was capable of fervid invective, vehement declamation, and scathing sarcasm; but strength, strength was the pervading quality, and there was argument even in his denunciation. "No giant form set forth his common hight," no stentor voice proclaimed a bully in debate; yet did he possess the power of impression, deep, lasting impression, of interesting you not only in what he said, but in himself, of stamping upon the memory his own image, in the most eminent degree, and in the most extraordinary manner, of any man of his age whom it has been my fortune to encounter. "*Bonum virum facile crederes, magnum libenter.*" Although removed the farthest possible from the affectation of mystery, or any asserted and offensive pretension to superiority over other men, and although his manner was exempt entirely from the charge of haughtiness, still, as he appeared at that time, he loved not familiarity and courted no intimacy. He was bland, courteous, and perfectly respectful in his intercourse; still, there was a distance, an undefinable sort of reserve, unmixed with pride, but full of dignity, keeping frivolity aloof, and attracting at once your curiosity and your interest. Upon his forehead, which was broad, and full and very commanding, were traced the indisputable lines of intellect and genius. His pale and delicate brow was stamped with the gravity and the care of premature manhood. About his lip and mouth were the slight, but living and indelible traits of a resolved and ambitious spirit. The whole countenance was that of a man who had suffered and struggled, but who had conquered the past and was prepared to grapple fearlessly with the future. But the master expression, the natural language which breathed from his face, form, step, gesture, and even the almost feminine tone of his voice, and which contrasted so strangely with the delicacy of the whole, was energy, unfainting, indomitable, though curbed and regulated energy, which could sustain him through all danger and under all fortune, and which would and must bear him on to the utmost mark at which his ambition might aim, and to which his talents were at all adequate. There was nothing restless or impatient about him. His was deliberate, concentrated, disciplined energy. He had that managed calmness of general manner, which so often betokens a fiery and excitable temperament, but under the most perfect control. Never man was more entirely master of himself than Mr. Menefee. His conversation corresponded with and deepened the impression made by his public speeches, and a close examination of his whole appearance. He had all the quickness and penetration of a man of true genius, but without a spark of wildness or eccentricity. There was no dreamy idealism, no shadowy romance, no morbid sentimentalism about him. The occasional splendor of his illustrations proved him to be sure possessed of an imagination not only grand and lofty, but exquisitely sensible of the beautiful and the soft, but it was the ally, not the principal; and an ally upon which his sovereign reason, abounding in its own resources, leaned but little and drew but seldom. His fancy drew her inspiration from the natural fountains around and within him. It was not even tinged with the sickly light of modern fiction. His whole mind was eminently healthy. His was the seriousness of determination, unmixed with gloom or melancholy. The purity of his language, which was remarkable for its beauty as well as its precision, declared a mind imbued with elegant letters, but there was an antique severity in his taste, a marble firmness as well as smoothness in his style, which spoke of the hardihood and muscle of the Grecian masters, those first teachers and eternal fountains of poetry and eloquence.* But neither Mr. Menefee's conversation, nor his attainments, nor his talents, eminent as they all were, surprised me so much as the matured and almost rigid tone of his character, the iron control which he exercised over himself, the cool, practical and experienced views which he took of the world, and the elevation, consistency and steadiness of his purposes. These were the qualities which made his talents useful; these were the qualities which, young as he was, gave him such absolute hold and command of the public confidence; these were the qualities which adapted him to the genius and bound him to the hearts of his countrymen, without which he might have been brilliant, but never could have been great.

He had early ranged himself with that great party in politics, whose protracted and arduous struggles have at last found their consummation, and whose principles have been ratified by the judgment of the nation in the election of General Harrison to the presidency. He belonged to that class of minds, who, in every country and under every form of government, are found the unflinching advocates of rational and regulated liberty, a liberty founded in principles fixed and eternal, and which is only safe under the shield and cover of a law changeless and inviolable by the government, equally supreme and binding upon the rulers and upon the people. The imperial

* That he was familiar with the historians and orators of antiquity, particularly of Athens, I am able to state of my own knowledge. Those who knew him at college, say that he won his academic honors by his superiority in mathematics and the languages.

maxim, "*voluntas principis habet vigorem legis,*" he rejected utterly. He loathed despotism in all its forms, and wherever lodged, whether in the hands of one, the many, or the few. Born in a monarchy, he would have died as Hampden died, in the assertion of legal limitations upon the prerogative. Born in a republic, he clung to the constitutional restrictions upon the rapacious passions of faction. He regarded the courtier cringing at the footstool of a throne, and the demagogue lauding the absolute power of a mob, as equally the foes of freedom, and the just objects of patriot execration. He understood the term people as comprehending every interest and every individual, and looked upon that system alone as free, which protected each against the arbitrary power even of the whole. He regarded government as something framed for the defense of the weak against the strong, of the few against the many, and considered human rights as only safe, where fixed laws, and not the fluctuating caprices of men and parties, were supreme. Strength and numbers are absolute in a state of savage nature; they need no laws nor magistracy for their support. The rights of the weak and the few, can only be secured by the incorporation of the eternal principles of liberty and justice in a constitution impassable to power and immutable by party. The splendid popularity of a favorite chief, blinded not his reason, the roar of triumphant faction deafened not his conscience, the proscribing genius of a power which punished with inexorable severity, or rewarded with unbounded profusion, appalled not his moral courage, nor shook for one moment his native integrity. Young, poor, talented and aspiring, still he followed where his principles led him, and battled long on the side of a feeble and almost overwhelmed minority of his countrymen. To the cause which he espoused, through all its fortunes, he adhered with unbroken faith and consistency, and lived just long enough to witness its final and complete success.

Mr. Menefee passed from the Legislature of Kentucky into the national councils, where he took his seat in the lower house of Congress at the call session of 1837. He is said to have exhibited during the canvass, extraordinary powers of popular eloquence, and an unequalled grace and facility in mingling with the great body of the people, demonstrating thereby the versatility of a mind whose strength alone I have been contemplating. The same destiny (for it seemed no less) attended him in Congress, which had marked his entrance upon State legislation. There were no gradations in his congressional history. He comprehended at once, and as if by instinct, the new scene in which he was called to act; and no sooner did he appear, than he was recognised as a statesman and a leader. The intrepid boldness of his character, and precocious strength of his genius, seem to have smitten all parties with astonishment. Some of the leading men of the political party to which he was opposed, pronounced him the most extraordinary man of his age, who had till then, appeared in Congress. He encountered hostility in his upward flight, (when did soaring genius fail to do it?) and meaner birds would have barred him from his pathway to the skies. With crimsoned beak and bloody talons, he rent his way through the carrion crew, and moved majestically up to bathe his plumage in the sun. Never did a career more dazzlingly splendid open upon the eye of young ambition, than burst upon Mr. Menefee. The presses teemed with his praise, the whole country was full of his name; yet did he wear his honors with the ease of a familiar dress. He trod the new and dizzy path with a steady eye, and that same veteran step which was so eminently his characteristic. Around his path there seem to have been thrown none of those delusions, which haunt the steps of youth and inexperience. All was stern reality and truth. He maintained his character undimmed, and his position unshaken, till the end of his term, and then this wonderful man imposed upon himself, his spirit and his ambition, that iron control of which I have spoken, and voluntarily retired from a theatre the most elevated and commanding, upon which genius and ambition like his could engage in the gigantic strife for undying honor. At twenty-nine years of age, Mr. Menefee found himself upon a summit to which the dreams of youth and hope could scarce have aspired. He alone seemed neither astonished nor confounded by the hight to which he had arisen. In 1837, an obscure young lawyer, scarce known beyond the precincts of his native highland district; in 1839, he stood forth on the world's great theatre in acknowledged greatness, the predictions of his first tutor realized, the prayer of his childhood granted. He stood on that eminence so long and so gloriously occupied by the man whose name he once bore, and whose fame had been the pillar of fire by which he guided his footsteps through the long, dark, perilous and unfriended night of his boyhood; and he stood there at an age which threw even that example into the shade. The draught which he drank, so far from intoxicating his understanding, served only to refresh and invigorate his spirit for the work set before him. He surveyed calmly from the hight on which he stood, the prospect stretched beneath him; he quaffed the full beams of the sun of glory which glowed above him, then turning to the gentle flower at his side, which he had vowed to shelter and defend, to her who had loved and trusted him in obscurity and penury, before the world, now ready to do him homage, had learned his transcendent talents and inestimable worth, and folding her, all bright and blushing in the light of her husband's glory, to his bosom, he descended without a sigh, to vindicate her confidence and toil for her support.

He was now, though steeped in poverty, in the full possession of fame. He was known universally. Over his character there hung no doubt nor shadow. He had but to select his ground, to choose his theatre. His talents, his acquirements, his habits, all fitted him eminently for the bar. A self-made scholar, he was of indefatigable application—with a mind of singular acuteness naturally, and now much enlarged and strengthened by the great topics it had grasped, and the powerful collisions into which it had been thrown, he was peculiarly fitted for the largest and most comprehensive views of jurisprudence. Of an integrity stainless as the untrodden snow, and without one vice to consume his time or warp his career, he was sure to devote himself to the interests of his clients. In the summer of 1839 he located himself in Lexington. There was no dreary noviciate with him. He stepped into the forum armed at all points, and business flowed in upon him in a full and rich tide. Never did any man occupy such a position in Kentucky as did Mr. Menefee in the opening of his professional career in Lexington. The public sympathies rallied around to cheer and to support him in a manner utterly unknown in any other case. Each step of his progress but deepened the interest and vindicated more triumphantly the opinion entertained of him. Men flocked in crowds to hear him speak, his counsel was sought and relied on, and his services engaged, when ever it was practicable, at points distant from the scene of his immediate operations. At a period of life when most men are just rising into business, he was steeped, actually overwhelmed with the weightiest, most honorable and most profitable causes. The sun of prosperity broke out upon him with a warmth and brilliancy entirely without example. All difficulties had vanished from before him. In the past he found nothing with which to upbraid himself. The rough road through which he had journeyed from childhood was marked throughout with trophies of his triumphant spirit. His country regarded him as public property, and waiting with fond impatience the attainment of that pecuniary independence which his erect and honorable nature deemed essential to his character, stood ready with open arms to receive him into her service and crown him with her choicest honors. Fortune was absolutely within his grasp. He was the slave of honor, not the drudge of avarice. It was independence that he sought, independence for himself and his nestlings. He had tasted the bitter fruits of early poverty, and although he had triumphed, he would not doom his little ones to their father's struggles and sufferings. He must have attained the object of his pursuit even before he had reached his manhood's prime, and then he could have turned him again without a crime, to the pursuits of ambition, again have mounted the solar hights whence his moral nature had forced his intellectual down. For one short year Mr. Menefee's delicate frame sustained the fiery energies of his mind. In the spring of 1840 in reply to a note from myself on professional business, he alluded to the decline of his health in a tone of sadness, not despondence—his was a soul that never desponded—which struck me as ominous and prophetic. Disease had indeed fastened its fangs upon his body, its force was vain against his mind. With rapidly declining health he persevered in his business, till in September, in a case of vast magnitude, in which Messrs. Clay and Wickliffe were both employed against him, he put forth, for the last time, his immortal energies at the bar. Like the Hebrew giant his last effort was the greatest. Oh, would to God that he had been or could have been induced to spare himself! But the occasion had come, and the ruling passion, strong in death, broke out with irresistible force, to throw its radiance over his funeral pile. Ambition has been called the last infirmity of noble minds. To me it seems to constitute their essence and their strength. I mean not the love of power, but that higher ambition, the love, the yearning after that imperishable fame, which shines through far generations, and with an increasing light over the memory of great and glorious talents, greatly and gloriously exerted in the cause of justice and mankind. This appeared to me to be the master passion of Mr. Menefee's soul. He must have been conscious of an extraordinary fate and an extraordinary genius. He must have appeared to himself as he certainly did to all others, a man marked out from birth for great actions and the most splendid distinction. What had he not achieved? His friends may challenge the history of this country for a parallel. I have said that I had observed him closely in 1836. I have had intimate opportunities since his retirement from Congress. I have conversed with him since his disease was distinctly developed, and the qualities which struck me with so much force upon our first acquaintance, appeared to gather strength with time. There was an unsparing intensity in his mind, a concentration of the whole soul upon his pursuits, a haste, a rapidity, as though he feared the sun of life should go down ere the goal assigned to his genius had been attained. Was he conscious, (such a suspicion has sometimes flashed across me, and from remembered conversations gathered strength,) could he have been conscious that the seeds of early death were implanted in his original constitution, and was it this which spurred his fiery soul to such gigantic and unpausing strides upon his road to greatness? Himself, at all events, he did not and he would not spare. This was his only crime; the generous martyr; for this, and this alone, can his country reproach him. Perchance the opportunity of measuring himself with that great genius, whom he had proposed originally as his standard, struck upon his heroic temperament, and roused the poetry of his nature, as being a meet finale to a life like his. Be that as it may, he dashed at the opportunity as new fledged eaglets dash into the sun. He did measure himself, and, in that effort, pouring forth his genius and his life, reached the consummation of his first wishes, the utmost point of his childhood's prayer. He was measured and found a match for one whose thunders long have shaken the American Senate and who was erst the monarch of the forum. Mr. Menefee sank gradually from September. His waning life sank, not his spirit. When apprised at last that his hour had arrived, "Brief summons," was the reply, and he manned himself to die with dignity. His sense of duty, the energy and collectedness of his nature and his cautious regard for others, were strikingly manifested by the last act of his life. He made his will, executed a mortgage to indemnify a friend who was responsible for him, and ere the next sun had risen, his own had set for ever.

Thus perished, in the thirty-second year of his life, Richard H. Menefee, a man designed by nature and himself, for inevitable greatness. A man of the rarest talents and of the most commanding character. A man whose moral qualities were as faultless, as his intellectual constitution was vigorous and brilliant. A man to whose advancing eminence there was no limit but the constitution of his country, had not the energies of his mind proved too mighty for the material elements which enclosed them.

> "'T was his own genius gave the final blow,
> And helped to plant the wound that laid him low.
> So the struck Eagle stretched upon the plain,
> No more through rolling clouds to soar again,
> Viewed his own feather on the fatal dart,
> And winged the shaft that quivered in his heart.
> Keen were his pangs, but keener far to feel
> He nursed the pinion which impelled the steel,
> And the same plumage that had warmed his nest,
> Drank the last life-drop from his bleeding breast."

SPEECH ON THE BILL TO APPROPRIATE THE PROCEEDS OF THE SALES OF THE PUBLIC LANDS, AND GRANT PRE-EMPTION RIGHTS,

Delivered in the House of Representatives of the United States on the 6th of July, 1841.

John Quincy Adams pronounced this the ablest speech he had ever heard upon the subject. This, especially just after having heard Mr. Clay's great land speech, is no small eulogium.

"The bill to appropriate the proceeds of the sales of the public lands, and to grant preëmption rights," being under consideration in Committee of the Whole upon the state of the Union, after Mr. Rayner, of North Carolina, had closed, Mr. Marshall, of Kentucky, obtained the floor at half-past five P. M., and spoke as follows:

Mr. Chairman:—I would apologize for entering upon the discussion of this question at this hour, and would, moreover, pledge myself to brevity, but that, in examining the speeches made upon this floor, I have uniformly observed that the longest of them have been preceded by such apologies and promises. I shall, therefore, proceed without preface, or exordium, to state the answer to the more important objections urged so eloquently against the bill yesterday, by the distinguished gentleman from Virginia, [Mr. Wise,] and in a very general manner the leading principles upon which it reposes for support in the judgment of its friends. I gave an attentive ear to the gentleman from Virginia through the entire space of three hours and a half. I listened to him (I had almost said with pleasure) at least with an interest, albeit a painful one, so absorbing as to destroy all consciousness of the length of time consumed by his speech. The gentleman premised, that he had on a former occasion fully discussed the principles of the bill, and that for the present he would confine himself to the objections which existed in his mind to the details; yet, when once embarked on this great measure, he found it impossible to confine himself within the limits prescribed. Borne away by the impetuosity of his own genius, he directed his fire at the whole measure, principle and detail—origin, progress, and ultimate effect; he struck at it root and branch; he raked it from stem to stern—hull, masts, and rigging. Such was the power of the gentleman's declamation, and such is the influence of genius even in its errors, that I found my preconceived, and, as I thought, well settled ideas, not only in relation to this bill, but as to the nature of this Government, and the relations of the several parts of our republican empire to each other, thrown into confusion, and my understanding so enveloped in the smoke from his artillery, that it was not till I sought my pillow in the calm and in the silence of the night, that I was enabled to recur to the habitual, and as I still believe, the clear and correct, contemplation of all the matters handled by the gentleman from Virginia.

Mr. Chairman, the bill upon your table proposes, generally, to distribute among the several States of this Union the proceeds of the sales of the public domain, in the proportion that their federal numbers bear to each other. It reserves to the General Government the management and administration of the sales. It fixes the maximum price, and provides for the cessation of the law in case of war. To nine of the new States it gives ten per centum on the net profits of the sales of the land within their territory, after the 31st December, 1841. These are the chief provisions which encountered the gentleman's denunciation and invective. To the right of preëmption granted to settlers under certain conditions, he was understood to make no particular objection.

The gentleman from Virginia sees consolidation in every thing. The sovereignty of the States is threatened by this Government in every mode of its action. There is consolidation in debt; there is consolidation in surplus; there is consolidation in distribution. Under this bill he detects the assumption of State debts, internal improvement, and a protective tariff; he treats it as in fact a distribution of the customs, and a declaration of war upon the part of free labor against slave labor. Sir, in what sense can the distribution of the proceeds of the public lands be considered as an assumption of the State debts by this Government? I understand by the assumption of the State debts, their consolidation into one, to be discharged out of the national funds raised by equal taxation. The States which, like North Carolina, owe nothing, or whose debts, like those of Kentucky, are comparatively small, would be taxed, not in proportion to their debts, but in proportion to their population, to pay off a debt contracted without their authority, and bearing no proportion in the several elements of which it is composed, to the amounts to be paid by the several States for its extinction. That a community shall be taxed to pay a debt contracted without its authority, is, in fact, taxation without representation. Practically, it were better, safer, more free, that the Legislature of Pennsylvania should have the power of laying an equal tax upon the whole Union to pay a debt contracted by the general authority, than that she should have the separate power to contract the debt, leaving Congress to impose the general tax. The war debt of the States at the close of the Revolution is very clearly and easily distinguishable from the present internal improvement debt. The war debt was really the debt of the Union, and, although contracted by the States separately, it was for the liberty and independence of the whole. It was for the common good, and should have been discharged from the common funds. Ingenuity itself can not liken the distribution of national property among the several States, upon a principle strictly of federal equality, the basis both of representation and taxation, to the consolidation and assumption of *unequal debts* contracted by State authority alone, to be paid out of national funds raised by *equal taxation.*

It is further contended, strenuously, and with an air of most triumphant confidence, that this is, in fact, a distribution of the customs. That the General Government proposes to levy taxes merely for the purpose of distribution. The gentleman from Virginia, treating the Government as trustee of two separate funds, files his bill in equity for an account between the customs and the public lands. He sits as master commissioner, and finds that the whole expense of the administration of the public domain exceed the whole receipts into the Treasury from the sales, and decrees that the lands must be charged with this difference, and that it must be reimbursed before there is any thing to distribute. I object to this mode of settlement. That the expenses of the sales and administration have exceeded the receipts from the public lands, may well be contested. Waiving, however, any dispute as to the fact, and admitting it to be as stated, nay, charging them with every thing, the purchase money paid for part, the Indian wars—every thing I say—and credit them with nothing by receipts from the sales, suppose them given away to those who have settled them, and political arithmetic still discloses a balance scarcely susceptible of numerical statement in favor of the lands against the customs. When the General Government grants its lands, although it is in fee, she reserves the right to tax, through her custom-houses, the consumption by the grantee of all articles of foreign growth or manufacture.

Suppose the vast domain comprehending the new States unsettled and unsold. Strike out both receipt and expenditure; hurl back, if imagination be capable of such an achievement—hurl back Ohio, Indiana, Illinois, into their primeval, yet recent wilderness, and what becomes of all the revenue through the custom-houses drawn from the enormous consumption of these States? I speak of revenue already received and expended, saying nothing of what is to arise through all coming time. In estimating the receipts of the General Government from the public lands, it is a most narrow mode of calculation to limit the revenue drawn from this source to the one dollar and one quarter per acre paid by the grantee. It is after the sale and settlement that revenue begins. The Government might, indeed, have settled the lands by donees, and still have established thereby a fund of credit upon which the customs might have drawn without limit and for ever.

This is a question of imperial policy and imperial equity, and must be settled upon other and more enlarged principles than govern such a suit in chancery as the gentleman from Virginia has instituted. Credit the public lands by all their countless tenantry have paid into the coffers of the State, and the balance would be fearful against the customs. But we not only do not claim this from the lands already sold, but we have surrendered it through the constitution to the United States, over all the eight hundred millions of acres yet remaining to be sold. Distribute the price paid for the land among the States hereafter, and still as they settle, and new members of the confederacy spring into existence, the General Government reserves to itself the exclusive possession of the most fruitful source of revenue through the duties, a source widening, deepening, becoming more copious and exuberant with the progress of settlement and distribution.

Mr. Chairman, the fund proposed to be distributed is no more raised by taxation than it is indebted to the customs. The revenue raised from the sale of the public lands is not a tax; it is distinct, eternally distinct, in its nature and its origin, from the revenue raised by duties, or in any other way.

The money which the Government receives from the grantee of a section of land is for a consideration of many times the value paid. The man who gives one dollar and one quarter for an acre of land, which, by the application of a moderate degree of his own labor, and the rapid growth of society around, must soon be worth twenty, thirty, in many instances one hundred times that sum, can scarcely be persuaded that he is paying a tax. The proceeds of the sale of the public lands, then, compared with the actual value of the grant made, the thing transferred, more nearly resemble a donation than a tax. It differs from the customs as much in its origin as in its nature. The gentleman from Maryland [Mr. JOHNSON] has saved all who come after him in this debate any trouble in the investigation of this branch of the subject. He has traced the title to the public domain back to the several deeds of cession from the States—deeds executed before the adoption of the federal constitution, and has shown that the rights both granted and reserved in them, remain unaffected by that instrument. The war of the Revolution was a common cause. It was held, at its close, that the vast unsettled territory within the chartered limits of the several States, having been rent from the crown of England by the joint exertions, blood and treasure, of all the colonies, did in equity become thereby the common property of the whole. To avoid all territorial disputes, and the interminable difficulty of a division of the lands themselves among States situated so widely apart, and many of them so remote from the territory to be divided, it was determined, in the magnanimous spirit of that immortal age, to cede the unsettled and almost boundless wilderness to the common Government, for the "use and benefit of such of the United States as shall become members of the federal alliance of the said States, and for no other use or purpose whatsoever." Such is the uniform language of the deeds of cession. In the preamble to the statute of New York, authorizing the cession, it is said, "That the waste and uncultivated territory within the limits or claims of certain States ought to be appropriated as a common fund for the expenses of the war."

Thus was the Government of the United States invested legally, formally, and by deed, with the title, as trustee, for the several States composing, or who should thereafter compose, the confederacy, and charged with the expenses of the war. The deeds are strictly and technically deeds of trust. They are not grants of political power, but conveyances of landed property charged with specific debts, and, for the use and benefit of specified communities, clear, precise, technical. A trust estate, in land, differs as much from the sovereign power to lay and collect taxes, duties, imposts, etc., as the revenue received from the sale of land does from that collected by a duty upon the importation of a cask of wine. But I will press this view no farther. I will pass by the legal and strict right of the States to this fund, incontestable as the gentleman from Maryland has shown it to be, and consider it as a great practical question, bearing upon the present condition of the people of the United States, their credit, their interest, and their general welfare. The gentleman from Virginia [Mr. WISE] assumes, as settled and incontrovertible, that Congress have no power over the internal improvement of the States; and contending that the money to be distributed by this bill is intended to be applied to that object, or to the payment of debts contracted on that account, argues that we are endeavoring to do indirectly what we are prohibited from doing directly. We shall not appropriate any thing to the connection of the several parts of the vast country whose commerce, foreign and domestic, we are appointed to regulate; nor shall we distribute among the local governments even that which is their own, lest they should apply it to the development of those hidden stores which Nature has every where provided throughout this favored land, for the comfort and enjoyment of men, and only concealed that she might stimulate his industry, and invigorate his nature. Internal improvement can not be carried on without revenue. The States are cut off from the easiest and most fruitful sources through duties upon commerce. Those who oppose this bill seem to dread any increase of the duties upon the part of the General Government, lest there should be revived a protective tariff. What are we to infer? Is it that the General Government has no power but over war and foreign negotiation? Is it that she is impotent in peace, without authority, direct or indirect, to advance the industry, facilitate the intercourse, strengthen the credit, and unfold the natural resources of the country? Is it that she shall be compelled to lean upon the public domain, granted under the conditions which I have shown, and to eke it out by direct taxation for the revenue necessary to the execution of the slender and circumscribed powers which the argument leaves it? Are the States prohibited from raising revenue from commerce? And shall the General Government leave idle and unexerted the sovereign and most productive power of impost and duty upon such a trade as ours—a power expressly and exclusively granted—about which even strict constructionists can not dispute, and throw the national expenditure upon the same resources, to which and to which alone the States are allowed to look for revenue? Is she to abandon what is exclusive, and resort to what is concurrent, and what will be sufficiently burdened by State necessities for a long time to come? And for what reason? Are we to abandon the clearest dictates of economical finance, lest, by the imposition of duties upon foreign commerce, incidental protection should flow to American industry?—lest, by restoring to the States property originally their own and ceded to a common trustee for their own use and benefit as States, their credit should be strengthened, and they enabled to prosecute those great domestic works which they alone, according to the argument, have the right to prosecute? This Government must not lean upon the customs for its expenditure, although they be exclusively by the constitution a national fund for national purposes—because, by so doing, they will leave other branches of revenue, to which the States are entitled, concurrently, untouched; and thus, by the action of this Government in the choice of resources, the States may be permitted to do for themselves that which we are told the General Government can not do directly. Sir, is not this a strange argument for States rights gentlemen to employ? Can it be better answered than by the statement of it? Gentlemen from the South have not always reasoned thus. The leader of the States rights party, the distinguished Senator from South Carolina, [Mr. CALHOUN,] once held that the General Government had the power over internal improvement under the right to make war. His great and expanded mind devised and recommended a general and magnificent plan of intercommunication by roads and canals between the several portions of the republic, as auxiliary and directly referable to the national defense. And, sir, should war's rude summons again awake our land, we shall feel that the facilities furnished by the State improvements for the transportation of troops and provisions, are of the very essence of military strength, are among the instruments of war, and the means of defense—as clearly as ships, or troops, or armor. Sir, there is an other party in this House who are opposed to this bill: surely it can not be upon any constitutional scruple as to the power to distribute revenue among the States, no matter whence derived. In 1830, General Jackson avowed himself in favor of internal improvement by the State authorities. He vetoed an appropriation made directly by Congress to a State work; but recommended, nay urged, the distribution of the whole surplus, customs and all, after the payment of the national debt, among the States for the purpose of internal improvement. He anticipated a large annual surplus for many years, and devoted it all to this greatest of all objects.

But, "*tempora mutantur et nos mutamur cum illis.*" We find these same parties now not only denying all power to the General Government over the subject directly, but resisting any form of national policy which may aid or encourage incidentally those States to whose rights they are so much devoted in the prosecution of their own works by their own authority. Sir, I mean not now and here to contend for the power of internal improvement by the General Government. But I do mean to contend that there is a difference in reason and in fact between the direct power over internal improvement by that Government, and the application of funds to the subject by the State authorities, nothwithstanding those funds may have been drawn from the national Treasury. I do mean to contend that this Government is bound so to shape its own financial policy as to interfere as little as possible with the resources of the States. Nay, more, in such manner as to strengthen and aid those resources, so far as may be. I say, that it is essential to the independence and the advance of these States to wealth, power, and population, that the power over internal improvements, as a political right, should exist some where. Without revenue the power is nugatory. The policy to which the argument I have been endeavoring to answer would seem to point, is practically a denial of it, both to the State and the General Government. It is to lay this country, her industry, and her institutions, prostrate at the foot of foreign nations. The genius of this age is utilitarian, mechanical. The tendency of its philosophy is to extend the power of man over nature, physical nature, to multiply the sources of human enjoyment, the objects of human industry, and the means of human subsistence. The jealousy which denies to the Government such an exertion of its powers, and such a direction of its means, as will effect objects to which individual strength and capital are altogether inadequate, dooms the people to embarrassment and weakness. The reasoning which dismembers revenue from political duty, which confers the great and welling fountains of the one exclusively upon the national, yet imposes the most expensive and burdensome portions of the other upon the State governments, which gives the sovereign and exclusive control over war and commerce, foreign and domestic, to the one, yet compels the other to furnish, unaided, the highways of trade and transportation, military as well as commercial, may be friendly to State rights, but is exceedingly unfavorable to State powers and interests. General Jackson conceded the principle, so far as the right to distribute revenue among the States is concerned, to an extent far beyond what is claimed by this bill or its advocates. He denied to the national Government the power to direct and control the internal improvements within the territory of the particular States; but was willing that it should be the collecting agent for the States, leaving to them the right of expending and applying treasure which they are constitutionally incompetent to raise. I have said, sir, that I did not go this length, nor is it necessary that I should.

Fortune, a most propitious and singular fortune, has placed at the disposal of this Government a fund, an enormous fund, independent of taxation, to which we have shown the States have something very like to strict title. Eight hundred millions of acres of land, at one dollar and one quarter per acre, one thousand millions of dollars—think of that, sir!—to be applied gradually and upon a principle of strict federal equality to the extinction of State debts, to the extension of State improvements, to the support of State credit! Oh! who can say, sir, that this measure is hostile to the rights of the States as separate communities? And this fund, too, conferring ten times its own value upon the individuals from whom it is drawn, and opening up new perennial and unfathomable fountains of revenue to the Government which distributes it! Who shall say that it is injurious to the power or the interests of the people as a nation, or to their national Treasury? This picture is not overdrawn—not in the least. It is the advantage, the peculiar advantage, of peopling and bringing new and fertile land into cultivation. Raise money in any other way, or from any other source, and it is taxation. Sell any thing else, the product of human art or labor below its value, and you are either robbed by the vendee, or you rob those from whom you derive it. But land, vacant, unsettled, unpeopled, fertile, uncultivated land, is the creation and the gift of God. When you sell it for the one-tenth of its value, you have enriched yourselves to that extent from the munificence of Heaven; and he who purchases has made one thousand per cent. upon his investment. You enlarge the national capital a thousandfold by the very act of filling the national Treasury; and, at the same time, and by the same operation, extend incalculably the sources of future revenue. But, sir, although all this is true, strictly and philosophically true, and the individual is enriched, American population increased, the national capital enlarged, and the national Treasury filled by this progress of emigration and settlement, still the money thus profitably invested is withdrawn from the productive industry of the States whence it was taken, and the power of that industry is, for the time, and to that extent, diminished. How beautiful the operation of this bill, which restores and renovates the fountains whence these streams were drawn, enabling them to flow on, and on, and on, without exhaustion, till the whole grand reservoir of the West be full of people and of capital—the perennial sources remaining fresh, and full, and vigorous as before! And it restores, in a form at once the most just, the most beneficent, the most useful. It was gone from the State entirely and for ever. It is taken by the General Government, as I have shown, without tax or oppression. It is given back in masses to the State treasuries to be expended, not unproductively, but in the creation of new instruments and vehicles of commerce and production; the people receiving again the money, the State receiving an equal value in works which are to be the permanent sources of revenue to the public, by conferring permanent and enriching facilities upon the industry of the people, at once preventing the drain of capital by emigration, and replenishing the State treasuries without taxation.

Mr. Chairman, the gentleman from Virginia [Mr. WISE] has told us that the effect of this bill upon the States will be similar to an effort to reform a spendthrift by filling his pockets with money. Sir, is it just to the States, is it quite consistent in those who claim to be the champions of their rights, their sovereignty, and the guardians of their honor, thus to stigmatize their character and their credit? Is it quite fair in a government, or any member of it, which, holding the imperial sources of revenue in exclusive property, and in possession but a few years ago of a vast surplus, repudiating all authority to advance the arts of peace, all power to extend domestic commerce, and to conquer the vast distances of its territory by quickening communication and intercourse — is it quite fair, after shuffling off these sovereign powers upon the States, and seducing them into their exertion by promises of aid and countenance, to brand as profligate and prodigal the generous efforts they have made to improve the face of their country, to bring themselves nearer to each other, to increase the objects of the industry, and enlarge and extend the markets for the productions of their people? No, sir, the internal improvement debt of the States finds no type in the wanton expenditure of the profligate. Theirs is rather the wise and far-sighted policy of the husbandman, who sows all his seed broadcast upon his fields, and even stints himself for the present rather than his lands should lie idle, awaiting with philosophic patience the rich and sure reward of the coming harvest.

But, sir, the gentleman from Virginia [Mr. WISE] found much to blame in the details as well as the principle of the bill. He considers the ten per cent. on the net profits of the lands situated within their territorial limits, which the bill gives to the nine States enumerated in the first section, over and above their federal proportion, as unjust and unequal—a mere bribe to those States. The principle which governs this provision seems clear and unexceptionable. In the first place, the land upon which this per centum is given is within the territorial limits and jurisdiction of the States to which it is given, and is, by the existing law, exempt for five years from taxation. In the second place, the States so enumerated are found to increase in population in a ratio of about ten per centum faster than the older States of the Union. So that the provision of this section is necessary to compensate the State for the loss of revenue occasioned by the exemption of the public lands from taxation for five years after the settlement, and to preserve the general principle of the bill, by apportioning the distribution, as nearly as possible, to the increasing ratio of population.

The section which fixes the maximum price which the Government shall demand during the existence of the laws at the present minimum of $1 25 per acre, has met with the severest denunciation. The wisdom and propriety of this provision seem to be equally manifest with the policy and justice of the preceding. The great national object is to promote, as fast as possible, the settlement, real and bona fide, of the public domain, and so to keep down the price as to place comfortable farms within the reach of the poorer class of emigrants. Under the distribution law, the necessities of some of the older States, or the jealousy of those who imagine that emigration drains their population, and ascribe their own decline, or at least inertness and stagnation, to the rise of the western States, might induce them to raise the price of lands so as to check the advance of that population which the General Government is most interested in extending. The one would kill the goose that lays the golden egg to get at the treasure;

the other would stop the national growth, in the vain hope of increasing thereby their own particular importance. Against either result, or either motive, the provision is aimed, and wisely aimed, as it seems to me.

And here, Mr. Chairman, I beg leave to differ not only from the gentleman from Virginia, [Mr. WISE,] but from my associate in this argument, the gentleman from North Carolina, [Mr. RAYNER.] I can not ascribe the want of progress, or at least the very slow advance of population and resources, in the Carolinas and Virginia to the settlement and growth of the western country. When was emigration ever known to diminish population at home, all things else being right there? Did emigration to America diminish the population of Great Britain? Has the population of New England diminished under the settlement and most wonderful advance of Ohio, Illinois, and Indiana? Has New York or Pennsylvania declined under the growth of the West? So far from it, the settlement of the western lands and the creation of the western communities have been the great source of the rapid advance and wonderful improvement of the States whence they have principally drawn their people. The power of increase in the human species is unlimited, save by the means of subsistence; the amount of which depends upon the amount and character of the industry employed, and the remuneration it receives. Population and labor move *pari passu*. The growth of the new States has furnished the demand for the products of the commerce and manufactures of the old, and the cultivation of the fertile lands of the West has afforded abundant means of exchange and payment. States which have neither commerce nor manufactures, and whose agriculture is carried on by those who have neither a property in the soil nor interest in its production, if they find themselves sinking into poverty and weakness, must look for the cause elsewhere than in the prosperity of communities differently situated. But this is dangerous ground, and I quit it.

Finally, the gentleman from Virginia [Mr. WISE] conceives this bill to convert the public lands into a fund of universal corruption: States, old and new, corporations and individuals, rich and poor, governments and people, all bid for and bought. In the power to resume the fund in case of war, when the necessities of the national Treasury and the interruption of our commerce may render it essential to the public defense, he detects a bribe to peace. The national honor is endangered; the States of this Union are tempted to bear with national wrongs and indignities; to prostrate their rights and their independence at the footstool of European monarchs; lest, in case of war, they should lose their annual share in the distribution of the proceeds of the public lands. It seems then, sir, that the great objection to the bill is the universal benefit it confers. Every class of persons, natural and political, find their advantage in it. Could a prouder commendation be passed upon any measure? Could human wisdom have produced aught more perfect in legislation than a law which promotes every interest, and rains down blessings upon every class; which reconciles jealousies and hostilities one with another, and binds a whole people by the strong cords of a common interest to their common country? It was a great and a just compliment which the gentleman paid to the bill. It does, indeed, contain bonuses in abundance. Blest bribery! which enriches the new States without impoverishing the old; which strengthens State revenue without increasing State taxation; which lifts the poor into opulence without plundering the rich; which renders the local governments strong and independent, without affecting the power or the resources of the national; which removes every cause of jealousy or uneasiness between them, by leaving the States in the uninterrupted power of locating and directing the improvement of their own territory, furnishing ample means, and deriving national strength, resource, and safety from their expenditure. Whence, Mr. Chairman, springs this jealousy of the Federal Government, and whither does it tend? One would imagine that it was created but to be feared and watched. It is treated as something naturally and necessarily hostile and dangerous to the States and the people. The powers with which it is armed are considered but as so many instruments of destruction. It is represented as a great central mass charged with poison and death, attracting every thing within its sphere, and polluting or destroying every thing which it attracts. It is represented as something foreign and inimical, whose constant and necessary policy it is to bow the sovereign crests of these States at the footstool of its own power by force, or to conquer and debase them into stipendiaries and vassals by bribes and corruption. Sir, while I listened to the impassioned invective of the gentleman from Virginia, I felt my mind inflaming against this mortal and monstrous foe, meditating such foul designs against public virtue and public liberty.

But the question recurred, what is this Government, and who are we? Is Kentucky to be bought and sold, that she may be corrupted and enslaved? Are New York, Pennsylvania, Virginia—all, all—to be brought under the hammer and struck off—honor, independence, freedom—all at a stroke? And who the auctioneer? who the purchaser? Their own representatives, freely chosen and entirely responsible? Nay, sir, they are doubly represented in this Government so bent upon their destruction. *We* come fresh from the hands of the people themselves, soon to return and account for our conduct. Those in the other end of the Capitol represent the States as sovereigns. Strange violation of all natural order, that we should plot the ruin of those whose breath is our life, whose independence and safety is our glory. Whither does this jealousy tend? Are the States only safe in alienation from and enmity to their common head? Are we most to dread the national authority when exerted most beneficently upon State interests? Sir, what can this mean, and to what does it tend, save dismemberment? Why continue a government whose only power is for mischief; which to be innocent must be inert; and which, where most it seems to favor and to bless, means the more insidiously, but the more surely, to corrupt and to destroy? I can understand why a consolidationist, if there be such a foe to reason and to liberty, or an early federalist, feeling an overwrought jealousy of the State sovereignties, and dreading the uniform tendency of confederated republics to dismemberment and separation, should feel unwilling to part with the power of internal improvement, and grant the revenue necessary to its exertion along with the power. I can understand why such an one, stretching his vision forward to that period when a sum approximating to the national debt of England shall have been expended by State authority, and the State governments surrounded with corporations of their own creation, and invested in perpetuity with the vast revenues in future to be derived from this vast and most profitable expenditure, shall swell into populous, opulent, and potent nations, the people looking up to them as the source whence the facilities of commerce have been derived; I can understand that such an one might apprehend that, under these circumstances, the more distant orb, the central sun, would grow dim, and lose its just proportions to the planets which were destined to wheel around it. But how a States-rights man, one whose jealousies are all in the other direction, who dreads, from the centripetal tendency, the absorption of the smaller bodies, and the consolidation of the system—how such an one can see aught in this bill to threaten the power and independence of the States, passes my understanding. For my part I see no danger on either hand. I see power, independence, and ample revenues for the States; but, as they swell, the nation which they compose can not dwindle. The resources of the national Treasury expand in exact proportion to the expansion of the population, the wealth, the commerce, and consumption of the States. Indeed, sir, as a mere measure of national finance, as a far-sighted mean of deepening the sources, the exclusive and peculiar sources, into which the States are forbidden to dip, and whence they as Governments can not drink, I should vote for the measure. Imagine the vast wilderness tamed into cultivation, eight hundred millions of acres of fertile land, teeming with people, studded with cities, and intersected and connected by highways and canals; compute the consumption if you can; imagine the revenue to be derived from it; concede, what is manifest, that, as the revenue increases, the burdens on commerce will diminish: and tell me—no sir, you will not tell me—that the effect of this bill is to weaken the national powers or to oppress the people.

But, sir, the provisions for resuming his fund in time of war is a bribe to peace. Surely, sir, no one desires to convert this into a military republic, to infuse into the States or the people a thirst for wars of ambition and of conquest. The meaning of the objection must be, that the pecuniary consideration in the bill—the distributive share of the States being limited to the time of peace—will emasculate the spirit of the States, will tempt them to bear with wrongs and indignities, to shrink from just and necessary wars, wars of defense—will, in a word, make slaves and cowards of us all. In this sense, this odious sense, is the bill considered as a bribe to peace. Mr. Chairman, I have shown, I think, that the necessary effect and avowed object of this bill is to increase the strength, enlarge the resources, establish the credit, and relieve the finances of the States, at the same time that it multiplies the means and instruments of military operations, and extends the sources of national revenue. It is a new philosophy which teaches that in proportion as you enlarge the objects for which men are most apt to fight, and improve the force with which they are to be defended, you destroy the courage which makes that force efficient. Peace, sir, is emphatically the policy of this country; peace is the true policy of the world; a policy into which religion and the most enlarged philosophy may yet indoctrinate mankind.

> "Oh! monarchs, did ye taste the peace ye mar,
> The hoarse dull drum would sleep, and man be happy yet."

In one sense industry and commerce are bribes to peace. The peculiar industry of the South is emphatically a bribe to peace. War, which would interrupt, if not destroy, our foreign commerce, and cut off the planting interest from their best customers, their most profitable markets—war would fall with aggravated hardships upon the agriculture of the South. Shall we inhibit the growth of cotton? Shall we break up all industry which has foreign consumption for its object? Shall we sunder the chain which binds the civilized nations of the world into one great commercial republic? Shall we undo all that art, science, reason, and religion, have achieved to change the direction of human genius, to soften and beautify the face of modern society? Shall we teach nations again to look to war, spoils, and conquest, for the means of subsistence, and the only true foundations of glory and of empire?

The gentleman from Virginia, in the prosecution of this objection, warns New York and Maine against the consequences of the bill. He exhorts New York, in an especial manner, to stand by her rights; to maintain inviolate her territory by her own authority. Try McLeod by your own laws and courts, and if you find him guilty hang him, said the gentleman, [Mr. WISE,] hang him upon the border, hang him high and within full view of the Canadian fortresses, that his dangling corse may flout the British cannon. Sir, I understood the gentleman [Mr. WISE] the other day to approve the ground taken by the American Secretary [Mr. WEBSTER] in that most dignified correspondence which he held with the British minister in relation to the case of McLeod. I understood that ground to be, that the course of the British Government on this subject had rendered it a national question. The jurisdiction of such belongs exclusively to the national Government. If wrong has been done, New York has surer remedy in the united force and constitutional guarantee of twenty-six States than she could find in her own arm, potent as it is. The soil of New York is the soil of the United States; the citizens of New York are citizens of the United States; the right and the power, constitutional and physical, has been surrendered to this Government to settle all questions touching the safety of either, in their collision with other countries, whether by negotiation or the sterner arbitrament of the sword. Surely the State of New York feels no diffidence in that Government of which she forms so important a part.

Surely she means not to answer the gentleman's appeal, and, throwing off the national authority, to draw questions of peace and war from the American Government to her own State courts. She means not to treat or war with England or any other country upon her own separate account. The duty to carry on war is surely in reason, as it is undoubtedly, in our fundamental law, intimately and inseparably connected with the power to declare it, and to decide all questions with foreign countries which may involve such a result. That the rights and the honor of New York are secure from violation or insult in the hands where the constitution has placed them, I should deem it akin to treason to doubt. Her rights, her honor, her territory, are the rights, the honor, the territory of the United States. She is part of my country. She is covered by the imperial flag, overshadowed every inch of her by the wings of the imperial eagle, protected by his beak and talons. For these sentiments I may be permitted to answer here for at least one State in the Union. Kentucky is placed securely in the center. So long as this Government lasts, her soil is virgin and safe from the impress of a hostile foot. Her fields, thanks to the wisdom of our ancestors, the goodness of God, and the guardian power of this imperial Republic—her fields can never be wasted by ravage, her hearths can never taste of military violation. She knows full well the source of her security, the shield of her liberties.

The exterior States are the bulwarks of her safety—the impregnable fortresses which break the storm of war, and keep far distant from her borders its ravage and its horrors. She views them as such, and regards their rights, their safety, and their liberty as her own. She is one of a system of nerves which vibrate at the least touch from without from the remotest extremity to the center. The frontier of New York is her frontier; the Atlantic seaboard is her seaboard; and the millions expended in fortifying the one or the other, she regards as expended for her defense. A blow aimed at New York is a blow aimed at herself; an indignity or an outrage inflicted upon any State in this Union, is inflicted upon the whole and upon each. To submit to such were to sacrifice her independence and her freedom—to make all other blessings valueless, all other property insecure. Not all the unsettled domain of the Union, in full property and jurisdiction, could bribe her to such a sacrifice. The blood she has shed on the snows of Canada and in the swamps of Louisiana, give ample testimony to her readiness to meet danger at a distance. She seeks no separate destiny; she feels no interest alien from the common country. She wants this money to strengthen herself, and, by strengthening herself, to make the whole country stronger and better able to maintain any future conflict in which its interests or its safety may involve it.

Sir, by the operation of that *generous* rule, for which I myself voted, the time for discussion is about to expire. No other western member has spoken, and now no other will have an opportunity to speak, on this subject. With their leave, and to this purpose, I will play the representative for the whole West. Believe me, sir, that when ever the national honor, the national safety, or the honor or safety of any State in this Union, which is the same thing, is menaced or trampled, the States from beyond the mountains whence I come will rush to the rescue. It is not, sir, in the power of three nor three hundred millions per annum to bribe from them what, in their judgment, in the judgment of all but slaves, is priceless.

Mr. Chairman, a few words in relation to myself personally, and I am done. The gentleman from Virginia, [Mr. Wise,] in the course of his argument yesterday, alluded to the discrepancies between this bill and the recommendations of the President, in his communication to the Houses at the opening of the session. The gentleman explained himself fully and satisfactorily, as not intending to press the Executive opinions with a view to influence the action of this House. I refer to the passage with the view of explaining myself in relation to some matters which passed some weeks ago on this floor, and to which I have not since had an opportunity of referring. Permit me to say now, sir, that my own warm support of this bill derives no additional motive from the fact of its differing from the recommendation of the President of the United States. Mr. Chairman, the letter writers and several of the public prints have represented me as assailing the President in advance. I have been made to say that my constituents would not have voted for him as President. The gentleman from Virginia, [Mr. WISE,] thought it necessary, by a note to the Intelligencer, to correct some inaccuracies in the report of what he said, in which he was kind enough to indicate that I also had been misreported. I would have been glad when the gentleman was rectifying in part what I said, if he had put me in my true attitude in relation to this matter. I do not of course complain of him; I have no right to do so. But the gentleman surely recollects what I did say.

Here Mr. WISE rose to explain, and said that the gentleman from Kentucky had said that "his constituents had not voted for Mr. Tyler as President—they had voted for Old Tip, as sure as you are born;" but that he had inferred more from the gentleman's manner than his words.

Mr. MARSHALL resumed: That is precisely what I did say, and the gentleman's memory is perfectly accurate. He has the right to draw what inferences he pleases, and I have the right to make what explanations I please. I stated on that occasion that Mr. Tyler had not been elected President of the United States; that he had not called this extraordinary session—a circumstance which he notices with some particularity in his message, and intimates pretty strongly that he would not have done so had the matter rested with him, and of course I argued that the reponsibility of its failure would not rest with him. I came not here as the enemy of Mr. Tyler; I voted for him as Vice President of the United States, and supported him warmly throughout the canvass. I came here hoping to find him coöperating cordially with the legislative branch in carrying out the wishes and the principles of that great and now victorious party, to whose cause I have devoted myself from my earliest youth. I came here prepared to support his administration, as a whig administration, and shall continue to do so till developments hostile to the principles I serve are made, and not a moment longer; developments which I trust, for the sake of my country, and what I believe to be her cause, may not be made.

Mr. Chairman, I have been described as setting myself up as the exponent of the opinions, of the personal views, of a great man in the other end of the Capitol. I have not been, and can not be, guilty of such impertinence. Coming from his district, and holding the relations political which I do to him, a most unworthy and insidious effort has been made to wound him through me, and to hold him responsible to the public for what I may say or do here. Sir, it is a rich idea that the great Senator from Kentucky should require an exponent, and he in the Capitol. He needs no interpreter of his opinions, no exponent of his designs or his course. And, if he did, he knows me far too well to select me for the office. When he wishes to be understood, he will explain himself. While he wishes to remain at peace, nor I nor all of us can disturb his repose; and should he desire war, he will, rest assured he will, be his own herald, and will wage it after his own taste and fashion. I am the exponent here of the known will of my constituents. I came to present their wishes, and to speak in their stead at this bar. To none else am I responsible; for none else do I act. I came here, sir, with no dream of raising, or of finding, or of leading, a third party. I had rather follow than lead—it is easier and safer. I have no earthly desire "to raise a whirlwind that I may ride it." I came to follow in the plain, well-known, and beaten path of whig politics. I shall pursue it, depart from it who may. Nay, should all desert it, I will trudge it alone. I want no new lights—I can not learn under new teachers, nor will I receive new doctrines from the old.

ADDRESS,

Delivered in the Hall of the House of Representatives, before the Congressional Total Abstinence Society, there assembled.

Dr. SEWALL, of Washington, having concluded an able and eloquent lecture, accompanied by plates illustrating the different degrees of wretchedness and disease to which the stomach of the drunkard is reduced, Mr. MARSHALL rose and addressed the auditory as follows:

THE world at large is under great and lasting obligations to the gentleman who has favored us with the able lecture to which we have just listened, for the inquiries he has instituted into the pathology of drunkenness. He has published one of the most interesting and scientific essays on that subject which it has ever been my fortune to examine. It is accompanied and illustrated by some splendidly executed drawings, similar to those exhibited to-night, portraying the various changes of the lining, or coats of the human stomach, from a state of perfect health to the last stage of gangrenous inflammation, produced by intemperance—imparting to the force of scientific reasoning the startling certainty of sensible representation. The style of the essay, as of the lecture, is admirable indeed. The doctor confines himself entirely to physical effects. There is not the least affectation of rhetorical display, not the slightest perceptible straining after stage effect, not the smallest infusion of personal or professional vanity, and not the faintest tinge of fanatical enthusiasm, in the matter or manner of his writing or discourse. The whole is simple and unadorned as truth itself. His demonstrations of his subject are as lucid, as conclusive, and as unpretending, as those of Sir Isaac Newton in mathematics. To call Dr. Sewall a man of *genius*, according to the modern acceptation of that much-abused term, were to insult his merit and lower his understanding. To designate him an *orator*, would be to sink science from the stars to the *stump*—to throw the tawdry drapery of an actress over the Florentine Venus—to clothe the cold, clear, naked, yet modest, symmetry of truth, in the glaring gewgaws of a harlot. He is, then, neither a *genius* nor an *orator*, but a learned physician, a profound, patient, and modest inquirer into the economy of nature, as exhibited in the animal structure of man, armed with the love of truth, to guide him in his researches, and stimulated by a regard for his kind to communicate their results, in language exactly fitted to be the vehicle of scientific ideas, untainted by the cant of religion or the dogmatism of ethics, though he be both Christian and moralist. The Doctor must excuse me if I love to praise a man who never, even in manner, vaunts of himself. He has succeeded in satisfying me that the conclusion at which he has arrived is certain and irrefutable. He has *demonstrated* that alcohol is a substance which no organ, with which nature has furnished the human system, is of power sufficient to appropriate as aliment to the body. It undergoes no change from the action of the gastric juice, the great solvent provided by nature to convert our food into nourishment for our frames. It goes into the system alcohol; it circulates through the system alcohol, irritating, inflaming, and finally gangrening all the delicate surfaces with which it comes into contact, from the coats of the stomach, to the membrane of the brain, till it is ejected with the breath through the pores of the skin, and with all the secretions—still alcohol unchanged, and retaining its original properties. Its effect is always to injure, even in the smallest quantity; to that extent it is injurious. Its excessive use necessarily and inevitably changes the appearance and prostrates the powers, not only of the stomach, but of every part and organ of the human body. As opposed to food, it is a poison—a poison not found in an original and separate state any where in nature. Diffused throughout the greater part of the vegetable kingdom, in another form, and with other qualities, it has been extracted, and changed into a poisonous agent, by chemical process and the ingenuity of man. Unlike food, it does not satisfy, but stimulates the appetite for itself, and leads, from this peculiar property, necessarily to excess. Although the melancholy observation and experience of every day, satisfy and confirm the experiments and inductions of pure science, still this poison is the subject of most extensive and everyday consumption among men, working all the fearful ruin of mind and health which has this night been so impressively painted to our view.

Our aim is to banish the use of it as a drink from society altogether. We declare, in our Society, openly, that we will not take into our systems a substance which the God of nature has rendered the human stomach unfit to receive, and incapable of digesting—a substance which has all the properties of a poison, the effect of which is not only to derange the animal economy, and to destroy life, like other poisons, but to work a still more melancholy ruin in the moral constitution of man. Yet, for my share, for the very small and obscure part I bear in this great moral effort, I have seen myself, within these few days, taunted in a public print as a fanatic in the cause of temperance! A cold-water fanatic strikes upon my ear as something strange and paradoxical. Be it so, however. Be this or any other title applied to me, so cold water and temperance go along with it. The object and the character of our Society have neither kinship nor alliance with fanaticism, political or religious. Ours is the cause of morals public and private, irrespective of rank, sect, or party; it is the cause of peace, of happiness, of virtue. Let me here, sir, put a case for the consideration of our colleagues in Congress. Let me suppose for a moment that the condition of the world were changed; that alcohol was but now discovered; that it had not yet commenced that career of ravage which has marked its course and progress. Let me further suppose that the Congress of the United States—the representation of the people of this great empire, the sober likeness of a sober nation, in the case imagined—were just now apprized of the discovery; that some great teacher, who had penetrated the qualities and effects of this substance, and its future possible bearing upon the fortunes of the human race, should here this night present, for the first time, before the mental vision, in long and appalling perspective, all the consequences upon this people which have in fact followed its use; that he should fully satisfy every man in this assembly that, poisonous as it is, and ruinous as its effects must be, this hitherto unknown evil was approaching our shores; that the only antidote was abstinence from the first contact; and that, if we once ventured to taste, nothing could arrest its progress, until it had wrought that entire mass of wretchedness, which he had, in living colors, pictured to our view. And then let us suppose that the proposition were made to Congress, not as a cure, but as a measure of prevention—as anticipating the commencement of an illimitable evil—as seeking to guard and preserve our countrymen in that glorious and happy state in which they would be were intoxicating drinks unknown—a sober nation—a republican empire containing seventeen millions of people, free, sober, healthy, and, so far as this prolific parent of miseries was concerned, happy!—all the disease, all the misery, all the long catalogue of crimes which have sprung from drunkenness, banished—no, not banished—unborn, unheard of:—suppose, I say, that, with this object in view, an appeal should be made to these members of Congress to come forward, each in his place, and, as an example to those who had commissioned them—to those whose image it was their duty to reflect—to whom they should be as a mirror—and whose virtue and happiness it should be their pride to guard—a proposition were made to take a solemn public pledge that they never would stain their lips with the polluting contact of a poison which must destroy their countrymen? I ask, sir, who would pause? Who would refuse? Who would reject a pledge, the impassable barrier against such an inundation of misery? I would not—I am sure I would not. So far from considering such a pledge as the "surrender of my freedom of action," I should exult in the deed as one by which I had secured my own, and preserved the liberties of my country.

The friends of the temperance cause, however, are, unhappily, not in the condition I have supposed. The demon has not only approached, but has been welcomed to our shores. He has already wrought among us an amount of mischief and misery which I am wholly incompetent to describe. It is our object to arrest and expel what we can not now prevent. We seek to secure, in aid of the most glorious moral and social revolution of which the world has any record—save only that which was effected by the introduction of Christianity—to enlist in this cause the countenance and support, and to throw around it all the dignity and influence which necessarily attach to the movements of those connected with the government.

We are sometimes told (for our cause, like every thing else that is great and good, has its difficulties and its enemies) that the pledge proposed subjects necessarily the man who takes it to the implied admission that he is himself laboring under the evil in question, and flies to this as a means of escape from it. This is a grossly unjust view of the matter, and as injurious to our cause as it is untrue. It is to the sober we here appeal. We call upon them to rally to the standard of sobriety; we invite the temperate to guard the cause of temperance. Shall shame interpose there? Can the man who loathes the bottle, and shrinks appalled from all the degradation to which the bottle leads, blush to profess openly the honorable principles which he practices? You who are temperate, how can you withhold your aid from us—the aid simply of your name and countenance?

Temperate men refusing to join a temperance society!—withholding their name and influence!—nay, throwing, by their refusal, the weight of both against us! it is unnatural, it is unintelligible, it is cruel. It is most cruel in those untainted by this destroying vice, to cast the whole weight of the cause upon its wretched victims, writhing and struggling with the chain which darkly binds their strength, nor stretch out the arm, free and unparalyzed by its might, to aid in rending its links asunder. You (Mr. M. here looked steadfastly and earnestly at Mr. WISE)—you incur no risk; you make no sacrifice; you brave no painful notoriety; your lives are as yet unstained; your good name unscathed. Not a shade darkens the fair field of your unsullied escutcheon. There is no room for shame. Nothing but honor to yourselves, and blessings to others, can follow your union with us. Ashamed of pure and perfect temperance! oh, no; true dignity surrounds her; the diadem of honor sparkles on her brow; and the flowing robes of virtue encircle and adorn her elastic and graceful form. Mine, sir, was a different case. Mr. President, we of the "Total Abstinence and Vigilance Society," in our meetings at the other end of the city, are so much in the habit of "telling experiences," that I myself have somewhat fallen into it, and am guilty occasionally of the egotism of making some small confessions, (as small as I can possibly make them.) Mine, then, sir, was a different case. I had earned a most unenviable notoriety, by excesses which, though bad enough, did not half reach the reputation they won for me. I never was an habitual drunkard. I was one of your spreeing gentry. My sprees, however, began to crowd each other; and my best friends feared that they would soon run together. Perhaps my long intervals of entire abstinence—perhaps something peculiar in my form, constitution, or complexion—may have prevented the physical indications, so usual, of that terrible disease, which, till temperance societies arose, was deemed incurable and resistless. Perhaps I had nourished the vanity to believe that nature had endowed me with a versatility which enabled me to throw down and take up at pleasure any pursuit, and I chose to sport with the gift. If so, I was brought to the very verge of a fearful punishment. Physicians tell us that intemperance at last becomes, of itself, not a habit voluntarily indulged, but a disease which its victim can not resist. I had not become fully the subject of that fiendish thirst, that horrible yearning after the distillation "from the alembick of hell," which is said to scorch in the throat, and consume the vitals of the confirmed drunkard, with fires kindled for eternity. I did become alarmed, and for the first time, no matter from what cause, lest the demon's fangs were fastening upon me, and I was approaching that line which separates the man who frolics, and can quit, from the lost inebriate, whose appetite is disease, and whose will is dead, I joined the society on my own account, and felt that I must encounter the title of "reformed drunkard," annoying enough to me, I assure you. I judged, from the cruel publicity given through the press to my frolics, what I had to bear and brave. But I did brave it all; and I would have dared any thing to break the chain which I at last discovered was riveting on my soul, to unclasp the folds of that serpent-habit whose full embrace is death. Letters from people I never had heard of, newspaper paragraphs from Boston to New Orleans were mailed, and are still mailing to me, by which I am very distinctly, and in the most friendly and agreeable manner, apprized that I enjoyed all over the republic the delectable reputation of a sot, with one foot in the grave, and an understanding almost totally overthrown. I doubt not, sir, that the societies who have invited me to address them at different places in the Union, will expect to find me with an unhealed carbuncle on my nose, and my body of the graceful and manly shape and proportions of a demijohn. I have dared all these annoyances, all this celebrity. I have not shrunk from being a text for temperance preachers, and a case for the outpouring of the sympathies of people who have more philanthropy than politeness, more temperance than taste. I signed the pledge on my own account, sir, and my heart leaped to find that I was free. The chain has fallen from my freeborn limbs; not a link or fragment remains to tell I ever wore the badge of servitude. Mr. President, the temperate members of Congress are exposed, as I have said, to no shame or annoyance from the act to which we invite them. It is to rescue others that we summon them. To rescue others—ay, sir, and to place themselves beyond the reach of a danger from which none are exempt. There are men of a stamp which secures them absolutely from every thing which can degrade, save only this one vice. There is no danger that a man of lofty mind, a high-spirited, well-educated gentleman, will stoop to other vices which sink and degrade humanity. He will not lie; he can not steal; he is incapable of dishonor. Death itself can not drive him to the perpetration of baseness. Poverty, want, starvation may assail him, he is proof against them all. This alone can drag his virtue down; and against it what genius can guard, what magnanimity shield us? Who has not seen the most towering, the most majestic, sink vanquished beneath its powers? Who has not seen genius prostrate, courage disarmed, manhood withered, before the march of this fell-destroyer of all that is great, and bright, and beautiful? It seems, indeed, as if, with the cunning malice of tyranny, and the ambitious policy of a conqueror, this grim king selects the loftiest victims, and from those who otherwise are formed to be the ornament and strength of their land and race. Certain it is, that political ambition or elevation is of itself no safeguard. I have been told that the last ghastly spectacle exhibited to us to-night—the ruined stomach of a dead inebriate, once the living receptacle of God's good and healthful gifts, and so by him intended to remain—was part of the frame of a distinguished statesman and member of this House, a man of genius and of eloquence, whose mind led once the councils of his own State, and whose voice has often resounded through this hall while listening thousands hung with rapture upon its accents. Look on that picture and imagine, if you can, the horrors which must have preceded a fate like that. But, sir, this poison stops not with physical destruction; it is over the intellectual and moral man that it achieves its greatest triumphs. The erect form, the muscular limb, the taper waist, oh! how they change under the transforming touch of this monster magician. But it is not the trembling limb, the bloated body, the bleared and dimmed eye, the sluggish ear, the blotched and ulcerated skin, the poisoned breath, the destruction of strength, and cleanliness, and beauty, which most effectually attest the terrible power, and mark the wrecks with which the demon strews his path—it is the overthrow of the moral principle, the extinction of conscience, sensibility to what is right and wrong, charity, domestic affection—all, all that makes us men—the utter dispersion of the moral elements which hold the world together, and the entire implication of the weak and the innocent, the mother, the wife, the infant, in suffering for crimes of which they are the most wretched, yet the guiltless victims. These are the proudest trophies, the most splendid fruits of the victories of the wine cup. Other vices, other crimes, leave the physical, the intellectual, the moral man capable of repentance, of amendment, and of action; but this destroys him throughout—body, mind and conscience—yet leaves the wretch survivor of himself.

Would, sir, that some of the thrilling confessions and narratives disclosed in those homely associations of ours, in a distant part of the city, could be heard by this audience as I have heard them—the confessions and narratives of men whom the indefatigable benevolence of the "Vigilance Society of Total Abstinence" has rescued from the very kennel. They are not your stately, refined educated gentlemen who quaff their rich and costly Madeira, old and mild and fragrant and sparkling and redolent of the true flavor of the cork—nectar, fit for gods to sip, taken down bottle after bottle, from day to day, till their complexions are purple as the crushed grapes whose juice they drain—till their trembling hands can scarce conduct, unspilled, the fluid to their lips—till their feet are swollen and agonized with gout, while untold horrors fill the region whose ruin has been to-night laid open to our view—and yet they are no drunkards! Oh, no, no, no, no. Drunkards! not they! it is not from such men that we hear in our humble ward meetings. No. They are the once wretched, but now rescued, victims of what, in our western world, is called "white-faced whisky"—children of the lowest intemperance who there appear. This tyrant alcohol, like him of whom it is no unapt representative, can suit its temptations to men of every grade of fortune, and to every diversity of human condition. He holds out an appropriate lure to every taste, and draws within his fatal snare the high and the low, the learned and the unlearned, the vulgar and the refined; it is to the story of the humbler and the poorer who have been reformed by means of that society, with which I was first connected, that I have listened with keenest interest.

It does appear to me that, if the loftiest among the lofty spirits which move and act from day to day in this hall—the proudest, the most gifted, the most fastidious here—could hear the tales I have heard, and see the men I have seen, restored, by the influence of a thing so simple as this temperance pledge, from a state of the most abject outcast wretchedness, to industry, health, comfort, and, in their own emphatic language, to "*peace*," he could not withhold his countenance and support from a cause fraught with such actual blessings to mankind. I have heard unlettered men trace their own history on this subject through all its stages, describe the progress of their ruin and its consequences, paint without the least disguise the utmost extent of degradation and suffering, and the power of appetite, by facts which astonished me—an appetite which triumphed over every human principle, affection and motive, yet yielded instantly and for ever before the simple charm of this temperance pledge. It is a thing of interest to see and to hear a free, bold, strong-armed, hard-fisted mechanic relate, in his own nervous and natural language, the history of his fall and his recovery; and I have heard him relate how the young man was brought up to labor, and expecting by patient toil to support himself and a rising family, had taken to his bosom in his youth the woman whom he loved—how he was tempted to quit her side, and forsake her society for the dram-shop, the *frolic*, the midnight brawl—how he had resolved and broken his resolutions, till his business forsook him, his friends deserted him, his furniture seized for debt, his clothing pawned for drink, his wife broken-hearted, his children starving, his home a desert, and his heart a hell. And then, in language true to nature, they will exultingly recount the wonders wrought in their condition by this same pledge: "My friends have come back—I have good clothes on—I am at work again—I am giving food and providing comforts for my children—I am free, I am a man, I am at peace here. My children no longer shrink cowering and huddling together in corners, or under the bed, for protection from the face of their own father. When I return at night they bound into my arms and nestle in my bosom. My wife no longer with a throbbing heart and agonized ear counts my steps before she sees me, to discover whether I am drunk or sober—I find her now singing and at work." What a simple but exquisite illustration of a woman's love, anxiety, and suffering! The fine instinct of a wife's ear detecting, from the intervals of his footfall before he had yet reached his door, whether it was the drunken or the sober step, whether she was to receive her husband or an infuriated monster in his likeness. I say, sir, these things have an interest, a mighty interest for me; and I deem them not entirely beneath the regard of the proudest statesman here. On my conscience, sir, I speak the truth when I say that, member of Congress as I am—(and no man is prouder of his commission)—member of Congress as I am, if, by taking this pledge, it were even probable that it would bring back one human being to happiness and virtue, no matter what his rank or condition, recall the smile of hope, and trust, and love, to the cheek of one wife, as she again pillowed it in safety, peace, and confidence upon the ransomed bosom of her reclaimed and natural protector, send one rosy child bounding to the arms of a parent whence drunkenness had exiled it long, I would dare all the ridicule of all the ridiculous people in the world, and thank God that I had not lived in vain. And, sir, I have had that pleasure.

Mr. President, it is really astonishing what a prodigiously great man a member of Congress is in the estimation of some people. Now, suppose all these members, who are themselves temperate men—and they constitute, thank heaven, an overwhelming majority in both Houses—would, by common consent, become members of this Congressional Temperance Society, what sort of influence do you suppose it would have, both within and without these walls? They would make no sacrifice in doing this—it costs such men nothing—and if they would only do it, I aver that, before the close of this present session, we should not have a single drinking character left in either branch of the National Legislature. They never could stand out against it—I know they could not. I was myself about as bold, and as open, and as hardy a soul as ever swallowed a julep. I did not care who saw me drink; and though, as I have already admitted, I joined the temperance society because I was scared on my account, and not for the purpose of influencing others, or under the influence of others, yet sure I am, that if all my fellow-members who are temperate had joined this association, (for they constitute a majority far greater than is necessary to suspend the rules of the House or to reverse a Presidential veto,) I should have found myself left in so very small and lean a minority as the drunkard's corps would have amounted to when the line was once drawn between the parties, that I never could have stood the shame. Why, it would be the weakest, meanest, poorest, most contemptible, powerless little faction that ever did appear in Congress. What a figure would half a dozen drunkards cut against the whole body of both Houses! Why there would not be enough to guard the obsequies—to form a decent funeral procession for King Alcohol—they would be ashamed to attend the remains of their dead master from the capitol. No, sir; they would have to stop drinking in mere self-defense.

Sir, if there be within this hall an individual man who thinks that his vast dignity and importance would be lowered, the laurels which he has heretofore won be tarnished, his glowing and all-conquering popularity at home be lessened, by an act designed to redeem any portion of his colleagues or fellow-men from ruin and shame, all I can say is, that he and I put a very different estimate upon the matter. I should say, sir, that the act was not only the most benevolent, but, in the present state of opinion, the most politic, the most popular, (looking down at Mr. Wise, who sat just under the clerk's stand, Mr. M. added, with a smile,) the very *Wisest* thing he ever did in his life. Think not, sir, (said Mr. M., still regarding Mr. W. with great earnestness,) think not that I feel myself in a ridiculous situation, and, like the fox in the fable, wish to divide it with others, by converting deformity into fashion. Not so; by my honor as a gentleman not so. I was not what I was represented to be. I had, and I have shown that I had full power over myself. But the pledge I have taken renders me secure for ever from a fate inevitably following habits like mine—a fate more terrible than death. That pledge, though confined to myself alone, and with reference to its only effect upon me, my mind, my heart, my body, I would not exchange for all earth holds of brightest and of best. No, no, sir; let the banner of this temperance cause go forward or go backward—let the world be rescued from its degrading and ruinous bondage to alcohol or not—I for one shall never, never repent what I have done. I have often said this, and I feel it every moment of my existence, waking or sleeping. Sir, I would not exchange the physical sensations—the mere sense of animal being which belongs to a man who totally refrains from all that can intoxicate his brain or derange his nervous structure—the elasticity with which he bounds from his couch in the morning—the sweet repose it yields him at night—the feeling with which he drinks in, through his clear eyes, the beauty and the grandeur of surrounding nature;—I say, sir, I would not exchange my conscious being as a strictly temperate man—the sense of renovated youth—the glad play with which my pulses now beat healthful music—the bounding vivacity with which the life-blood courses its exulting way through every fiber of my frame—the communion high which my healthful ear and eye now hold with all the gorgeous universe of God—the splendors of the morning, the softness of the evening sky—the bloom, the beauty, the verdure of earth, the music of the air and the waters—with all the grand associations of external nature, reopened to the fine avenues of sense;—no, sir, though poverty dogged me—though scorn pointed its slow finger at me as I passed—though want and destitution, and every element of earthly misery, save only crime, met my waking eye from day to day;—not for the brightest and the noblest wreath that ever encircled a statesman's brow—not, if some angel commissioned by heaven, or some demon rather, sent fresh from hell, to test the resisting strength of virtuous resolution, should tempt me back, with all the wealth and all the honors which a world can bestow; not for all that time and all that earth can give, would I cast from me this precious pledge of a liberated mind, this talisman against temptation, and plunge again into the dangers and the horrors which once beset my path:—so help me heaven, sir, as I would spurn beneath my very feet all the gifts the universe could offer, and live and die as I am, *poor*, but *sober*.

REPORT OF DEBATE BETWEEN HONS. JOHN J. CRITTENDEN AND L. W. POWELL,

Versailles, Kentucky, July 10, 1848.

THE gubernatorial canvass of 1848, in Kentucky, was quite exciting throughout the entire State. Mr. CRITTENDEN, the Whig, and Mr. POWELL, the Democratic candidate, came frequently in contact, and never failed to draw large assemblages together. The pending Presidential election attached additional importance to the canvass of these gentlemen, and afforded fruitful source of controversy between them. Early in July they met in debate in the town of Versailles, Kentucky. Mr. MARSHALL was present, and with acuteness of perception and tenacity of memory unsurpassed, reported substantially the arguments of each for the Press. The Report, though it appeared over the signature of "Senex," carried with it the patent of the author's genius, and left no room even for conjecture as to its source.

THE last week has been one of unusual stir and interest in this village. The gubernatorial candidates addressed an immense crowd, Monday, in the Courthouse. Mr. Powell's appointment had been made for some time before. Until a few days prior to Monday, Mr. Crittenden had not been expected here. The former gentleman was hitherto an entire stranger in this part of the country, and curiosity was on tiptoe to see and hear the candidate concerning the mode and circumstances of whose nomination so much had been said. In relation to Mr. C., though long and well known, and well beloved in this county, scarcely less curiosity was felt. His course and his conduct in relation to the candidates for the Presidency; the Taylor convention in February, at Frankfort; the convention at Philadelphia in June; his alleged letters to members of the first; Mr. Clay's card; the result of the second, etc., etc., had occasioned a great deal of speculation, and many persons had anticipated from Mr. Crittenden some explanation in relation to matters in which he had been supposed to have borne a leading part, and which had excited such intense interest in Kentucky for months. Mr. C., in the course of his remarks, avowed his preference of Mr. Clay, for the Presidency, and alleged *availability* as the ground of General Taylor's selection by the party. To the other matters referred to, he made no allusion whatever. Of this debate, marked as it was with ability, and even more highly distinguished by a kind and graceful courtesy, I will, in the course of this letter, attempt an analysis. In the meantime, I hasten with the outline of our week's history. Mammoth bills had been posted up for several days in the taverns, barbershops, etc., appointing Saturday for the arrival and exhibition of a caravan of wild beasts, of all sorts and sizes. Anticipating the menagerie, and the crowd to be attracted by it, some gentleman of Versailles, with rare tact, selected this as the most appropriate occasion, and the one most likely to secure a numerous audience for the display of ex-secretary Hardin's peculiar qualities. This man was known to be in Frankfort, was apprised of the expected show and crowd, and invited to take a hand. The temptation of such society was to him irresistible. The proximity of a caravan of his brethren aroused sympathetically all his instincts, propensities and appetites. As a suitable finale, and one in admirable keeping with the foregoing part of that day's show, the speech, Saturday evening, is above all praise, and the community hereabout — nay, the public at large — can never be sufficiently thankful to the managers who procured them so rich a treat. So you perceive, we have had an uncommon week here, with men and beasts. Zoology has poured forth her stores upon us for the entertainment of the vulgar, and the instruction of the wise. We have seen, from specimens living and before us, in one short week, a mighty chain of animated beings, comprehending, in its vastness of range, the distant extremes of humanity, exhibiting, at one end, how nearly man in reason, sentiment, and speech, can approach the gods, and at the other, how shadowy, thin and undefined the boundary which separates him from the brutes. As it is my purpose to fling you a sketch of these speeches, particularly of Crittenden and Hardin, and to give a faithful transcript of the impression they made upon an attentive, and, I think, unprejudiced mind, I will begin in the historic order of time with Mr. C., as I saw and heard him, together with the thoughts and associations, his presence and his words, suggested and awakened.

About half-past one o'clock, the bell struck the notice, and the Courthouse, which is a spacious one, was, in a very few moments, crowded to a jam. When I entered, the candidates were already on the stand, and the whole array was imposing even to solemnity. One glance at that crowd of freemen sufficed to prove that Woodford had done her best that day, and the air and the countenance with which the candidates eyed the assembly, showed that they thought, wherever either of them might have spoken before, whether in court or senate, they were upon a theatre, and before an audience not unworthy of the first actors. The population of Woodford is indeed a striking one, and when brought forth upon their public days, and on any occasion of strong popular interest, has always arrested the attention and remark of strangers. Never did the independent yeomanry (for they are truly such) of this little county, present a more respectable appearance, and never did they wear a countenance of keener intelligence, interest and curiosity than on that day. They are, from long experience, competent judges of oratory. Midway between Lexington and Frankfort, a very rich county, and fruitful heretofore in important litigation, Woodford has been, for forty years, the theatre and the arena upon which the best speakers in this or perhaps any other country, have struggled for victory and for fame. It was here that Mr. Clay won much of his early forensic reputation, and is said to have made some of his most brilliant efforts. Mr. Crittenden was born in this county. Its soil is hallowed to his imagination as holding in its bosom the dust of both his parents and several of his family. Before he went into the Senate of the United States, it was his favorite court, and had been for years the theatre on which he was wont and delighted to exhibit those beautiful talents, and exert that peculiar and fascinating forensic eloquence of which he is so consummate a master. He stood, after years of absence, (but years of great distinction, upon a theatre far more elevated and august,) he stood at last upon his native soil, in the midst of men, every one of whom was familiar with his countenance, loved his person, reverenced his virtues, and was proud of his talents and fame, being a portion of their own moral wealth, and of the public inheritance. He stood, too, among a people two-thirds of whom are of his own political party, and with the whole of whom (so tested in his honor) the clearest text of scripture is not of more unimpeachable veracity than his smallest assertion. To look upon that beaming and ingenious and manly face, and doubt his word, were indeed difficult even for a stranger. How much more so for men who have known him all his life.

He commenced the debate, and when he rose, you might have heard a pin drop. Milton speaks of "darkness visible," to express intensest want of light. You might, with a similar freedom of speech, have termed that deadly stillness, "silence audible." His mind and his heart seemed to labor under the memory of his own past history, and the personal relations he bore to the men he addressed. He spoke of Woodford as the heart of Kentucky, and of Kentucky as the heart of the Union, and of the ties which bound his own to this "heart of hearts." He alluded to his birthplace and his present position with graceful propriety, with a taste, a delicacy, a beauty and tenderness of which I think he alone is capable. To report him is impossible, and the attempt is always grossly unjust, unless you could use words as colors, and paint along with his expressions the tone, the action, and, above all, the countenance, the eloquent, the indisputable countenance with which they are accompanied. He said it was unnecessary, and would be impertinent, to give a detailed account here of his own history, political opinions, or public acts; they were all known. There could not be a tribunal on earth, were he under arraignment, more competent to try him from their thorough knowledge of all the facts, and from whom he in particular could invoke or expect a more indulgent or merciful judgment. As to him, his judges that day were beyond all challenge. "Sixty years ago he said, (he was sorry to acknowledge so long a period of life,) sixty years ago, within two miles of that spot, he had been a child; a nursling in what was then a cane-brake." Since that time through what vicissitudes he had passed, what changes he had witnessed, what revolutions had swept over the beautiful face of the beautiful country where he was born, lovely in its original wilderness, still lovelier perhaps under the forming hand of taste, art and culture. He stood at last upon the spot whence he set out, his starting-post and his goal, in the midst of his brethren, "a child of Woodford, and proud of his nativity." He said he was then, under all those circumstances, as a candidate for the chief executive office of the Commonwealth. They, the men before him, were the best judges of the facts. On the present occasion they should be the sole judges, without assertion or proof, or argument from him. They were well acquainted with his past courses of life, they knew how unprofitable they had been to himself personally. (We thought here Mr. C. manifested the smallest conceivable bitterness in his tone, and by a slight movement of the mobile and eloquent muscles of his face. We may readily have been deceived. We felt bitterly ourselves, and may have mistaken our feelings for his expression.) They were aware, he said, of the position he had just quitted, the Senate of the United States, and he referred it to them whether personal ambition, taste or preference for the office he now sought at their hands, could possibly have impelled him to the pursuit. They knew how and when, under what circumstances, his friends had called him to his present position. Kentucky had honored him over and over again, in times past, and far beyond his merits. She had never denied him any thing he had asked. She had now drawn him from a post which was the utmost mark and bound of any ambition he had ever cherished. He must refer the fact to them, whether he had or had not quitted that post with reluctance, and in simple deference to those who from former generosity had acquired the right to control his own wishes, and to command and direct his services. Mr. C., after an exordium somewhat like this, proceeded to consider and answer certain objections, which he understood to have been urged against him in the country, in relation to the bill introduced by himself some years ago in the Senate, to prevent the interference of federal officers with elections, sometimes called the gag law; as also his connection with the bankrupt law, and his opinions and vote upon the State convention of Kentucky. He was brief on each of these topics, and said nothing which I recollect that has not been before the public through the prints. He vindicated the first bill as sound in principle and conformable even to English precedents. He contended that something of the kind was indispensable to curb the growing and corrupt influence of the executive, through its army of officeholders, upon popular elections. He explained that the original penalty of $500 had been stricken out, and when the bill was finally passed upon, the penal consequence of interference in the elections, by way of persuasion or influence with the voters, was removal from office. The right of suffrage, he said, had been left untouched. The law only required that when the people, the sovereign, the master, came forth to exert his highest prerogative, the servants should be silent. At the session when he voted for the bankrupt law it had fallen, and his vote did no harm; when it subsequently passed, he was not a member of Congress. He afterward returned to the Senate, and, under the instructions of his State, voted for its repeal. In relation to the convention, he stated precisely what is contained in his letter recently published.

He then passed on to the approaching Presidential election, drew a rapid and masterly sketch of the biography of General Taylor, pronounced an able eulogium on his military talent and services, and sat down, after a speech of exactly one hour. There was no stamping or noisy applause, but a low, deep murmur came up from the bosom of the crowd, which spoke plainly enough how profound the sentiment of affection and respect which they cherished for the speaker.

Mr. Powell's person has become familiar to the people in this part of the State, and needs no description here. He rose evidently impressed with the difficulties of his situation, and the advantages his adversary, or competitor rather, had over him before that audience. His appearance and countenance and manners were modest and conciliatory, slightly embarrassed, perhaps, but perfectly firm. He noticed, with great propriety, Mr. C.'s relation to the people there, paid a just tribute to his abilities and character, and in a strain neither fulsome nor overwrought, avowed his own admiration of the man, and the pride he felt, in common with all Kentuckians, in the genius and reputation of one so distinguished. He complimented the county of Woodford in the same vein of good taste, and proceeded with his argument. Mr. Powell limited himself exactly to the time consumed by Mr. Crittenden, and it was evident that, in doing so, he necessarily abridged and crippled his argument. Indeed, he did not pretend to discuss the peculiar doctrines of his party, or to unfold and vindicate the principles upon which he relied for success.

Mr. Crittenden had not himself stated any particular measures of policy, or avowed the principles by which General Taylor's administration would be guided, should the nation elect him. There was yet no position to be assailed, no ground for political discussion. Mr. Crittenden had not assailed the present administration. He had spoken personally with great respect of the President of the United States, and of both the Democratic candidates, Cass and Butler. He had confined himself to General Taylor's qualifications as they were to be gathered from a long and honorable life, passed entirely in the service of his country, during which he had shown himself equal in ability to every emergency in which he had been placed, and of an integrity never yet doubted. He claimed the Presidency for him as the just reward of long and preëminently glorious services. His principles were to be presumed.

Mr. Powell seemed to feel the want of an antagonist; he had nothing set up, against which he was to contend, and of this he complained.

He stated the existence and the past struggles of the two great political parties in the United States. He contended that they had been divided upon and struggled for principles of government and measures of policy. They had been heretofore avowed by both, they had in every contest based their respective hopes and their appeals to the people upon the supposed strength and soundness of the principles they advocated. The Whigs, in 1844, had confidently unfurled their banners to the breeze, with their measures for their motto emblazoned in full. Had they abandoned them? Did they yield to the truth of the Democratic creed and doctrines, under the force of their experiments? If so, why change, why wrest the government of the country from the men and the party whose policy and principles, now predominant, had been justified by events, and were no longer assailed by their former adversaries? Or did the Whig party, still retaining their organization and peculiar views of government, studiously conceal them, and hope thus, through a popularity won in the field, the popularity of a military chieftain, without party or principles political, to raise into power and then force a system of government upon the country, which, when openly proposed, had been openly and unanswerably condemned by the nation? This is the substance of Mr. Powell's speech. He enlarged upon the nature of elective and representative government, and the absolute propriety and necessity that the people should be fully acquainted, not merely with the private character, moral worth, personal virtues, or great talents even, of their candidates, but with the practical measures and system of legislation and policy, bearing as they did upon the prosperity, the industry, the liberty of the people, which were to be advocated and enforced. He pressed these views upon his own party, and illustrated them forcibly and happily. He warned, somewhat humorously, the Whig party themselves, of their disasters under Tyler, and bid them beware of a second delusion. They ought to be sure of their man this time; he was certain a no-party no-principle man would not suit them.

Mr. Powell avowed himself in favor of a convention, and a radical revision of the State Constitution. He wished to see every aristocratic and monarchical principle stricken from it, but did not particularize the changes he contemplated. He disavowed having made any allusion, in Mr. C.'s absence, to his course upon the bankrupt law or the bill respecting elections.

Mr. Crittenden explained that he had not alluded to Mr. Powell; he had always understood and took pleasure in stating it, that Mr. Powell, in his absence, had treated his name with respect and courtesy, and that he had not pressed either of the subjects alluded to.

Mr. Powell proceeded to observe, however, that he differed with Mr. Crittenden upon both the measures. He had been always opposed to the bankrupt law, and thought the principle of the election law, as proposed, at war with the genius of our institutions and the rights of our citizens. He had been unable to perceive how or wherefore a citizen, by taking office under his country, forfeited or should be deprived of any of his civil rights as an individual, and particularly the precious one of entertaining, discussing, and sustaining his political opinions or preferences. Mr. Powell's speech was evidently well received, and the impression with respect, both to his abilities and his temper, was highly favorable. I have not attempted to report his words, and have omitted many smart but good-humored hits he gave the Whigs. In relation to the Florida war and General Taylor's blood-hounds, he was particularly happy.

When Mr. Crittenden rose to reply, his manner had undergone a great change. He was evidently roused, if not stung, by the remarks of his competitor, and seemed to feel that they demanded an answer. The genius of the debater, the keen, dextrous, pungent debater was up. His countenance wore that expression, half comic, half sarcastic, midway between a smile and a sneer, with which benevolence curbs and half conceals scorn, and which a soul, naturally kind and generous, flings like a graceful and delicate vail over unbounded powers of raillery and ridicule. Nature has conferred upon Mr. Crittenden, among other gifts, some of the highest qualities of an actor, and a comic actor. It requires all his dignity to retain within just limits his perceptions of the ludicrous, and his exquisite powers of mimicry. Those who remember (and I am sure none who witnessed it will ever forget) his introduction that day of the committee to General Washington, demanding an account of his principles, and his impersonation of General Cass, when he received his nomination by the Baltimore convention, will understand perfectly what I vainly attempt to describe. The weapons of his wit, if wielded by malignity, would suffice to kill. In his hand, however, and guarded by fraternal charity, they are used as instruments of defense and chastisement. He never strikes at a vital part, nor aims a mortal blow. The knife he employs has a guard about the edge which prevents an incision deeper than the cuticle, and the wound, though it cause the patient to writhe for an instant, so keen, so smooth, so exquisitely polished is the instrument, heals by the first intention, without inflammation, suppuration, or gangrene.

In giving a sketch of Mr. C.'s reply, I shall follow his thoughts rather than his words. I do not attempt to report him literally; some of the most effective passages in his speech, (and they were astonishingly effective,) were I able to repeat them, were nothing without the look, and the peculiar accent and half-mocking pronunciation he put upon the words he used. Yet all was tasteful, and he felt himself pursuing this vein too far, stimulated by the evident delight and *gusto* of the crowd. He checked the tendency to ribaldry, and, observing "but this is badinage," resumed the air and post of the statesman. He said the gentleman claimed a great advantage for his candidates over General Taylor, for they had principles—oh yes, and printed too—printed principles, and a platform to stand upon, a broad, strong, Democratic platform, with printed principles for its foundation and support, and poor old Rough and Ready presented himself, his naked self on foot, on his own foot, without principles, or without any that were printed, and without any platform at all. There was a great convenience in these principles made by printing, and candidates shaped and manufactured to order. These creatures of the type and the press could be changed to suit circumstances, and new editions could be struck every four years with various amendments and corrections. There was some times a little inconvenience (for good and evil are mixed together in this world) in having a President of the United States fast nailed to a platform by a convention of architects appointed by, nobody knows whom, and responsible to nobody at all. I remember, he said, that the principal printers and platform builders of 1844 laid down the boundary of 54° 40′ north latitude, as one of the principles of Democracy. Oh, yes! the parallel of 54° 40′ was one of the planks of the Democratic platform, and Mr. Polk, poor fellow, was nailed to it without discretion, or power of motion, or change of position. They tried to persuade me, gentlemen, that the frozen and sterile waste between the 49th and 54th degree of latitude on the far shores of the Pacific was my native country—aye, and General Cass was willing, so stubborn and stiff was this plank in the platform, so binding upon him was the authority of the builders, to involve his country in a ruinous war with the greatest power on the globe, in defense of an unpeopled desert three thousand miles off. Mr. Polk thought better of it; he had to think better of it; he found that in the varied, extended and changeful relations of his country with foreign nations; relations, the management of which were intrusted to him, he found that the ligatures bound about the President of the United States by a set of men unknown to the law and irresponsible to the people, destroyed a necessary discretion, fettered his just freedom, and might ruin the State. He consulted the Senate, his natural constitutional council of advisers, and they relieved him from his difficulties, and saved the public peace. I do not blame Mr. Polk, he said; I am only showing how mischievous and embarrassing sometimes, how inefficient always, how unlawful, how unwise this modern doctrine and practice, of having printed principles and rules drawn up by an unauthorized body of men, to govern and control, for four years in advance, an officer intrusted with the discharge of duties, the just and wise discharge of which requires a prudent adaptation of his conduct and his policy to the ever changing face of the public affairs of a changeful world.

Does the gentleman really think that it is in the power of a Baltimore convention, or of any convention, to make, to manufacture principles for this government or this people? And if it be so, who are these men armed with this great, this transcendent power, above the law, and claiming to bind in advance all the functionaries for its interpretation and execution? Practically, gentlemen, our institutions seem to me to be undergoing a thorough, radical, and ruinous revolution. The President of the United States is not to be chosen by the electors, nor the electors by the great body of the people; and when chosen, he is to be armed, not merely with executive powers, but with the power, a power which he is compelled to exert, of annihilating all legislation upon all subjects, the raising of revenue and appropriation of moneys, among others, unless it accord exactly with his principles, views, policy, or wishes. And these principles and this policy are not to be his own, not the fruit of his own patient reflections and labored examination of all the circumstances surrounding the country and attending the law when passed, but they are to be laid down for him by others, and he compelled to subscribe, if not swear to them, before he is permitted ever to come before the people as a candidate. Laid down for him, and by whom? The old plan of choosing candidates was in Congressional caucus. Then, at least, it was done by men who had been actually and fairly elected by the people, every man having a vote, and the elections held by law. Now the electors are first chosen by conventions in the States, and pledged to vote for the gentlemen nominated in a national convention to be held at Baltimore, or somewhere else. This convention, chosen by, nobody knows whom, representing nobody knows whom, and responsible to nobody, appoints a committee on principles; yes, sir, a committee to manufacture and have printed a set of principles. They meet at a tavern over a basket of champagne, and fix the principles of the government; of the government of the United States for four years, appoint as candidates such persons as will subscribe to these preliminary articles, and as in other respects may be suitable, and having doubtless made various other little arrangements in relation to the patronage, offices, etc., adjourn to meet no more, leaving to the people the sole right of voting for electors appointed by others, and the electors the sole right of voting for the candidates thus selected for them. This is popular government with a vengeance. Why, gentlemen, by taking away all discretion, it levels all capacities. One man who signs the principles is just as good as another. It takes from the people the power of election, for the power of nomination thus exercised is virtually the power of appointment. It destroys the distinction of power among the several departments of government, and, by the use of the veto, confounds all legislation, placing for four years the law, the policy, and the people in the hands of a single man, and he the pledged slave and instrument of a self-constituted cabal of lords and of articles.

But the gentleman's candidates have principles, principles drawn up and printed as asserted. General Cass has signed them. I have no doubt he would have signed them in the dark, and that he would have signed them if there had been twice as many more. I am told that he was delighted when he received them, and the news of his nomination by the Baltimore Convention. I am told, and doubt not, that he stroked himself up and down, (here Mr. Crittenden rubbed his hands up and down over his abdomen, after the manner of an old gentleman of goodly proportion, upon the receipt of the most gratifying intelligence;) yes, he rubbed himself up and down, and he exclaimed, oh, but this is truly a great nation!

But General Taylor, I suppose, gentlemen, has no principles, because he has authorized nobody to write them out for him. The government can not be trusted to his hands, because he says, if elected by the people, he will be President of a nation, and not the instrument of a party. He does not think that principles, or at least his principles, can be manufactured by a committee over their wine. He has other ideas of the principles of a President of the United States, and of the evidence of their existence and quality. So have I, said Mr. C.; I can not regard the occasional opinions of party meetings upon party measures as deserving the name of principles. I have considered a principle, whether in morals, politics or philosophy, as a great, all-pervading, general truth, impressed by the divinity upon man or nature at the moment of their creation. I have considered it as a rule, something fixed fast in the nature of things. Not a measure, not a fact, not an individual object, but an invariable standard in morals and politics, or a general type in nature, to which actions and objects are to be referred, and by which they are to be tested as to their class or quality. The principles which guide a man's understanding and control his actions are discoverable by an observation of his whole life; and the result of the observation is likewise to be more or less correct, according to the variety and severity of the circumstances under which he has been called to act. Tried by this test, gentlemen, has General Taylor no principles? Has he not the very principles ground into him, compounded until inseparably with his moral being, the very principles and qualities a sensible and sober-minded people should desire in a Chief Magistrate? Is he just, is he faithful to his word, is he brave, does he love his country? Has he been clothed with power, and accustomed to high command? How has he exercised it? Has he been placed in a subordinate station? how has he demeaned himself to his superiors? Has he moved in difficult circumstances, surrounded with dangers, pressed with enemies, clothed with supreme command with thousands of his fellow men, dependent for life and safety upon the steadiness of his nerves, and the combinations and decisions of his judgment; how has he borne himself? Has he seen battle, has the storm of war broken over him, has it been his stern duty to direct the murderous charge and gaze on fields of slaughter; how did he lead? Did he blench from the helm when the wind blew highest; did his spirit sink or soar as the whirlwind swept over him? Has victory perched upon his standard? When flushed with triumph, and fresh from the bloody conflict, with what countenance has he regarded the vanquished? Let his life, his long, his honorable, his glorious life, answer these questions. And is there no principle involved in justice, truth, courage and patriotism? Can a committee manufacture these? or is there any guarantee for them so sure as the whole life and entire conduct of the man? General Taylor, said Mr. C., is a soldier, a successful soldier, yet fond of peace. He fears no danger and courts no quarrel. Is there not pledge enough in the character of such a man for his conduct; aye, and his principles, too, if elevated to power? Is there not a peculiar and beautiful adaptation of that character to the present condition of the world and the circumstances in which he will be called to act? The surface of European society is disturbed beyond example, it is heaving as under the first throes of an earthquake. What agencies are at work, or what fiery elements exist within its bosom, we know not. The volcano, so long tranquil, may be again in action—may again break forth in wasting war, and vomit crime and blood upon the world. Who, in the midst of the troubled and heaving nations, who so fit to guide our own as the man whose renown in war commands the respect of all Europe, and who, although he has shown himself invincible in arms, courts for his country and himself the fame of justice and the charms of peace?

Rely upon it, gentlemen, General Taylor has principles. He has principles like General Washington. Do not understand me, he said, as claiming for him equality with General Washington. That man stood and stands alone in this world's history utterly unequalled; but we may strive to imitate what we can not equal. But General Taylor has won the confidence of his countrymen by the same means; he has travelled the same road with General Washington. Now only fancy, in the year 1789 a committee of politicians, a little squad of party organizers, a clique of gentlemen, who had risen into their then state of august distinction, by figuring at county meetings, or it may be by discussing principles in debating societies, fancy such a body convened by their own authority, voluntarily assuming the onerous duty of selecting for the whole nation a suitable and proper person to undertake the guidance of our public affairs under the new-made constitution. Fancy further, if you please, that first and foremost, before they could trust any one of the great men with which the country then teemed, they must draw up a creed, a catechism, in which the fortunate and honored object of their august choice must be examined and found perfect, and subscribe, as the rule of his faith and practice, before this same self-created committee could permit him to appear before the people as a candidate at all, or the people be permitted to vote for him, whether a candidate or not. Imagine, if you please, they had taken the precaution to have their code of principles printed, that there might be no mistake, and then, after mature deliberation, it had occurred to them that, may be, General George Washington might do, might answer their purpose, if he would only sign the printed principles. Go on, gentlemen, and figure to yourselves the shades of Mount Vernon—the lawn, the trees, the hights where still stands, in simple majesty, the hero's homestead, unchanged since last its walls resounded to his tread; the noble river, which there spreads itself out like a broad mirror to receive and fling back, as if in grateful pride, the image of the most beautiful and affecting scenery in the world—surround, steep yourselves in the very genius of the spot, and there, in the cool of the summer evening, in the portico which looks to the East, dedicated to his solitary musing, seated with thoughtful brow, and all capacious eye, bending its deep, tranquil gaze upon the deep and tranquil stream he loved so much, behold the grand, the awful form of the Father of his country. The war was over, the anarchy which followed, a danger far more terrible than war, had passed away. The mighty elements of prosperity and power, which nature had scattered over the land, were united at last; concentrated and safe under a constitution which bound the States together without constraint, and only disproving them of the power to hurt or annoy each other, left every member and muscle of this new and glorious body free to exert itself in all useful labor and every peaceful exercise. Liberty was established. Imagine *him* thus seated and thus musing, the curtain which vails the future uprolled by Providence, and all the coming glories of his country spread out bright, glowing, palpable before that same deep and tranquil eye. Shall we disturb him, dare we break in upon his solitude, or interrupt his mighty thread of thought? Yes, let us finish the picture our fancy has begun. A knock, a servant—General Washington, a committee of gentlemen request an audience. Show the gentlemen in, and with a grave politeness and a dignity which never through life deserted him, a dignity which was with him in death, when he turned his face to the wall in conscious pride, that the last agony which convulsed and distorted the hitherto heroic calm of his features might have no witness, with that same dignity which triumphed over death, he rises to receive a committee of his countrymen. They come, all fearless and unblushing, with printed principles in hand. General, say they, we have an important commission to execute, and proposition to lay before you. We are, sir, a committee, appointed by a convention, appointed, we believe, by themselves, whose right and undoubted office it is to represent and speak for the democracy of this land. The new constitution is about to be launched into practice, we want a steady and valuable hand at the helm in the commencement of the voyage. The first election of President is at hand. We do not think it entirely safe to leave the choice of this office to the electors directed by the constitution. It is the particular business of the convention to nominate before hand such person as they may think most suitable for the electors to choose, and the electors, at least such as hold pure democratic principles, will be pledged to support our nominee. That there may be no doubt, no doubt at all, sir, what these democratic principles are, and that the future President, whoever he may be, may be saved all trouble of thinking, all doubt and difficulty under perplexing circumstances, we have been appointed a committee on principles; yes, sir, a committee to whom was referred the business of manufacturing principles and having them nicely printed, to be signed by our candidate, and to serve for his guidance during the first four years. We have discharged that duty, and have been sent to notify you that you shall be the nominee, upon condition that you sign. We have the principles along, printed on the best paper and with imperial type. The face long used to vail emotion, and never apt to kindle under light or transient excitement; the face of the hero remains fixed, rigid, impassive marble. Proceed, gentlemen, if you please. Well, general, you may suppose that the constitution, with your own good sense and honest purpose, is a sufficient guide; or you may imagine, that upon any doubt or default of your own judgment, you will have a council of legal advisers, able men, to be selected for their integrity and intelligence, their knowledge of the intricate sciences of government, and their pure and tried devotion to their country. Men who are known to the country, who will be filling high official station, and will be responsible to the country and to you for the advice and opinions they give. Or you may imagine that there are two branches of the legislature, one chosen directly by the people, and coming from small districts of country with the rights, wishes and principles of which, each representative must, of course, be acquainted; and the other chosen by the States, upon a principle of perfect equality among sovereigns, the smallest State being equal to the largest in weight and power in the

Senate; now possibly it may have occurred to you that these, too, are among your counsellors and advisers, and a source whence you may draw sound expositions of the law, and the most authentic evidence of the state of popular opinion, and the public will; or you may imagine that there is a fourth council, judicial in its character, the Supreme Federal Court, appointed by the constitution as its very oracle, priest, and keeper, and that in case both branches of the legislature and the President, and his cabinet to boot, should all, after the purest intentions, and the most laborious thought, commit a blunder, and transcend the commission of the people as expressed in their constitution, why this court, this council of old men, whose only business it is to study and expound law, who have no connection with, and who are not afraid in the least of any other branch of the government, inasmuch as the people have secured their independence, by rendering their salaries and commission safe from the arbitrary action or caprice or resentment of both President and Congress, that they may judge the law free from any sort of apprehension of the law makers, why this court have the power, in the last resort, to assert the paramount authority of the constitution, and to set aside as void any statute which Congress and the President may have enacted contrary to its provisions, whether from rashness, inattention, ignorance, passion, or even corruption. Or you may think that your whole life passed in the service of your country, and under the full blaze of the public eye, under the searching scrutiny of the whole world, is pledge enough for your principles, even though all the other guarantees, cabinet council, house of representatives, senate and court, should fail in their duty. This is a very natural mistake, general; you are a soldier, your business has been war, you have not studied politics; there is an art, a mystery in politics which you men of the sword do not understand. Indeed, general, we have understood that you yourself have doubted your ability to guide the intricate and complicated affairs of a government like ours, and in the present threatening circumstances of the world, so diffident are you of your political abilities, it has been hinted by some that you can not be induced to accept the office, though the people themselves, thoughtless creatures, should have more confidence in you than you have in yourself, and elect you any how. But you are very right, general, military men do not understand politics.

Now we are anxious to give you this nomination; you are decidedly popular, and if you will only sign, if you will only pledge, if you will only be our man, if you will only satisfy the honorable body we represent, that you have principles, why here goes: You are the nominee of Democracy. We know your history, general, we believe you to be honest, we have heard a great deal about you from your youth up; but we do not know any thing about your principles; we have heard it hinted, nay, it has been broadly asserted, that you have no party and no principles—no party and no principles? Why, general, a man had as well have no country—better. Now, as to your past life, general, that will not do. To be sure we understand that you are of good family and well raised, that you derived your first impressions—and they were impressions of truth, honor, piety—from a mother of rare discretion, intelligence and virtue. We understand that you have received an excellent, plain, practical English education: we have heard, that when quite a boy, you were a capital surveyor—we know that early fame gave notice of that rare combination of qualities, which, through a long course of the most wondrous events, have never failed in any particular, and attracted to you, while yet a boy, the attention of the colonial government; we know that you were early employed in the most difficult, the most delicate, the most dangerous service, and that the result of each employment only increased the confidence, already great, in your precocious character and extraordinary talents. We know full well that ere the down upon your lip had ripened to virility, aged men sought your council, that when the notes of savage warfare sounded from the forest, and its deadly whoop broke over all the border of your native colony, grown men rallied to the call of the youthful avenger, and that age, and sex, and infancy reposed in safety under the shield of your lion arm, and slept securely under the vigilance of that young eye, which knew no sleep when danger was at hand. We know that war upon a larger scale broke out, and that your veteran reputation, then in your first manhood, again made you a leader under the standard of him who was then your king. Again the danger roused your genius; again that prodigious capacity, that vast strength of judgment, that wonderous sagacity, that rare, that marvellous prudence, which weighs all probabilities, masters and ponders all circumstances, deliberates with the caution of the most rigid philosopher, risks nothing upon chance, or from the thirst of glory, yet combined with that fierce courage of action, which sweeps to its object, when decided, with the speed of the eagle and the daring impetuosity of the forest king, we know that under the spur of powerful circumstances these qualities broke through the shackles of a subordinate position, and the thick cloak of a modesty which haunts you yet, and would now, you being judge, shroud you from the gaze of an admiring world, and bar you from the service of a grateful country, broke forth, we say, and proclaimed the young provincial the first general of the age. We know, too, general, that though occasion always found your genius ready and armed at every point, you never sought occasion for its display. Heaven, which shaped you for its instrument, furnished, however, the precise occasion, and man had wit enough to hunt you even in the depth of that obscurity you seemed so studiously to seek. We know too, general, that with all your military talents and experience you are a considerable farmer, and have ever been, for a great man, remarkably devoted to agricultural pursuits. Another war, the last, the grandest, the boldest, the most just in its purpose, the darkest and the most portentous, the most dangerous in its progress and execution, but most inconceivably magnificent in its results, of any that has been waged since man first began to shed his brother's blood, this war, which broke the frame, and dismembered the parts of the greatest empire on earth, found you at the plow. It was the war of a member, a weak and infant member, against the fullgrown and powerful head of a powerful State. The long-established code of public morals, the venerated sentiments of all existing governments, were against it. It was waged for objects, and upon principles that were new and forbidden by every political canon of the prevailing faith of the world. It was, in its inception, a war of rebellion against lawful government, it was disloyal, it was according to the statute book, the common law, and the then prevailing science of government, the darkest, the most damnable of crimes—high treason, patricide. The bold spirits who commenced the conflict, fought in defiance of the whole system of the world, they fought with halters—felon's halters—round their necks.

"They sought a leader equal to the feud." The invitation to command in this desperate strife against such desperate odds was, in fact, an invitation to mount the scaffold. We know they turned to you and found you, as ever, attentive to the call of honor and of danger, still distrustful, however, of your own capacity for so high, so responsible a trust. It was indeed most high, most responsible. The fate of the human race depended on the result of that conflict, and that result depended, to all human seeming, then and now, upon the character of the leader. The principles and objects for which it was declared and waged, involved the rights of human nature and the freedom of nations. In its results was involved the extinction of those principles, of their triumphant and eternal establishment. You brought to that struggle and to that post the same great qualities which we have described; qualities, no doubt, originally impressed by the hand of a beneficent God, developed in early life by the peculiar circumstances of your youth, strengthened in the hard stern school of practice, and now matured into perfection, by long years of patient, deep reflection. We know, the world knows, coming ages, the latest generations of men, will know and bless the result of that struggle, and the name of the leader who conducted it to that result. It conducted your country to liberty, true liberty, we believe, general, and it has conducted you, General Washington,—a result unsought, unexpected by you, we believe; a result, so far as your aim or efforts were concerned, entirely collateral,—but it has conducted you along a dark, steep, precipitous road, right up the mountain of fame, to its very summit, to the topmost pinnacle, never trod before by mortal foot, with just breadth enough of pedestal for a single figure, and there, on that far and unapproachable hight, it has left you, immeasurably above the crowded world of history, in eternal solitude, without a peer, without a rival. General, we do not mean to flatter, we are democrats, and never flatter great men—great men are very dangerous articles in a really democratic country—they break that dead level of equality, the establishment and maintenance of which is one of our *principles.* Their greatness most frequently makes them ambitious, and when the public danger has for a time silenced envy, and driven into retirement and silence the convention men, and committee men, and stump speakers, when the shrill call of the bugle, and the hoarse roar of the drum and the deep-toned thunder of the artillery, has hushed or drowned the voice of the real simon pure democratic orators, and made them pocket their principles for a while, and promote men to posts of danger without too close inspection of their politics; these great men that no body ever dreamed of for office in peace, by the splendor of their achievements, and their hardihood of valor, sometimes turn the people's heads, and when the danger is past, and peace has come, and it is time for people to think about principles again, these fellows start up, or somebody starts them up with their ambition, and the real democratic principles are endangered by these *military chieftains.* Now, we do not think you are exactly of the stripe of usurpers, or have ever designed to overthrow the liberties of your country. We know you surrendered your commission, and disbanded your army, though it was devoted to you; and grumbling terribly about pay, yet you disbanded them, and threw away your sword the moment peace was restored and Independence acknowledged. We know all this, and think better of you than of most great men, so do the people. But, general, to make short of a long story, we do n't know your principles, and a candidate without principles will not do. There are some things in the new constitution we are afraid of—we are afraid of the Federalists, we are afraid of a leaning to the British model, we are afraid of that fellow Hamilton; to be sure he fought through the war, and was your aid-de-camp, and all that, but they say he admires the British constitution, and is no better than a Tory and an Englishman at heart, and worse, they say you have spoken of him with respect. We are afraid of British banks and their doings, we are afraid of Congress, they have too much power; a President can't have too much, if he is one of us, and will sign our principles. Now, general, let us know your principles, speak out like a man, or rather sign ours, you are nominated in a jiffy—we will stump it for you, puff you, praise you, and you will be our President by force of our nomination. Imagine, if you can, the long gathering storm now concentrated in all its mass on that Olympian brow. Turn to yon committee; look at them, they perceive their blunder too late. Great God, said Mr. Crittenden, we can not measure or imagine unearthly punishment, (and his look toward where the committee were supposed to stand, a look full of sublime, superhuman, unutterable contempt, a look such as his excited imagination brought to his face; the copy, the exact copy, doubtless, of the Washington that was in his soul, overpowered the crowd, and they burst into one loud and long-continued roar of applause, which drowned the residue of the sentence; it was never finished.)

Mr. C. proceeded to remark, that he could not perceive why his competitor should feel any anxiety on the score of General Taylor's principles, as he would not support the general upon any terms. General Taylor had said he was a whig, though not an ultra whig. General Taylor had said that he would not interpose the veto in ordinary cases of legislation. He deemed that power to have been conferred to protect coördinate branches of the government from legislative assault, to guard the constitution from violation, and the country from hasty legislation. It was a high power to be exerted on rare occasions, and with great caution. It was the extreme medicine and not the ordinary diet of the constitution. The gentleman had asked Mr. C. what General Taylor thought of the Wilmot Proviso. I have not been authorized, said Mr. C., to speak for General Taylor, but I can answer the gentleman, that General Taylor was born in Virginia, was raised and educated in Kentucky, now resides in Louisiana, is the proprietor of 155 slaves, and is an extensive sugar and cotton planter. I should imagine the slave States had a better guarantee in all these circumstances, that General Taylor was no enemy to their just rights, than a pledge extorted under the hope of a party nomination could possibly afford. And since the gentleman seemed inquisitive on this point, he could tell him, that whatever General Cass might be now, two years ago he was known to be warmly and decidedly in favor of the Wilmot Proviso. He had complained of the adjournment of Congress on that ground, alleging that if the session had been protracted somewhat, the proviso would have been adopted. He, Mr. C., had been informed by Mr. Winthrop, speaker of the House of Representatives, that he had heard General Cass in the stage, openly and warmly among the passengers, vindicating the Wilmot Proviso.

Mr. C. rejoiced, if General Taylor came into power, that he would approach that high place unfettered and unpledged to any other rule than the constitution, and his own good sense under the circumstances in which he might be placed; General Taylor had said (he, Mr. C., had seen it in his own hand writing) that if it was expected of him to reward or punish men for their political opinion, to proscribe from office and civil preferment any portion of his fellow-citizens on party grounds, men would find themselves grievously mistaken. That Whig and Democrat had flocked together to the standard of their common country—under his eye, and by his order, they had poured out their blood together in its defense, and that for himself, he would as soon turn his back upon an enemy as exert the power with which the law might clothe him to punish a citizen for his free opinions.

Mr. C. wound up by saying that a President of the United States should, if possible, discard from his mind all former prepossessions, prejudices, or principles, if you please, such loose opinions as he may have formed in private life, or in a different position where they were not to be practically exerted, and could have no bearing upon the public, were to be all rigorously revised, or rather thrown away. A President of the United States should be regenerated, actually made over, and approach the discharge of his duties with a new mind, or a mind exempt from all bias, washed clean of all prejudice, and free to examine all objects in the new points of view in which they must present themselves from the new and elevated position from which he was to behold them.

Mr. Powell rejoined in a speech of some twenty minutes. He said a great change had come over some people in this nation upon the subject of military rulers, since the days of General Jackson. Once it had been held by the whig party, if he remembered right, that one of the greatest dangers to which a republic was exposed, was the excessive admiration of the people for mere military leaders. Now it seems they have selected as their political head a man whose only claim is military service—a man who has been in the army all his life; whose civil qualifications have been subjected to no test, whose political opinions, so far as the great practical measures of the government, heretofore, and still the subject of deepest interest with the people of the United States are concerned, are unknown or unavowed. The gentleman had directed the powerful artillery of his wit and rhetoric against "printed principles." For the soul of him, Mr. Powell said, he could not conceive that printing a principle made it any worse. The democratic convention had never claimed to create a principle by printing it. The principle existed before, the printing only made it known. His competitor seemed to think that "printed principles were very convenient, as they might be changed." Now he humbly submitted whether principles, unprinted and unavowed, might not be more easily shifted to suit the occasion, and be more readily adapted to party purposes. His competitor's definition of principle he thought entirely too general and abstract for any practical political purpose. He had as well confine a candidate to the Declaration of Independence, or to a belief in the decalogue. He rather apprehended, after all, that General Taylor, if elected, would find himself in the hands of men who would hold him, and hold him strictly, to principles, which, though not printed now, were snugly laid away for the present, to be produced in due season. He was authorized in this by the history of the past. He remembered that when the Harrisburg convention nominated General Harrison and John Tyler in 1840, they put forth no programme of the measures or principles of that administration. The thing worked then admirably, he acknowledged; the no principle candidates were elected in a perfect whirlwind. But mark the sequel; no sooner had the administration commenced its career, and Congress convened, than we hear enough of principles, of party principles and party measures. Why was John Tyler so bitterly denounced, and by whom? The whig party, and their great leader in Congress, Mr. Clay, alleged that their principles were betrayed by the administration, the very measures defeated which they had been elected to carry out. Mr. Tyler denied that he had been pledged to any set of measures, denied that he was elected to carry Mr. Clay's peculiar system into execution, claimed to be the President of the United States, and by virtue of his high office to be entitled to the free exercise of an unfettered judgment. *He* may have been *regenerated* after his election; I know not; but I put it to my competitor whether printed principles, aye, printed and subscribed to, would not have been of main utility in settling that question of treason. I am not defending Mr. Tyler; I believe he betrayed his party, and I condemn him for it, but I am only showing the propriety of having the opinions of public men made public, and am showing it from the history of that very party to whom I am opposed. Publicity, I have been in the habit of considering, as of the life and essence of popular institutions, secrecy, and mystery, and intrigue and fitness, for the cabinets of princes. It is possible, that with a candid avowal of the principles afterward attempted to be enforced, Harrison and Tyler may not have been elected. The whigs, however, would have lost nothing by this; they could not have been worse off than under that administration. Warned, however, by their fate, then, they came forward again for the contest in 1844, under a leader of whose principles and objects there was no doubt. He was, indeed, a distinguished statesman; he had just endeavored to force upon the acting President of the United States a set, a system of measures well understood. He had denounced and crushed that administration for its recreancy to him.

Over him there hung no mystery—not a doubt. His principles had been avowed, proclaimed, pressed through a long life. They had formed the subject of bitter controversy and fierce struggle for twenty years. They were published, then printed. Bank, land distribution, protective tariff, anti-annexation, "the veto power," were written all over the folds of every whig banner, and every whig press groaned under argument and declamation in their support. The democratic doctrines, their views of the constitution and the true policy under it, were set forth with equal clearness and in direct opposition. The issues were fairly made, the battle was manfully fought. Never was the nation brought up to decide with more distinctness upon national measures. Never could a people be called upon to decide upon opposite systems of policy with a clearer knowledge of the points in dispute. The whigs had won without principles; they lost upon their avowal before the nation. What means the present guarded silence? Is the experiment of 1840 to be tried over again? That was indeed the most extraordinary event I ever witnessed. That successful campaign of hard cider, log cabins, long poles, and coon skins, without principles, was a phenomenon. Struck with it rather as a diseased convulsion, than the regular action of the public mind, to be accounted for upon any known laws of the moral or political world, I consulted a physician on the subject. He told me that it was undoubtedly a disease of the public mind, epidemic in its character, but it was of that type of epidemic which, like the small-pox, the people can only take once. It looks very much, however, as if our whig friends expected to inoculate the people with it a second time. Indeed, their preference for Mr. Clay is avowed, if they had any hope of electing him. General Taylor is second choice, and taken upon the sole ground of availability. What means this? Why is Mr. Clay less available? He is a civilian of high attainments, a statesman of large experience, an orator of unrivalled powers, and a leader of unflinching firmness, and preferred even by my competitor as President. Why is he not available? What means that word availability? What can it mean but that Mr. Clay's system of government is known; that it is known, if he were elected, and his party are brought into power, they will reverse the whole policy of the past administration, and that when brought fairly before the people, that system has been steadily rejected. What can it mean but that by a cautious concealment, or entire silence as to the future views of party, a dextrous avoidance of unpopular issues and questions, democratic votes may be won to support a man whose renown in arms has raised the reputation, extended the power, and excited, as it ought to have done, the gratitude of his country. The democratic President of the United States is to be charged as the sole author of the war alleged to be declared by him, in violation of the rights of Congress, and in the teeth of the constitution. The war itself to be denounced as unnecessary, unconstitutional, unwise, unjust. The administration to be thwarted, crossed, opposed, villified in every stage of its progress. The example is to be set of pitting a general in the field, even while in the field, in opposition as a candidate for the Presidency to the government which he serves. The dangerous example of making it the interest of the chief commander of armies to throw blame and disgrace, if possible, upon the administration at home, to become the champion and the instrument of political opposition, is to be introduced by a party heretofore signalized by their dread of military men. The singular spectacle is presented, of a party condemning a war throughout, warning the country of the growing love of conquest, of the danger of fostering the military spirits, of the damnable character of the recent war, and at the same time bringing forward, as a candidate for the Presidency, a gentleman whose entire claims rest upon his vigorous and successful prosecution of this very war, a gentleman who has never held civil office, and refuses to avow a political principle. It would be scarcely uncharitable to question the sincerity of our whig friends. Let the democracy be upon their guard; let them not be deceived. I need not vindicate their principles here; they have not been assailed.

I can not attack General Taylor's principles; none have been avowed save those great principles of morality to which all men profess obedience. Perhaps his declaration in the Allison letter, upon the subject of the veto, may be considered as the avowal of a principle. It is, however, so vague and undefined as not to be taken hold of. He leaves us utterly in the dark as to what he would consider unconstitutional, or hasty legislation. My competitor is not authorized, he tells us, to pledge him on the Wilmot Proviso, further than the circumstances of his position and private interests pledge him. This, it seems, has not convinced the northern people. I see the northern papers claim him as a friend of the Wilmot Proviso, and urge him upon the people upon that ground. I do not say he is: far from it, I only refer to it as showing how the mystery of his silence is calculated to mislead or to confuse the public. If, however, the general be opposed to the Wilmot Proviso, the slave States gain nothing by his election under his views of the veto power, unless he chance to think that Congress can not constitutionally legislate on the subject.

My competitor has ridiculed the platform of 1844, and has exhibited the awkward dilemma of the President upon the compromise line at 49° of north latitude. I do not understand that the platform fixed, or that Mr. Polk was pledged to, the parallel of 54° 40′ as the fixed boundary, and his ultimatum in the negotiation. I am very confident he was not. The title to Oregon was an unsettled one. The British government had theretofore refused, or at least evaded a settlement of it. The American government had offered, over and over again, to fix the boundary at 49°, and the proposition had been steadily rejected. It was a question of great and growing interest. There was, before the last Presidential election, a strong party opposed to pressing the negotiation. They dreaded bringing it to an issue. The democratic doctrine was, that the question should be settled, and settled upon the American ground—the British claim to the mouth of the Columbia being held as inadmissible. The American proposition, for twenty years, had been the line of 49°. Mr. Polk, when he brought the subject up for negotiation, renewed the same proposition. That was his original position on the question. It was rejected. The compromise failing, he did not drop the subject as former administrations had done, but, true to his pledge, claimed to the extent of our title, and brought the matter before Congress. The British Cabinet, under the energetic conduct of the President, who was preparing for the military occupation of the country, and, if necessary, the forcible assertion of our whole right, the British Cabinet, under what the opposition in Congress considered as a threat, came into Mr. Polk's original proposition, and yielded under a threat, what they had steadily refused for twenty years. Mr. Polk violated no pledge to his friends, and yielded no ground to a foreign nation, when he carried, by a threat of war the very terms which had always been offered in negotiation. Mr. Powell said that Mr. C., in his admiration of General Taylor, had almost overlooked the other part of the whig ticket, Mr. Fillmore. He warned the democracy to remember, that, in voting for General Taylor, they must take Mr. Fillmore along with him, and vote against General Butler, a gentleman somewhat known in peace as well as war, and entitled, in the judgment of a great many, to be regarded with pride and admiration by all Kentuckians.

His competitor had said that he, Mr. Powell, would not vote for General Taylor, at any rate, or upon any terms.

He must confess, as matters now stood at present, he did not think he could. But if General Taylor could undergo the regeneration of which his competitor spoke as being necessary for a President of the United States, and the whig party along with him, of which he thought the latter stood much in need, why, after the new birth, it might be a very different affair. The debate here closed. Mr. Powell was frequently cheered loudly during his remarks. The whigs spoke of him with respect and kindness. They were surprised, and, to do them justice, rather pleased to find him so very different from what he had been represented. No matter what they expected, they found a modest, well behaved, fine looking, sensible man, entering into the arena with Mr. Crittenden, duly and properly impressed with the greater weight of the age and reputation, and fully sensible of the real merit and virtues of his competitor, returning his courtesy, if not with equal grace, at least with equal kindness, and notwithstanding his inferiority in renown and his modest sense of it, buckling to the work his party had set before him, and giving and receiving blows with knightly courage as well as knightly courtesy. One main inducement to the preparation of this report was to correct the misrepresentation of a most unjust and paltry notice of this debate, which appeared in the Louisville Courier a few days afterward, in which, among other things, it was stated, that by an arrangement among Powell's friends, a noisy effort was made to prevent Mr. C.'s reply; and that after the reply, Mr. Powell vanished, and had not since been heard of. From whatever motive, or from whatever quarter the call may have proceeded, which stopped for a moment Mr. Crittenden's reply, rest assured it was not from Mr. P.'s friends exclusively, and so far from vanishing, he rejoined substantially in the terms above set forth.

The writer of this owes a slight apology to the gentlemen, and a brief explanation to the public, in case you should think this letter worth publication. He differs from Mr. Crittenden upon several grave political questions, deemed by them both of vast importance to the greatness and prosperity of their common country. He regrets Mr. Crittenden's past, and some of his present political connections, but entertains for his personal character the highest respect; and for his talents, his virtues, and his noble temper, admiration the most unbounded. Should this report, purporting to be a full one, of his speech, which all men who heard it acknowledged to be splendid, ever meet his eye, I dread his censure of the presumption which dared such a task, though the offender be for ever unknown. Mr. Crittenden has suffered, and does suffer, more from reporters than any great orator I have ever known. Lest it should be thought that the speech I have put into his mouth is literal, and he be responsible for, or judged by the precise words and style of it, I state that it is a free translation, not, by an immeasurable distance, an accurate report. The writer took no note whatever at the time, and did not commence writing from memory for some days after the debate. If I have fully embraced the thought, the scope, the meaning of the speech, if I have represented him as employing no argument, or uttering no sentiment which he did not or would not have employed or uttered in the connection in which he spoke, I am satisfied Mr. Powell is more easily reported, and I am sure I have not done him injustice. In that fine, surpassingly fine episode, of Mr. Crittenden's, of General Washington and the Committee, I fear I have failed most and erred most. There are portions of it which he did not speak. In some instances I have ventured to translate his looks, when he looked volumes perfectly intelligible to the crowd, yet spoke never a word. In other instances my memory had lost the words. The remains of his speech in my memory lay there entombed, and petrified like the fossil bones of geology; and it required the aid of comparative anatomy to bring out the entire skeleton perfect and complete. The reader will have no difficulty in making out the genus of the noble animal I have endeavored to preserve, and will easily detect those parts which are genuine remains from those which a clumsy artist had added. If the supplied parts are sufficiently in keeping to identify the whole frame, he is satisfied. The translation, of course, does not approach the original in grace and spirit. In those instances—and there are several in the interview between the committee and General Washington—when I undertook to interpret his countenance, and to write what he looked, in addition to what he said, I feel that I have elaborated some of the sentences into fustian, and covered them with ambitious ornament—a literary offense, which he never commits, and one which before the tribunal of his severe and simple taste is never forgiven. With this explanation, he will not as an orator be held responsible to the letter, and if I have not misrepresented his meaning, or misstated his facts, he will forgive false taste, and even the impudence of reporting him at all. I promised at the outset a sketch of Mr. Benjamin Hardin. I design a full length portrait of that gentleman, but not here; his figure will spoil the piece; he has no business in such company. I will give him a separate canvas, when he shall stand alone in his glory. Forgive the garrulity of an old man.

THE OLD GUARD—NEW CONSTITUTION.

NO. I.

Edited by Mr. Marshall, *at Frankfort, Kentucky, in* 1850.

The first number of the "Old Guard" was issued at Frankfort, Ky., on the 6th of February, 1850. The main object of the publication was to investigate the New Constitution, and give to the public an analytic exposition of its defects. That instrument had just been drafted and signed by the members of the Convention. At the ensuing election it was to be submitted to the people of Kentucky for their adoption or rejection. Some of the most talented men in the State arrayed themselves against it. Among these was Mr. Marshall. As editor of the "Old Guard," he came into the battle champing like a war-steed, his whole armor on, impatient to measure strength with the most chivalrous veterans of the opposition. The Old Guard, with "up Guards and at them" for its motto, went into the struggle gloriously and gallantly. Mr. Marshall, in a series of leading editorials addressed "To the people of Kentucky," gave the proposed Constitution a most thorough and searching analysis. To use one of his own expressions, (applied to Mr. Wise in Congress,) he "struck at it root and branch; he raked it—hull, mast and rigging." More than one experienced combatant shrank from the keenness of his lance and the power of his saber-stroke. The following are the letters referred to, published in their original order. The first, or opening address, is a general examination of the body of the instrument. In the succeeding articles, skilfully as a surgeon, he applies his pen, keen as a dissecting knife, to the deformities of its parts.

In pursuance of the promise given in our prospectus, issued some weeks since, the Old Guard commence to-day their examination of the plan of government submitted by the Convention for your approval or rejection. Before we proceed to that minute and detailed scrutiny of the particular parts of the instrument, or begin that rigorous analysis, to which we have pledged ourselves, we desire to take a general survey of its outline and figure—to determine the outward form, dimensions and proportions of the building, before we cross the threshold, to examine its interior distribution, the arrangement and relations of its various courts, passages, and apartments. We design to compare it first, as a whole, in its general plan and features, with the old building, whose walls and roof, still stanch and stout, without leak or crack, have sheltered you and yours in tolerable security from flood and fire, and kept you sound and safe amid every storm which has swept the political atmosphere during the last half century. We mean, too, to compare it with itself, and assuming for a moment, as just, the object at which the architects profess to have aimed, and the plan and principle upon which they profess to have wrought, as wise and true, we will labor to trace both, through the details of their work, to ascertain, if possible, whether the means they have employed be adapted to the end they had in view, or conform to the plan and the principle upon which they set out. It is for you that we write. It is to you we address ourselves. It was professedly for your superior convenience and greater safety, the new edifice was constructed. The builders were appointed by yourselves. They had full powers, ample credit, and the whole storehouse of the past and present, thrown wide open, whence to select and draw their materials. History has preserved full and accurate drawings of the ancient structures. Philosophy has plunged into the ruins of ancient civilization, gathered, from the study of its dead relics, its forms, its peculiarities, its genius, explored and unfolded the principles upon which States now past away were founded, and penetrated and unfolded the causes of their rise and fall, their glory and their shame. Modern times, so fruitful in examples of every kind, their own country, their own State, not without its share of instruction, lay full before them, not in the dim twilight of legend or tradition, not to be traced through broken columns and crumbling ruins, and to be brought before the imagination by the reconstructive energy of comparative anatomy, but full and complete in every member, and bathed and basking in the broad light of present history. Your workmen were not without models. Committing to them a mighty task, you clothed them with mighty powers. The trust was great, the discretion large. They were empowered to examine the old edifice thoroughly, to decide whether it was radically defective, and unfit for modern use, and the present size, taste and condition of the family, or whether it would admit of slight alterations, or only required repairs cheap and easy. They have rejected it as no longer suited for your habitation; they propose razing it from turret to foundation—from dome to cellar nothing suits them. They have built again, or propose to build, and not upon the same foundation. If they have agreed to use some of the old materials, to work in a stone here, or a beam or rafter there, they have preserved nothing of the character of the old homestead—every thing is new, bran new, we believe, in this world. One thing, however, they have done, for which we thank them. They have submitted their model for your revision, and the work of ruin, if achieved, must be by your own hands. It is here, and now that we ask you to pause. It is here, and now that, notwithstanding all the circumstances which surround the question, notwithstanding this building committee, this Convention, (that we may drop a figure perhaps continued too long,) was called by a majority so overwhelming, as to leave no doubt that a change in your political organization was demanded by yourselves, still here and now, we implore, we expect, that you will pause and ponder.

There is a wide difference, we apprehend, between the call of the Convention and the acceptance of this Constitution. If indeed a distinct plan, either as to principle or detail, had been in the first instance laid before you, and your delegates had assembled fully instructed to carry it out, and they had done so, then indeed the present submission had been mere matter of form, opposition would have been fruitless, hopeless, and we would never have written. It was this evident temper of yours to introduce some change into your organic law, that has inspired the Convention with such extraordinary boldness. It is the same cause, which inspires with dread many, very many, wise and good men, who regard the plan of the Convention as the worst imaginable, and overawes their opposition. The people have decided say they, we must submit. The people have not decided, say we. The Convention are not the people. They have striven, to be sure, to reverse the natural relations between themselves and their constituency. They have sought to introduce a new principle, to wit, that the Constitution can derive neither life nor authority from your sanction, nor does it necessarily fall by your condemnation. It is from the Convention it must derive its living energy, its imperative character, its binding force. The submission to you, in the language of a leading member of that body, is in the nature of an interlocutory order out of chancery. Your decision is in the nature of the report of a commissioner, a report which binds not the sovereign Judge, which may be reversed or sent back, which may or may not become the foundation of the final decree. They alone are empowered to make a Constitution say they, to alter or amend, or reädopt the old one, and this they can not delegate to you. The Convention delegate power to the people! Verily, verily, freemen of Kentucky, we are likely to be involved in strange questions. This reasoning of theirs is with them not an abstraction. They have deduced from it a concrete idea, full of meaning and terribly practical.

They have raised upon it a new structure of power, a political body and authority, hitherto unheard of in American legislation. After they had finished their work, round and complete in all its parts, approved it, so far as they were concerned, and signed it, by means of this submission of it to you, they have contrived to render their own existence perpetual, or at least terminable only at their own will. We will treat this branch of the subject more at length hereafter, and shall invoke to it, in connection with other matters, your earnest and undivided attention.

We have said that we designed to compare the leading object, as avowed by the Convention, with the means they have employed to effect it, and the principle upon which they profess to have wrought, with the results produced. In the first instance, we shall not argue the propriety of the object, or contest the force of the principle.

The Convention and their admirers seem to be well aware

of the force of the old maxim, that sometimes words are things. They have christened themselves as the friends of "Constitutional Reform." They are the pioneers and the champions of the progressive democracy. They have all confidence in the mighty principle of self-government, and the absolute sovereignty of the people. They seek to extend through every department of political administration, supreme or subordinate, discretionary or ministerial, the popular and elective principle. Though the trunk of aristocracy has been hewn away, the roots of that detested tree still linger, they say, hidden in the undersoil of our free institutions, still living, and ready, under favorable circumstances, to shoot up with renewed vigor, and fling its dark and blighting shadow o'er all the land. They come to extend, to broaden, to make complete the power of the people. The old idea of constitutional restraint and limitation upon the power of both government and people, coupled with the reasonable delay of changes in the organic law, imposed fetters unworthy of the age, and derogatory to the wisdom of the democracy. They sought to place the fundamental law itself nearer to the people, and more immediately within their reach. In these glorious days of experiment and progress, it was insulting to the human understanding, and implied distrust of the democratic principle, that any part of the social polity should be put beyond the reach of amendment even for an instant. Whatever progress may have been made in other arts, or other departments of knowledge, however much human science may have extended itself over the realms of nature, and human power grown along with it, in the arts of demagogueism, there seems to have been neither advance, nor improvement, nor change. The same cringing servility, the same honeyed flattery, even to the phrases, which marked the courtiers of the people in democratic States twenty-five hundred years ago, distinguish them yet. The fawning sycophants of power, the supple slaves of a master, whose confidence they have ever sought to win, by soothing his vanity and flattering his worst passions, they have paved the way to their own elevation and to the ruin of States, by the same means and with the same materials, throughout the whole period of human history, and will, to "the last syllable of recorded time."

Aristotle said long ago, that a courtier in a monarchy, and a demagogue in a republic, was made of the same stuff—the same animal placed in different situations. The one cringing at the footstool of the throne, the other bowing into the very dust of adulation, in the presence of the multitude, each seeking to make power absolute and unlimited, wherever they found it, whether in the crown or in the people, and each alike the fatal enemy of human liberty, of law, and of the wise restraints which reason and justice every where impose upon human power. Had the Stagirite lived till our times, however much he may have changed other branches of his philosophy, modern experience would have sustained him fully in this political maxim. Communities of men are subject to the same passions and the same temptations with individuals. They are liable to the same faults, and they are capable of the same prudence and the same courage. As they display the capacity of self-restraint, which is the true meaning of that "pet phrase," self-government, as they exhibit the power of studying and comprehending their own nature, and the nature of the things which surround them, and the firmness to pursue the rules deducible from both, they will be found to flourish or to fail, just as individuals, by the same course and under the operation of the same causes, are lifted to prosperity, or overwhelmed in ruin. The spectacle now exhibiting in the Commonwealth of Kentucky is the grandest which the moral world affords. A whole people, not through representatives, but in their own proper person, armed with absolute and irresistible power, with no authority or magistracy, or law, to compel or restrain them, save that curb alone which their own sense of reason, and justice, and right may impose, a voluntary obedience rendered to principles only made obligatory by their truth and their importance—a whole people are about to sit as a Convention, with original power to frame a fundamental law henceforth to be binding upon all. It is indeed a grand spectacle, and at the same time a searching test of the moral and intellectual qualities which fit men to govern themselves. You approach this sublime task under very peculiar circumstances—circumstances artfully thrown in to obscure the true questions before you, to darken and perplex the judgment you may form. Elements will be strenuously sought, to be mingled with the subject of your deliberations, which, in truth have nothing to do with it. The worst passions of particular men, and the most dangerous of the community will be appealed to in behalf of the new instrument. The clamor with which faction always assails, and sometimes deafens the public ear and maddens the public mind, will peal its highest notes. Every prejudice will be appealed to, every art, every stratagem employed. The great heart of Kentucky needs all its firmness, the great mind all its clearness, to carry her safe through the impending crisis. Among other and serious difficulties thrown in your way, is the brief space allowed you by the terms of the Convention, to examine maturely so great a work and to form your judgment upon it. These champions of reform, these worshipers of the people, after having consumed nearly three months, although there were but an hundred in council, and they together in one room, and after argument and discussion filling a volume of some 1200 pages in the formation of the instrument, have allowed but a few weeks more of time, for nearly a million of men scattered over a surface of 40,000 square miles, to examine, deliberate and consult on the same work. They have fixed too upon that precise season, when it is least likely that the whole people can be drawn together, to hold the election. These patriotic gentlemen, so regardful of majorities, so careful to exclude the possible rule of a minority, that they have prohibited the representatives of the people, under the new government, from appropriating any sum over one hundred dollars, unless a majority of the whole number elected assent—who have required repeated majorities, not of those who vote, but of the entire people through a period of seven years, before their new form of government can be touched by the innovating finger of progressive experience. These same gentlemen have directed that a simple majority of the votes cast at a season so near, and so unpropitious, and not a majority of the entire people, shall be sufficient to rivet upon the whole body, a law, next thing to impossible ever to be changed. These are among the difficulties which surround you.

Having promised a comparison, first between the general scheme of the two instruments, we proceed to redeem our pledge. Those who imagine that the Constitution of 1799, by which the Commonwealth of Kentucky has been governed ever since, was framed by rude and ignorant hands, know nothing of the matter. The men who formed that Convention will challenge a comparison with any who have appeared in American affairs. The early History of Kentucky—her separation from the State of Virginia—her first Constitution in 1792—the causes and motives which led to the change in 1799—her subsequent history down to the present time, are matters into which an abstract philosopher might look with interest, and emerge from the study with enlarged views of human nature, and an increased admiration of human virtue. The men who settled Kentucky first, and framed her early institutions, were not savages. Society when established here, was not in its infancy. Those who laid the foundations of the first State on this side of the Apallachian mountains, the foremost crest of that great wave of civilization, which has since spread over the Mississippi valley, were matured in the science of liberty. Fresh from the revolution, and reeking and imbued with the mighty principles of the greatest event recorded in the history of men, they understood well the grounds upon which human right and human freedom according, at least, to the genius of that age, were supposed to rest. With them, government was not a mere matter of guesswork, an affair of experiment, a business of empiricism and quackery. They worked by rule—a rule deduced from ten thousand experiments made before their time, the origin, progress, and results of which had been thoroughly studied, and were thoroughly understood.

Had their names perished, had they left no other monument than the Constitution of Kentucky, subsequent inquirers would have been at no loss to determine their genius and their character. We have said in our prospectus, that we were not opposed to cautious reforms in the Constitution. The changes we contemplated, however, had reference to the original character of our government. They should have been adapted to it, and designed not to reverse and destroy the groundwork and principle of the institution, but to perfect and carry out more fully the original plan. That principle and that plan, though perhaps not thoroughly executed, were, in our judgment, perfect. Our ancestors sought to raise a republic upon a purely popular basis, and they did it. Averse to absolute power in any form or in any hands—recognizing fully the great body of the community sought to be *governed* as the only source of *government*, and the thorough political equality of each member of the State, they still felt the necessity of imposing limitations, legal limitations, even upon a sovereignty thus constituted. Here lay the difficulty. This is the mighty problem in political science, the solution of which had been sought for centuries by the founders of States and systems, in the halls of practical legislation and in the schools of philosophy, and sought in vain. The founders of the American Constitution hoped they had found it. Universal suffrage, frequent and direct elections by the people, a prompt responsibility upon the part of the representatives to their constituency, seem to be ample guarantees, they are, at least, the utmost which the wit of men has been competent to devise against the violation, or at least the continued violation of the public will, in the exercise of that great mass of political authority included under the idea of the legislative power. But that public will itself, may become perverted. *Quis custodiet ipsos custodes*—who shall keep the keepers—who shall guard the guardians. We are in the habit of speaking of the people as an unit, of the right and the sovereignty and the will of the people as though it were a single individual, whose action, beginning and terminating in himself, operating upon no person or interest save his own, with its results confined to himself; the most unrestrained power of will may be accorded to a being thus isolated, without danger or cause of complaint to any other right, interest, person, or thing in the universe. This, however, we apprehend, to be a very mistaken view of the subject, and leads to great mistakes in reasoning upon government. Society, or the people if you please, is composed of a vast number of distinct individuals, very unequal in strength, faculties, fortune, means of influence, and all the natural or acquired instruments of defense against wrong, oppression or violence. It is a great co-partnership among a multitude of members with very unequal stakes in the firm. This inequality of interests and condition, rooted in the nature of things, an essential and unavoidable condition of the institution of property, and of the civilized state, is the groundwork and the cause of the jealousies and the divisions which exist in every community of men; it is the parent of faction in free States; it is the hidden fire, the smoldering volcano which, however deeply buried, lurks in the bosom of all societies, even to the most despotic in their form, and ever and anon breaks forth to sweep before the burning terrors of its path all the monuments of human power, art and civilization. It would involve us too deeply in the discussion of principles, which, to many of you, we fear, will appear too abstract for an address to the people, to show that this social inequality of condition is the legitimate offspring of equality, the natural equality of right. Were not each man rendered secure in his acquisition, with the power of transmitting them to his offspring, industry would cease, and men relapse into barbarism. This social inequality has a further consequence. It naturally and at once divides mankind by its own line into two great classes, the rich and the poor; those who in the enjoyment of previous accumulations, wield the capital which stimulates, employs and rewards labor, and the great and perpetually increasing class of those who win from nature by the sweat of their brow the means of subsistence. To preserve each class from the oppression or injury of the other, and each individual from both, or all combined, to protect property on the one hand and personal liberty to the fullest extent upon the other, to reconcile perfect equality of right, with vast inequality of strength, intellect and wealth among individuals, is the rational end of all government, the great philosophic and humane object of all political arrangement. It is an end oftener sought than found. It were easy for us to demonstrate, that this inequality in human condition, this great division of mankind to which we have referred, is founded in the order of nature, and therefore unavoidable; but we feel assured that those who read us, will appreciate fully the truth and the force of the principle without farther illustration. Carefully observed, it will be found to explain all the political phenomena exhibited in history; it is the secret force which has caused all the social revolutions that are recorded. The operation and the progress of the principle, has originated, modified, changed and finally overthrown every form of polity whose history is complete. It is more rapid, or slower in its operation and its results, but it never slumbers, it is an incessant agent in human affairs. The management of it, the reconciliation of that strange system of antagonism and hostilities upon which society, like the universe and every organized thing in it, seems to be built, with order, and harmony, and freedom in the parts, is the grand desideratum, the mighty problem, the attainment and solution of which requires the sublimest efforts of human genius.

We glance at these principles now. They will be of prime importance in settling the difference between the Convention of 1799, and the Constitutional reformers of 1849, in relation to the constitution of the Judiciary. We design to probe that question to the very bottom, but must defer its thorough examination to another number. Although we have shown that society is not an unit, but it is composed of various distinct individuals, with various and separate and often clashing interests, and with separate and absolute rights, which ought to be inviolable even by the whole power of the State, still, in some respects and for some purposes, it must be regarded as a whole and one. There are matters common to all. In relation to these, in the guidance of its public policy in the management of its public affairs, the community, upon the principle of self-government, is supreme. A very slight examination of the two forms of government now submitted to you, will satisfy you that the old one manifests infinitely more confidence in the popular and elective principle than the new. The restraints put upon the legislative power of the people, through their representatives in the old Constitution, are only such as to protect the absolute rights of individuals, and the rights of private property from infraction or violation by the government. It leaves the people, through their Legislature, the amplest discretion, and the fullest power over matters of public policy, finance, revenue, internal improvement, the organization of the courts inferior to the supreme, the superintendence of the administration of justice, every thing indeed, of a public and common character. It secured prompt responsibility by annual elections, and kept alive and vigilant and for ever active, the popular principle, by this call for the frequent exertion of the popular power in the choice of one branch of the legislature—a circumstance, in our judgment, of vast importance. The new Constitution provides for biennial elections, and has almost annihilated the legislative power. Biennial officers, clothed with legislative powers, and the number of days they are to sit, prescribed in the fundamental law, seems to be no great advance of the democratic principle from 1799. They have cut down the Executive till he is a mere cipher in the Constitution. It would seem from the manner in which the Convention have handled those branches of the government heretofore elective, that they considered representative government as a failure, and that they had no confidence whatever in the elective principle. Indeed, all the abuses complained of seem to have been committed by the representatives of the people. Those branches of the government heretofore elective, are they whose powers have been most curtailed, and conduct most severely arraigned. It is a strange compliment to the representatives of the people, and through them to the capacity of the people to choose their representatives to put a constitutional veto upon any appropriation of public money over an hundred dollars. We mean by a constitutional veto, such a veto as the Executive now wields, to-wit, the requisition of a majority of the whole number elected to pass a law. They have made the judges and clerks elective by the people, but they have shown, in both instances, that they have no confidence in their capacity to choose either. They send the people to the courts for a certificate of the qualifications of a clerk, thereby demonstrating their sense of the truth, that the courts who have now the appointment of clerks are not only the best, but the only proper judges of the necessary qualifications. They give to the people the election of judges, but they limit their choice to a particular profession, thereby, again demonstrating that in their sense the people whom they flatter so much, if left free upon the subject, would wander wide of the track. It would be a strange thing if the Constitution required that the President of the United States should get a certificate of his learning and qualifications from some college before the people could vote for him. Under the old Constitution, when a man became a citizen of Kentucky, he carried his franchise with him wherever he went. A residence of an hour, a minute, in any county, gave him the right to vote. He was a Kentuckian, and wherever he resided in the State, by virtue of his citizenship, he had a voice in selecting those who were to govern him! By the new Constitution, each county is to be laid off into precincts, and the voter must have resided within the precinct sixty days next preceding the election, to be entitled to a vote, and can not vote out of his precinct. He may have been born in the county, resided in it from birth, be perfectly known to the judges of the election, still, unless he has been a citizen of the precinct sixty days he is disfranchised. Thousands in Kentucky will be disfranchised by the operation of this rule, and thousands of the laboring class—the very class for whom our patriots profess most regard. They have dismembered Kentucky, broken it into a number of petty municipalities, and made the right of citizenship local instead of general. They have required a new qualification, and abridged, most seriously, the former right. They have made the Judiciary elective by the people, yet in the arrangement of the supreme court, they have shown that they have no confidence in the elective principle. They have directed the State to be divided into four districts, and each district to choose a judge, so that of a court composed of four judges, no man in Kentucky will vote for more than one. It is not a State court chosen by the people of Kentucky, each man voting for the whole court, but a number of district officers representing fractions of the community. Take each separate voter in the State, and of a court which is said to be elected by the people, there will be three in the choice of whom he has had no voice. And the reason assigned for this arrangement evinces the most profound distrust of the elective feature in the judiciary.

They say the pernicious influence of party ties and personal connections between the judge and the friends who elect him is thus avoided. That whenever a cause comes up, no matter from what district, three of the court will be independent of the parties, and can render a judgment, without the influences which the argument admits will operate upon the mind of the judge elected by the district whence the cause comes. Thus, in the constitution of the supreme court, the Convention themselves admit the mischief of their own principles, and have striven to paralyze it. In the constitution of the circuit courts, however, they abandon altogether the ground upon which they have placed the court of appeals, and give the most full and sweeping effect to the evils there sought to be parried. The circuit judges are to preside in the districts where they are chosen. They must reside there also. Reeking from an electioneering conflict, the judge ascends the tribunal to administer justice among the very persons who have just been engaged in a hot struggle for and against him. His ardent friends on one side of him, his bitter enemies on the other. Had the Convention followed out the principle upon which they seem to have organized the appellate court, they would have directed the circuit judges to have been chosen by one district, and to have presided in another.

Retrenchment of expenditure and a more economical government were among the leading objects of the reformers. They have created four hundred new officers, three judges of the court of probate, and one lieutenant circuit judge for each county in the State. Whether justices of the peace are to form a part of the new county court for all purposes, or only in the court of claims, and for adjusting the county levy, and making appropriations, we have been utterly unable to determine from the language of the instrument. The expense of this machinery, if it be contemplated to obtain officers of competent ability, will be very great.

One of the leading objections urged by the "reform party" against the old Constitution, was the difficulty of changing or amending it. It was too remote from the people. The plan of calling a Convention by successive votes of the people, and submitting the whole instrument for revision, was too slow. As experience might suggest particular defects, they professed, as one of their most prominent principles, the purpose to place the fundamental charter within easy reach by specific clauses, without hazarding the entire scheme of government. This was the text. The commentary is, that the time within which the people can reach the instrument, the mode remaining the same, is exactly doubled. These votaries of progress march at a quick step to the point of improvement which limits their own genius, and, beyond this, forbid the advance or the return of the human understanding for ever. The scheme of government they propose is not an experiment to be abandoned, if it should prove false or hurtful, but an immutable law, a fixture, an iron bed upon which society is to be stretched and bound for ever, without the power of turning.

Professing unlimited confidence in the democratic principles, and claiming to have extended popular power, they have, in their action, insulted representative government, declared the legislative branch, emanating from the very bosom of the people, as unworthy of trust or confidence, and stabbed popular sovereignty in its very heart.

You are so conscious of your strength, you are in the full enjoyment of a liberty so perfect, that you will be likely to regard with contempt, or receive with ridicule, the pretensions of an usurping assembly, which among a people differently situated, might well awaken emotions both of rage and fear. They have assumed, distinctly, the power to continue their own existence indefinitely. They have exerted the power over the public purse, and asserted their complete independence of the existing government and laws upon the vital matter of the appropriation of money. They have laid down the proposition clearly, that your sanction or refusal of their work amounts to nothing. That they, not you, are the sovereigns. They have decided, under these circumstances, and upon these principles, to reässemble, with powers not conferred by your decision, whatever it may be, but fresh and ample to build up or pull down as they were in October. They have decided that the legislative branch of the government expires in June, should they determine upon adopting this Constitution. They will be here in existence, without other limit to their term or powers than they may choose to impose; and for two months, Kentucky will be without any other legislative government than that of this single assembly, without a Senate, without any law defining their powers, or limiting their existence. They have referred the Constitution to you, not as the principal, the sovereign, the master, whose agents and servants they are, but have condescended to consult with you, to take your opinion, reserving to themselves the sole right and power of entering up the final decree according to their own supreme discretion. As they did not intend the judgment of the people to be final and decisive, it was well enough, perhaps, certainly of a piece with the rest, that they should not have allowed you time for examination and reflection, nor required the voice of a majority of the whole people, in sanction of an act so solemn, so important, so enduring. The advocates, par excellence, of democratic progress, of speedy and continued reforms in government, professing the most profound and unlimited confidence in the masses, they have imposed a law, around which they have thrown an impossibility of change.

In our opening address, our remarks are designed to be general. In future numbers we will examine more minutely the particular provisions of the Constitution, and in our next will commence the examination of the principle upon which the Convention have constructed our judicial system. Their whole scheme, in our judgment, in relation to this branch of government, is founded in a great and fatal misconception of the nature and object of the judicial magistracy. The subject is one of such incalculable importance that we have determined to consider it alone, and apart from any other. We will devote a considerable portion of our next number to the discussion of the elective principle, when applied to the judiciary, and compare the system proposed to you, with what has been heretofore held, in Kentucky, the true philosophy.

THE OLD GUARD—JUDICIARY.

NO. II.

The succeeding numbers of this series of leaders examine the Constitution more in detail. On the judiciary they are quite elaborate. These articles evince the closest powers of reasoning, perception vigorous and acute, and a mind every way clear, compact, and rigidly analytic. Junius-like, he wielded his pen against power, and dropped with every stroke a pearl of his genius.

In our opening address to you, we promised, in the present number of the Old Guard, to examine the scheme of the Convention in relation to the Judiciary. The elective principle, as applied by them to this branch of magistracy, we have stated to be founded in a great and fatal misconception of the nature and object of the institution. We again invoke your attention, while we proceed in the discussion of the most important and interesting branch of the whole subject submitted to you. We have, in our first number, endeavored, and we think with success, to show, from a general view of the new Instrument, that the framers had themselves no sort of confidence in the elective principle, the extension of which they profess to have been their leading object. We admit here, however, that their distrust does not demonstrate the badness of the principle. They may themselves have had no confidence in the rule by which they wrought, and yet the rule be sound. We have endeavored, and we think with the most perfect success, to show that the Convention have trampled upon the existing law—law which, while it continues to subsist, binds us all, the Convention and yourselves—that they have inverted the just and natural relations which subsist between the people and themselves, and transferred, or endeavored to transfer to their own hands, the most unlimited sovereignty of which we can conceive. And yet we admit, that all this may be true, and still the instrument of government they have proposed may be worthy of adoption. It must be examined and tried by itself, without reference to the motives, conduct, or present position of the Convention itself. We seek not to excite or enlist any prejudice or passion of yours, either past or present, against the instrument. It is to your reason, your clear, cold, unclouded, and we hope determined reason, operating upon and strengthened by your own rich and ample experience, that we appeal, and shall continue to appeal. The principles from which we shall reason, and to which we shall constantly refer throughout the entire course of our argument, we know to have been once cherished and held sacred by you, as so many fundamental and indisputable truths, interwoven with, and running through the whole texture of your opinions, planted firm and fast in the deep soil of your moral and political ideas, as they are rooted and fixed in the eternal nature of things.

We have said that the great problem in government was to reconcile, in one society, perfect equality of personal and political rights, with vast inequalities between individuals, in wealth, strength, intellect, and all the means of influence and of power. We have said that it was the institution of property, and the consequent rise and growth of industry which distinguishes the civilized from the barbarous condition of mankind. And that the just and humane aim of all political arrangement, is to protect property on the one side, and personal liberty to its fullest extent upon the other. Justice and peace are the legitimate ends of government among men. Is it, can it be necessary for us to argue in proof of the proposition, that the whole scheme of American legislation, the radical, fundamental, all-pervading American idea, from the revolution down, has been, that the more perfect security of individuals, is the great end of all political association? And that liberty, individual liberty, can only be found in a limited government? Is it, can it be necessary for us, at this time of day in Kentucky, to show that absolute power, whether in the hands of one, the many or the few, is equally despotic, and inconsistent with all American ideas of freedom? Is it, can it be necessary for us, here and now, Kentuckians ourselves, and in the midst of Kentuckians, to explain the meaning of constitutional government? We had hoped not. But in the strange confusion of ideas, the utter revolution of system and opinion with which we are surrounded and threatened, we feel the necessity of recurring to original principles, to re-explore, explain, and establish upon the everlasting foundations of immutable truth, the grounds of the faith of our ancestors. In the general, we abhor abstractions. Government is a practical affair. It has to do with men in their business, their homes, their every-day pursuits. Its operation and its results, bearing directly upon the rights, the interests, the happiness of men, are eminently practical. Yet when the whole frame and principle of social organization, when the source and the object of power, the end and the means of political authority are involved in the question, we feel our utter inability to discuss it without mounting to the original and apparently remote causes of the social Union, the rational and philosophic fountains of all human authority over human beings.

In the arrangement of the judicial power, the Constitution of 1799 directs, that it shall be vested in one supreme court, and in such inferior courts as the General Assembly may, from time to time, erect and establish. The judges of these courts shall be appointed by the governor, by and with the advice and consent of the senate. They shall hold their offices during good behavior, or in the Latin of the English law, *dum bene se gesserint*—with the proviso, that the governor shall remove any of them, on the address of two-thirds of each branch of the General Assembly. They are liable for malfeasance, to be impeached by the House of Representatives, and for the trial of charges urged by that body, the Senate is constituted the court. The judges shall receive an adequate compensation for their services, at stated times, to be fixed by law. This is the brief and general outline of the judicial constitution, as traced by the masterly hands of the patriots of 1799. Let us examine the end they had in view, and ascertain first whether that end was wise and just. Let us afterward study, and observe how far the means they employed are naturally calculated and adapted to produce the results they sought. Let us further look back upon our own domestic history, and see how far the system, in its practical workings, has actually produced those results. And lastly, let us examine and compare the principle, the end, the object of the arrangement under the new Constitution with the old. The probable results of the change designed, can be ascertained, or conjectured rather, only by reasoning. We have no experience, no history to guide us in relation to it. With us, it is sheer experiment, and in direct opposition, as we will show, to the ideas and principles upon which our institutions have heretofore reposed, as on a foundation.

It is evident at a glance that the aim, the end of the framers of the old Constitution, was to render the Judiciary independent. It was to place this class of magistrates in such a position, in relation to every other, that they could approach the discharge of their peculiar functions, unawed by any other power, and uncontrolled by any other authority in the State. They did not leave the Judiciary irresponsible. They are made responsible, not to party, not to passion. They are not left in a condition to be swept away at the arbitrary discretion of the executive, to be overwhelmed by heated and factious majorities in the General Assembly, impatient of constitutional restraint, and chafing under the curb of a law designed to restrain and to regulate their will, nor finally to be removed at the mere pleasure of the sovereign constituent body—the people themselves. But they are made responsible, for malfeasance, misfeasance, neglect or violation of the high duties imposed upon them, responsible, in the most solemn form of trial, before that high constitutional court composed of the representatives of the people, and liable there to be removed and degraded, but upon proof and conviction.

Whether in a free government, resting on a purely popular basis, with powers defined and limited in a written Constitution, the judicial department ought to be independent—whether the appointment of the judges in the mode prescribed by our fundamental law, and the tenure of office there fixed, be a violation of the republican principle and an infraction of popular rights under it—whether the means selected by the founders of our particular Constitution to secure the independence of the Judiciary be the only, or the best means, by which that end can be attained—whether the appointing power may not be transferred to the people, and the elective principle may not be applied to the Judiciary, and under what modification, and whether the tenure of judicial office may not be limited, and how, without impairing that independence of the courts, heretofore held so important, are the questions we mean to discuss.

What then is the meaning of an independent judiciary? What is the object for which, and the means through which it is to be attained? What are the elements in this great idea, so deeply graven in the mind, so concentrated in the heart of the early American legislators? They should have known what despotism meant—they had felt it, they had looked it full in the face, and studied well its features and its countenance—they had grappled with it in the struggle of life and death—they had brought it to the earth, and with armed heel upon its neck, had trampled, as they supposed, the last spark of life from the prostrate trunk. They should have known what a republic meant, and something of the means by which liberty was to be won and secured. They had won their own, and thought they had secured it, in the establishment of a government which is the admiration of the world. They turned to an independent Judiciary as the basis of their system, without which constitutional limitations upon power, were an idle effort, to bind the limbs of a giant, or restrain his strength with bands of paper. What is this master idea, of the wise and brave, and good, who have thought and struggled for liberty every where? Why is it that in those countries where freedom is best understood and most thoroughly enjoyed, patriots and sages have united in the belief, that of all the contrivances of human wisdom, this invention of an independent judiciary affords the surest guaranty to a limited constitution, and the amplest safeguard to personal liberty and the rights of individuals? Let us examine the term—let us measure the idea. We have sought for ourselves, laboriously, painfully, through long years of thought, with such means of information as lay within our reach, and the application of the whole of the limited faculties with which heaven may have endowed us, with candor and with caution, to penetrate thoroughly the idea we seek to analyze—to grasp it in its whole dimensions, and all its mighty meaning. We ask you now to go along with us patiently, while we endeavor to unfold the views, and to state the great general truths upon which our reasoning is founded, and from which we deduce our theory of liberty, our idea of a republic.

There are certain elementary principles in government which are admitted by both the parties to this discussion—they may be assumed as established and indisputable—they are to be stated, not proven, in the argument. Among these is the axiom, that the concentration of all powers known to government, legislative, executive and judicial in one depository, no matter whether it be a single person, a select number, or a simple majority of numbers told by the head, constitutes absolute, instead of limited government, and is inconsistent with the idea of liberty and safety. Hence arises the necessity for distributing the political authority of the State into different departments, of dividing it among different branches of magistracy in such manner as to make them operate as checks upon each other.

We can not conceive of any political authority that may not be classed under one or another of the three great heads, to which we have referred, and into which the entire mass has been divided in our Constitution. It is very easy to perceive, and in this country will be readily admitted, that the power to make the law, to interpret its meaning, and to carry it into effect, if united in a single person, constitutes despotism, and subjects the society, so situated, to the absolute will of that person. The same powers united in a small number of persons, becomes equally absolute, equally subjects the residue of the society to the unrestrained will of a fraction of the community and constitutes an oligarchy—a worse form of absolute government, in our judgment, than the other. A worse form, because that responsibility which at last attaches to every form of power, in the latter case, is divided among a number of individuals and is thereby weakened. The abuses and the oppresssions, the wrongs and injustice practiced under it, can not be brought home to any single individual. Men have ever been found, and will ever be found to practice enormities when associated together, and shielded by this association from direct and single and individual responsibility, which no one man would have dared, if exposed singly to the full glare of the public eye, the full weight of the public indignation. These simple forms of government—an unlimited monarchy, which is a despotism—an unlimited aristocracy, which is an oligarchy—will find no champion here—they are universally rejected with us as loathsome and intolerable to human thought. But shall we, the inheritors and votaries of constitutional liberty, pause here in our detestation of absolutism? Is there not another form of unlimited government, equally formidable to the rights of human nature properly understood? Suppose in any community of men all these powers united and wielded by a simple majority of that community—with no rule but the will of that majority for the hour—is it not obvious, that the remaining individuals of a community, so situated, the minor and weaker portion of it, is subject to a dominion absolute, unrestrained, irresistible? This is the despotism of mere numbers—this is not a republic, but a simple democracy—and, according to human experience, the most terrible form of oppression, under which one portion of mankind have ever been subjected to the lawless and unrestrained will of the other.

Had we time now to cite historical examples, we could easily show you, that of all the experiments yet made in social polity, that of simple democracy has proved, without a solitary exception, the most disastrous failure. The efforts to preserve civilization and liberty—to protect persons and property—to keep a great number of individuals, unequal in strength, fortune, intellect, all the natural instruments of power—the rich, the educated, the proud, bound together upon a principle of equality, with the poor, the ignorant, the laborious—under a system which gave to a simple majority of numbers absolute power in the management of all that relates to social affairs—such efforts, and they have been frequent, exhibit the most awful lessons in history for the instruction and the warning of mankind.

We claim to be republican thoroughly. We assert and maintain the right of communities of men to rule themselves; but we will for ever assert and maintain their obligation to rule themselves according to the principles of a justice eternal in its nature, principles not alterable by the voice of majorities or minorities, a justice ascertainable, to be sure, by reason—but having its origin and terminus in the bosom of God—it is for ever obligatory in reason and in morals upon the whole human race.

We have already shown that absolutism in government is not an avowed doctrine, as yet, of any party in Kentucky. That, to avoid the concentration of power destructive to freedom and subversive of the great ends of the social union, the mass of political authority entering necessarily into the idea of government, has been broken and divided, by all our schemes, into three great departments, the Executive, the Legislative, and the Judicial. We can not now review, even cursorily, the various plans resorted to in other countries, to balance the antagonistic principles, which we have shown naturally and necessarily to exist in the bosom of every community of men where property is established—and their efforts from that balance to attain a tranquil equilibrium in society, in which the right of each class might be established, and by which the peace of the whole might be secured. We must hasten briefly to state the leading principles upon which our own systems have been framed.

Our fathers rejected the hereditary principle altogether. They refused to recognize monarchy as a necessary and independent element in their political system. They refused to give to hereditary property a separate, and permanent, and independent weight in the constitution of the State—a separate and independent voice in the passage of the laws which are to bind the whole community. They struck out of their scheme the idea of an aristocratic body, in the shape of a hereditary Senate. Throwing the community into one great mass, without distinction of classes, without rank or privilege, we have carried the representative principle throughout the executive and legislative branches of government. They established the democratic principle as the only power known to our institutions. But they did not design even that to be absolute. They sought to limit it—not by a king sustained by a house of peers, a body of hereditary nobles, a bench of bishops—but by a fundamental and written law, embodying the great and eternal principles of private right and justice, established by authority of that very democratic power, and for the very purpose of imposing limitations upon itself. This fundamental law they placed in the keeping, and made subject to the interpretation of an unarmed and powerless magistracy—a body of men without purse or sword, army, navy, or revenue; without either force or will; with no power but to decide upon laws established by others; no discretion, no faculty, no function but judgment. That same democratic power has sought heretofore to lift this body of magistracy above the reach, and place them out of fear of those other elements, which they are designed to curb and restrain. This is the outline of constitutional government sustained by an independent judiciary. It is the system of our fathers. It is the system which we will endeavor to show, that you are now called on to abandon.

We have already given you the outline of the judicial system, as established by the new Constitution; and if we had not, we make no doubt you have examined and are acquainted with its leading features. In the discussion of the elective principle as applied to the Judiciary, in the particular mode in which the Convention have applied it, it is in reference to its bearing upon their independence, that we wish particularly to draw your attention. We can not take a step in this inquiry without carefully considering, in the first place, the difference in the political functions, the nature of the duties to be discharged, by the legislative and judicial departments of government. The Legislature represents the collective will, and wields the collective force of the community, expressed through a majority of its members. It is the community acting through agents of its own appointment, in the direction of its public affairs, the guidance of its public policy. It is like an individual managing his own estate, directing the investment of his funds, the cultivation of his lands, indeed exercising the fullest control over his own property, through his agent or attorney. Individuals have the right of self-government within fixed limits, in an equal degree with communities. Indeed it was to secure this right that communities were formed. In both cases, the agent of the individual or the representative of the community, is bound to obey and to execute the will of the principal in the one case, of the constituent in the other. But suppose the individual has a dispute with some other person, in relation to some right or property claimed by both. It becomes necessary to save the peace, and to adjust the question, to appoint an arbiter, and to appeal to a law binding upon both. Can it be conceived that this arbiter represents either of these parties, that he is the agent of either of them, bound to obey the instructions of either or both? Is it not at once perceived that he represents a fixed law above them both, which he is to apply to the case, and that the nature of his office, and the ends of justice require that he should be independent of them both, fearless of them both, and responsible to neither. No man shall be judge in his own cause, is the maxim of eternal justice. No man shall appoint a judge responsible to and dependent upon himself, to settle his controversies, is a principle equally obvious. There are some things common to all, public, appertaining solely to the will of the community, and under their absolute control. These are to be managed, regulated and controlled by agents whose duty it is to represent their will, their reason, nay, even their passions. To secure their obedience, and to establish the supremacy of the public will in public affairs, it has been found necessary that these agents should be chosen, and at short intervals, by the people themselves. This is legislation, representative legislation, the only safe basis of political liberty, by which we mean the right of the community to govern itself in relation to its general affairs. But there are things not common to all. There are personal and private rights, involving individual liberty and individual property, subject to invasion by the community, or by other individuals. These are protected by the Constitution of the State, and by a system of fixed laws, defining those rights and appointing the remedies by which they are to be preserved and guarded even against the combined force of the whole community. This is civil liberty. The Legislature represent the community, reflect their will, obey their mandate. The judiciary represent the law, the fixed inflexible law, giving to each man the same weight, the same measure. The nature of their office requires that so far from consulting the will or obeying the instructions of any man or any number of men, they should have neither will nor discretion of their own. It is their duty to study a rule, and to apply it with inflexible and unswerving rigor, to weak and strong, to rich and poor, to the powerful and the defenseless. This is evidently the nature of their office, the character of their duties. Should they not be independent? Is it not clear that there is nothing representative in their character or functions? Is it not demonstrable; that so far from being subjected to the will of either government or people, they are the agents of a law intended to protect individuals against that very will, against any will or any force in the universe?

The importance of an independent judiciary, among any people hoping to enjoy the smallest portion of civil liberty, is admitted, we believe, by many of the friends of the new Constitution. They contend, however, that judges elected by the people, according to their plan, can and will be as independent of improper bias or influence as when appointed by the governor and senate. In our judgment, the new Constitution has changed the whole principle and character of the judicial institution, mistaken its nature and functions, prostrated its independence, destroyed its usefulness, and converted it into a mere supple engine of political intrigue, party passion and violence, and individual oppression. The arrangement they have made is, in our judgment, the very worst imaginable. It is shaped in exact opposition to every principle upon which judicial independence and the stability of jurisprudence have been heretofore supposed, by wise and good men, and by many of the most distinguished members of the Convention itself, to rest. They have made them in the first place representatives of the people by direct election, and for short terms. They have made them district and not State officers, compelled to reside and administer justice among the people who choose them. They have made them re-eligible, so that the hope of continuance in office, and the consequent fear of whatever power and influences, party or personal, may be able to promote or prevent a reëlection, will be for ever before their eyes. An institution could not have been more perfectly shaped to subject the mind of the officer to the passions and the will of others. In what will a circuit judge or a judge of the court of appeals, differ from a member of Congress, or a member of the Legislature, save in the greater length of his term, and value of his office, which circumstances will only render him the more intensely servile or obedient, if you prefer the term, to the influences which can retain him in it? He becomes a representative of the people, subjected in the most intense degree to the will of the majority of his district, in the decision of private causes between man and man, involving the rights of person and property. Is this what you have heretofore meant by judicial independence?

We are frequently met with the question, are not the people capable of electing judges? They elect the governor and the senate, who now appoint the judges; they elect members of Congress, who wield the purse of the nation, and make laws to bind an empire stretching from the Atlantic to the Pacific ocean; they elect the President of the United States, who commands the armies and navies of a republic, before whose dawning glories the meridian spendor of the Roman and the Greek grows pale; are they not competent, capable to choose a constable, a clerk, a scrivener, a circuit judge, or even so august a functionary as a judge of the court of appeals? Are not these public officers? Are not the people supreme? Who should appoint the servants but the master? These be the terms of flattery and of praise by which our demagogue reformers, with their short catechism, for ever on their lips, would drown our voice, and bar us all access to your ear. Hear us, people of Kentucky, hear us at least, though you repudiate our argument, and reject our prayer. When the haughty chief of the confederate Greeks drew his baton of office over the Athenian Themistocles, pressing his advice with patriot urgency—Strike, said the Athenian, presenting his shoulder to the blow, strike but hear me.

We do not doubt, though the Convention do, your capacity to select suitable persons as judges and clerks. We would not have confined you by constitutional restriction to a particular profession in your choice of judges, or sent you to the court of appeals for a certificate of qualifications for a clerk. We would not have insulted your understanding by a constitutional presumption, that unless the convention guided and restrained you, you would or might have selected men to administer the law who had never studied jurisprudence, or clerks, to keep the records, who knew not how to make an entry, or to write their names. Learning and talents of any sort were of no use, unless the community, the people, were judges of them. It is the reputation, the public admiration, that follows great attainments and great genius, in any department of social life, that makes men seek attainments, and that stimulates genius. Go into any community and seek the most profound lawyer, the ablest physician, the most erudite scholar, the orator who can rouse the understanding or stir the hearts of men, the people will tell you the man. Public opinion is the test of human merit. What is fame but the breath of the people? To what does genius, learning, poetry, eloquence, art, look at last, save the immortal wreath which fame holds forth to crown their labors? Holding in simple verity all these opinions—looking to you as the sovereign and master of our glorious country, which you are, and that same breath of yours, which we call fame, as the only hope which cheers us on through life—wè still urge it upon you to decline the power proffered you, and with manly candor which best becomes you and us, to give ear to our reason.

It is not the capacity of the appointing power which is the real subject of controversy. It is the effect of that power, and the relation which it bears to the judiciary. In this argument, by mutual concession, the independence of the judiciary is the thing sought. When the Governor and Senate make the appointment under the old Constitution, their power over the officer is exhausted. They can not remove him, they can not reappoint him—he holds his office during good behavior—he has nothing to hope or fear from that source, whence he derived his commission. So far as his judgment is to be influenced by them, according to the ordinary run of human motives, he is independent. The Governor is a single person, with himself a limited term of office. The Senate is a small body of men, with an equally limited term. So far as any influence which they might exercise over the court indirectly from their dignity or official station is concerned, it must soon expire. Being few in number, it is not likely that they would be before the judge as suitors. At any rate, that is a difficulty which can not be avoided by any mode of appointment, and is reduced infinitely, as you reduce the number of persons concerned in the appointment. It is utterly impossible, but that a judge must come, when elected in the district where he is to preside, to decide causes between the friends that elected him, and the enemies who opposed him.

If any other power than your own were concerned, we are confident that you would perceive at once, under the arrangement of the Convention, that judicial independence was utterly prostrate at the foot of that power. You are the people, the sovereign, who, like the king, never dies, and, like the king, "can do no wrong." You are not like the governor and the Senate, representative officers, with short terms—you are eternal. Now suppose a monarch, (and there have been such, in the various experiments of mankind in government,) clothed with your powers, but still supposed in the administration of justice among his subjects, bound by certain laws, fixing and defining private rights of person and property. If he had the appointment of these judges, removable at his pleasure, do you not at once perceive that he could not only rule the State, but that he could come upon the person, into the bosom of the family, and upon the private estate of every subject in his dominion, through his agent and slave, the judge? Has not history, English history, with which we are best acquainted, demonstrated the truth of our proposition? Has nobody in Kentucky heard or read of the Star Chamber, or of Jeffreys? Suppose that, instead of removing him at pleasure, he had the power of appointing him for a limited term, but in case the judge during this term pleased his master, he could reäppoint him, would not the judge, in such case, be equally the slave of the appointing power—is there the slightest difference? If the king could appoint during good behavior—the question of good behavior to be tried by some other tribunal than himself—or for a limited term, the judge not being again appointable, in either case the officer would be independent, and might be just if he willed it—at least he would be free from influence. Predicate the same state of things of an aristocratic council, the Senate of Venice for instance, and you will instantly perceive, that you have made an absolute government. Take a democratic assembly—history furnishes examples of every sort—take the French Convention from 1792 to 1794, with its revolutionary tribunal, and you will see the principle fully exemplified.

The organization of the reign of terror—the awful power of Robespierre and the Jacobin club, bloody, boundless, murderous, wielding the guillotine, and leveling society with the ax, would have been incomplete without a dependent judiciary—a court appointed by the supreme democratic power, and removable at its pleasure. Tyranny, rapacious power, throughout all time, has felt its aims incomplete, until it has acquired the absolute control of those tribunals which decide upon private rights, and administer law to the people. The effort of the new Constitution, to fix the term of office, within which term, the advocates of that instrument contend the judge to be independent, is a perfect delusion. If I appoint an agent for a limited time, with a salary upon which he is to furnish bread to his wife and children, with the power, at the end of that time, of reäppointing him, or putting another in his place—is he not, during that period, by the hope of continuance in his office, as much the slave of my pleasure and my will, as though I had the power of removal at any moment? It is evident, too evident for argument, that the Convention have prostrated the judges at the foot of what they call the people, that is the majority, the ruling party or influences in the district where they are chosen. To make our view of this great subject perfectly intelligible, we must refer again to the natural distinctions between the legislative and executive, and the judicial functions. You are empowered by your constitutions, State and national—constitutions established by your own authority—to elect your executive and legislative officers, and they are reëligible. They are your representatives, the slaves of your will, and they ought to be so. They are made so by this feature of reëligibility, a feature left out of the executive department, and, in our judgment, improperly left out, both in the old and the new Constitution of Kentucky.

We will take our examples, for argument, from the highest of these functionaries, the President and the Congress of the United States. They are your representatives. Are they not your servants, the slaves of your will? Did you not design to make them so? They ought to be so. They are so. Now look at the President of the United States, the highest public functionary, in our judgment, in this world. How is he appointed? A party convention meets and nominates their candidate, upon certain avowed principles of public policy, to which he is pledged. Another party convention meets, and upon opposite principles, nominates another candidate. The people choose between them. The majority decide the controversy, and the person elected represents this majority. Do we object to this? Not at all. The powers of this officer relate to public affairs, and they should be administered according to the public will, which can not be gathered so fairly from any other source as the voice of a majority. Observe, though, how perfectly he represents that majority. To execute their will, and carry out the system of measures and policy which they have decreed, it is necessary for him to appoint a number of officers subordinate to himself. He appoints ministers, embassadors, consuls, etc., to conduct our foreign relations. Let any one who voted against him, not of his party, opposed to his political views, we care not what his abilities, his learning, his reputation—let such an one apply for station or appointment under the government—will he get it? You know he can not. Do we complain of this? Not in the least. No man has a right to office. Offices were created for the public good, not for the advantage of private individuals. If a political friend of the President be appointed minister to France or England, who has a right to complain on the score of private injury, and what boots it to the public, so the duties be discharged. But when the question is, whose land, or house, or money is this? When a charge of treason or felony hangs over me, and my life or liberty is involved, these are private matters, to be decided by a fixed law, and not according to the discretion or caprice of men or parties, of president or people.

Between the legislative, the representative branches of government, and the judicial, there is this ruling distinction. The first under the instruction of the community should have the most absolute discretion. They should be free to choose, according to circumstances, the course to be pursued. The latter is without any discretion at all. We beg leave to explain this distinction somewhat at large. There are persons among us who complain of the voluminous and complicated nature of our jurisprudence. They seem to regard it as the contrivance of lawyers, for the purpose of obscuring what might be rendered plain, and thereby making themselves necessary to the community for the purpose of unraveling a labyrinth, which they themselves have devised, and to which they alone hold the clue. A voluminous body of law is a part of the price of liberty. It may be an inconvenience, but a very little reflection will satisfy any one that it is the absolutely necessary consequence of the first idea and principle of civil liberty. In a despotic government, the judge, the creature of the prince, need not decide by any anterior rules. His decrees are but the arbitrary decisions of his master. They do not form a rule either for himself or future judges in the administration, not of law, but of a capricious will in the settlement of disputes among men. In a free country, that is in a country where civil and personal rights are defined, and where law is not an arbitrary decision of the magistrate, but a fixed rule which controls the judge himself, law becomes a body of precedents. The rule which has been applied by previous judges must be pursued. It is not so important what the law is, as that it should be fixed. Certainty and stability are the great requisites in a jurisprudence for freemen. The successive decisions of judges must be published and known, for the guidance of future judges, that like law may be administered in like cases, that the course of justice may be uniform. Were it otherwise, the power of the judicial magistrate would be arbitrary. His own will, and not the precedent rule, would guide him. This voluminousness and apparent complication of jurisprudence, is a necessary consequence of free institutions.

In reply to all this reasoning of ours, our adversaries say, you have shown that the judicial power, if controlled by any other in the State, becomes the most formidable and oppressive. That under its exercise, when guided and controlled by any other authority than its own, power becomes absolute, and the rights, property and liberty of individuals are left without security.

How happens it, they say, that the judges, with a power so

formidable, left in their own hands independent and uncontrolled, do not themselves become absolute and despotic? In avoiding absolutism in other branches of government, or in the people themselves, you are piling the most absolute power in the hands of a magistracy which you seek to make irresponsible. We state these objections to our own argument with more force and fairness than any of our adversaries with whom we have fallen in. In truth, they seem to know, or to have thought little of the matter. We do it of purpose, that you may have the whole subject before you. We could not deceive you if we would—we are very sure we would not if we could. We reserve for our next number the consideration of those circumstances, in the nature of the judicial office, which make it the safest of all the depositories of power, when left free from fear or favor, and the most dangerous and terrible if controlled by other powers than its own.

THE OLD GUARD—JUDICIARY.

NO. III.

In our last number, we think we have shown the importance of an independent judiciary to the limited constitution of a free people; indeed that is admitted on all hands in the argument. The real question is, how that independence is best to be secured. We endeavored to show in our previous reasoning, the natural distinction that exists between the legislative and judicial powers and functions, in a free State; that the first represents the will of the community, and ought to represent that will in relation to matters that were common to all, that were naturally public and political—that the latter represented a fixed law that was designed to regulate disputes about private rights, either of person or property, occurring between different members of the same community, or between the State, the whole body, and a private member.

We have endeavored to illustrate our idea by the case of a single individual, managing his own estate and those affairs peculiarly his own, and the case of the same individual having a dispute with some one else in relation to a matter of property or right claimed by an other. In the latter case, we have endeavored to show that the common arbiter, to settle the difference and adjust the question, should be independent of the parties to the dispute, and appointed by some other power. Since the appearance of our argument, it has been suggested that we have made a case against ourselves. That we have, in the private dispute, used for illustration, made the very case in which the parties may choose an arbitrator or arbitrators, and are authorized to do so by the existing laws—and they liken this choice to an elective judiciary. We thank our adversaries for the suggestion. In the case of a dispute between two private individuals, the law does, indeed, wisely authorise a reference to arbitrators. But in this case, each party concerned chooses a judge. Each judge represents the party selecting him, and the rule refers the appointment of the ultimate arbiter—umpire as he is called in law—not to the parties, but to the court so constituted. Now this arbitration, by the vote and consent of the parties to the dispute, is to be distinguished most evidently from an elective judiciary, in the following particulars. In the case of arbitrators, each party is represented, and when they differ, the decisive voice, the umpire, is selected by the court. In an elective judiciary, where the community, of course, is divided in the choice of a judge, the majority alone is represented. The voice of the minority is lost. If you would, in every instance, let the majority choose one-half the court, the minority the other, and, in case of a difference of opinion, let the court itself choose an umpire, you would liken an elective judiciary to a board of arbitrators chosen by the parties. But what mortal, whose rights were involved in a dispute with an other, would be willing to refer the question to a court chosen entirely by his adversary? Yet this is precisely the position of the minority, or any member of a minority, in a State, where the judges are to sit upon the trial of private causes, or of causes in which the constitution of the country is involved, causes which can never occur, except upon alleged violations of the fundamental law, by a majority, and are themselves chosen by, and represent that majority.

In a dispute between an individual asserting the constitution of his country against the will of a majority, which he asserts to have violated that constitution, how, in the name of the ordinary principles of human nature, can he expect a fair trial of the question from judges appointed by, and dependent upon the very party whom he is accusing, and against whom he is seeking justice. We think we are understood. We shall recur, however, to the same principles, and retrace the same argument when we come to consider the legislative power and examine the manner in which this truly elective branch of free government has been handled by the convention.

If it be not evident, from our previous argument, that the election of judges to private causes and constitutional questions, coupled with their reëligibility, by a simple majority of the community, subjects the will of the judges and the constitution of the country to the will of that majority for the time—that it destroys all idea of a fixed jurisprudence—that it breaks down all limitations in government—that it makes the will of the majority supreme, absolute, uncontrolled, despotic, not only in the direction of public affairs, but in the administration of justice and the decision of causes between man and man—then we despair of our powers of argument or discussion—and if we have shown this, then it follows that an elective judiciary, for a limited term, and reëligible, makes a simple democracy, and destroys the great leading fundamental idea of American liberty with which we set out.

We might, perhaps, rest the argument here. In the close, however, of our last number, with the utmost fairness, we stated certain difficulties thrown in our way by our adversaries, or, rather, we stated certain objections which fair and philosophic opponents might be supposed to urge against our position. We proceed to answer them. We will endeavor to answer them fully, and in doing so, must sometimes recur to, and rely upon principles heretofore stated, and, we think, proven by ourselves.

We proceed with our argument in answer to the objections, the strongest we know of, as stated by ourselves in the close of our last address to you. We are constantly told, we are annoyed with the oft-repeated tale, that our mode of reasoning is too profound, that there is too much the air of science, too much of the scholastic about our method of handling political subjects for the people. Various persons, even among our friends, say that we lay the foundation of our reasoning too deep for the popular comprehension. Such persons wish us to split our articles into short paragraphs, cut up to suit what they call the popular appetite. They conceive the people of Kentucky incapable of comprehending a regular and consistent argument upon government. They may be right. If they are, however, our hope is lost. A people who can not comprehend an argument upon government are not fit for self-government. The brutal ignorance which those who oppose us suppose to exist in the community, presupposes a state of things which would render democratic government the most execrable form of dominion ever exercised over men—the dominion of brute force and brute ignorance over intellect and property. We have, ourselves, an abiding confidence in the general intelligence and good sense of the people of Kentucky. We address ourselves to it, and shall continue to do so—should we fail, the consciousness of having discharged our duty will afford some consolation even in defeat.

We state then to you, as an American idea, lying as the broad basis at the bottom of our whole institutions, that an independent judiciary is the foundation of our peculiar system of civil liberty.

This system of courts which are to decide between man and man upon questions of private right—upon matters of property between individuals, or upon matters that may arise between the citizen as an individual and the government—between the entire community and a single man, should be independent of the parties between whom they are to decide. This is our proposition. We know that many of you, probably a large majority of you, object to the present constitution, because you say that the judicial office under it is a life estate. You considered the liability to impeachment and trial, through your representatives, or to removal by an address of two-thirds of the legislature, as an insufficient guarantee of good conduct in your judges. We know this. You wished your judges appointed for a limited term. We will discuss this matter with you as reasonable men arguing a great subject with a great and sensible people.

We have already said, and we take occasion to repeat it, that the real question does not involve the capacity of the appointing power. The question is as to the independence of the Judiciary when appointed. Were the governor and the senate permanent bodies, with the power of appointment and removal, or what is the same thing, of reäppointment in cases the judges pleased them, we would die in opposition to such a a government—no hell could be worse. It is not that the people are incapable of judging of personal worth or merit—it is not that they do not understand the qualifications of distinguished citizens, for public office of any sort, legislative, executive, or judicial—it is upon no such ground that we found our objection to the plan of the convention.

The old constitution designed to make the Judiciary independent—that was the object. We have, in part, reviewed and commented upon the means they employed. There is an imperfection, an evident deficit in the mode of their work. They have left the Judiciary, so far as their salaries are concerned, absolutely in the power of the legislature. It is competent for the legislative branch, by reducing the salaries, to starve the judges off the bench, whenever they become obnoxious or disagreeable to that arm of the government. He who holds another's bread in his hand, who can furnish or withhold the means of subsistence to himself, his wife, his children, is the master, and can command the services, and lord it over the will of the person so situated. Had the old constitution placed within itself a minimum judicial salary below which the legislature could not reduce it, or declared that the legislature should have no power to reduce the salaries of the judges when once fixed by law, during their continuance in office—the means would have been all shaped to the end, and, we could have tested fairly and certainly the wisdom of the design.

We desire to make this point entirely clear—it is urged as an objection to the old constitution on the ground of a departure from its own principles, or rather a failure to adjust the means precisely to the clear and avowed object of the instrument. In the constitution of the Judiciary, according to the principles which we have stated, and from which we reason, there are two leading objects, two great ends to be attained. One is to secure, in the most important of the branches of political administration, the highest talents, learning and character. The other is to place these high qualities, when secured to the public service, in a position to exert their most beneficial influence and action, by removing every sinister motive resulting from hope or fear, from favor or affection, from love or hate.

The State can not secure to her service the highest talents without paying what the commodity she requires will command in the market of the world. The qualities necessary to complete the character of a great judge are not so abundant as to glut the market. They are rare, they are of exceeding value, and must needs be costly. He who will follow out the principle strictly, and means to secure a Judiciary at once able and free, will provide an independent support for the judges, and place their pecuniary compensation beyond the reach or control of those whom the Judiciary are designed to curb and to restrain. Under our reasoning, it would, at first blush, seem that the new constitution was an improvement, in this particular, upon the old. The proposed instrument provides that the salaries of the judges, when fixed by law, shall not be reduced during the term of office. High salaries, so efficient to attract great talents, and the independence of those salaries of the legislature, so mighty to make the judges free from fear of other branches of the government, under the new constitution, become aggravated, and intense causes of dependence, fear and servility on the part of the judges. We beg leave to explain this position and this distinction somewhat at length.

Under the old constitution, offer a permanent and ample salary, sufficient to attract men of the first order of learning and talents, and you have them—at least, you can have them—and they are independent judges. Under the new constitution, give high salaries to your judges, and what is the consequence? You will, no doubt, have men of the first order candidates for the judicial office. But when elected, with the understanding that, if agreeable to the party that elected them, they can be reëlected, and hold on by this tenure of pleasing their friends or masters, who does not at once perceive, that the larger the salary, the more valuable the office, the more intensely you subject the functionary to the power that appoints him. Fair salaries, salaries sufficient to command the services of men of the first order, under this arrangement, become the very means of corrupting the Judiciary to the last degree. We mean to deal with you and the question before us with the utmost candor. We will not say that it was the precise aim of the convention to destroy the republic. We will not charge upon that body the deliberate purpose to destroy all limitations in government, and to break down a free commonwealth to the level and condition of one of the miserable, jarring, wrangling, banishing, proscribing, murderous, faction-ridden democracies of ancient Greece or modern Italy—Athens or Florence, if you please. But this we say—whatever they mean, the effect of their measures and their plan terminates in that result. We have said the people were as capable of electing judges of competent ability and learning as the governor and the senate. We have said that we believed that you were dissatisfied with the tenure of the judicial office, as established by the present constitution—that you desired a limited term—a fixed period at which the judicial office should terminate.

The people of Kentucky were satisfied with the principle upon which their constitution rested in relation to the Judiciary. The error, the defect, was such as we have stated. It is not fair to charge any failure in this branch of our government—if, indeed, there has been any failure, upon the appointing power. To have made the old instrument complete, to have carried out its purpose, it would have been necessary to have given constitutional salaries, to have rendered the judges independent of the legislature. We speak of this as a defect, because it was a failure to carry out fully the design, the end of the framers of the constitution, by an exact and perfect adaptation of the natural and appropriate means to that design.

There are various conceivable modes of constituting the Judiciary. They may be considered in reference to the tenure of office or the mode and source of appointment. The present method, in relation to both tenure and appointment, might be changed or modified, and the great principle, the ruling object which is, if not conceded, at least assumed in this argument, still be preserved. This great principle, this ruling object, is the independence of the courts, no matter how constituted. We have said so often, in the course of our argument, that we surely need not repeat it; that, in our judgment, the people are competent to select judges. If they elected their judges during good behavior, which is the present tenure of office, the only difference between that mode of appointment and the present, as bearing upon the independence of the Judiciary, would be this. The governor and the senate being few in number, and with a limited term of official existence, could hardly be expected to come before the judge in the character of parties. By the act of appointment their power is exhausted. To them the judge is not, and can not be rendered responsible in any way for any decision he may make. There is no permanent relation, no continuing tie between the appointing power and the officer, which can influence his will or enslave his judgment in the discharge of his duties. The governor and the senate cease, in a short time, to be governor and senate, and there is no conceivable source of influence or corruption from the appointing power, unless the very remote one, that some of them may become parties in a suit before the court, and the judge be swayed or affected by gratitude for the vote he may have received, or anger from the opposition to his nomination. In an election by the people, the judge presiding among those who chose him, it is obvious that he must be swayed, even though he hold his office during good behavior, by the feelings engendered by the popular contest through which he has passed in his way to the bench. This is the only difference between the two modes of appointment, the tenure being as at present. This difference operating upon the independence and impartiality of the courts was the reason why the present mode of appointment was preferred. The people of Kentucky, we verily believe, without wishing to destroy the independence of their Judiciary, desired to change the tenure of office, and fix it at a limited term, instead of during good behavior. We will not, it is not necessary that we should, discuss this question. We have already said enough to show that the old constitution was imperfect on its own principle. That for want of fixed and independent salaries, the appointing power was, to some extent, crippled, and could not command, to the service of the State, the highest talents and the richest qualities required. If this provision were incorporated in the present constitution, if a constitutional salary, independent of the legislature, were provided for the courts, and the appointing power thus enabled to select the highest talents from the bar, we would be enabled to judge fairly the soundness of the principle adopted by the convention of 1799. Even with this manifest imperfection, this departure in a very important particular from its own principle, the practical working of the machine has been eminently successful. The Judiciary of Kentucky, taken collectively, will challenge a comparison with that of any State of the Union. The decisions of her highest court are cited as authority every where. They form a part of the library of distinguished lawyers every where in America. New editions of our reports are publishing in other States, and are sought after with an avidity that prove their importance and their value. Kentucky has no reason to blush for her Judiciary. Indeed the convention itself has paid it the highest compliments, at the expense of those branches of the government which have always been elective.

Were you to change the present constitution in relation to the Judiciary, leaving the appointing power where it is, but limiting the term of office to a stated number of years—mark the consequences. In the first place, if you desired (of which we have no doubt) to command to your service the ablest men among you, you would be compelled to give higher salaries than you do at present. The machinery, if it were made effective, of necessity would be more expensive. No man would quit his business, abandon the lucrative pursuit of his profession, to serve the State for a limited time, at the same price for which he would undertake the same office during good behavior. We do not deny in this argument that you might have an independent judge for a limited term. It is evident, however, to your common sense that he would cost you more. If you preferred electing him yourselves, to having him appointed in the present mode, you might still preserve his independence. He would, to be sure, as already indicated in our argument, be exposed to partial judgment, from his affections and passions, springing from the popular contest through which he had risen to the bench—in other respects, and as far as the appointing power had any continued authority over him, he would, or at least might, be free. The convention, however, have done nothing like this. They have made the judges elective by the people. They have made them elective for short terms. They have made them reëligible. They have not fixed a minimum salary in the constitution, but they have declared that the salary of a judge, as fixed by law, shall not be reduced during his term of office. This latter principle, so important to an independent judiciary, becomes not only powerless, but absolutely mischievous under the new arrangement.

We beg leave to explain this idea of ours somewhat at large. We have explained until we fear we have wearied you, that the power of reäppointing an officer or agent, is precisely the same in effect, with the power of removing or displacing that officer or agent at pleasure. A king, or an aristocratic council, who could appoint a judicial magistrate for a limited term, but with the power to reäppoint him indefinitely, provided he pleased his employers, has precisely the same control over the will and the actions of that magistrate, as though the same king or council could remove the officer at pleasure. There is not the slightest difference so far as the question of freedom or dependence is concerned. The salaries given to the judges under a system designed to secure their independence, are the most powerful among the instruments shaped to secure this result. Under the new Constitution, should the legislature give high salaries, they will be the means of corrupting the Judiciary to the utmost extent, of this most extensive scheme of corruption. Give to a circuit judge, or a judge of the appellate court, an annual allowance sufficient to support himself and family, his wife and children, in comfort. Give him enough to educate his offspring, to indulge them while rearing, in the luxuries, the pleasures of life, and place him in a position that all this is to be lost, that he is to be thrown back upon his own resources, his own efforts, with the disadvantage of having been removed from the scene of contest, of having lost his business, is it not at once perceived, that the amount of the salary, the value of the office, becomes an intense source of influence, a powerful and overruling motive, by which a magistrate, so situated, is subjected, absolutely, to those who have appointed him, and can continue him in his office. The worst feature in an elective and reëligible Judiciary is, that the high salaries, so necessary to secure the highest order of talent to the service of the State, become, under this system, the very means of corruption. The aliment, the food of an independent judiciary, under a sound system, becomes under this, the poison which taints, vitiates corrupts and destroys.

High salaries, under the present constitution, are the means by which you can attract to your service the ablest men of the State. High salaries, if the legislature choose to give them, are the means by which your new judges will be bought and bribed to serve the power which elects them. If you do not pay them well, you will have a worthless set of servants. If you give the compensation necessary to secure talent, you will have, by means of that very compensation, a set of slaves bowing to the will and obeying the mandates of the power that appointed, and can continue them in office, and will, upon the condition of obedience.

We have reasoned thus far to show the importance of an independent judiciary. The difficulty suggested by ourselves, that a Judiciary constituted upon our principle, holds a power dangerous in any hands, that it is itself a despotism, and a despotism coming into the very bosom, the every day rights and pursuits of men, remains to be answered and removed.

Take away fear or hope, and remove the dread of consequences—and of all the functions to be discharged in life—that of deciding questions of mere right between individuals with neither of whom the arbiter is connected, is the least exposed, according to the ordinary principles of human nature, to abuse or corruption. There is not a man in the world, who would not, if you will remove all temptation, of fear, or interest, prefer right to wrong. Go to the antipodes and bring me a human being, I care not how corrupted, how debased—he may have been exiled, transported to Botany Bay for his crimes—he may have been cast in a state of society where all the higher walks of life, all the nobler avocations by which fame is won, and honor and wealth and reputation earned, are crowded, till in despair he has become a wretch and turned in wrath a felon against his species—but bring him, outcast, exile, felon though he be, to decide where he has no interest, no hope, no fear, between two men upon a question of property, of liberty or of right, and he will decide according to the promptings of truth and justice. The very crimes in which he may have been steeped; the very infamy in which he may have been overwhelmed; the very curse of his species, the condemnation of mankind, which rests upon his name, will form a motive in addition to the instinctive love of truth and justice which forms a part of our nature, to insure a righteous judgment. Bring a man from the other side of the globe, let the parties between whom he is to decide be strangers to him; let it be understood, that so soon as the judgment is rendered, he is to be carried back, that there is to be no further connection of any sort between him and the litigants, and what is there to tempt him to a corrupt judgment? Place the Judiciary in a position where they are unawed by power, and free from the influence of affection or of hate, and it would seem impossible but that they should be pure.

Powerful as are the judiciary for good, they seem to be impotent for mischief. They can levy no tax, raise no revenue, command no army. They have no purse, wield no sword. In the judgments they pronounce they are governed by a fixed law, which excludes all arbitrary discretion. The parties who come before them are represented by men whose profession and business it is to understand the law, and who scrutinize, with sleepless and searching vigilance, the decisions of the court. There is no department of government exposed to so watchful an observation as the Judiciary. They are sometimes said to be irresponsible. It is an utter mistake. No branch of government, no public functionary whatever, no agent in human affairs is subjected to a closer and more constant observation, to a scrutiny so thorough and searching.

If we have not failed utterly in our purpose, we have established clearly two or three very important political propositions. We have striven—and we hope not in vain—to show that there is a distinction growing out of the nature of their respective functions, between the legislative and judicial departments of government, which renders the one representative strictly in its character, but which requires the other to be independent, or it fails in the object of its creation. We have shown, we think, conclusively, that in any form of government, other than the democratic, if you render the Judiciary dependent upon the ruling political power of the State, you have destroyed every security for individual rights, and subjected the community absolutely to that power. The plan of the convention subjects the Judiciary constantly, intensely, to the will and the passions of the party which elects them. It converts the judge into a politician. It makes him the representative and instrument of faction, instead of the organ and mouthpiece of a fixed and stable law. It carries through every part and parcel of the social order, absolute, irresistible, irresponsible power. It will convert a free republic, with a limited constitution and a fixed body of law, into a simple democracy, without check or balance, restraint or responsibility.

And this they call progress. They throw off all the guards, that the accumulated experience of thirty centuries have shown to be necessary to every form of human power. They go back to the first crude experiments in government; experiments made in the infancy of society and of knowledge, and from which men have every where fled with terror, and vaunt of these long exploded errors, as grand discoveries, the wonderful inventions of modern genius.

Had the convention limited the judicial term of office with the appointing power where it is, they would have imposed upon the government a more costly machinery, but the courts might still have been independent, and capable of performing their appropriate functions in the social economy. Had they wished to change the appointing power, as well as to alter the tenure and limit the term, they might have made them eligible by the people in a manner and upon conditions that would have preserved the great principle of independence. The plan they have adopted, however, is shaped with the utmost ingenuity to destroy all that has heretofore, in this country, been considered as constituting the purity and usefulness of the courts, the stability and certainty of jurisprudence, the supremacy of the constitution, the safety and the liberty of individuals.

THE OLD GUARD—JUDICIARY.

NO. IV.

We resume to-day our own discussion, in our own way. We have already argued the general question of an elective judiciary at such length, that we fear we have wearied you. In this number, in which we design to conclude the subject, we shall go more minutely into the particular provisions of the new Constitution, and examine them more in detail, in relation to the judicial branch of the government, than was consistent with our previous general view of the general question. We have discussed separately the various propositions involved in the single question of an elective judiciary. In the further prosecution of our argument, we shall consider the principles on which we rely, as proven and established, and shall proceed to compare the details with the principles. We desire further to collect together—to sum up the result of our argument—to present, without further discussion of the particular principles, in one general view, and in connected order, the sum of all the propositions we have sought to establish. When we have done this, we shall have closed the regular and elaborate examination of this branch of the great subject before us. Should we touch it again, it will be incidentally, and only by way of illustration, and as it stands in natural and necessary connection with other portions of the new Constitution which remain to be handled.

In the detailed examination upon which we are entering, we regret that our limits will not allow us to transcribe the entire article in relation to the judicial department. It is the fourth in order in the instrument itself. We shall cite from it, in some instances at large, the sections to which we wish more particularly to invite your attention.

In the constitution of the supreme court, you have doubtless observed that it is not a court chosen by the State at large. The commonwealth is to be broken into four districts, as nearly equal in voting population as may be, in each of which the qualified voters shall elect one judge. The term of office of these judges, after the first election, shall be for eight years. The judges at the first term of the court after the first election, are to determine by lot the length of time each shall serve. And in such manner that the term of one shall expire in 1852, the next in 1854, the third in 1856, and the fourth in 1858. After this, it will be perceived, that an election of one judge will take place every two years. The legislature are further empowered to reduce the number of judges and districts to three, upon the occurrence of a vacancy on the bench—in which case the term of office shall be so changed as to preserve the principle of electing one judge every two years. Should this reduction of the number of judges take place, you will at once perceive the necessity of reducing the term of office from eight to six years—in no other way could the principle be preserved. When a vacancy shall occur on the bench, from any cause, the governor shall issue a writ of election, to the proper district, to fill such vacancy for the residue of the term. We have cited with the utmost exactness the provisions of the Constitution in relation to the supreme court upon which we mean particularly to comment. There is, however, before we pass to the consideration of the other and inferior branches of the Judiciary, one provision in relation to the supreme court, so curious, so mysterious, so utterly unreachable by any power of legal construction, or philological criticism of which we are masters, that we must claim your patience and your pardon for introducing the section at large. It is the 15th section of the 4th article, and is couched in these oracular words:

"Whenever an appeal or writ of error may be pending in the court of appeals, on the trial of which a majority of the judges thereof can not sit, (*or*) on account of interest in the event of the cause, or on account of their relation to either party, or where *the judge* may have decided in the inferior court, the general assembly shall provide by law for the organization of a temporary and special court, for the trial of such cause or causes."

The judicial power of the commonwealth is declared to be vested in this supreme court, thus constituted, and the courts established by this Constitution, and such inferior courts as the general assembly may, from time to time, erect and establish.

There is established by the Constitution, a circuit court for each county now existing, or which may hereafter be established. The general assembly, at their first session after the adoption of the new Constitution, are required to divide the State into twelve judicial districts, having due regard to business, territory, and population. In each district a judge shall be elected for the particular district, and shall hold his office for the term of six years, with the proviso, however, that the term of the first judges, elected in May, 1851, shall expire on the first Monday in August, 1856. The general assembly are empowered to establish an additional district every four years, till they amount to sixteen, after which there shall be no increase in the number until the population of the State shall exceed one million five hundred thousand. The judges shall, at stated times, receive salaries to be fixed by law, which shall not be diminished during the term for which they were elected. If a vacancy shall occur, the governor shall issue a writ of election to fill the vacancy for the residue of the term, provided that if it be less than one year, the governor may appoint for the remainder of the term.

"The general assembly shall provide by law for some person to preside in each of the circuit courts, when from any cause the judge shall fail to attend, or if in attendance, can not properly preside." The qualifications of the judges of the court of appeals and the circuit courts are the same. Citizenship of the United States; two years residence in the district for which he is a candidate, next preceding the election; thirty years of age, and eight years practice of law or service on the bench, are the tests established for both. The removal of a judge from his district vacates his office.

A county court shall be established in each county, now existing, or which may hereafter be established, to consist of a president and two associates, any two of whom shall constitute a court for the transaction of business—they are to be elected by the qualified voters of the county for the term of four years, and shall receive such compensation for their services as may be provided by law. Their jurisdiction is to be regulated by law, and until changed shall be the same as is now vested in the county courts. The qualifications for these offices, are citizenship of the United States, twenty-one years of age, and residence in the county one year next preceding the election.

The several counties shall be laid off into districts of convenient size, and two justices elected in each district by the qualified voters, for the term of four years. The qualifications of these are, citizenship of the United States, twenty-one years of age, and residence in the district for which they may be chosen. The general assembly are empowered to make these justices members of the county court, at the court of claims, and in laying the county levy and making appropriations. The general assembly are also empowered to abolish the office of associate judge of the county court, and make the justices, in that event, members of the court for the transaction of all business. Removal from the county or district for which they may have been elected, vacates all these offices. These officers are all reëligible. There is a peculiarity in the arrangement of the periods at which the various elections are to take place, to which we would call your attention. The first election of the legislative branches of the government under the Constitution, is to be held in August, 1851, which will throw the election upon the odd year always for those officers, as 51, 53, 55, etc., which will happen in the case of both Senate and House of Representatives. The elections for all the judicial officers, from the supreme court to the justices of the peace, with their ministerial officers, clerks, sheriffs, constables, etc., are so arranged, that the first election is to be held not in August, but in May, 1851, and infringing the terms assigned to them by the Constitution at the first election, their respective officers are to be vacated the first time in the even years, as 1852, '54, '56, '58, etc. As in the case of the court of appeals—one judge elected in 1851, goes out in '52, the next in '54, the next in '56, and the next in '58, shortening the term by one year; and so with all the rest. The object of this arrangement is obviously to prevent the political and judicial elections from being thrown together. The meaning and spirit of it was a distrust of the elective principle, not upon the grounds which we have assumed, not for reasons growing out of the different nature of the political and judicial functions, but from real distrust of the people themselves, and a vain effort by separating the time, to sever the connection between the judicial and merely ministerial officers, and the party and political passions which for ever prevail in democratic societies. A happy device this most certainly, and at the same time a large concession to the opponents of the new Constitution.

Although not in exact connection with the view we are taking of the judicial department, we here call your attention to the condition in which the Convention leave the electors, the people themselves. Each county in the State, as you are aware, is to be laid off into precincts of convenient size, with regard to the qualifications of voters, the most invaluable of the franchise of the citizen; we beg leave to quote the section entire. It is the 8th section of the 2d article, and is in the following words:

"Every free white male citizen of the age of twenty-one years, who has resided in the State two years, or in the county, town, or city in which he offers to vote, one year next preceding the election, shall be a voter; *but such voter shall have been, for sixty days next preceding the election, a resident of the precinct in which he offers to vote, and he shall cast his vote in said precinct, and not elsewhere.*"

We have reason to believe that there are many places in the State where the new Constitution has not been circulated to any great extent. And by consequence, and from the shortness of the time allowed by the convention before the election, a great number of you have had no opportunity of examining its provisions minutely for yourselves. We have been, therefore, thus particular in going into its details, and, in some instances, quoting it literally and at large. For those who have had leisure and opportunity to study it carefully, this synopsis and these details are unnecessary—a hint or an allusion, in most instances, would be sufficient to make our argument intelligible.

From this review of the judicial department, it is evident that the revolution is thorough, complete, radical. There is scarce a vestige or feature left of the scheme and plan of the old instrument by which we are enabled even to trace its ruins.

Not only is the appointing power and the tenure of office changed—not only are the judges made elective by the people, and the tenure of office limited to a term of years—changes which we have admitted, and shown might have been made, and if connected with ample and permanent salaries, might have secured at a greater expense, and at some greater exposure to the influence of the passions, an upright, an able, and an independent judiciary—not only is the independence of the Judiciary utterly broken down by the feature of reëligibility, but the commonwealth itself is broken to pieces. There is no State judiciary, deriving their offices from a common source, and acknowledging a common authority. The representative principle is not only carried throughout the system —not only are the judges changed from passionless organs of a fixed law, into the political servants, necessarily, aye, and rightfully, according to the new theory, the mere agents of the will of those who elected and can reëlect them—but the last hope of a stable law, of the unity of our jurisprudence, is destroyed by breaking the State into fractions, and making the judges the representatives of the various wills or passions of these various little independent judicial democracies. We have said that we would not reärgue the propositions with which we set out—we will consider them as proven. We do beseech you, however, rigorously to apply the principles which your ancestors and yourselves certainly, until within these few years, deemed essential to your security and your freedom—to apply them rigorously to the system of government now submitted to you, and if it be found to reverse them all, to fail in every demand made by them, all and singly, in every part and in every form to fail, in the name of experience and your own history and memories, and of all the consistency becoming a great and free and stable people, fling it from you with scorn and disgust. What is there in your recollections of the past that should make you weary of interpreters of the law, rendered as independent as the nature of things will admit, of the overbearing influence of wealth and power, placed as far above the sweeping fury of the storm of parties as the strong scaffolding of the constitution can be made to bear them up. The convention are evidently disgusted with those branches of the government heretofore elective. They have sat as a legislature, not as a convention—they have run out their constitution into all the cumbrous detail of a statute. They are afraid to trust your representatives to assemble more than once in two years—they have taken from them all discretion as to the time they are to occupy, and fixed and limited it themselves. They have left them nothing to do when they do assemble—but chalked out for them, in the most minute detail, the whole career of legislation upon the most important subjects. They have fixed the taxes and the system of taxation—they not only will not permit the legislature to appropriate over an hundred dollars, save on conditions equivalent to an executive veto, but have put it out of their power to lower, to modify, or alter the taxes. They have deprived your real representatives almost entirely of all discretion in the management of your public affairs. They have made no complaint of the judges—they have not abridged their powers or jurisdiction. In the constitution of the Judiciary, indeed, they have shown their usual distrust of the legislature. The old constitution made the supreme court a constitutional court, and made it independent entirely of the legislature, but left the circuit courts and subordinate tribunals subject to legislative reorganization, according to the changing circumstances of the country, the demands and the convenience of the people. The new constitution has made the circuit courts constitutional courts. They have reduced the judicial districts to the number of twelve. They have pointed out, as if endowed with omniscience, the precise times at which any increase may be made—one in every four years may be added, till they reach sixteen, and then stop, till the population attain to a million and a half. Never, never did any body of men manifest so deep a distrust of the representative and popular principle. And yet condemning, branding it where it existed, they have carried it into a department where it was not before—a department to which, organized as they found it, they attached no blame, and whose powers they have not curtailed. But we were borne away by the current of our thoughts into a branch of the subject not now under review; we will consider the legislative department hereafter.

But this same distrust of the people, at whose feet they seem to fawn, and upon whose sovereign robes they spew the slaver of their insincere and filthy flattery, marks the arrangement of their elective judiciary. Although they have shown no distrust of the Judiciary, and expressed no censure upon its past conduct—imposed no restraint upon its powers, as they have done upon the legislature—yet, the moment they make it elective, they manifest the profound contempt and want of confidence they feel for the capacity of that very power in whose hands they have placed their appointment.

Why is it that they will not allow the elections of judges to come on the same year that political elections take place? Why? but that they suspect the judges will be placed on party tickets, along with candidates for congress, the senate, the legislature. Why? but that they dread the result of the tremendous experiment to which they urge you. Why? but that they have no confidence in the people in any thing. We have already, in a former number, examined the constitution of the supreme court in relation to the peculiar mode of choosing them by districts—the result of which is, that no one of all the qualified electors of Kentucky votes for more than one of a court composed of four judges. They are not elected by the State at all—so far as the court is concerned, there is no State. There is no authority common to the whole tribunal, and to which they all owe obedience. They are the representatives of distinct communities, formed for the purpose of electing judges, who are to carry out upon the bench the peculiar views of their own constituency, to whom alone they are responsible upon all matters of law or politics involved in the cases which may come before them. We have already briefly examined the structure of this court, and shown that the convention intended it as a conservative principle—a guard thrown around the terrible experiment they are making. We hope you will excuse us for recapitulating what we have said elsewhere, and for examining the form the convention have given to the supreme court with more particularity, and a narrower scrutiny than heretofore.

In our first number, we showed the grounds on which the friends of the new constitution vindicate this election of the supreme court by districts—grounds which we also showed, that they abandoned utterly in the constitution of the circuit courts. If, say they, you elected the whole court by the State at large, it would all be responsible to the dominant party in the State, and being reëligible, it would be the slave of that party, a mere political engine in the hands of a ruling faction. Very well, but this is a tremendous admission, say we, against an elective and reëligible judiciary. They proceed to argue, that they have parried the mischief inherent in the system—warded off the danger to which the elective principle, by their own admission, is for ever exposed by the district system. Each judge is responsible only to his own district—the remaining three are independent as to the fourth district, and so all round. A case comes up from the first district—the argument admits the judge from that district to be unfit to try it, for the very sufficient reason that he was chosen by it, and can be rechosen by it, and therefore will be subjected in his judgment to the ruling influences there. Instead of the law, he will represent the will of his constituents. But, say they, there will be three other judges on the bench exposed to no such influences. Those three will be independent, and can try the cause fairly. But we answer, each of these three are exposed to the same thing as it regards causes coming from their respective districts. Your conservative scheme, based upon a false and rotten principle, corrupts, necessarily, the whole court. Each of the four judges has a set of causes, coming from his own district, in which he is a partizan, not a judge. Each of the four judges has, therefore, in his hands, the means of purchasing the support of his associates. Says the first judge to the second, third and fourth, "gentlemen justices, here is a cause from my district which my interest requires should be decided in a particular way. One of the parties is very powerful in elections. He is leader of the democratic party—he has a large interest at stake in this cause, and if I go against him, at the next election he goes against me, and I lose my seat on this bench. There is no rivalry among us. Whether you be whig or democrat is immaterial. We represent different districts and can not interfere with each other. The beaten party in this cause can not hurt you. But remember, that each of you are precisely similarly situated in relation to causes from your own districts. Let us therefore understand each other. I will go for you if you will go for me. We never can be rivals. We represent different constituents, and if we will only help each other, can perpetuate our own power, and defeat all opposition that may arise against any of us at home, by union and mutual assistance here." In a court so constituted, there is no ground for jealousy. It will be the most magnificent theatre for log-rolling ever devised. Were they all dependent upon the same constituency—were they all elected by the same people—if three or one were inclined to play the rascal, the other or others could avail themselves of, at least, the aid of a minority at home, in the prosecution of an honest opposition. The argument which justifies the dismemberment of the commonwealth, and constitutes a court of four members, nominally elective, and yet no citizen voting for more than one, upon the ground alleged, at once destroys the representative principle, and admits that which proves the whole institution corrupt. We have already shown the glaring departure from the principle relied upon in this argument in the constitution of the circuit courts. We will not repeat what we have said before. We recur to the eternal truths founded in the nature of things, with which we set out. Truths, from which, the more our adversaries depart, the more they prove. The object of government among civilized men is peace and justice—the security of property, and the protection of personal liberty. Society has the right to govern itself.

But there are matters common to the whole society—there are other matters peculiar and belonging to individuals of right. The former are political, the latter are judicial. For the regulation and control of the first, a common council—call it a legislature—should be appointed by the free voice of the whole community. No restraints should be imposed upon such a council, except those necessary to protect private and individual rights and property from aggression. The judicial power being designed to decide, to arbitrate, under a fixed law, between the whole force of the community and a single individual, or between man and man, unequal in strength and influence, should be independent of the parties between whom it is to act as the umpire. In a most especial manner, it should be exempt, not only from the direct control, but from the indirect influence, from hope or fear, that may be held out by the ruling power in the State, in whatever hands that power may be placed. Without such a magistracy, there can be no security for persons or property. Without it liberty is brute license. With it, even in a despotism, there is some security for the fruits of industry, the earning of labor, and the great ends of civilization may be obtained. With a Judiciary independent of the emperor, China were preferable to Athens with judges chosen by the mob. These be our principles, openly avowed, boldly maintained, sustained by history and the experience of mankind, backed by reason and philosophy, and heretofore championed and borne aloft in the terrible struggles through which we have passed, by the votes, the sentiments, and, if need had been, by the valor and the poured out blood of a majority of the people of Kentucky. People of Kentucky! what are, and have been, since your commonwealth was founded, your favorite principles? What, we ask you again, what? We answer for you, and you will not dispute our response. The right of instruction and universal suffrage. If you make the Judiciary elective, will not the principles to which you are most attached, apply equally to this branch of magistracy with every other? You know they will. You know your demagogue reformer would flatter you into support of the new Constitution, by the very hope, that you will hereafter rule the courts, as you have ruled the legislature. In every case, be it treason, felony, or the right of property—a will upon which a large estate may be depending—whatever the feeling, real or supposed, of the people may be—the judge, the future representative of the people, bound by the will of his constituents, and deriving his power from the voice of universal suffrage, will be bound, not by the law, not by a long course of adjudications, but by that will and that voice.

Can you, gentlemen of Kentucky—can you be caught with this bate? There is a hook under it against which you have struggled for twenty-six years, within our memory, and struggled manfully and triumphantly. You have ruled yourselves, and you have ruled yourselves gloriously, prosperously, against all the principles contained in this infernal document. If we were inclined to be personal, we could very clearly show you the prime actors in this murderous tragedy—actors against whom it were easy, by past memories, to stir your utmost wrath. We could show you the same, the very same elements, once congregated and arrayed against the principles for which we are contending, under leaders now dead—once more assembled under the lead of those then in the ranks, but deeply, darkly, terribly imbued with the Jacobin spirit—a spirit rebuked, cowed, crushed by you in 1825—a spirit "scotched not killed," reäppearing under the prominent lead of one then a subaltern, a private—now a President, trampling on, overthrowing, Attila like, all the monuments erected by his former enemies.

Is the memory, and the sense, and the experience of Kentucky obliterate and lost? Have we forgotten relief and anti-relief, new and old court, and all the struggles that have followed since?

We understand—the Old Guard well understand the causes which led to the call of this convention—and others, we fear, will understand, before we are through with it, the dangers of that call. The majority in Kentucky, were in the minority in the Union; the minority in Kentucky were in the majority in the Union. The minority here, of course, called out for a change. Aristocracy was the cry. They mistook the cause of their local grievances, as the Whigs did their national. Whigs and Democrats are, in America, (the Guard fears no body, and speaks truth,) like Democrats and Aristocrats in Greece, Plebeian and Patrician in Rome, Guelf and Ghibeline in Italy, Whig and Tory in England, Royalist and Republican, Republican and Jacobin, Jacobin and Conservative in France—eternally seeking power, and vindicating their claim to power, by an appeal to the only legitimate source of power—the fountain of justice.

Human nature is always the same, and the Guard draws its maxims from the philosophy of mankind. Our principle is, (as we will demonstrate in the progress of our paper, if we have not already done it,) that men in the civilized state are necessarily, by the doom of nature, unequal. That the object of all law is to preserve equality of right, under inequality of condition; and that this can only be achieved by a system of fixed jurisprudence, interpreted by an independent judiciary. We have heretofore explained our idea of what an independent judiciary means. We shall even yet enlarge upon that subject, when we come to consider the legislative power, as treated by the new Constitution. We profess to believe in democratic progress. We trust, (God knows we do,) to that same progressive democratic power, for the ultimate liberation of mankind, from every chain but that of reason and prudence—from all thralldom but that which the divinity of justice and truth within him, necessarily imposes.

We have reasoned at some length, and with great pains, against a party who are determined to overthrow what we consider the true commonwealth. Do they answer us? Not at all, except by clamor and abuse. "Office-holders," "Old Hunkers," "Emancipationists." This is their whole cry—their only defense.

Do they interpret the new Constitution to the people? Not a bit of it—they suppress the paper. They resort to clamor. They cry out the right of the people. We acknowledge that dominion. Ah! say they, you deny the right of the majority to rule—you dispute the capacity of the people, of mankind, for self-government—you have thrown yourselves full across the path of popular progress, the march of the democratic principle in government.

What mean these men by self-government? Do they mean the right of each human being to control himself, to regulate his own actions, to shape his own conduct, by his own will, unconstrained by any other being? If so, how happens it upon the principle that men, all men, have a natural right to govern themselves—how happens it that a majority have a right to govern a minority, any more than a minority have a right to govern a majority? This rule of a majority is not self-government, it is the government of other people. Suppose thirty men thrown together, whence do sixteen of them derive their right to make the other fourteen obey their will? Upon the principle of self-government, the sixteen would have a perfect right to rule themselves; but surely upon the same principle the fourteen would have the same right to rule themselves. Suppose a million of men, or any other number, how happens it upon the principle of self-government, that of these, five hundred thousand and one, have the right against their consent and will, to subject the remaining four hundred and ninety-nine thousand nine hundred and ninety-nine, to whatever rule of action this larger number may choose to compose? Is this self-government in the majority? Certainly not, it is the government of others, against their consent. It is the subjection of the will of one set of men to the rule of another set of men. All government is the exercise of power by a portion of men over others. When men congregate together and form a social union, they agree to abandon the natural principle of self-government, and to submit to a control out of themselves, a control which is the result of convention and compact, and not of any fixed right. According to reason and nature, each man is his own master, with a perfect right to employ his own strength and faculties, for his own support, and in pursuit of his own ideas of happiness, but every other man having exactly the same right, there might arise collisions. Liberty, either natural or social, consists in the right in each individual, to do exactly what pleases himself, to regulate his own conduct according to his own will, provided he does not interfere with precisely the same right in others. The rational end of society is to render this liberty more perfect and secure. It should be an arrangement by which the strength of the whole is pledged to secure the rights of each, by which the weak should be protected against the power of the strong. In entering into society, men have a right to establish any form of government they please. Monarchy is as legitimate as aristocracy, and aristocracy as legitimate as democracy. It is a question of prudence. With the great end of the social union in view, to wit, the security of property and the protection of individuals, the maintenance of justice and peace, it is a matter of sound discretion for the societies of men, to throw themselves into any form best calculated to attain these objects. We are met perpetually with the question, have not the people a right to elect their own officers of every sort—judges, sheriffs, constables, clerks, every thing? Certainly they have, if they choose so to arrange in their fundamental law. But have they not a right not to elect them, if they choose, and if they judge their own peace, safety, property, and liberty will be better secured by a different mode of appointment? You have all power over the subject. It is a matter of prudence and discretion. It is for you to determine what mode will best secure the great ends of society, the rights and the liberties of individuals, and your right and power to adopt and pursue it can neither be disputed nor resisted.

THE OLD GUARD.

NO. V.

THE Legislative Department—Ben Hardin—Public Debt—Internal Improvement—The Public Expenditure—Sinking Fund.

WE commence to-day another branch of that mighty subject, which still stretches in unmeasured length before us. In imitation of our correspondent, "the Citizen," we put at the head of our leading article the matters of which we shall treat. We offer you the bill of fare, before we invite you to such a table as our means enable us to spread.

A very slight examination of the Constitution, and the most cursory glance at the published debates of the Convention, will satisfy any one that the Convention aimed their heaviest blows, that their real rage was directed against those branches of the old government heretofore elective and popular. They have not exactly assailed the representative principle in terms—but in the reörganization of the representative departments, they have manifested the most profound detestation and contempt for its results, after an experience of fifty years.

With the judges, sheriffs, clerks, jailers, constables, assessors, they have no fault to find, except that they have not been elective. The lists of property have been fairly taken, and valuations fairly made, the revenue faithfully collected and paid in, law process impartially executed, persons liable to imprisonment strictly confined according to the law, the records fairly kept, and justice faithfully administered. The whole machinery, judicial and ministerial, has worked steadily and smoothly upon the principle established by the Constitution of 1799. If the legislation has been excessive, confused, contradictory—if the taxes have been oppressive and unnecessary—if the expenditure of public money has been wasteful—if a wretched and useless system of public works has been projected as the mere means of creating unnecessary offices, extending executive patronage, and wasting the substance of the people upon worthless pets and favorites—a standing army of lazy drones, producing nothing, and consuming the treasure wrung from the toil and the sweat of the people, and which ought to support and to stimulate the labor which created it—should these things all be true, where lies the fault? Can the judges and the sheriffs, the clerks and the constables, do any act of legislation? Can they alter, modify, repeal the statutes? Can they impose taxes? Can they borrow money? These things are sovereign, these powers are legislative. The old Constitution, following in the track of free and popular government, so considered them, and left them all—all that relates to finance and legislation, to public policy, and public administration—in the hands of the people themselves, to be devised and executed according to their will and pleasure, their instructions, their judgment, nay, even their caprice, by magistrates freely chosen by themselves at short intervals, and directly responsible—removable, too, without accusation or trial—removable by reëlection of others, at the mere pleasure of the master. Representation and taxation, said they, go together. The money of the people is their own, it can be raised in any quantity and for any purpose which they may direct, through representatives thus chosen, and bound to obedience by every motive which can sway the human mind. Were they mistaken? Is the principle of self-government, through a representation purely democratic, so disastrous a failure, that the people can not dispose of their own property?

or are they so incompetent to choose from among themselves, persons properly qualified to execute these powers, that the powers themselves must be abandoned? Are all the guards thrown around the principle of democratic representation by the nature of things and the organization of men, found so utterly impotent, that the principle itself must be thrown away, or so crippled as to render it impossible for the community, in this form, to direct its own means for its own advancement? If so, there is no hope in this world. The man or the community of men, who can not, through their own agents, manage their own affairs, direct their own means, is powerless and a slave, and requires a master, or he is an idiot, and demands a guardian.

But be it so. What shall we think of the celestial genius which has penetrated, and the bold spirit which has disclosed this terrible secret to mankind? When questioned as to the remedy, it is all too true is his reply. This representative government is a sad affair. These annual agents of yours, in the course of less than twenty years, have brought you to the very verge of ruin—the very brink of perdition. This legislative power, of which we were all once so proud, is the most stealthy, dangerous, infernal contrivance, that the wit of rogues ever devised to gull and ruin fools with. I once thought as some of you do. "I was myself one of your representatives, in one house or the other, during a period commencing in 1810, and ending in 1833. I have no doubt during that whole period, I voted every year against a bill to take the sense of the people on the proposition to call a convention. I left the legislature, however, in 1833. Every thing was then straight, and right, and fair. It was in 1834, the very year I quitted the legislature, that all this deviltry began. In 1833, your taxes were 6¼ cents on one hundred dollars, yielding you a revenue of $64,758 58. This tax, with some trifles in the treasury, as tavern licenses, tax on seals, on legal instruments, etc., etc., sustained this government from 1792 up to 1834 inclusive. Well, an *economical* set of men got into power, and somehow or other, without your knowing any thing about the matter, by little and little, your revenue and expenses have risen in this year, 1850, to $562,000. 'Was there ever such an increase?' They have raised your taxes from 6¼ cents to 19 cents; and this is the result. But this is not half. These representatives of yours, these delegates of the people, have run you in debt about seven millions by little and little, and without your knowing any thing about the matter." (Jack Falstaff said once, "Lord how this world is given to lying." We throw our own comments into parenthesis, after the manner of reporters.) "As Tom Paine said to Lord North," (our champion studied the Bible under Tom Paine,) "you know, in overloading a horse, it is the last feather you put on that breaks his back. I will give you the philosophy of all this, it is of no use to know facts, without understanding the reason of them." (Now we have it.) "There is an eternal lust in mankind to grasp at power," (there is, is there, Mr. Philosopher?) "there is a love of domination, a love of gold, a love of governing." (Any other lusts you know of, old gentleman?) "I remember reading a publication published by Matthew Lyon, when he was a candidate for Congress, and in it he said: (This is charming:)

"There is such a tincture in the blood
That all men would be tyrants if they could,
And if they did not their neighbor devour,
It is not from want of will, but want of power."

And there never was said a truer thing than that. Well, what is the remedy? Will you let the wagon go on in the old road? No—what must be done? What caused the revolution in the time of Charles I? Why, excessive taxation; by his endeavoring to force money out of the people under the head of "ship money." They rebelled and fought him on many a bloody field, and it ended by bringing the head of Charles to the block. What caused the revolution in France in the days of Louis XVI? Among the many leading and prominent causes was the deranged condition of the finances of the country, and the expenses attendant on providing for the numerous hangers-on on the government. What are we to do here? Are we to have a revolution? No, because a revolution is an anomaly in a republic." (Our champion of reform is an historian we know—he knows there was a bloody revolution in England in 1640, and in France in 1789, when a couple of fellows, they call kings, lost their heads; but this last remark, "that a revolution in a republic is an anomaly," is news to us; but we will compare notes with this most profound of living philosophers after a while—let him proceed.) He proceeds:

"No, we are to have a recurrence to *first principles;* then, and not until then, will the people be enabled to brush from off their coffers the miserable flies that have been sucking their blood for years. We must reörganize the government; we must reconstruct it; we must make a new constitution, (applause, says the reporter,) and by doing that we will drive these old hunkers out. I will give the meaning of the word hunker. There had been a set of men in New York, like in Kentucky, who held their offices, and held on—and held on—and there was no getting them loose; they were the greatest patriots that ever lived." (Laughter, says the reporter; and we think there was cause. The people must have been thinking of the convention. The way they hang on to office is a sin.) "Well, a convention was got up for the purpose of establishing a system of rotation in office." (Ah! That is it, is it? We thought it was to correct legislative abuses, and surely there is rotation enough there.) "A young lawyer got up in the convention and made a flaming speech in favor of the rotation plan, (old ones do the same in Kentucky,) and finally he said, that these old office-holders, or hunkers, were like rats in a barn, they could not be driven out, nor trampled, nor beaten out; so the only way to get them out was to burn them out. But he would not burn the corn;" (oh, Lord! No, the new rats might suffer, poor things, for winter provisions:) "he would build a new barn and remove the corn into it, and then he would burn the old barn. Thence the word barnburner arose. There never was a more thorough barnburner than I," (we believe you, 'pon honor; Van Buren, No. 1, was a chap of the same sort,) "although I have held an office." (Ah!) "*I was Secretary of State under Gov. Owsley.*" (The devil, you say.) Egad, we thought you would have steered clear of that rock, under such a press of canvas as you were carrying. You have run foul of yourself. You have been in office, eh! my barnburner? and how did *you* get out? Were you driven out, or trampled out, or beaten out? Was there any tar burnt under your nose, (rats hate tar,) or were there any feathers added, to break the back of such a *horse* as you. We have no allusion here, of course. We have understood that you hung on as long as possible by the old Constitution, and that it shielded even the like of you, the rotten old thing, from an illegal exercise of executive power; and that it was the people, whom you love and praise so much; the people, who, in the deep and swelling tide of their awful indignation, rose wave-like under you, broke your holts, as the boys say, and washed, or would have washed you out, if you had not turned tail (rats do n't love water much better than fire) and absquatulated of your own accord. Query. Why did n't you make the secretary of state elective by the people? They seem to be prime judges of the article. Perhaps as you *run from* it once, you do n't care about running *for* it. It is an uncomfortable place any how, and you care not who fills it. We beg pardon for the length of this parenthesis, but we were full, and could not contain ourselves. That last feather broke *our* back.) "I use the word barnburner in its metaphorical sense," added Mr. Hardin.

And here we close our long extracts from the celebrated speech of that *gentleman*, (we mean to be polite,) delivered in the capitol at Frankfort on the 25th and 26th of January, and inserted in the second number of the Champion of Reform. We inserted the last line of our extract, from a sense of justice to an adversary, who seems to have thought it necessary, even after his long account of the pedigree of the word, to make the explanation, in order to protect himself from a supposed confession of the crime of arson. We did not suppose (nor do we imagine his audience were in the least exposed to such a supposition) that he meant to avow himself literally an incendiary. We knew he was metaphorical—in truth, we had heard this story, as we have most of his, some hundred times before. The figure is a good and apt one. He means to illustrate the idea, not that he would really fire a neighbor's barn, but that he would apply the torch to the constitution of his country—that he would wrap in flames a structure more precious than the Ephesian dome, a temple at whose altar he was wont to worship, in praise of whose glorious proportions he used to exhaust his utmost powers of language, which contains within its time-honored walls, and shelters beneath its lofty roof, deposits more precious and costly than all the treasures which Grecian or Asiatic superstition had heaped upon the shrine of Diana. Ay, we understand him, and his motives—he would spread conflagration and death any and every where, to wreak the passions of his vindictive soul, by expelling certain subordinates who are allowed to minister within its precincts, so long as they demean themselves according to the law of the temple. No zeal like that of the convert of revenge—no fury like that which scorches the brain and consumes the heart of the renegade from a faith he has professed and deserted; a cause he has served, and learned to hate.

Similes are sometimes better than arguments. An apt illustration of a thought, drawn from a striking and just resemblance to something known and familiar, is often more forcible than the naked idea brought forward in the abstract form of logical statement. Mr. Hardin seems to have some confused notion of this sort, and hence he constantly labors in his discourse, instead of arguments, to employ such figures of speech as his memory has been able to retain. To his imagination he is indebted for nothing but his facts.

Though no indigenous flower was ever known to spring from the bosom of that cold and sterile soil, and exotics, when planted there, lose all their beauty and their fragrance—still, as the region of mere fiction—in the production of notions which have no type in nature or in truth, it becomes the very mint of invention. Genius has been defined by writers on the mind to be the creative faculty; taste, to be a fine perception of the beautiful; and wit, the power of combining, by remote and fanciful but striking resemblance, objects apparently different. Genius is the spider which draws the material of its web from its own bosom; taste the bee, which extracts and enjoys the sweets of every flower; and wit, the subtle artist, who perceives a likeness lost to the common eye, and with the touch of his delicate pencil makes that apparent, palpable, which before was hidden and unknown. The pleasure its exhibition affords is produced by the surprise it excites, combined with its truth. Truth is the master element of all intellectual greatness, and in every kind. Mr. Hardin seems to us to possess none of these faculties—yet is he a man of boundless fancy, but his fancy holds the same relation to that noblest power of the mind, imagination, that Baron Munchausen sustains to Shakspeare or to Walter Scott.

But what are we to think of the reasoning of this barn-burner, considering him as a physician called in to ascertain the disease of the State, and to apply a remedy. The machine, says he, is worn out, worthless. We can apply no remedy. You were made up wrong from the beginning. We must reconstruct, and give you a new Constitution. You must die, and resurrect. We will cut you up—put you into Medea's cauldron—reduce you to *first principles*—your original elements—boil you over again, and you will come out rejuvenised, and fitted for a glorious immortality—subject to no further change, and never to require medicine or physician again through all eternity. All very fine, doctor. But before we go through this process of regeneration—before we venture on this untried state of being—before we doff this present form of vitality we wear—tell us, if it please your wisdom, the fatal poison that lurks in our present being, and the antidote in the new vital organization, upon which you rely against the recurrence of similar disorders. Perhaps, after all, we are not as badly off as you imagine. We are subject at times to disorders—but this is the law of life and nature—of all life, and of universal nature. We have occasionally indulged too much in stimulants; we have sometimes abused things in themselves good; but abstinence and temperance will soon restore us. A slight headache is nothing to die about. Upon the whole, the organs seem vigorous, and well adapted to perform their appropriate functions. It will not do, says the doctor. You must die, and be born again. Unless you be regenerated, you shall not see my face. But I will tell you what is the matter; the human heart is sinful above all things, and desperately wicked. In the new Constitution we will put it out of your power to take any more stimulants. You have managed your affairs through various agents. Some of them have behaved themselves pretty well; but others have abused your confidence, wasted your property, flattered, gulled, fooled, imposed upon you. The worst of it is, this latter set of rascals are the very class of servants whom, by your present miserable constitution, you appoint yourselves, and who act under your own immediate orders. The fault is, therefore, your own. Now the remedy is, that as you have evidently shown yourselves incapable of choosing proper men to do your business, and guide your larger and more important concerns—and as you can not possibly manage them in person, henceforth they shall not be managed at all. You may still appoint the agents, but they shall do nothing. They shall have opportunity to come together to counsel about your affairs, but very seldom; and when they do, they shall not be permitted to remain together long enough to plot any mischief. No danger of their running you into debt any more. We will advertise them as having no credit. We will prevent your hurting yourselves hereafter, in spite of you. Now, as to your other agents, who have behaved themselves very well, so far as we know, inasmuch as you have shown yourselves utterly incapable of selecting proper persons in the higher departments of power, you may try your hand on the lower; but should they play the same game on you, you must stick to it, for, by my wisdom, I swear I will trust to no physician that shall ever come after me. Like Lycurgus, I will bequeath you an everlasting constitution.

The patient has not answered. He is still master of himself, however, and can dismiss this bold doctor, if he please.

Mr. Hardin has seduced us by his example into the figurative. We mean not to be understood as acquiescing in Mr. Hardin's charges on the government. We will yet find time to lay before you the whole history of the expenditure of the government. We shall do so with the utmost candor. Where there has been fault—and that there has been, there is no doubt—we will candidly admit it. The grossness of his errors, however, shall all be exposed. We will show his own participation in the legislation which led to that increase of taxation he denounces so heavily, and which he thinks demands a revolution. Perhaps there is not in the world so glaring an example of insincerity as in the brief history Mr. Hardin has given of the expenditures of the government, and her system of taxation since 1792. These are grave and profound matters. We have some knowledge of them from our own connection with the legislative department, during the very period when the taxes were raised, and the debt, or the major part of it, contracted. We have full means of information within our reach. In subsequent numbers, we will sift these matters to the bottom, and lay before you the truth, the simple truth, and nothing but the truth. The remainder of the present we must devote to Mr. Hardin, who vaunts himself the author of the Revolution, and is heralded by his party as the Cœur de Lion of Reform.

We had never expected to have been under obligations to Mr. Ben. Hardin for any thing. But although we are tired enough, as we suppose every one else to be, of this history of the word barnburner—of this joke, so stale, flat, and unprofitable, we are exceedingly indebted to him for one variation he threw into his threadbare jest, in the speech from which we have extracted some portions. "But he would not burn the corn," he said, "he would build a new barn and remove the corn into it, and then he would burn the old barn." Whether intentionally or not, this figure illustrates most forcibly the motives of Ben. Hardin and the Jacobin party, and their ultimate purpose in the novel, and, we hope, most hazardous position they have assumed, in regard to the powers of the convention. We shall take the liberty of employing and carrying out his own metaphor to illustrate our meaning, which we think it does thoroughly. That we may be understood thoroughly, we refer to this man's argument upon the question of the recess till the first of June, and will quote literally several passages from it. He says there, "I say that we have the power; that we can adjourn from day to day, if we choose; that we can adjourn for a month, if we choose, or six months, if we choose; but if we ever dissolve, there is an end of it." (See printed Debates, p. 1055, first column near top.) Again: "I rose and read from this book to show that we can not delegate our power, which is given on account of our skill; when an apprentice is bound to a master on account of his skill, and the master dies, he is free; because he was bound for a particular purpose. A judge can not act by deputy, because he is appointed on account of his skill. A clerk can, because his is a mere ministerial act; but a judge can not appoint a deputy. A legislator can not act by his deputy. Why? Because he is sent here on account of his skill, etc. What do we propose to do? Why we propose to appoint *another set of gentlemen* to make this very thing which we are sent here to make. We are to submit our work to the people, and they vote upon it. Can they make a constitution? No, sir, etc." (See page 1079, 2d column, near top.)

Mr. Hardin gives his usual account of his own great feats, and their astonishing results. These details are in no wise interesting, except as illustrative of the particular character of the man. We can not forbear, however, to give you a specimen of the true Falstaffian style. "*I* have had," he says, "this question very much at heart for a long time—a long time. *I* repeatedly mentioned it in public speeches made last summer, and where ever *I* named it, it met with universal approbation. *I* knew the opposition which the constitution would have to encounter. When *I* first started this question of a convention, it was doubtful whether we would have a majority or not, etc. When *I* first went to Washington, there was William Booker, and the judge his brother, who mounted the rostrum and spoke against *me*. In Green, Judge Buckner *was* present, and I expected they would mount *me*. But at last, they all agreed with *me*, except the clerk and his family. Then *I* spoke the whole week in Nelson county, and on Saturday night at Bardstown *I* was haunted by the clerks and their families. On Monday morning a clerk asked the judges at a precinct to open the polls at 8 o'clock, and when the judge asked what is the reason, he answered, to prevent HARDIN from speaking, for *he* will get the people to vote for a convention. After *I* spoke, every man but three voted for a convention." (See page 1080.)

We question whether before such an assembly, and on such an occasion, human vanity ever produced any thing like this. There is one, and but one important statement in it, and that is, that he was the author of the revolution. He evidently had great influence in the convention, especially on this question of the recess.

He afterwards says, "We have all the opposers of the constitution to fight. We have all the emancipationists, and all the office holders for life, or a great body of them, to fight. These will all combine, and thousands and thousands will be raised to defeat us." At this stage, Mr. Marshall, of Fleming, inquired of Mr. Hardin if the people should reject the new constitution, and the convention reässemble in June, whether it were competent for this convention to make a new constitution or amend their work?

Mr. Hardin said "*we should meet with the same powers as at first.*" (See page 1080.)

On the next page Mr. Hardin proceeds with these remarkable words:

"Sir, I was unhappy from the day this convention was called till last night. I was afraid all these discordant interests, the emancipationists, the old hunkers, and the old constitution men, would combine and raise money—which is the sinews of war, politically as well as civilly—and no man would subscribe one dollar for the constitution, and that they would mash it up. A dark cloud hung over our prospects till last night. The lightning seemed to flash and the thunder to roll; but thank God it is past, and I see the bright sun of Austerlitz now bursting on the people. Yes, sir, the bright sun is shining on us, and as sure as the Lord liveth we will have a constitution, and the people will take it. Where will be the emancipationists? Will they undertake to kill you, friend Meriwether? (Laughter.) Never, they will not be a thorn in your side. Where will be the old hunkers? They will swear they were with us from the first. Where will be the old constitution men? Like the rest of the horses when they ran against Flying Childers, they will be no where in the race. We will have an easy time of it if we determine to come back here. Did not the world say that Sampson was a fool for permitting his hair to be cut off by that woman Delilah? Why? He was shorn of his strength. If we adjourn *sine die*, we shall be like Sampson with his hair cut off."

We have laid before you these long extracts from this remarkable speech, not for the purpose of responding here to the monstrous propositions they contain as to the powers of the convention, and the relations that body hold to you. We do it to satisfy you that he maintained them distinctly, and carried his point too, in the face of the strenuous opposition of the very ablest men in the house. These propositions are—First, that the convention has the power of continuing its existence indefinitely. There is no term to their office save their own will. Secondly, that when they meet in June, even should you reject the constitution, or if you adopt it, as it is, their power is as complete over the subject as when they met in October. And these propositions rest upon a principle never before broached in this country, so far as we have heard or read, that a constitution submitted to the people for their ratification or rejection, can derive no obligatory force from the one, and is not in the least invalidated by the other. It seems to us, people of Kentucky, you should look into these things. This man claims to be the leader in this revolution, the author of the movement, the conqueror of the battle, which was in fact no battle at all. The question went by default. From various concurring causes, the people of Kentucky in 1847–48 were willing to submit their constitution to the revision of a convention, reserving to themselves the right, by pledges taken from every candidate in the State, to submit it to the people—reserving thereby to themselves, as the sovereign, not the delegate—the master, not the apprentice—the principal, not the agent—the right to approve or reject the instrument by which they were to be governed.

Mr. Hardin says he had thought of these things a long, long time. He says "he was unhappy from the day when this convention was called, till last night," the night it was determined to reässemble in June—the celebrated night in which the principles for which he contended were established, so far as they could be established by that body. He tells us the reason of the movement, in terms not to be mistaken. He tells us the grounds upon which he had long determined to reverse the precedent set by Washington, Madison, Marshall, etc., etc., for all of whom he professes the utmost respect, but all of whom he contends were mistaken in this matter, of the binding character of a ratification by the people. The Federal Convention, with General Washington for its President, equal, we think, to the President of the late convention—we mean no disparagement to Mr. Guthrie—the Federal Convention never dreamed that they must reässemble and give to the instrument they had submitted, its vital energy. Under this argument, the national constitution is, in fact, a dead letter. We will not cite examples. We have said we would not argue the proposition. The astute lawyer, who has discovered a resemblance between master and apprentice on one side, and the convention and the people on the other—who thinks that because the convention were appointed by the people on account of *skill*—(ye gods, what a basis for the argument)—therefore they are converted into an eternal sovereignty, and the people who gave the power, or rather lent it, are merely "another set of gentlemen," (this is his language,) to whom they can not impart or delegate it, because gentlemen of their skill can not act by deputy—the people of Kentucky—you, ye proud and jealous sovereigns, the deputy of James Guthrie and Ben. Hardin, in the ratification of your fundamental law!! This astute lawyer, however, has condescended to explain the real grounds which urged him to so portentous a position. It is to these grounds that we wish to call your earnest attention. He says that the opposition to the constitution they have made, will be great and formidable. He cites the elements of that opposition, and hurls the venom of his infernal malignity—pours the whole torrent of his devilish epithets upon each and all, yet admits that the new constitution would have been beaten, unless the convention had retained, notwithstanding the submission, the absolute power over the subject in their own hands. Had they adjourned *sine die* after the completion of their work, and submitted it fairly and fully, and finally to the people, he admits, in distinct terms, it would have been beaten. They would have been like Sampson, shorn of his hair. As it is, they are reveling in the full might of their gigantic power. The hosts of the Philistines will be dispersed without striking a blow. And why? And why? Has that opposition, which he admits would have been victorious, had their decision been permitted to be final—has that opposition lost its strength—has it, *secretary like*, fallen into the lap of some Delilah, to be led forth bound and blind, to make sport for the worshipers of some Dagon Deity? Has its great courage quailed? Has its mighty heart ceased to throb in the cause of constitutional liberty? Oh no? That is not the hope of this scoffer. We will be defeated, because in our case, he says, victory itself were hopeless. Why fight, when even if you conquer, your enemy is master of the citadel? Should you defeat the new constitution in May, we meet in June, armed with full power to make such an one as we please, or to rivet this upon you, despite of your struggles and strength.

This is the subtle contrivance by which the friends of constitutional freedom, strong enough to conquer, are to be defeated, because, dispirited from the consciousness that victory will be fruitless, they will not contend. Vain hope on your part. You know us not. Despair itself only gives a more deadly character to the resistance of the brave. When liberty is threatened with ruin, when every breeze is tainted with oppression, a patriot courage makes no compromise with danger. But we gather hope, fresh, vigorous hope, from your policy and its motive. We are any thing but desperate. This is what Mr. Hardin meant when he said he would not burn the corn; he would build a new barn, and remove the corn into it; and then he would burn the old barn. The convention, we know, have not only claimed the right, but exercised it, to pay themselves not only without, but against law. Never does their power cease till they adjourn *sine die*, and that is entirely within their own discretion. The people not only can not control or remove them, but can not even be deputized by them. There never was any thing so tremendous in theory as the power claimed and thus far exercised by this convention. The power over the treasury, the recess till June, are the text—Mr. Hardin's speeches are the commentary. They have built the new barn, and they claim the corn. They have had a nibble already. It seems from Mr. Hardin's ingenious metaphor (we fear we did injustice to his wit—when we spoke of his want of taste, however, we did not mean his taste for corn) that the two barns are to stand together till all the corn is removed into the new one, and then the old is to be fired. This is precisely the state of the case at present, and this pleasant simile explains the whole transaction. The builders of the new barn evidently mean to hold possession of it. They can not be ousted till the old one is burnt, and they alone can apply the torch. We have, under the figure of these two barns, two governments at once. The one held by the hunkers, constitutional, limited under strict legal restraints: the other composed of barnburners, absolute, interminable, save at their own pleasure, independent of all human authority, save their own, and under the name of corn and old barn, claiming the right, having exercised it in part, and asserting the purpose of drawing, at discretion in future, the money from the treasury. They avow their hunger. Their great leader metaphorically declares this to be the great object of the revolution. It is a mere question of food among the rats. Corn, corn, corn, is the cry. In the enthusiasm of victory, in the flush of anticipated triumph, Mr. Hardin speaks too plain. He has converted his convention into a Rump Parliament, and thinks there is no Cromwell here with his bayonets to force them from their seats. With all his shallow and pedantic parade of names and dates, I fear he knows little of real history. He has never penetrated into the great deep of moral and political science. He is a man of progress, but he has a long, steep road to travel up, before he is on the level of the knowledge of his own age. He has joined the Jacobins, yet knows little of the real democracy. He aspires to lead—there are abler men of that party, ten to one, than he—they will use, then discard him. Within a narrow and vicious circle, he is a good judge of bad men. A scoffer and a cynic, with no deep moral sense himself, with neither relish nor perception of the sublime and great, he has studied human nature in its shameful parts, and thinks he knows the whole anatomy of man. A shrewd man he certainly is, but shrewdness is not wisdom. He thinks every man has his price, and can not conceive of the disinterested at all. He conceives himself a statesman and a philosopher. He is about as much of either as he is of an orator or poet. He could not become the latter, for he has no imagination; nor the former, for he has no heart. He knows the names of the most celebrated nations of antiquity, and of the more remarkable men who flourished then, and has a smattering of modern history and geography. But of the great and steady movements of human society, and of the causes which have retarded or impelled them, of the real *progress* of the human understanding, of the political problems which have been, or which remain to be solved, of the philosophy of history, or the science of government, he knows nothing. He talks of Charles I, and Hampden, and Cromwell—he knows nothing about them. He compares the existing government of Kentucky and her system of taxation with the oppressive levy of ship money, and the tyranny of Charles Stuart—he is either very ignorant or very insincere. Professing democracy in the extreme, he has taken ground for his party in opposition to every democratic principle and democratic prejudice. He thinks there is no Cromwell here to hurl him and his Rump Parliament out of doors. He thinks, or at least talks so to the people, that this is a mere squabble among rats—the hunkers and the barnburners—the office-holders and office-seekers—and calculates that as but one man holds each office, and ten desire it, the barnburners must carry the day. Of the real proprietors of the barn—the growers and the owners of the corn, who are neither hunkers nor barnburners—who are no rats at all, and might not feel inclined to have a fine, stately, capacious old barn, built by their ancestors, which has kept the grain of generations sound and dry, burnt to the ground, merely to get rid of a few old rats who had lived comfortably and grown fat, if you please, on grain which the proprietor never missed—of a few old servants, rather, who had worked well and faithfully for their living, and between whom and their master there was an agreement—a standing law of the estate—that they should not be driven out so long as they behaved themselves. Of these Mr. Hardin has not thought. There is a greater than Cromwell in this land. Rouse that power, and Mr. Hardin will soon see who is master and who is apprentice—who is the principal and who the deputy. Public opinion is the master and the principal here, the supremacy of which reposes upon foundations in this country, dug deeper than those of the palace of the Cæsars, and surrounded with instruments of power more irresistible than all the legions of Rome. It is to this we appeal—it is upon this we rely for the triumph of reason, and of truth, and of constitutional liberty.

THE OLD GUARD.

NO. VI.

This is, perhaps, the best review of the financial condition of Kentucky, during the time it embraces, to be found anywhere.

Ben. Hardin—The Public Expenditure—Internal Improvement—Public Debt—Sinking Fund.

WE resume this week the subjects of our eighth number, then left unfinished. We gave in that paper extracts from various parts of Mr. Hardin's speech, delivered in Frankfort on the 25th and 26th of January, thrown together by ourselves, not exactly in the order in which they appear in the 2d number of the Champion of Reform, from which they were taken, but according to the subject matter to which they relate—and of which we were then treating, to wit: the legislative power. Before we proceed to review, and to correct from authentic sources, the apochryphal account he has there given of the revenue and expenditures of the government from 1792 to the year 1834, we must be permitted to transcribe verbatim, and in the exact connection in which it stands in the report—that portion of the speech upon which we mean to comment—that our readers may understand thoroughly the enormity of his accusations, and the completeness of our answer. Our readers may remember to have read the greater part of this extract in the eighth number of the Guard, but as we propose to-day not to deal in personal satire, but to give a detailed and grave answer to the charges by which this man is laboring to spur the people of Kentucky into a thorough, and as we most devoutly believe, ruinous revolution in the whole structure of their government, we must lay before you, together with our remarks, though you have seen them before, these remarkable statements. Mr. Hardin pretends to great knowledge and accuracy in his statistics and figures. He assumes to have made the finances, the revenue, the expenditures of the government, his particular study, and for the very purpose of enlightening you upon the subject of its stupendous corruptions. Many persons believe that a man in his position, and of his aspirations after reputation and influence, would not dare to misrepresent facts, open to the examination of any one, and spread upon the archives of the State. Whether he has done so or not, will more fully appear by noting and comparing his statements with the public records. He proceeds, in the passage which we extract entire, to give the following history of the expenditures of the government, and for the purpose of inducing the people to overthrow their present constitution. He says:

"In a republic, the people did not revolutionize, but there was a recurrence to first principles, and there was a reconstruction of the government. As in the governments we found in Europe, the hunkers hung on until the taxation became so excessive that the people would rise in their strength and revolutionize the condition of their government. What caused the revolution in the time of Charles I? Why, excessive taxation; by his endeavoring to force money out of the people under the head of 'ship money.' They rebelled, and fought him on many a bloody field, and it ended by bringing the head of Charles to the block. What caused the revolution in France in the days of Louis XVI? Among the many leading and prominent causes was the deranged condition of the finances of the country, and the expenses attendant on providing for the numerous *hangers-on*, on the government. What were they to do here? Were they to have a revolution? No, because a revolution in a republic would be an anomaly. No, they were to have a recurrence to first principles; then, and not until then, will the people be enabled to brush from off their coffers the miserable flies that had been sucking their blood for years. (Applause.)

"He would refer to a few of the expenses of this government. The revenue collectable by the sheriffs in 1829, was $61,357 05; in 1830, $66,309 98; in 1831, $62,351 44; in 1832, $70,598 82; in 1833, $64,758 58. Now, up to, and until the end of 1834, the revenue tax collected never exceeded $74,000 a year. They might begin at 1792, and come down year after year, and they would find that the expenses of the government were steady, and provided for by that amount of revenue. Besides which there were some incidental taxes in the treasury; as tavern licenses, tax on seals, on legal instruments, etc., etc. Those incidental receipts, together with the regular revenue, sustained the government from 1792 up to 1834, inclusive. Well, an *economical* set of men got into power. The expenses of the government in 1834, were $74,119 93; in 1835, $124,518 80; in 1836, $139,381 02; in 1837, 169,864 35; in 1838, $205,783 62; in 1839, $218,-363 53; in 1840, $255,009 76; in 1841, $261,898 98; in 1842, $370,843 05; in 1843, $325,413 88; in 1844, $284,-084 45; in 1845, $315,413 35; in 1846, $348,744 38; in 1847, $350,838 39; in 1848, $346,000 22; in 1849, $415,-004 20.

"From that period (1834) the expenses increased continuously, until at last the expenses for the present year were estimated at $562,000. Was there ever such an increase? Beginning in 1835, and in fifteen years running up from $74,000 to $562,000. How was it done? Why, by increasing the taxation from 6¼ to 19 cents, from time to time putting on a little of the load. By what else? By taxing spectacles, which they had a foolish fancy to have made of gold; their watches were taxed; carriages, if their ladies had grown too old or fleshy to ride on horseback, were taxed; and buggies were also taxed. And not only that, but by increasing and diversifying the objects of taxation, every thing they possessed was taxed, with a very small exception. Horses were once taxed, but now they were taxed higher; their cattle were taxed, and he (Mr. H.) supposed, if they had a dollar in their pockets, it would be taxed; but it was well taxed already; and, before long, they would have their hearths taxed, as they used to be in Great Britain; and, finally, they would tax the very means by which the light of heaven was let in upon them.

"Well, what was the remedy? Would they let the old

wagon go on in the old road? No. What must be done? They must reörganize the government; they must reconstruct it; they must make a new Constitution, (applause;) and, by doing that, they would drive those old hunkers out. He would give the meaning of the word hunker. There had been a set of men in New York—like in Kentucky—who held to their offices, and held on, and held on; there was no getting them loose; they were the greatest patriots that ever lived. (Laughter.) Well, a convention was got up for the purpose of establishing a system of rotation in offices. A young lawyer got up in the convention and made a flaming speech in favor of the rotation plan; and finally, he said, 'that those old office-holders or hunkers were like rats in a barn, they could not be driven out, nor tramped, nor beaten out; so the only way to get them out was to burn them out. But he would not burn the corn; he would build a new barn and remove the corn into it, and then he would burn the old barn.' From thence the word barnburner arose. There never was a more thorough barnburner than he, (Mr. H.,) although he had held an office. He was secretary of state under Gov. Owsley. He used the word barnburner in its metaphorical sense.

"There was no way of getting rid of those old hunkers, unless the people reconstructed and made anew their government from beginning to end. There were other things he wanted to see done. He wanted to see the State debt paid."

You can not fail to observe that he likens the system of taxation in Kentucky, and the financial embarrassments growing out of it, both in principle and oppressiveness, to the tyrannic exactions and hopeless confusion, the consequence of the same thing in England, in the 17th, and in France in the 18th century, under Charles Stuart, in the first instance, and Louis of Bourbon, the 16th of the name, in the second. According to him, the experiment of a republic, purely representative, has, in fifty years, brought a free people to the same practical result which an absolute monarchy of a thousand years standing in France, had at last attained, and an arbitrary line of princes of some seven hundred years had reached after that interval in England. It is a case to justify such revolutions as he thinks a republic alone can undergo—to wit, the overthrow, without blood and by the deliberate voice of the people, the constitution of the State, and to return to what he calls first principles. We have been examining these principles, to which he would carry us back in the preceding numbers of the Guard. We would only remark, that this is a queer sort of progress which he recommends; it reminds us of the movement which the fellow said he made at the battle of Guildford—he advanced backward some distance. But it is not with the principles of the new Constitution we now have to do, but with Mr. Hardin's facts, upon which he justifies the havoc which the convention have made, he leading, of all that we in Kentucky have been in the habit of considering as constituting a republic.

You will remark that Mr. Hardin gives first a statement of the revenue collectable by the sheriffs, the proceeds of the taxes, from 1829 to 1834, beginning in the former year with $61,357 05, and ending in the latter year with $74,000 in round numbers. You will further remark that Mr. Ben. Hardin states distinctly, that the expenses of the government were defrayed out of this amount of revenue, with some incidental taxes, such as tavern licenses, tax on seals, etc., which he does not consider worth estimating. We must repeat the passage, in which he alleges distinctly, after stating the amount of the revenue each year, that that amount limited the expenditure of the government. "They might begin at 1792, and come down year after year, and they would find the *expenses* of the government were steady, *and provided for by that amount of revenue.* Besides which, there were some *incidental taxes* in the treasury; as tavern licenses, tax on seals, on legal instruments, etc., etc. These incidental receipts, together with the regular revenue, sustained the government from 1792 up to 1834 inclusive." Starting, then, from this basis of $74,000 in 1834, he gives us a progressive increase of what he calls expense, till in 1850 it swells to $562,000, thus rising in the ordinary expenses of government, in the course of fifteen years, from $74,000 to $562,000. He inquires into the cause of this great increase of revenue and expense, and ascribes it solely to the stealthy march of taxation, rising, by little and little, from 6¼ to 19 cents on the hundred dollars. We are thus particular, even to tediousness, that you may comprehend this man before we proceed to answer him in every particular of his statements.

On the 26th of October, Mr. Hargis called, by resolution of the Convention, on the second auditor, for a tabular statement of the receipts and expenditures, annually, of the government of the State of Kentucky, from the year 1823 until the end of the year 1849, showing the receipts and expenditures from each source. Mr. Page, the second auditor, furnished a tabular statement the next day, running back to 1829, with an apology for going back no further, with which Mr. Hargis was satisfied. Mr. Hardin begins with the year 1829, and cites with an approximation to accuracy, the receipts from the sheriffs for each year. There is no doubt he took his statements from the auditor's table furnished to the Convention. That table will be found on page 111 of the Journal of the Convention. On page 112 is given the total expenditure of each year, and the objects of the expenditure. From these, we think, we will convict the gentleman.

For the year 1829, as you have seen, Mr. Hardin states the revenue collectable by the sheriffs to have been $61,357 05, and tells the people of Kentucky that that limited the expenses of the government for the year. The auditor's table shows $61,390 05. The difference is trivial, and was, no doubt, an error in transcribing. But the table shows a total revenue from all sources of $154,065 80 cents—and gives the sources thus: from clerks, $11,494 73; miscellaneous, including surplus revenue, State bonds sold, etc., $81,175 02. This exhibits a difference between the actual revenue of the State, and the sum to which it is limited by Mr. Hardin, of $92,669 75. He must have known better—the tables were before him—and this suppression was merely for the purpose of deceiving you, and calumniating the government. If you will refer to the Journal of the House of Representatives, 1839–40, page 33, you will see the several sources of this revenue more minutely stated—they are as follows:

Bank of Kentucky, for distribution of stock,	$29,835 00
Profits of the Bank of Commonwealth, . . .	23,116 00
Sales of lands west of Tennessee river, . . .	23,196 15
General receipts of revenue, vacant lands, etc.,	77,917 90
Total, ...	$154,065 80

Examine the expenditure of the same year, at page 112 of the Journal of the Convention, and you will find it amounting to $177,578 16. If you will examine the more minute report of 1839–40, you will find there was a balance against the treasury of $30,958 09—on account of money overpaid by the treasurer on the 10th October, the year before—there having been in that year a deficit to that amount in the revenue from all sources. Add this to the annual expenditure of the year 1829, as an outstanding charge against the treasury—and you will have the sum of $208,531 41 to be met by $154,065 80—leaving a deficiency in the revenue of $54,465 61, a sum nearly equal to what Mr. Hardin represents the whole expenses of the year to have been. This deficit is marked in the auditor's report, to which we have referred, "as a balance overpaid by treasurer, on 10th October, 1829, in Commonwealth's paper, of $54,463 61," and stands, of course, as a charge against the revenue of the next year, though, in the auditor's statements, these balances are never included in the annual expenditure, but are charged as so much money overpaid the preceding year.

Thus we perceive, at the start, that Mr. Hardin, with the evidence all before him, misrepresents the actual amount of the revenue of the State, by the difference between $61,357 05 and $154,065 80; and misrepresents the expenditure by the difference between the same sum of $61,357 05 and $177,573 16—

being a blunder only to the tune of $116,221 11. The expenditures of that year only lacks about six thousand dollars of being three times as great as he represented them. In 1830, he represents the revenue and expenditure as being $66,309 38. The auditor's report, from which he quoted, found in the Journal of the Convention, pages 111, 112, shows a total revenue of $146,050 86, and the same report shows a total expenditure the same year of $175,961 47—exhibiting a blunder upon the part of Mr. Hardin, for this year, of $109,652 09. In 1831, he states the revenue and the expenditure to be $62,351 44. The tables whence he drew the amount of the tax collectable by the sheriffs that year, show him first—that the total revenue from all sources amounted to $215,415 50, and the total expenditure to $243,541 47—exhibiting the enormous mistake of $181,190 03, in his estimate of the expenses of the year—the actual amount being very nearly three times what he represents it. In 1832, he states the revenue and expenditure to have been $70,598 82. The Journal of the Convention shows, in the same tables so often cited, a total revenue for this year of $175,199 22—and an expenditure of $236,059 27; showing another mistake of $165,460 45. In 1833—the last year of the service of this renowned master and most veracious historian of statistical finance—he represents the revenue and expenditure to have been $64,758 58. His own tables show the total revenue of that year to have been $341,976 10. The total expenditure of the government was $169,410 51—being again mistaken to the amount of $104,651 93. In the history of the revenue and expenditure of the State during five years—for the most part of which he tells us, he was himself a member of the legislature—he has erred to the amount of $697,175 61. He adds, as we have already quoted, that till 1834, the revenue tax collected never exceeded $74,000 00. "*From* 1791 *down, year after year, they would find that the expenses of the government were steady, and provided for by that amount of revenue.*" Whoever will examine the report of the second auditor, made to the legislature in 1839–40, of the receipts and expenditures of the government from 1823, beginning at page 29, Journal

House of Representatives, will find the expenditure for the years 1824, 1825, 1826, to be $305,562 38—$392,092 33—and $239,100 90, respectively.

We have gone through this long detail to show you Mr. Hardin's great and astonishing unfairness. We have, in one instance, given all the elements of the revenue, the lands west of Tennessee—the vacant lands—the banks—and shown you how far they exceeded the ordinary revenue from taxation. You must be satisfied that 6¼ cents on the hundred dollars could never have defrayed the expenses of the government. These resources were gradually exhausted. But the strangest part of Mr. Hardin's statement is that when he shows a steady and vast increase in your revenue he should attribute it purely to increased taxation. In 1829, he says your revenue from tax was only $61,396 05—in the present year it is estimated at $562,000. All this vast increase is owing to increased, burdensome, unnecessary, ruinous taxation. In 1829, your taxes were 6¼ cents, in 1850, they are 19. But Mr. Hardin's 19 cents is only three times the amount of 6¼—the revenue from all taxes now exceeds what it did then 9⅓ times—how does this happen? In some of those years—those glorious, free, happy years—take the year 1831 for instance, when the revenue from taxation at 6¼ was $62,351 44, and the total expenditure $243,541 47—19 cents on the hundred dollars would not have begun to pay it. Make the calculation: if 6¼ cents, on a given valuation of property, yield $62,351 44, what will 19 cents on the same valuation yield? You will find it would only be about $187,054 32—it would not begin to pay the expenditure of the year. Now, it yields $562,000 you say—10 cents, a little over half of what the country pays, supports the government, and achieves what 19 would not have done in your boasted time, to which you would carry us back. The other nine sustains the sinking fund—goes in support of common schools—and supports our *glorious convention*. You can not fail to observe, from the careful and detailed statement we have given of the total revenue, and total expenditures of the government, within the five years cited by Mr.

Hardin, down to 1834, two facts—first, that but a small portion of the means of the State was drawn from taxation—and, second, that there was almost constantly a deficiency in the revenue. Even in the year 1834—the account stands thus:

Revenue from sheriffs, ...	$74,119 93
Revenue from clerks, ...	20,242 68
Miscellaneous, ...	67,646 07
Total, ...	$162,008 68

The total expenditure of that year was $230,340 82, exhibiting an excess of expenditure over income of $78,332 14. These deficiencies of each year are marked in the auditor's tables of the next year as balances overpaid by the Treasurer on the 10th October (which is the close of the fiscal year) of the year before. The mode in which it is done is, that the annual deficiency of one year is paid by anticipating the revenue of the next—by which means a public debt was in the gradual course of formation.

You will further perceive that Mr. Hardin's statement contains two gross delusions, the extent of which is ascertained by the foregoing statement—1st, That the revenue from taxes was within a trifle of embracing the whole revenue of the State—and 2d, That the whole expenses of the government were met or limited by that revenue. These are the two propositions with which he set out, both of which are utterly false.

But, says Mr. Hardin, with a sneer, an *economical* set of men then came into power—and then proceeds to show the steady increase of the revenue, down to the present period, which he ascribes solely to the insidious and stealthy march of taxation. He compares, with his usual accuracy, resulting from his profound knowledge and careful study and comparison of the causes which have led to the great social and political revolutions recorded in history, the present financial embarrassments, and onerous taxation of Kentucky, with the similar state of things which curbed the English and overthrew the French monarchy.

He talks of the stealthy march of taxation, as though the acts and counsels of a representative republic were vailed from the public eye, hidden in the mystery which shrouds the movements and the motives of the cabinets of princes.

The archives of your State are no secret. The acts of your government are open to your inspection at all times. The history of your revenue—your expenditure—your taxation—your finance—is spread out full and fair upon your records—is subjected annually to the rigorous inspection of your representatives.

Most men measure the freedom and prosperity of communities, by the standards from which Ben. Hardin deduces their decline and ruin. A steadily increasing public revenue has been regarded by some persons, claiming to be philosophers and economists, as entirely consistent with public prosperity—as marking, nay as proving incontestably, the growth of industry, the enlargement of capital, the increased and increasing value of the property of the people. They will do this without the aid of statistics. We will endeavor to prove, before we close this article, that the theory squares with the facts.

We have exhibited to you the state of things down to 1834. The resources of the State, independent of taxation, were declining, and must soon have ceased entirely. Her lands and the funds derived from her banks were not permanent and perennial sources of supply. The tax of 6¼ cents, the sixteenth part of one per cent., one-sixteenth of a cent upon the dollar, was known to be insufficient to support a government at all competent to any political object.

No man perceived this more clearly than Mr. Ben. Hardin. We have shown you, in the close of our eighth number, and pointed you to the proof, that feeling the insufficiency of the then amount of the revenue, he led upon the subject, and met directly and manfully the question. He looked to the true source of revenue—an equal ad valorem tax upon the property of the people. A bill came from the House of Representatives, taxing stores and merchandize; Mr. Hardin offered the amendment, to raise the general ad valorem tax to ten cents, and carried it through the Senate. The House rejected the amendment, and it fell, the Senate receding. This was the session of 1832–33—the last of Ben. Hardin's legislative service, till he came to overthrow the State in the convention. The next year—1833–34—the legislature yielded to the necessity which Hardin foresaw, and did what he attempted to do before. This tax remained stationary till 1841, when five cents were added in aid of the sinking fund—a matter which we will explain when we come to that branch of the subject. In 1848, the people ratified at the polls the tax of two cents in aid of the school fund. In the session of 1848–49, the legislature directed two cents additional to meet alleged defalcations in the treasury, and to defray the expenses of the convention. The convention seem inclined to use up their share of it, and to make it perpetual, by continuing their existence and their power. Should they ever adjourn—the tax itself, from its nature, will cease—it was not designed to be permanent. The tax of 17 cents is permanent, and is composed of the three elements into which we have distributed it—imposed at the times, and in the manner, and for the purposes we have enumerated—purposes to which it has been heretofore faithfully applied by the present government, as the public accounts fully demonstrate.

The statement of the revenue for 1849—its amount and its application—is as follows:

Gross revenue, 1849, - - - - -		$561,382 43
Commissions, delinquents, etc., - - -		43,507 13
		$517,875 30
Sinking fund, - - - -	$137,676 60	
School fund, - - - -	54,407 92	
Convention, - - - -	54,407 92	
		246,492 44
Leaving for expenses, - - - - -		$271,382 86

[For proof, see second auditor's report, 1848–49, page 23, statement No. 9.]

It will be seen from this statement, that a tax of five cents, ad valorem, yields $63,666 60 more in 1849, than 6¼ cents did in Mr. Hardin's boasted year 1834.

It will be further observed, that, deducting every thing else, expenses of collection, delinquencies, sinking fund, school fund, convention, the regular revenue tax of 10 cents, which covers the whole expenses of the government—appropriations and all—amounts to $271,382 86, and yields to the State $197,382 86 more than the tax of 6¼ cents yielded in 1834. This is the increase of revenue in fifteen years, by the addition of 3¾ cents upon the hundred dollars of property. A little more than one-thirtieth part of a cent to the dollar—a back-breaking business, to be sure, to the tax-payer—but to the State, this mite, for which we have no coin or denomination to express it, has turned out a mine of support and credit. The tax of five cents for the sinking fund was laid in 1841, though it does not appear in the auditor's report till October, 1842. The tax stood at ten cents from 1835, when it was first collected, to 1841, making seven years. We will help Mr. Hardin to the true reason of the increase of the revenue during these years. It can not be explained by increased taxation—for the taxes remained the same; we must look elsewhere for it, and we think we shall be able to find the explanation without difficulty. In 1835, the year after the ten cents were imposed, the revenue was $124,518 80. In 1841, before the five cents appear in the accounts, $261,808 00—exhibiting an increase of revenue upon the same basis of taxation, within seven years, of $137,290 18—an increase of nearly double of what the whole revenue receivable from sheriffs in 1834 amounted to. This looks like ruination.

But how did it happen? Examine legislative report, No. 10, communicated at the December session, 1849, page 276, and you will find the valuation of taxable property for the year 1835—the first year the ten cents were levied—to amount to $149,273,972. Cast your eye down to 1841, and you will find the valuation to be $263,845,749, showing an increase in value in seven years, of one hundred and fourteen millions, five hundred and seventy-one thousand, seven hundred and seventy-seven dollars. This is horrible—the more the revenue thrives, the richer grow the people; the more the State robs, the more is the capital of the people enlarged.

The expenses of the government, exclusive of the public debt, the school fund, and the convention—including every thing else—in 1849 is shown to be $271,582 86 cents.

The expenditure in 1834, for the same objects—there being then no sinking fund, no school fund, and no convention, (in that they were, we acknowledge, in advance of us; here, and here alone, have we retrograded,) was, as we have already shown, $230,340 82—showing an increase in expenses, not from $74,000 00 to $562,000 00, but from $230,340 82 to $271,382 86. An increase in the expenses of a government for a people in the course of fifteen years of $41,000—whose capital has increased one hundred and fifty millions within the time, and whose numbers have advanced proportionably—would seem to be admirable ground for a thorough political revolution. It was not on account of an increasing revenue that France went into a revolution. Louis the Sixteenth would never have called the Assembly of the States-General in '89, but that his revenues had failed. All the politic machinery of despotism could squeeze no more out of the dried husks of oppressed and exhausted indigence. The question with Charles the First was certainly very like that now pending in Kentucky!

What must we think of the historian who compares the revenue system of the French monarchy—when two-thirds of the lands of the kingdom were held by the nobility and clergy, and they exempt by the fundamental law of the empire from taxation—when trade was crushed by the most oppressive regulations—when labor, in every department of it, was held in contempt, and yet the whole burdens of the State thrown upon the industrious classes—what must we think, we ask again, of the historian who compares this system with ours? Or what shall we say to the lawyer and statesman, who sees, in the effort of the English nation, in the seventeenth century, to wrest from the hand of an hereditary monarch the power of arbitrary taxation, and to assert and make fast and eternal the principle of frequent parliaments, and the right of the people to tax themselves through their own representatives, in any mode, and to any extent they please—who fought to put down arbitrary laws and dependent tribunals of justice—who saw, in the court of Star Chamber, a court dependent upon the will of the prince, a sure instrument of arbitrary power—who fought, and kept fighting, for half a century, through all sorts of confusion and difficulties and sufferings, till they succeeded in establishing these great truths—that the king was a constitutional officer, and held his power from the gift, and by contract with his people—that the people, through their representatives, had entire control of the purse of the nation—that the law was supreme, above all, until altered by parliament—and that to give it strength and efficiency, it must be interpreted and applied by judges, appointed by the king, paid by the parliament, and removable by neither, but holding their offices during good behavior? Is it not marvellous to hear a revolutionist, who seeks to strike down the representatives of the people, and to degrade their character—who holds them up as unworthy of all trust or confidence—takes from them all power over the public purse, and strips them of the entire direction of public affairs—fixes the revenue, the finances, the taxation for ever, in bar of all future discretion of the representative body—splits the commonwealth up into separate little *elective* and reëligible judicial dynasties—is it not wonderful to hear such an one compare himself with, or seek to draw his principles from, Sydney, or Milton, or Hampden?

There is a marvellously striking likeness between Ben. Hardin and John Hampden—fully as great as between John J. Crittenden, our despot, and the 1st Charles—fully as great as between our free commonwealth and the French despotism—but we must pass to another branch of the subject.

P. S. Since writing the above, a circumstance has occurred to us, which we had omitted to mention in its proper place—we do so now, and our readers will bear in mind and apply the correction. The subjects of taxation were enlarged in 1837 by what is commonly called the equalizing law, which took effect in 1838, and is included in the valuation of 1841, and was not in that of 1835, between which two years we have instituted the comparison of the taxable property of the State. It follows that to make the comparison a fair one, we should deduct from the sum of the valuation of 1841 the amount of property given in under the equalizing law. We have no means within our reach to ascertain with precision what it was at that period. The auditor's report for 1848 is before us, and furnishes the amount in 1848. It has, however, certainly increased very much within the seven years—but as we seek no advantage in the argument, we will deduct the amount of the last year from 1841, and measure the valuation thus reduced with that of 1835. The auditor's report shows an increase of the capital valued under the equalizing law, between the years 1848 and 1849, to be about a million and a half—if this increase has been steady since 1841, it would make a difference of five or six millions of dollars; as we do not know, however, with precision what it has been, we will assume the amount given in 1848. The auditor states it to be $32,361,752. Deduct this from the total valuation of 1841, which we have shown to be $263,845,749, and it will leave $231,584,097. The increase, then, in the six years from 1835 to 1841, in the valuation of the same subjects of taxation, will be $82,210,025, instead of $114,571,777, as we stated in the body of this article—this makes the comparison perfectly just.

We have fixed upon the year 1835 as being the date when the increased revenue under the ten cent tax is first exhibited in the auditor's report, and the year 1841 as the close—the five cents additional not appearing till 1842. The law raising the tax to ten cents was passed in February, 1834, and the law imposing the additional five cents, in February, 1841. This may produce the impression in persons not familiar with the mode of settling the accounts of the revenue, that the revenue of the year 1841, which I have given, ought to include the receipts of the additional five cents, inasmuch as the law authorizing its collection passed that year. Such is not the fact, however, as will be readily perceived by a reference to the auditor's tables. The explanation is this. The calendar year terminates with December—the fiscal year the 10th October. The taxes collected in 1834 are paid in January, 1835, or must be paid in by that time, and appear in the auditor's account at the close of the fiscal year 1835, which is October. The taxes collected in 1840 are paid in in January, 1841, or must be paid in by that time, and do not appear till October, the close of the fiscal year 1841. Thus the revenue from ten cents, authorised and collected by law in 1834, were not paid in till the next January, and, of course, do not appear on the auditor's books till October, 1835—and the revenue from the additional five cents, though collected in 1841, is not paid over till January, 1842, and does not appear till October, 1842. Hence, the statement which I have made of the year 1835, first exhibits the increase under the ten cents collected the year before; and my statement of the revenue in October, 1841, as exhibiting the last year of the ten cent tax, and not including the five cent tax, is also correct—because the five cents, though collected in 1841, is not paid over till January, 1842, and does not appear till the close of the fiscal year, 1842, which is October. Any one who will examine the auditor's table will see the fact of which this is the explanation.

THE OLD GUARD.—INTERNAL IMPROVEMENT.

NO. VII.

During his connection with the Old Guard, Mr. MARSHALL discussed this subject in the following article. It is handled with the same superior skill and judgment that characterize his other productions. No one can read the article and think of the remarks upon the practical workings of things it contains, and compare them with subsequent results, without being struck with the penetration—almost prophetic—it displays. The reader will also admit the masterly manner in which the portraiture of Mr. GUTHRIE is drawn.

YOU will have remarked that Mr. Ben. Hardin, to whom we are replying, fixes the year 1834, when the taxes were at 6¼ cents on the hundred dollars, and when he says the total revenue (which we have shown to be false) was $74,000—and the expenditure of the government (which we have also shown to be false) was limited by that revenue—and the value of property assessed for taxation (which we have shown to be true) amounted only to $136,703,999—as the close of the halcyon days of Kentucky, the culminating point whence her decline commenced. The additional tax of 3¾ cents on each hundred dollars, which marked her entrance, according to him, on the career of ruin, first took effect in 1835. It was in 1833 that Mr. Hardin closed his career of legislation. The *economical* set of men came in afterward—the internal improvement system was begun and prosecuted—the public debt was contracted—the taxes were raised again, and the result is a tax of 19 cents on the hundred dollars—a debt, as he somewhere says in his speech, (which is false,) of seven millions, and a revolution in government, with a total overthrow of the constitution of Kentucky, as he hopes. Before we consider the public debt and the sinking fund, we beg leave under a separate head to treat concisely this subject of internal improvement. It was in 1835–6 that the system of internal improvement may fairly be considered as entered upon and shaped. The act providing a sinking fund for the payment of loans for internal improvement, bears date February 29th, 1836. This celebrated act was the real initiation of the system, the evidence of the purpose of the State to prosecute it as a fixed policy.

We have shown in our eighth number, that in the session of 1832–3, Mr. Ben. Hardin did what he could for internal improvement. He did a good deal—and attempted a good deal more. We published his report in favor of advancing the State credit to the Lexington and Ohio railroad company, as guaranty in a loan of $300,000. In that report, the extreme ground is taken in favor of the system—the ground that the State holds a sort of *parental relation* to private corporations, and is bound by every consideration of policy, duty, and humanity, to guarantee and cover their undertakings, in this way, with her credit. We have shown that he reported, and carried bills for subscribing stock to two other companies, to the amount of $50,000 to each—and that he reported an amendment, and carried it through the Senate, for raising the taxes to 10 cents. We wish you to bear these things in mind when you read this man's tirades. But we quit him for the present.

The year 1832, and the session of 1832–3 were epochs in the domestic history of the United States—and marked a change in the internal policy of the State of Kentucky, which demands at our hands a brief comment. The election of General Jackson in 1832, settled the questions of the bank of the United States, and of any internal improvement upon the part of the general government. His vast popularity—and his complete and overwhelming triumph, rendered it more than probable that he would transmit the succession to some man of his own party and his own principles. The national debt was about to be paid off, which it was known must leave a vast surplus in the treasury of the United States. The United States Bank it was known must soon begin to wind up its affairs, and to withdraw its capital. The commercial operations of Kentucky had been mainly conducted through the credit of the branches of that institution, located at Lexington and Louisville—a credit out of all proportion to the capital employed, which was only two millions. The sudden withdrawal of that capital and that credit, it was easily foreseen, would press upon Kentucky with a force and acuteness, the extent of which could not well be estimated. The legislature of Kentucky at once perceived the necessity of providing a substitute—of adopting some means of alluring capital to the State, to occupy the place of that about to be withdrawn. They commenced chartering banks at the session of 1832.

The attention of the State became keenly awakened to the subject of internal improvement by the State itself. All hope from the general government was gone for years—if not for ever. An appropriation had been made by Congress to the first great work attempted here, the Maysville and Lexington turnpike—the president had vetoed it. Mr. Clay's land bill, by which he hoped, upon a principle peculiar to itself, to divert that much of the national revenue, which the nation did not want, and could not use, into the coffers of the States, to enable them to provide the means of easy commercial intercourse and transit between them, passed Congress. The president put that in his pocket.

The time was fast approaching when it would be absolutely necessary to decide what was to be done with the surplus revenue of the nation. Between 1832 and 1835 Kentucky incorporated ten millions of banking capital, in a mode and upon principles which will be explained when we come to treat of the public debt and the sinking fund. The popular enthusiasm in favor of the system in Kentucky continued to increase, and never did the popular enthusiasm run so high within our knowledge on any subject. Building roads, and opening the navigation of rivers—improving the old—and finding new avenues for commerce, seemed to occupy the public mind to the exclusion of every thing else. President-making itself appeared, for a brief season, to be forgotten. The people were far in advance of their representatives upon this subject, we know. One of the editors of this paper was a member of the House of Representatives, during the sessions of 1832–3, 1835–6, 1836–7, 1838–9, 1839–40. He participated largely in the guilt, if guilt it was, of what was done. He refused absolutely, however, to follow some, who are now denouncing the system, and seeking to overthrow the legislative branch of the government, for the length to which they went, under the spur of the people. That spur was put to him, and put to him in vain. He resisted obstinately, as they know, the urgent enthusiasm of his own constituency—who would have impelled him to embark his State in enterprises utterly beyond her means—and contrary as he believed to her interests. Does any body remember the project, and the leading projectors of the Charleston, Lexington and Cincinnati railroad and quasi United States Bank—the great four States monied institutions to be connected with it. Does any body remember Col. Memminger, and the winter 1838–9. If any one does, he will understand what we mean. Does any one remember the course pursued by the Wickliffe family in relation to that matter? If he does, let him compare their effort now to strike down the government for abusing State credit for contracting a public debt for internal improvement of their own territory—with the efforts of the same men then, to involve her in a wild scheme of connecting Lexington with Charleston, by a railroad six hundred miles in length, across mountains and rivers, at a cost probably of thirty millions—let him make the comparison; it will throw new light upon human nature—it will be good for his soul. Oh! these cousins—my conscience! Hear Chas. A. Wickliffe, in 1838, on the convention project, and an independent judiciary. Robert Wickliffe, sr. and jr., on the Charleston road and bank from 1835–6 to 1838–9—and cousin Ben. Hardin on internal improvement, advancing State credit to private companies, raising the taxes, etc., in 1832, and now listen to all four, raving in unison about public debt, and internal improvement, denouncing the whole affair throughout—annihilating the legislative power, and parceling out the commonwealth into little elective judicial bailiwicks, without an executive head, without a common council, armed with a full legislative power to represent the sovereign people, guide their policy, superintend their public affairs, and inspect the conduct of their subordinate agents. These men, banded together in a firm family pact, and the leaders, as they boast, of the revolution. Compare their present declarations and objects with their past, and who can trust or follow them? Amid the shameful renegadism of the times, there stands one man firm to the tenor and darling objects of his whole life, obstinate even in the midst of his concessions—consistent, even in his very inconsistencies. We mean Mr. James Guthrie, of the city of Louisville—the president of this convention. We shall speak more particularly of this gentleman, in our next number, when we come to examine the public debt and the sinking fund, of which last he was the author—we know what we say. We are not so indiscriminate, or so unjust, as to class him with such men as Ben. Hardin. He is a man of another stamp—more dangerous, because he is endowed with really more intellectual power—because he is the acknowledged head of a powerful party—and because, though unscrupulous in his ambition, and careless of the political means he employs. As a private gentleman, he commands the respect of society, and is a *man* of truth, honor and courage. Of an exterior, cold, proud, haughty, often supercilious and repulsive—still he is endowed with a spirit of craft, and a genius for intrigue, subtle, cautious, and profound as Machiavel himself.

Mr. Guthrie's original education, that is the education obtained at schools, is limited. He is what is termed a self-made man. He owes very little to early instruction, and his matured manhood has been too busy to allow of his reading books. Of what may be properly called science, out of his immediate profession, he has none, and with elegant letters, he is not even tinctured. But that sort of knowledge, which is won, from a cool and close and continued observation of the men and things, with which we are surrounded, is his. With a naturally strong mind, and a singularly clear and accurate judgment—he has made himself what he designed to be, a thorough man of business. He is a man of vast ambition, and vast tenacity of purpose, and obstinacy of will. If he had been endowed with those fascinating qualities of conversation, wit, eloquence, and above all, of manner, which render men pleasing to the crowd, and lay the foundation of what is called popularity—his history, and his character might have been different. He would undoubtedly have been a more splendid—we doubt whether he would have been a stronger man than he is. He felt his deficiencies, and has courted power, instead of popularity. He was a relief man, a new court man, a Jackson man, etc. He has adhered steadily to that party in all their political struggles—and yet his history as a legislator for Kentucky is in singular contrast with the principles of the party of which he is now the unquestionable head. Mr. Guthrie has seemed to us—and we have observed him somewhat, to have had three grand objects in life. First, to build for himself an enormous fortune. Avarice with him is a form, a very elevated form of ambition. He regards fortune as one of the instruments of power—and he employs it as such freely—lavishly on some occasions. There is nothing mean or miserly, about James Guthrie. He has done many kind and generous things—even where he had no political end in view. His second, was to make Louisville the first city in the west, and his third, to rule the city, which he considers in some sort a creation of his own—and through a power, and influence, central and commanding, to place his party in possession of the government of Kentucky, himself at the head of it.

He has attained one of these objects certainly. It is said that when he came to Louisville he was not worth $100. His estate is now estimated at a million of dollars. If he has not made Louisville the first city in the west, he has, at least, placed her in the front rank, and such as she is, he has long ruled her. For years he was Louisville—the corporate Louisville. He guided her whole municipal concerns, and ruled her with a rod of iron. With a dead party majority of 600 against him—he could be elected when ever he pleased. It was at one time thought he had lost his influence—popularity he never had. The call of the convention was a democratic call—the cry of abolition was a democratic cry, to crush the whigs with. Louisville was a whig city—Louisville was supposed to be an emancipation city. Every body who knew any thing, knew that the democrats, as a party, expected to rise into power in the State, after an exile of twenty-five years, over the ruins of the old constitution. Mr. Guthrie himself had been the uniform friend of the law of 1833 in relation to the importation of slaves—that law became in these days the badge of abolitionism. None so loud as he in denouncing emancipation. Under these circumstances, he contrived to be returned from a whig city, found his party in a majority in the convention, became its president, has offered to the whig State of Kentucky a constitution which prostrates for ever every principle in politics, for which they ever contended, and if it be accepted—his old party to which he has adhered so long, and through such evil fortune in Kentucky, will again be brought into power, he at its head—under a constitution of their own making—and radical thoroughly. Thus he seems likely to obtain the third great object of his life.

Throughout this whole career, at least since 1832, he has stood in his legislation in decided and glaring opposition to the general principles of his party. He has yielded at last, and agreed to carry into the constitution, a prohibition of those very powers, which he, as a legislator, has carried farther and wielded more effectually than any other man.

However others, when the system was popular, may have struggled for the honor of being its authors—he was the real efficient author of it. He projected the scheme of finance, and of the sinking fund, by which alone it could have been carried on—and with characteristic pride, even when with his locofoco spade—he was extirpating from the constitution the last fiber of the last root of the system, he was too proud, too true, to deny his agency—or to condemn the grandest work of his life. He avowed his approbation of the thing he was forced to destroy, and vindicated the wisdom of what he had projected.

LETTER TO THE LOUISVILLE JOURNAL OF NOVEMBER THE 27, 1851.

In 1851, the claims of both Mr. Crittenden and Mr. Dixon to a seat in the Senate of the United States from Kentucky, were being urged with zeal and warmth by their respective friends. The rivalry of two such champions created indeed quite a breach in the Whig party of the State. Mr. Marshall, being a warm personal and political friend of Mr. Crittenden, urged his claims to the position with accustomed energy and ability. Misrepresentation grew out of his course, and he was more than once charged with being mainly instrumental in bringing about the unpleasant disruption. In defense of himself, and to give more fully his views in regard to the senatorial contest, he wrote the following letter to the Louisville Journal in November, 1851. Aside from its value as an epitome of then current political history, it is one of the happiest literary successes to be found any where. Bold in its originality, in conception grand—of elastic brilliancy, searching depth and classic finish, it will vie with similar productions of the ablest masters.

Gentlemen: I met to-day with your paper of yesterday, containing two letters from Frankfort—the one signed "Alpha," the other simply with the letter "M." These letters undertake to review the state of the parties to the contest now going on for a seat in the Senate of the United States. My name figures in both communications, and I am charged distinctly as the author of the breach in the Whig party, or at least as the irritating cause which has rendered that breach incurable. Mr. Crittenden's friends, in the judgment of your correspondent, committed "an egregious blunder in intrusting his interests to the hands of Mr. Marshall." The divisions of the Whig party, and all the mischievous consequences resulting thereform, are ascribed to the factious and imprudent and bitter character of my remarks made upon the floor of the legislature. Until then, it is alleged that the friends of Dixon and Crittenden had been acting in good humor and friendship, but the inappropriate and uncalled for sarcasms, the severe and mortal thrusts aimed by me at Mr. Dixon, have exasperated the friends of that gentleman till all reconciliation is hopeless. The mischief I have done is not confined to exciting Mr. Dixon's friends against Mr. Crittenden, but it seems I have brought down upon him the vengeance of Mr. Clay and his friends, by insinuating that he was indebted to Mr. Crittenden for his escape from the wreck of Mr. Adams' administration. Your correspondent thinks that "Old Hal" (as he somewhat familiarly styles that great man) may possibly admit his obligations to Providence; but, save that, it is insult to ascribe his greatness, elevation, and power to the support of generous and devoted friends, or to any thing short of his own great and unaided genius. As if it were not enough to pluck down the wrath of Mr. Clay and Dixon upon John Crittenden's unoffending head, your correspondent makes me run a muck upon the Democracy, so as to leave my friend no support under heaven. My dear sirs, I have, for the last ten years, been so accustomed to misrepresentation of myself, my actions, opinions, words, and motives, that however I may have writhed at first, I have at length, so far as myself am concerned, given over resistance and ceased to struggle with falsehood. Were the effect of your correspondent's statements limited to myself—were their aim and consequence simply to hold me up as laboring to distract and ruin a party with which I pretend to be acting in good faith, I might and certainly would have borne it in silence, however false, unjust, and injurious.

That I should strive to scatter the seeds of a feud between Mr. Clay and Mr. Crittenden, to exasperate the former gentleman and his friends, and thereby procure the present defeat and future ruin of the latter, would be certainly the surest road to the dissolution of the Whig party in Kentucky. If I had any wrongs to complain of at the hands of that party, here were a revenge deep, sure, ample, and for the malignant treachery involved in the time and mode of its execution, entirely worthy of a fiend. Were the effect of these charges limited to myself, I have said that I should maintain unbroken silence. But the accusation has a wider scope, and is intended to reach other heads than mine. Your correspondent says that Mr. C.'s cause and interests had been entrusted to my hands by his friends. Whatever course I may have pursued in debate, whatever I may have said, is therefore chargeable upon him. It is to make him responsible for all evil consequences that my conduct has been arraigned—it is to reach him, and to hold him responsible for the calamitous divisions of his party, that these severe censures are piled upon me. That Mr. Clay and his friends will so consider it, is distinctly alleged by "Alpha." "This speech," says your correspondent, alluding to mine, "although an exceedingly fine one, will have the effect of widening the breach. The thrust made at Dixon was very severe, and he and his friends can not help feeling sore under it. *And I am sure that Mr. Clay and his friends will never consent for it to be understood that Mr. Crittenden dragged him out from under the ruins of Adams' administration. 'Old Hal' may be willing to admit he is under some obligations to Providence for his success in this world; but that indomitable spirit which has borne him up under all the political reverses, which in a lony and eventful life have befallen him, will never permit him to ascribe his elevation to any thing short of his own bright, glowing, and powerful genius.*"

It is to this latter view of the bearing of my course that I wish to draw your attention particularly. It is from the implication of my motives here made, and from the disastrous consequences here clearly predicted, that I mean to vindicate myself, and if truth can ever prevail, to rescue John Crittenden. This charge upon me—this false, mischievous, unfounded charge, that I had represented Mr. Crittenden as the founder of Mr. Clay's fortunes, came first from one of the leaders of the Democratic party on the floor of the House. Dr. Green, of Henry, rose when I had finished, and with skillful misrepresentation, adapted admirably to the views and tactics of his party, alleged that he had never understood, till he had heard it that day from the gentleman from Woodford, that Mr. Clay owed his elevation and his fame to John J. Crittenden. He had always understood that the sage of Ashland was the architect of his own fortunes, and indebted for his grandeur and his influence solely to his own great genius and indomitable energy.

Coming from this quarter, this was all quite natural, and the motive too obvious, as I supposed, to be dangerous, and the misrepresentation of my words and meaning too glaring to require then and in that presence explanation or denial at my hands. That a Democratic leader should, with humane and benevolent fingers, fall to scratching with all his might what every body knows has long been considered a sore place on the Whig body—a spot right over the heart, which the common enemies of Clay and Crittenden have long hoped to see terminate in cancer—was natural and politic.

It is true, my dear sirs, that until I spoke, explaining the reasons why I desired Col. Williams to withdraw Mr. Crittenden's name from the ballot, nothing had been said on the floor of the House in open debate upon the exasperating topics connected with this senatorial election. That "the two divisions had been acting in good humor and friendship until the factious speech made by Mr. Marshall," as alleged by your correspondent M., is utterly false. If your correspondent knows any thing about the matter, or knowing, cares to tell the truth, he will admit that every rumor to Mr. Crittenden's prejudice, every charge against him, and more, which I noticed and attempted to answer, had been made, circulated, pressed against him out of the House, and that, after I spoke, they were openly urged in the House, by Mr. Mitchell and Mr. McKee, and the charge of Abolitionism and the pardon of Fairbanks thrown in, by way of supplement, by Mr. Bates, of Barren, one of the aspirants to the Democratic leadership.

In withdrawing Mr. Crittenden, or requesting his withdrawal, I was compelled to explain, or be exposed to misconstruction myself, and risk irreparable injury to him.

The facts existing at the time are briefly these: That portion of the Whig party who desire to restore Mr. Crittenden to the Senate, whence he was withdrawn in 1848, to make the gubernatorial race against Mr. Powell, sorely, as it now appears, against his own political interests, did not desire to involve him in a contest on the floor with any member of his own party. They were willing to discuss his claims upon national, State, personal, or party grounds, before the Whig party alone, in a free and equal party council. They did not know, by any count they were able to make, what would be the result. They pledged themselves over and again to abide that result, whatever it might be, and to go in solid and unbroken phalanx for the nominee by a majority in a council of seventy of the party, the whole seventy binding themselves to such submission. On joint-ballot, seventy votes are necessary to an election. They were willing to this, and proffered it before any ballot was had. Every candid man will acknowledge this, who knows any thing of the party movements in Frankfort from the beginning of the session. Among those willing to submit the decision to a party majority, were several of Mr. Dixon's friends. Forty-six Whigs had tendered such a meeting, and submission to such a decision, before any thing had been said by me on the floor. If "Alpha" or "M." know any thing of what was said or had occurred out of the House, they know it was insisted that Mr. Crittenden should be run before the Democratic party, and his strength tested with the Whig party in a race, where several dissentient Whigs, if the Democratic party could be induced to unite with the minority, even thus feeble, would be able to elect any body over Mr. Crittenden, though he should be supported by sixty-eight Whigs. It is known that it was said in open council, that Mr. Dixon's friends would be willing to come into such a council, provided no name should be placed before it other than such as had been on the ballot in the House. That they feared to trust the gallant leader of the chase, who had, in the heat of the sun, borne the brunt, and strained every nerve and sinew in the contest, reeling with fatigue, and reeking with perspiration in every limb, to a new contest with an old hound, who had lain quietly in the shade, without even straining himself the least, that he might come in at the eleventh hour, and snatch the game which had been run down by others. In the face of taunts like these — I quote them substantially throughout, and in many instances literally — Mr. Crittenden was put in nomination. In the judgment of his best friends, it became my duty to urge his withdrawal. I could not do so without explanation. So much for the circumstance under which I acted; now for the mode in which I discharged my duty to the party, the entire Whig party, with which I am pledged to act. In allusion to Mr. Crittenden's course in 1830, '31 and '32, in the senatorial election, my motives, sentiments, and words, about which there could have been no misunderstanding or misapprehension in the minds of candid men, of whatever party, were substantially, and as near as I can report, literally as follows: If there could have been any doubt, or if it had been possible for any Whig to have been misled as to me, by the ingenious glosses of Dr. Green, on Friday, I am sure I dispelled every, even the faintest resemblance to a vapor, from the mind of every friend of Mr. Clay or Mr. Dixon not determined to misunderstand me. It had been said by distinguished, perhaps the most distinguished, men in the Legislature — men aspiring to a seat in the Senate of the United States themselves, and no friends of Mr. Dixon, though some of them are found voting for him — that Mr. Crittenden seemed to think that Kentucky was made for him; that she had done every thing for him, to the detriment and neglect of others of her sons equally meritorious; that he had been in the Senate; that he quit that high station, and run for governor, to the exclusion of other distinguished gentlemen, who had been anxious for the latter place; that he had resigned the government of Kentucky, before the expiration of his term, to take a prominent and profitable post in the Cabinet at Washington; that now, in the grasping spirit of a monopolist of all the honors of his country, he was seeking to provide himself a seat in the Senate two years in advance of the vacancy; that Mr.

Dixon had been thrust aside, in 1848, to make room for Mr. Crittenden; that, in 1851, he had encountered the full storm of the contest with the Democracy; that he had been overborne by a union of Old Hunkers and Abolitionists; and had fallen the victim to his devotion to the New Constitution, and to the rights of the Southern slaveholders; that he should be rewarded for his toils, his sufferings, and his defeats. These things had not then, though they have since, been said in debate. Every body knows, however, that they were urged incessantly and with powerful effect against Mr. Crittenden, out of the House, in every circle.

In scanning the elements of opposition to Mr. Crittenden, and in tracing the sources of division among the Whigs, those which I have enumerated are open, and lie upon the surface. There is another deeper and far more dangerous, which is working at the vitals, which, if not healed or eradicated, will, in my judgment, disorganize the party, and scatter its elements, never again to be united under a common head, with common objects, and upon its ancient principles of social organization, law, and policy—at least during this generation. This sore I endeavored to touch, when I spoke, as I shall do while I write, with tenderness and caution, but with truth. I did it then, as I do now, with a sincere desire to vindicate historic accuracy, and to prevent the mischief which must inevitably result to a common cause, from the misunderstanding and heartburnings among the respective friends of two of the greatest, at any rate the most renowned, statesmen which this age of Kentucky has produced.

This spark of contention which other men, not I, are endeavoring to fan into a flame of conflagration, had its origin in the action of the convention at Philadelphia, which nominated General Taylor for the Presidency in 1848, and in the course pursued by the Kentucky delegation in that convention. Those who remember the incidents of that day, will be at no loss to recall the efforts made by sundry Democrats, and a few Whigs, to fasten upon Mr. Crittenden the authorship of a letter to Mr. Anderson, of Cincinnati, in which he was made to assail Mr. Clay. The letter was published; its contents will be remembered, as also that it was proved a sheer forgery. The effort proved that it was designed to fasten upon Mr. Crittenden the charge and the guilt of insincerity and intrigue. The design was to sow distrust, and to plant the seeds of future alienation and quarrel between the two great men, from whose thorough union and coöperation the Whig party in Kentucky had been preserved in one unbroken and victorious column, firm in power and purpose, through all the disasters and defeats which it had sustained in the national conflicts. It was the reserved corps—fresh, unbroken in ranks and spirit, upon which the oft beaten line of battle, with its baffled, though still unconquered, leader, could always fall back, and under the cover of its well-trained guns, repair the disasters of every hard-fought field.

Divide and conquer was the maxim of the Romans, by a rigid adherence to which they steadily marched to the subjugation of the world.

In the contest of 1848, the double contest—first, between the two parties, and, secondly, between the friends of General Taylor and Mr. Clay—Mr. Crittenden's position was, in the last degree, delicate and distressing. No man, endowed with a spirit less pure, sensitive and disinterested, could have extricated himself from such a position with grace and honor, nor could he, without sacrificing for himself every hope of power and distinction, connected with the struggle, or growing out of its successful termination. Truth is a jewel always, set it in what case you may. On the present occasion, it must be exposed naked, to the fullest light in which it can be placed.

After General Taylor's first glorious successes in Mexico, every body knows that the eyes of the Whig party, including Mr. Clay's warmest and most devoted friends and admirers, were turned to him, as the man most likely to restore the fallen fortunes of the party. The questions of the annexation of Texas, and the war with Mexico, which grew out of it, were popular. The election of 1844 was decisive upon the questions of boundary and extension. Nothing else could have borne Colonel Polk to the Presidency. Conquest, war and aggrandizement are always popular. These were peculiar elements in the quarrel with Mexico, and the acquisition of Texas and the Pacific coast, which made our late successes doubly dear to the nation. Who so likely to command their suffrages and admiration as the dauntless soldier who had carried forward in triumph the banner of his country, and advanced the boundaries of her empire along with it.—the hero who had executed, with the most complete success, in the field, the resolves of the people at the polls—the fixed policy of the nation? General Taylor was a Whig, and had consented that his name might be used in the Presidential contest. Every body knows that, for a long time, it was believed that Mr. Clay would not be, and did not desire to be, a candidate. By a reference to the card which he published over his own name, upon his return from the east, in 1848, it will be perceived that he states himself such had been the impression with regard to his own personal views; that, under that impression, many of his friends, he had no doubt, from "patriotic motives," had turned their eyes and hopes to another citizen. From the observations he had made, and the information he had received, however, during his visit to the east, he had become satisfied that there were several States, which he there enumerates, that would cast their votes for him, and for no other Whig. One of them, Ohio, a State always steady to Mr. Clay, did actually vote against General Taylor. Under these circumstances, and under the urgent solicitations of his friends, Mr. Clay thought it necessary to announce, over his own signature, his purpose to permit his name to be placed before the convention. These things show, what every body, however, knows to be true, that when General Taylor was taken up so generally by the party, Mr. Clay was not expected to be a candidate. He says so himself, and explains the course of some of his friends upon that hypothesis. This determination of Mr. Clay found Mr. Crittenden in the same position, with many, very many of Mr. Clay's other friends. To him it must have been peculiarly embarrassing. To Mr. Clay and his cause, he had adhered with unshaken constancy through all his fortunes. He had been tried by every test. He had been buckled to the breast of the giant leader of the opposition, General Jackson, with hooks of steel. He found himself now in a situation not sought by himself, and for which he was in no wise responsible. He found himself the cynosure of all eyes. He found himself suspected and watched by both parties—hostile parties within his own camp, led by the most renowned soldier on the one hand, and the most renowned civilian and statesman on the other—both Whigs—and the friends of each struggling for the truncheon of command, and looking to his influence as decisive between these rival friends. Mr. Crittenden stood aloof; he could not, as an honorable man, do otherwise; he awaited, without interference, the decision of his party, prepared to aid to the utmost that decision, for whomsoever it might be cast. He had certainly aided General Taylor's cause, when no man expected Mr. Clay to become again a candidate; he certainly informed General Taylor, so soon as Mr. Clay's name was before the public, that he could go no further; that habit, friendship, duty made him prefer Mr. Clay to any one else. He certainly declared this preference, after General Taylor's nomination, and within my hearing, in a public speech at Versailles—the most brilliant, the most beautiful that even he ever delivered. I questioned him in private as to that declaration—whether I had understood him correctly. He answered with a rebuking eye, the third rebuke that I ever received from that glorious and eloquent eye, that he preferred Mr. Clay, and had said it. He said it, and I so reported him. The sketch of the debate between Mr. Powell and himself that day, published afterward in the Yeoman, signed "Senex," was taken by myself. He said it, AND HE CAN NOT LIE.

General Taylor was nominated without Mr. Crittenden's interference. He was withdrawn from the Senate against his wishes and his interests to make the gubernatorial race.

Who can suppose that Mr. Crittenden desired to quit the Senate of the United States to become governor of Kentucky—to withdraw himself from the eye of the nation, and from a scene where he was winning golden opinions from all men of all parties? When he retired, the entire Senate, men of all parties, met at a public dinner, tendered to the Kentucky Senator, as a voluntary homage rendered to his graceful character and generous nature — a character and nature which, amid the heated conflicts of party, for many years, in which he had ever borne a prominent and distinguished lead, had left, at their close, this beloved and stainless gentleman without an enemy.

Who can believe that John J. Crittenden could voluntarily, or from motives of selfish ambition, have quitted such a situation, and such a scene, to enter the lists with Lazarus Powell; to traverse the State of Kentucky, making stump-speeches, at his age, for the gubernatorial chair, and that, too, pending a revolution, which was to cut that chair from under him before his term expired? The idea is absurd — the charge is false as it is cruel. It was an act of sacrifice, complete self-sacrifice, to the wishes of his friends, and for the salvation of his party. There were many of those who said, and many who believed, that, in the result of General Taylor's election, Crittenden would become secretary of state; that he had sacrificed Mr. Clay to his own ambition; that General Taylor was his friend and relation; that conscious of his own inexperience in public affairs, and ignorance of public men, he would lean entirely upon Mr. Crittenden; that he would organize an administration of his own friends, and under his own lead; that he would keep Mr. Clay out of the Senate; that he had "scotched" and would kill that leader; that he would be President, *de facto*, and in a situation where he could play for the succession, with ample means, and the surest prospect of success. Kentucky had declared, in convention, against Mr. Clay — it was falsely ascribed to Crittenden's influence. He was judged by vulgar men and vulgar maxims. Time and his own actions have proved that he was falsely judged, as he will ever be by such men and such maxims.

The post of secretary of state was tendered to him, as it ought to have been, and rejected. More anxious to vindicate his honor, and preserve his party, so far as he could, entire, than to extend his power, or play for a crown, he remained, like a sentinel, on the post where he had been placed, negligent, as he has ever been, of self, and firm, as he will ever be, to honor and to duty. Mr. Clay returned to the Senate. Calumny itself is dumb here, and dare not whisper that Crittenden tried, or could be induced to try, to prevent it. Efforts, it is said, were made to tempt him to such an exertion of his influence. God knows—I know nothing — but I would have been sworn in advance that such efforts, if they had been made, would have been fruitless. This man is utterly without selfishness. I know him well, and have known him long in every relation of life. He is without the hardness which ambition, to be eminently successful, ought to wear. "Ambition should be made of sterner stuff." In struggles for his friends, he is game and fearless — he is the very type of courage; though even there, in the rage of warfare, and the din of conflict, his bearing is marked by some thing of the gentleness and courtesy, which distinguishes for ever the knight and the gentleman, even in the shock of war, and the storm of battle.

In a struggle among or against his friends, he is powerless and unresisting as an unweaned lamb.

Even now, in the conflict of mighty passions and mighty interests going on in Frankfort, where there are congregated so many elements to crush him — when men who have heretofore hated each other (examples are at hand, but I will not be personal), and hate each other now, are firmly combined to pull him down, and are ready to fly at each other's throats the moment the sacrifice is completed — even now, when his own personal stake, in the game which is playing, is so tremendous, he is "led as a lamb to the slaughter, and as a sheep before its shearers; he is dumb, and opens not his mouth."

It was in this connection, and in view of this charge of infidelity to Mr. Clay, that I spoke of Mr. Crittenden's conduct in the senatorial election of 1830–31 and 1831–32, to show his steady support of Mr. Clay for twenty-five years. With the events of that period, and with Mr. Crittenden's motives and conduct at that time, my position made me perfectly familiar, and my memory has treasured well the facts. The Adams' administration had fallen in 1828, and Kentucky had cast her vote, by a majority of eight thousand, in favor of General Jackson. The principal point of attack on that administration, was a charge of corrupt bargain between Mr. Clay and Mr. Adams, by which the vote of Kentucky in Congress was to be cast for Mr. Adams, and, in the event of his success, Mr. Clay was to be made secretary of state, and thereby placed in the order of succession. Mr. Clay was made secretary of state, and the attack upon the administration, of which he was the chief in the Cabinet, was kept up on this charge alone during the four years of its existence. The course of that administration was blameless, nor to this day can any censure be pronounced against it, even by that party who hunted it to the death, save this only charge as to the manner in which it was formed.

This is history, though your correspondents seem to think it sarcasm. In 1830–31, an election of United States Senator was to be held, to fill a vacancy which was to occur the following spring. At that time, John J. Crittenden was in the very prime of his manhood, younger, by several years, than I am now. He stood, at that time, next to Mr. Clay, *proximus magno intervalo*, as some thought, but certainly next to Mr. Clay he stood in popularity, and in reputation for genius and oratory. I had completed my legal studies under his tuition, and was, at that time, connected with him as his partner in the practice of law. He was in the prime of manhood and the flush of early fame. He had commenced his professional career in the Green river country, at Russellville. He was beloved, in that ardent region, above all the men of his time. He had been sent to the Senate of the United States several years before, to fill a vacancy in an unexpired term, when, as well as I remember, he was barely of the senatorial age. He had retired from the Senate at the expiration of the term, under the pressure of narrow circumstances and an increasing family, and subsequently removed to Frankfort to prosecute his profession in the superior courts held there. For several years he ran for the legislature, at the earnest solicitation of his party, to his own great inconvenience and loss, against a clearly ascertained party majority of one hundred and fifty votes; yet was always victorious—his political enemies voting for him from personal admiration and regard. Under all these circumstances, and when there was a party majority of several votes — four I think — in the legislature against Mr. Clay, who was to be, and did become the next candidate for the presidency, Mr. Crittenden was put in nomination against Colonel Richard M. Johnson, and tied him. That session there was no election. At that time, Woodford, the county which I now represent, was represented by a Democrat, a devoted friend of General Jackson. He was instructed, by a majority of his constituents, to vote for Mr. Crittenden, and disobeyed. The next year the elections in Kentucky were made to turn upon the choice of a Senator. Mr. Crittenden was every where considered as the candidate. The state was revolutionized, and a majority returned favorable to his election. Mr. Clay was not staked, nor his name periled in this race. If defeat had been sustained, it would have been Mr. Crittenden's defeat. This is exactly what I said in debate, and these are historical facts. In 1831–32, with a majority thus won and constituted, in the judgment of Mr. Clay's friends throughout the Union — in the judgment of Mr. Crittenden, at least, here — the interests of the opposition would best be served by placing Mr. Clay himself in the Senate of the United

States. Had Mr. Crittenden pressed his own claims, had he been selfish, it is certain, beyond question or controversy, that Mr. Clay could not, and would not, have pushed his younger friend and second from the place for which he had contended. Mr. Crittenden must have been elected, or divided and distracted his party, as it is now divided and distracted, running at the head of a minority of his personal friends, playing for the support of his enemies, and crying out that Mr. Clay had had honors enough; that it was time for him to give place to younger men; that it was time for the young chivalry, who had borne the brunt and blows of war, to wear its laurels, and enjoy its honors. These things were said. Mr. Crittenden had friends who believed that, with equal opportunities, and upon the broader theatre of the National Legislature, his talents would soon place him abreast with the foremost in the race of glory and fame. He recognized Mr. Clay as the great head of opposition. He deemed his presence in the Senate necessary to its organization and success. In his judgment, Mr. Clay ought to have been the man. He silenced and satisfied his own devoted friends, and gracefully and voluntarily yielded to the national leader a seat which that leader would not have claimed, and for which he could not, without indecency, have contended with a friend.

This is the substance of what I said, and said it to prove that John J. Crittenden was twenty years ago exactly what John J. Crittenden has ever been, and what he is now. This has been construed into a boast of Mr. Crittenden's friends through me, that he is the founder of Mr. Clay's fortunes—the architect of his fame and greatness. He the founder of Mr. Clay's greatness and fame, and this from me, who have studied Mr. Clay's political history as I have studied that of no other statesmen, living or dead. From 1806 to 1851, he has written nothing, said nothing which has been published, from his speech on the line of the Perdido to his great letter the other day on Secession and the Union, which I have not conned and pondered. I charge that Mr. Crittenden was the founder of his fortunes—the architect of his fame! Mr. Clay was in the Senate then, as now, the thunderer of the scene, when John J. Crittenden was at college. I cited, as matter of history, with every portion of which I was familiarly acquainted, to show that Mr. Crittenden had never considered himself the rival of Mr. Clay, whatever others might have thought, or desired him to be or attempt. That Mr. Clay was before him in age, in glory, in the race of ambition; that twenty years ago he recognized the fact; that, so far from timidity in the cause of a friend, he was willing to peril his young fame, and did peril it, in a cause which had just been beaten at home; that, so far from being a selfish monopolist of honor, insensible to the just claims of others, he had recognized the position and the claims of a man then more distinguished than himself, the indisputable head of his party, and after contending with the courage of the young shepherd of Israel against the Goliah of the Philistines, had voluntarily and modestly laid his trophies and his spoils at the feet of his commander-in-chief. I charge that Mr. Clay owes his greatness and his influence to Mr. Crittenden, or any thing else but his own genius! My object, if I were sane, would certainly be to reconcile, not inflame — to attune this jarring string to harmony, that the whole Whig instrument, from bass to treble, swept by the great master of the band, may again swell into one soul-stirring peal of sympathy.

I risk offending Mr. Clay's friends, or seek to add that influence, that commanding influence, to give consistency, direction, dignity, and force to the beggarly elements at work to ruin that man, to whom I am known to be devoted on personal as well as political grounds — to love as though he were my elder brother! I said that the Adams' administration had fallen, and that Kentucky, among others, struck a fatal blow. Is not this historically true? Was this statement, under the explanations which I have given in the House and here, aimed as a sarcasm at Mr. Clay, or can it be wrested into an assertion that Mr. Crittenden was the author of his greatness? Mr. Clay did fall in 1828, and from a lofty hight; but sprang, as he always springs, like the antique wrestler, the stronger from his fall, more terrible on the rebound than he was ere shaken from his feet. I have studied his life, his speeches, his actions, his character; I have heard him at the bar and in the Senate; I have seen him in his contests with other men, when all the stormy passions of his tempestuous soul were lashed by disappointment and opposition to the foaming rage of the ocean, when all the winds are unchained, and sweep in full career over the free and bounding bosom of the deep. He owes less of his greatness to education or to art than any man living. He owes less of his commanding influence to other men than any great leader I have ever known, or of whom I have ever read. He consults no body, he leans upon no body, he fears no body; he wears nature's patent of nobility for ever on his brow; he stalks among men with an unanswerable and never-doubting air of command; his sweeping and imperial pride, his indomitable will, his unquailing courage, challenge from all submission or combat. With him there can be no neutrality. Death, tribute, or the koran, is his motto. Great in speech, great in action, his greatness is all his own. He is independent alike of history or the schools; he knows little of either, and despises both. His ambition, his spirit, and his eloquence are all great, natural, and entirely his own. If he is like any body, he does not know it. He has never studied models, and if he had, his pride would have rescued him from the fault of imitation. He stands among men in towering and barbaric grandeur; in all the hardihood and rudeness of perfect originality; independent of the polish, and beyond the reach of art. His vast outline, and grand, but wild and undefined, proportions, liken him to a huge mass of granite, torn, in some convulsion of nature, from a mountain's side, which any effort of the chisel would only disfigure, and which no instrument in the sculptor's studio could grasp or comprehend.

I have acquitted myself, I hope, from what I consider the most serious charge urged against me by your correspondents—that of having indirectly assailed Mr. Clay's reputation, or of irritating the friends of that gentleman against Mr. Crittenden. As to my taunts and sarcasms, and thrusts at Mr. Dixon, which, it seems, are the cause of this now envenomed and incurable quarrel, a few words, and I am done. Here, as before, I shall write, as nearly as I can, what I said. If I was understood as assailing the character of Mr. Dixon, or the feelings of his friends, I was grossly misconceived. I certainly prefer Mr. Crittenden for the Senate to him, and, if I did not, my constituents most certainly do. I certainly do not approve the course of himself and his friends in this contest. Claiming, as they do, to be members of the Whig party, and anxious for the unanimity and success of that party, as they claim to be, they ought, in my judgment, most certainly, to have submitted their favorite, in the first instance, to the common law of all parties and communities of men, that is, the will and judgment of the majority of the members. Their preference for Mr. Dixon I have never censured, and am not surprised at. It can not, however, be greater, more ardent, nor do I think it better founded, than the preference of Mr. Crittenden's friends for him. I do not think their demand, that Mr. Crittenden should be balloted against Mr. Dixon in the Houses, was either generous or just, as a fair mode of ascertaining the respective strength of the two gentlemen before their own party. It is no disparagement to Mr. Dixon to say that Mr. Crittenden has more of national character and a wider fame than he. Mr. C. has been long in the national councils. He has been twice a member of the Federal Cabinet, and has been recently named as a probable candidate for the first or second place on the Presidential ticket. These things alone, independent of any comparison between the original talents or personal merits of the gentlemen, make it perfectly obvious that Mr. C.'s defeat would be more an object with the Democratic party than the defeat of Mr. Dixon. Any other comparison I never instituted, nor do I now. I never understood, nor can I now understand, the motive of Mr. Dixon's friends in refusing a caucus, unless it be that they are conscious of being in a minority, and that they hoped, by dragging Mr. Crittenden into a contest before the Houses, the Democracy might determine to select the weaker candidate, and claim a party victory in the defeat of a gentleman who is certainly considered, throughout the United States, the strongest man in Kentucky after Mr. Clay. I stated, in the House, that I had known Mr. Dixon twenty years; that I had often served with him in the legislature; that I enjoyed his acquaintance, and I hoped some portion of his personal friendship; that for personal honor, and especially for firmness and high personal gallantry, I did not know his superior. I stated that I had voted for him myself for governor; that, in the county which I represented, he had polled the full Whig majority; that I was then, and had always been, before I knew Mr. Crittenden's strength, prepared, and had avowed it in a large meeting of the Whigs, to vote for Mr. Dixon for the Senate of the United States, if he received the nomination of the majority of the party to which he belonged, and with which I was acting. More than this, I could not say—more than this, I could not do. As to my unlucky allusion to Lazarus and the resurrection, it was playfully done. Governor Powell was himself in the lobby at the time, and heard it all. It has, I am sure, not given him the slightest offense, nor does he consider me as having insulted him, or outraged propriety or decorum. In sober earnest, and in simple historic verity, Mr. Crittenden beat Mr. Powell, and Mr. Powell beat Mr. Dixon. There is no denying this, and I, at least, am not to blame for it. It is strange justice, to say the least of it, to reward Mr. Dixon for his defeat by giving him the seat which was Mr. Crittenden's, and which he quitted with reluctance, and at great loss of position, to obtain a victory over this same Lazarus. It does look to me like tearing the well-earned laurels from the victor's brow to adorn the triumph of a vanquished leader. It would be to strip the wreath from Fabius or Scipio to bind the temple of Terentius Varro. Thanks and gratitude and sympathy are certainly due to Mr.

Dixon for his untiring exertions in an unfortunate campaign. His own defeat was the defeat of his party; but I am unable to perceive that it will be bettered or atoned for by the prostration of Mr. Crittenden.

I can not conceive how your correspondent could understand me as taunting or thrusting with ill-natured and ill-timed sarcasm at Mr. Dixon, unless they consider the praise liberally but justly bestowed, I think, upon my friend, as so much subtracted from theirs. They forgot to mention the terms employed by Bates, the Democrat, and by the Whig gentlemen, Mr. McKee and Mr. Mitchell, in their replies to me. They could not have been originated by my remarks. Suffice it to say, that, notwithstanding my efforts to withdraw Mr. Crittenden from nomination, the Senate balloted for him before they were apprized of his withdrawal in the House. In this state of the case, I withdrew my opposition, and the ballot went on in the House of Representatives. Contrary to my fears, the Democracy disdained to abandon their own standard, and to side with a minority of their enemies. They would not steal a victory. The result was, Mr. Crittenden beat Mr. Dixon twelve votes with the Whigs. In that most impassioned and eloquent speech, delivered by Mr. Mitchell, of Montgomery, the young gentleman who nominated Mr. Dixon, he stated exactly what I had previously said was alleged by his party against Mr. Crittenden. He charged that we were running a parcel of bob-tailed nags from our stable (these were his precise expressions) against their gallant steed, till we tired him down, when we would bring out our favorite horse, fresh and unblown, to make the best heat, and take the cup from their courser, exhausted by this jockeying system. He said that Mr. Crittenden had stood one ballot, to be sure, but he knew that he would be immediately withdrawn, and the old game renewed. These taunts and this opposition to Mr. Crittenden, took me, from the first, by surprise, nor do I now fully comprehend their motive, or their cause. He is not here, and his friends are charged with a heavy responsibility. They have never been afraid to trust him before the Whig party in the legislature, and have always offered to do so.

They are not afraid to make the question in the elections of 1853, and to throw him before the people of the state, Democrats and all. These reiterated taunts, however, that he is skulking—he, John J. Crittenden, afraid to trust himself before the Whig party; that his friends rely upon finesse, and manœuver, and intrigue; that the lion's skin has failed, and is now to be eked out by the fox's; that, although not at all afraid of Mr. Powell in 1848, in 1851 he had suddenly lost all nerve and manhood, and trembled in the presence of Mr. Dixon like a whipped school-boy—have roused the metal of Mr. C.'s friends at last. They did not wish to involve their champion in a quarrel with one of his own party. They desired, and they labored to keep the peace, and preserve the harmony of the party. They were willing to submit themselves to its judgment and its will. But this oft-repeated charge, that Mr. Crittenden shrunk from a conflict to which he was exposing his friends, one after another—although John B. Thompson was the only friend of his balloted for before his own nomination—has roused his party at last. In reply to Mr. Mitchell, I was instructed, by those who had the right to give such instructions, to announce that Mr. Crittenden's name would never be withdrawn. Our leader has quit his tent, and is in the field, at the head of his friends, an undoubted majority of his own party. We have hung his banner on the outer wall—he will die at least with harness on his back. He is a candidate for the Senate of the United States, and will so remain, till the Democracy slaughter him here, or the people decide against him in the election of 1853. I called him Bayard, I believe; that ought not to have enraged any body. I call him Bayard now, the knight without fear, and without reproach. He is, as Bayard was, adorned with all courage and all courtesy. He is (I love to praise a great and good man)—he is a mirror, in which the young chivalry of Kentucky may glass and fashion itself to all manly virtue, and every gentlemanly grace.

There are examples enough in the history of heroes to cheer us on. We have rendered retreat impossible to our chief. Agathocles, in ancient times, when he invaded Africa and Sicily, burned his ships, and showed his troops there was no safety but in victory. Cortes, when he invaded Mexico, did the same, and cast the wide Atlantic between him and safety, without a prow or sail to bear him off. The last of the great barons of England, king-making Warwick, when pressed to his fall, brought to the front of his line the noble charger that had borne him in triumph over a hundred fields. The good steed bent his frontlet to his lord, who kissed the forehead of the generous animal, then plunged the dagger to his heart. The troops saw that their leader could not fly, even were he base enough to attempt it. Taunt us no more. Our leader's ships are burnt—his horse is dead. He can not fly if he would—he would not if he could. The banner which floats over him is broad, and bright, and spotless, as Bayard's oriflamme adorned with the lilies of France. I will not push out the parallel—I will not name Charles De Bourbon, high constable of France.

Should Bayard fall, he will be found with his feet to the foe, and his face upturned to the heavens. We will wrap him in his own banner for a winding-sheet—stained with his blood, it shall wave no more.

Consider you these as taunts? They are, however, the head and front of my offending.

Mr. Prentice, in my humble judgment, the defeat or withdrawal of Mr. Crittenden at this time would be the greatest disaster that has befallen the Whig party in twenty years. All hope of reconciliation in the legislature is impossible, I think. In my judgment, the majority of the Whigs should adjourn promptly and at once this vexed question to the people, to be decided by the elections of 1853. The Democrats will close with this proposition, I believe. If it is not done, the session will be wasted in the struggle, and the Whigs will be saddled with the whole responsibility. The Democrats will not sit beyond the sixty days, and the session will close with the most important business untouched. Adjourn the senatorial election till the next general assembly, I say. The people are never vexed by the reference of such a question to them. Without reference to Mr. Crittenden, I should be of this opinion; with reference to him, I would rather trust him in the hands of the people than to the personal factions now raging in Frankfort. I have long been an exiled and a branded man; for myself, I scorn to beg or to apologize for aught I have thought, said, or done in times past. I have never betrayed or sought to divide any party with whom I professed to act. When I could not act with the majority—when I could not, with a safe conscience, pursue their decisions, I have quit them openly and fairly, and acted with the other side. I hope you may find room for this letter, long as it is.

SPEECH IN OPPOSITION TO THE PRINCIPLES OF THE KNOW-NOTHING ORGANIZATION,

Delivered at Versailles, Kentucky, June 25, 1855.

Mr. MARSHALL, during his political career, adhered with marked consistency to the principles of the old Whig party. In our introduction, we have noticed the causes that produced the separation in 1844. Subsequent to that time, he has regarded the party as abandoning their principles on several important national questions. He was opposed to the repeal of the Missouri Compromise. When the American organization was originated, he urged the Whigs of his State to plant themselves firmly on their old principles, and stand aloof from it, telling them that, otherwise, disruption would be the result. His counsel was not heeded—the Whigs, in the main, identified themselves with the new party. During the canvass of 1855, for the purpose of discussing the subject before the people, Mr. MARSHALL announced himself a candidate for Congress in his old district. He reached Versailles on the 25th of June, and addressed a large and attentive audience. After reading and commenting upon the Philadelphia platform, and expressing himself satisfied with its resolves upon the slavery question, he spoke in substance as follows:

IT seems strange that the existence of the Deity, and his superintendence of the world, should be among Sam's secrets. I had supposed these matters were extensively known, and generally received among men, before the advent of the new party. It is strange that there should be a *Protestant* party in this country, bound together by an oath of secresy, under a thorough and complete organization, whose objects are political, owing allegiance to a government unknown to the constitution and the laws, with objects and with men concealed from all but the initiated. An *imperium in imperio*, seeking to grasp all power in this country, legislative and administrative, from a constable to the president of the United States.

I look around me upon a crowd of men, familiar to me all my life. I see men who have been the tried friends of my bosom

—the companions of my heart—men who have stood by me in every variety of fortune, through good and evil report—men who have wrapped themselves about me like the traveler's cloak in the fable, to shield and to shelter me when the storm had raged the loudest and the fiercest, and these men, bound by an oath not to reveal, even to me, the fact, the simple fact, that they are members of this order until the dispensing power of the general council authorize the disclosure! The order, so far as I understand it, seems an exact copy of that instituted by Ignatius Loyola. Its objects were universal empire, and the establishment of a religion by *political* authority; Loyola's was Catholic; this is Protestant Jesuitism. Popular institutions can not subsist without entire publicity in political transactions.

The new organization has promised a national platform. It calls itself the "American party." In this they have failed signally. The convention at Philadelphia were certainly know-nothings—all know-nothings. There must have been some principles, common to the entire order, which united and made them one. These principles did not relate to slavery—on that point the party broke into two. The party North were abolition; the party South held no principles upon the subject peculiar to themselves—they held nothing that had not been avowed, aye, and acted on by the national democracy for many years, and through fierce contests. What was it upon which northern and southern know-nothingism agreed? What was the point of contact between them? Nothing that I can discover but the repeal of the naturalization laws, and the imposition of political disabilities upon men of the Catholic communion, whether of American or foreign birth. Upon these points, the party North and the party South agreed. This is all their nationality—this is all their Americanism. These are anti-American ideas. Religious toleration and the right of expatriation are peculiar to this republic. These are the features that distinguish our institutions from every form of polity that has ever been known among men. I admit that they could repeal the naturalization laws, by act of Congress, without violating the Federal Constitution. Whether they should do so or not is a matter of sound discretion and policy. Religious liberty, however, in its largest and widest sense, is established by the Constitution. If the party succeed in its organization, it will be really and practically abridged. When a party has a particular object—a single idea, paramount to all others, the distinguishing feature of their system—all experience has shown, that whenever they acquire the political power, they carry this idea into legislation, and seek to make it permanent by the sanctions of law. Catholic disabilities is their leading object. They are sworn never to vote for a Catholic for office. They consider such unfitted by his religion to hold office in a republican government. They consider this republic as seriously endangered by the practical operation of that principle in the Constitution which declares that "no religious test shall ever be required as a qualification to any office or public trust under the United States." They seek to establish a religious test. They can not do so, permanently, without changing the Federal Constitution. If they get the power, they will be inconsistent and stupid, unless they graft upon the Constitution, and make a part of the fundamental law their great idea—the idea upon which "Protestant civilization" and the hopes of the world, in their judgment, depend. They can only reach their object through a revolution in the government.

There is, in my judgment, an awful significance in the recent letter of Rev. R. J. Breckenridge to the Commonwealth. It throws out, in distinct outline, the dark shadow of coming events. The writer is a man of great genius. As the representative of the religious element, he scorns to wear a mask, and writes over his own proper signature. Whatever emanates from that source, on many accounts, is worthy of the most attentive consideration. Mr. Breckinridge, after asserting that the nationality of America is to be sustained, her Protestant civilization to be perpetuated, and her Federal Union to be preserved, by destroying the foreign and Catholic influence, which he considers as in a great measure now controlling our government and politics, proceeds in the following ominous language: "There is but one possible method of dealing with the subject. The organized power of society must be taken out of the hands of those who have betrayed these vast interests, and must be put into the hands of those who will cherish them. Public opinion is the only instrument by which this great change can be effected. *The first step of the revolution is political; the second is legal.* The first step involves the organization, and the triumph of a party commensurate with the country—'The American party'—and that involves the overthrow of every party that resists its ultimate objects, *or resists the necessary means of attaining these objects.* Indeed, if this step were fully achieved, it would be of less consequence to take a second one; since the laws, though bad, are endurable, and society is safe as soon as it has finally put out of power *all men and parties hostile to our nationality*, to our Protestant civilization, and to our Federal Union; *out of power with an overthrow incapable of being repaired.* And this is the reason why this great movement excites such excruciating bitterness of hate, in its political aspects, on the part of all against whom it is directed. Its success is seen to be a finality and a fatality to them, etc." This language, and the ideas thereby conveyed, are most portentously distinct. Taken in connection with the character of the author, and his vast and controling influence in what he calls "the religious element," in this great movement, they become of the most intense importance. Mr. B. knows very well that a party victory in a single election, a transient political success, would go but little way in the road he wishes to travel. Mr. B. *calls* it a revolution. "The first step of the revolution," he says, "is political; *the second is legal.* Our nationality is endangered; our Protestant civilization is endangered; our Federal Union is endangered; the preservation of these constitutes our mission on earth." The country, of whose purpose know-nothingism is the manifestation, has determined to surround these great interests with "additional safeguards." They who are opposed to the methods proposed of furnishing adequate safeguards to nationality, civilization and union, "ought, in the judgment of the country," as Mr. B. thinks and writes, "to be indiscriminately crushed." "We, and our fathers," Mr. B. says, "have an unsettled account with popery, many centuries old." It is clear, very clear, that *the revolution* aimed at by the new party, and in the contemplation of Mr. B., involves the total repeal of the naturalization laws, and the change of the Constitution of the United States, in relation to religious tests as qualification for office. It is uncandid in the extreme, in the American party and their order, to endeavor to deny or obscure their real objects. There is nothing else but this legal revolution which discriminates them as a party. "*Americans shall rule America.*" So say I, so says every one. "But who are Americans?" By our constitution and laws, persons of a certain color born in the United States, and others "naturalized" by law, are citizens and Americans. They do rule America, and for some seventy years have ruled it more peacefully and prosperously than any other people ever were ruled. I contend that our immediate ancestors have suffered nothing from papal oppressions. The rival sects, the offspring of the Reformation, have alternately persecuted each other, and as they have alternately conquered, have held political power at home. The Churchman persecuted the Puritan, the Puritan and Presbyterian persecuted the Churchman, and both have persecuted the Catholics. New England, Maryland, and Virginia, were settled principally by exiles and refugees from religious intolerance in England. The tolerant spirit of the gospel, the true genius of Christianity, which is universal charity, the principle of Luther, the true principle of the Reformation, never had practical life till it was established here in our republic, and by those institutions which they seek to overthrow. The body politic, the grand corporation which is styled the United States of America, is the only state or society of men ever known, which, as a government, has no religion.

The Hindoo, Persian, Jew, Egyptian, Greek, Roman, Barbarian, had all, their religious establishments, with their orders of priesthood existing by law, and sustained by the power of the State. Christianity, after it triumphed over paganism, and had sustained terrific persecutions from the Roman emperors, formed a political alliance and became a part of the imperial establishment. We know the result. The reformation of the sixteenth century did not cure the evil. The three great divisions of the reformed church, the Lutheran or German, under the confession of Augsburg, the Calvinistic with the Presbyterian model of government, and the peculiar system of dogmas tortured from the writings of St. Paul by the French Reformer, and the Episcopal church of England, each sought a political establishment in the several countries where they obtained. Each considered itself as peculiarly intrusted with the cause of Almighty God, and dealt with Catholics, heretics and dissenters from what the dominant party called orthodoxy, as though clothed with infinite judgment in divine things, and with the mission of infinite vengeance for speculative errors and sins of opinion. Luther, perhaps the greatest personage who appeared in the church after its founder, was far, very far in advance of the age in which he lived. He taught the doctrines of religious toleration, and practiced what he taught. But he was not understood by his own times. Men had to be educated to a truth so sublimely simple, through centuries of mutual intolerance, suffering and blood. It was reserved for the founders of this republic to proclaim and establish the great truth, that political government had nothing to do with speculative opinions, religious dogmas, or forms of ecclesiastical polity. Of these matters the law "knows nothing." The Bible is the only standard of religious truth. Each individual man is an interpreter for himself. He needs no priest or mediator, but Christ in Heaven, and God is the only judge and avenger of sin. Political government guards life, liberty and property. It takes cognizance of human action, only as it affects others, in some one of these rights. It restrains the liberty of no man, only where such liberty trenches upon the equal rights of another. It interferes with opinion not at all upon any subject; least of all in religion. That is an affair between the individual man and his Maker.

To a free Bible, a free Press, a free Pulpit, and a system of religious belief and discipline absolutely voluntary and free, without restraint or interference, our law has intrusted the truth. Orthodoxy is an affair for the preachers, not for statesmen. The preacher is the advocate, the individual is the judge. The law takes no part. Argument is the only coercion in this world. No torture, no civil disability is allowed. The convincing reasonings of fire, or social degradation, or political disfranchisement are repealed here, and it was hoped for ever. Penalties for heresies in opinion, for speculative errors, are referred to the power who formed the human mind, and who alone can judge it with perfect knowledge and perfect righteousness.

The Catholic religion in this country is a perfectly voluntary system. The priesthood of that communion, have no means here of enforcing this system, or punishing disobedience or disbelief. The Catholic may stay away from the confessional, as the Protestant may from preaching, there is no law or magistrate to make him afraid. Right or wrong, this is our system. In my judgment, it bears the impress of consummate wisdom. Sam, however, judges differently. He affects to be afraid of the temporal power of the Pope. I allege that the temporal power or political authority of the Pope was never acknowledged by any State or people out of his own dominions, never, not in the times of Gregory, or Innocent, or Boniface. As a temporal prince, the Pope treated, negotiated, fought. He made alliances or waged war with Catholic States and princes within the Peninsula or beyond the Alps on terms of perfect political equality. No citizen of Venice or Florence, no subject of Milan or Naples during the middle ages, and after Italian wars and politics became interwoven with those of the transalpine nations, as part of the general history of Europe, no Frenchman, German, Englishman or Spaniard, though all Catholic, ever dreamed that he owed allegiance to the Pope as a temporal monarch, or was bound to his holiness by any tie that interfered with his duty to his own government, or made it sacrilege to bear arms against the Pope in war. Charles V, the greatest Catholic monarch of his day, the most devoted to the spiritual claims and jurisdiction of the Pope, the most decided and dangerous enemy to Luther and the reformation, after endeavoring in vain, by a long and subtle course of negotiation, in the sixteenth century, to draw the Pope into an alliance against France, declared war against him, sent an imperial army of German, Italian and Spanish Catholics, commanded by a Catholic Prince, Charles Bourbon, against the holy city itself. It was taken and sacked with merciless ferocity—the Pope himself taken captive, and confined, till the Emperor extorted such an alliance, and such guarantees as pleased the victor. The temporal power of the Pope in the nineteenth century is indeed a ghost wherewith to frighten the North American Republic. Sam is indeed scared, timid youth, at shadows—shadows thrown by no substance in existence, either now or in the past; shadows the new creation of his own fears, or the inventions of his wit, to frighten others, as malicious boys scare babies, with stories of raw heads and bloody-bones. Persecution is ever found to multiply the persecuted sect, unless you exterminate them. Leave the Catholics where the Constitution left them, or treat them, as the inquisition in Spain and the Papal States in Italy treated heretics—burn them, and burn them all. It is mere trifling in this organization to say that to exclude a man from office or honor in a free state, to place a whole class of native citizens in a rank below others, on account of their religion, is not persecution on account of religion, is not an abridgement of his religious liberty. They say, in one of their resolves, that they do not mean to interfere with the rights of conscience or religious belief. The Catholics may worship God, after their own fashion, but they will degrade them for it below the condition of free citizens. They will place them in the caste of mulattoes, free negroes and Indians. They had as well say, that they might imprison or burn for religious opinions, and the victims might still believe as they pleased. Gallileo when thrown into the dungeon, still enjoyed philosophic freedom—he still believed that the earth revolved. Huss, when expiring in the flames at Constance, and Servetus, at Geneva, *enjoyed* their religious belief, and shouted and proclaimed it as though triumphing in death. "An American Party" should be ashamed of such wretched and shuffling sophistry. Shift the shoe to the other foot. Gore the other ox and the party will shift its arguments in a trice—they will roar you out civil and religious liberty, loud as a young lion when roused from his jungle by the spear of the hunter. Indeed, they tell you now, that for a Catholic to hold office in this country, is an infraction of their Protestant liberty. What would they say—ye gods! what would they say, if the Catholics were actually banded together, as they seek to band the Protestant sects together against them, for the avowed purpose of excluding all American Protestants from office, and all native Americans not Catholics, from suffrage, as being inclined naturally to Protestantism. Let Catholics and foreigners treat this party as they are actually trying to use them, and you would hear the cry of persecution raised lustily. They would obtest Heaven and earth, they would rush to arms in defense. The badge, the universal badge of Anglo-Saxon freedom, the right of representation, would be torn from them only with their life. This right, if extinguished, would be extinguished only in their blood.

In relation to the naturalization laws, there is, undoubtedly, just cause of complaint for abuse and frauds practiced under them. The true spirit of those laws is evaded, and their real object defeated in very many instances by their defective execution, growing mainly out of the defective mode of proof of the preliminary fact as provided by the laws themselves. In this particular, I am and have long been in favor of their amendment.

The intention of those laws, was that no alien should be admitted to the rights of citizenship, or take the oath of abjuration and allegiance, till he had actually resided within the limits of the United States or some of her territories, five years. Moreover such alien must have declared his purpose to become a citizen three years before his admission to take the oath. In point of fact, according to the present mode of executing the laws, and the mode of proof under them, aliens are in very many instances admitted, who have not been in the country six months. These evils and abuses could be completely corrected, and the naturalization laws enforced according to their real intent, by revision and amendment. The object could be effected by means of offices of registry in which all aliens coming into the country should be compelled to enter their names, with the date of their arrival, and the further provision that a certified copy of such entry under the seal of the office, should be filed in a court, either district or circuit, of the United States or some of her territories, at the time when the party makes his declaration of intention to become a citizen, and that both the declaration and entry should be recorded in a federal court. When, three years thereafter, the party should apply for admission to take the oaths, the certified copy of the date of his registration and his previous declaration of his intention to become a citizen, from the office of record, should alone be received as evidence of either fact. It would be a matter of no great difficulty to prevent the importation or landing upon our shores of paupers and felons, without touching the real objects and spirit of the naturalization laws as they stand.

The object of the Know-Nothing secret association is to repeal the naturalization laws altogether, and to admit none but natives to the elective franchise, and to exclude even natives, if they be Catholics, from every office under government: "Americans and Protestant Americans by birth shall alone rule Americans." The Pharisaic Philadelphia Platform announces, as its third great cardinal principle, "The maintenance of the Union as the paramount political good," and by way of corollary from, or exemplification of, the principle, "Obedience to the Constitution of the United States as the supreme law of the land, sacredly obligatory upon all its parts and members; *and steadfast resistance to the spirit of innovation upon its principles, however specious the pretexts.*" This lip-service to the Union and the constitution is exceedingly fashionable, and marvellously cheap and easy. The abolitionist, when he takes his seat in Congress, swears to observe the Constitution and maintain the Union. The nullifier does the same. Your man from Massachusetts, who is both abolitionist and nullifier, swears to their doctrine. We must go a little further than these general declarations, even when backed by oaths, before we can know whom to trust with the Union and the Constitution. The new organization avows "steadfast resistance to the spirit of innovation upon the *principles* of the Constitution, however specious the pretexts." This is their text. One of the principles of the constitution is that "no religious test shall ever be required as a qualification to any office of public trust under the United States." They have sworn, upon the holy evangelists, to exclude all men of the Catholic religion, whether citizens by birth or naturalization, from every office of public trust under government. This is their commentary and proof of "steadfast resistance to innovation upon the *principles* of the constitution" upon any "pretext, however specious." The constitution declares that Congress shall have power to establish a uniform rule of naturalization, and further, that "the citizens of each State shall be entitled to all the privileges and immunities of citizens in the several States."

There is abundant evidence, from the highest and most indisputable sources, that if this party is not able to repeal the laws of naturalization established by the national legislature in pursuance of the constitution, they mean, wherever they have the power, by State laws or constitutions, to repeal the naturalization laws, and set up by State authority different tests of citizenship from those established by Congress, producing thereby a beautiful uniformity on this subject. The source whence I draw my proof of this latter proposition is no less high and indisputable than the official efforts of the Hon. Garrett Davis, of Bourbon, backed with all the powers of argument and eloquence of which that gentleman is so conspicuous a master. The resolutions which he offered when a member of the convention, which formed the new constitution of Kentucky, and the speeches which he made in support of them, are now before me. Mr. Davis, in fixing or attempting to fix the rights of citizenship, and the qualifications of voters, under the new constitution, sought to confine them in Kentucky, as to persons of foreign birth: 1st. To such as, at the time of the adoption of the amended constitution, should be naturalized citizens of the United States. 2d. To such as, at the time of the adoption of the amended constitution, should have declared their purpose to become citizens of the United States, in conformity to the laws thereof, *and who shall have become citizens.* 3d. Those who, *twenty-one years previously thereto shall have declared their purpose*, according to the existing provisions of the laws of the United States, to become citizens thereof, and who then shall be citizens of the United States, etc. The true meaning of the third provision is, perhaps, not perfectly clear. It is differently interpreted by different readers. Some persons consider that it was Mr. Davis' intention, through all time, to confer the right of suffrage upon foreigners born, who had declared their purpose to become citizens of the United States twenty-one years previously to their application to vote, and who should be actually citizens at the time of the election at which such application should be made. Such persons consider the words "previously thereto," to mean, previously to any election which might be held in Kentucky, at any distance of time from the adoption of the amended constitution, while that constitution remained in force. To me it appears that the plain grammatical construction, taking all the clauses together, is that the word "thereto" refers to the adoption of the amended constitution—no other point of time is referred to or named in any of the clauses. The first clause begins, "those who at the time of the adoption of this amended constitution," etc. The second clause commences with the same words—and the third proceeds immediately without any other phrase or reference, "Those who, twenty-one years previously thereto, etc." Previously to what? To the adoption of the amended constitution, undoubtedly. Whether Mr. Davis meant to confine the right of suffrage, in the case of foreigners born, only to those who were naturalized citizens of the United States at the time of the adoption of the amended constitution, and who had been actual residents of the country and declarants of their purpose to become citizens twenty-one years previously thereto, or meant that twenty-one years residence and naturalization under the laws of the United States shall at any time confer the right of suffrage, without reference to the date of the amended constitution, is immaterial. In either event, it is the purpose of the resolutions to exclude from office and suffrage in Kentucky naturalized citizens of the United States, who had every other qualification of a citizen of Kentucky but birth. The Constitution of the United States and the laws of Congress in relation to the important subject of citizenship, recognize no distinction between citizens by birth and citizens by adoption. The rules of naturalization must be uniform. The language employed, the word used to express the act of conferring the rights of citizenship upon an alien born, whatever those rights may be, is singular and exceedingly impressive. The law is said not to convert him into a denizen or citizen, or to confer any limited or specified rights upon him, but to *naturalize* him. Such is the transcendant power intended to be conferred upon Congress, that the law passed in pursuance of it is supposed to abolish the fact of foreign birth, and to stand in the place of nativity. The new born republican is regenerated by an act of paramount and all sovereign grace. In the language of the theologians, he is born again. Now, these naturalization laws require only five years' residence. Mr. Davis' resolution requires twenty-one, and therefore, in Kentucky, renders null and imperative the law of the United States.

I admit Mr. D.'s talents, firmness, and purity. I avow accordance with the general views of that gentleman, in relation to social organization and fundamental law as maintained by him in the convention. I can never sufficiently admire or laud the political heroism and self-sacrificing zeal with which he threw himself alone into the wide breach made by the convention in what I hold with Mr. D. to be the true principles of constitutional freedom, and opposed himself singly to a torrent which had proved irresistible.

If there has ever been personal unkindness between us, it was long since healed and obliterated. Still, in my most decided and deliberate judgment, Mr. Davis' resolutions contained a great radical and mischievous error; an error which, if carried into the legislation of the States, is fatal to the constitution and the Union upon this point of citizenship. It would prove fatal, too, to Mr. Davis' own darling scheme of repealing, by the national authority, the naturalization laws. If the new party, during the existence of those laws, can establish, by State constitution or law, a different rule of citizenship, within a particular State, how shall they say that a State where they are in the minority, may not disregard their repealing act, and establish for itself any rule of naturalization the State may see fit? The doctrine, in its practical operation, destroys, in my judgment, the fundamental idea of the republic. It annihilates the nationality of the people. It falsifies the first words of the Federal constitution—"We, the people of the United States." It abolishes the provision that "the citizens of each State shall be entitled to all privileges and immunities of citizens in the several States." On the one hand, a citizen of the United States can never become a citizen of Kentucky; and on the other, a citizen of Illinois or Michigan is not recognized as a citizen of the United States. This is nullification up to the handle. It is the resuscitation of the South Carolina doctrine, or theory of the government as laid down in her ordinance of 1832. The Federal compact, as they term our national constitution, will not be, under the idea considered an union of the people of the several States in such manner as to make them one, but a confederation of sovereignties, whose citizens are alien to each other, and only connected through their several State governments. To be a citizen of the United States will mean nothing, since each and every State in the Union can deprive such of every right and franchise which marks citizenship, or makes it valuable. If Mr. Davis can declare, by his State constitution, naturalized citizens of the United States for ever incapable of office or of suffrage in Kentucky, because they were not born in the United States, he can declare, with equal right, that a citizen of the United States, born in Ohio or Massachusetts, should never vote at the polls, or be eligible to office in Kentucky. He might declare that a citizen of Virginia, Carolinas, or any slave State, upon a residence of two years, might vote in Kentucky, but a citizen of any other State migrating to Kentucky should be disfranchised for ever. The doctrine denationalizes us, makes each State sovereign upon this subject within its borders, and makes the citizens of each State aliens to each other. There is no such thing as the people of the United States.

To refute this idea it would seem only necessary to indicate the consequences which flow inevitably from it. The confusions which will follow this effort to disturb the great principle of the constitution, and the laws of the Union made in pursuance of it in relation to naturalization, are not confined to their side of the question. If they succeed in repealing those laws, and overthrowing that principle, in pursuit of their favorite scheme of nationality, they will gain nothing by it, unless they carry and retain every State in the Union, an event not to be anticipated. Their opponents meet them on Mr. Davis' ground of the right of State interference with the subject. Many distinguished men of the democratic party contend that among the rights of the States, that to fix the qualifications of electors or voters for the members of the State legislature and all State officers, is unbounded and absolutely unqualified by any condition or exception. They say that the Constitution of the United States recognizes the right fully in the second section of the first article, where it fixes the qualifications of electors or voters for members of the House of Representatives in Congress. It is in these words: the electors in each State shall have the qualifications requisite for electors of the most numerous branch of the State Legislature." As the Federal constitution no where undertakes to fix or define the qualifications of voters for any officers in the State government, the argument is, that the whole matter is left to the unrestrained discretion of the State laws. If this be so, it is evident that a State, or any number of States, may have any number of citizens, who are themselves not citizens of the United States, not covered by the flag, or entitled to the protection of the United States government either in peace or war, not entitled to the rights or immunities of citizens in any other State, foreigners and aliens, according to the law of nations, and the constitution and laws of the United States, and if taken in arms in the service of the United States against the prince or government in whose allegiance they were born, liable to be hanged for treason, yet authorized, by virtue of State laws, to vote for members of Congress and President of the United States; officers whose powers extend far beyond the limits of any particular State; powers which bind for good or for evil the whole people of the United States, and challenge the obedience of the entire republic.

It matters not, whether the argument upon which this right is claimed by its advocates be well or ill founded. Should the naturalization laws be repealed, this right will be practically exercised in many States. The new States, the territories of the United States not yet organized into States, will be crowded with men of foreign birth; the repeal of the naturalization laws, will disfranchise almost the entire inhabitants, at least a large majority in some sections of the United States. All such will frame their own rules of naturalization, and will fix their own qualifications for electors. The scheme will rend the constitution to shreds and tatters. The purpose of the organization to revolutionize the domestic policy of the United States upon this subject is ridiculous, unless they intend to make it uniform. Have they thought of the means by which they are to enforce this system? They might find it easy enough to crush a few insurrectionary ebullitions of Irish turnpikers, but when they come to grapple with powerful and organized committees, States asserting their sovereign powers under the constitution, Know-Nothing mobs will not answer the purpose. They must put on armor of another sort and temper. They feel the difficulty of their situation, and contend stoutly that the laws of naturalization must be uniform. That if they repeal them, they must be repealed every where. They aver that a State can not naturalize a foreigner, but in the same breath maintain that a State can disfranchise or *unnaturalize* a citizen. They are inconsistent. The democrat argues that his position is in favor of liberty, and extends a right which the national laws are bound by the constitution, but refuse to provide for, but that the new party, by their doctrine of State interference, deprives a citizen of a franchise actually conferred by the national authority. There seems to be at least more of liberality, more of the generous spirit of American freedom in the democratic position. I disagree entirely, and protest most solemnly against either doctrine. Differing in object, they are the same in principle. Nominated by no convention, representing no particular body of men, no one has the right to complain of me. My own nominee, and representing my own ideas, I am free to follow where ever my own free reasoning may lead. Sam, if he obtain a majority in both houses of Congress, and make a President who will sign the bill, has, in my judgment, a legal right under the constitution to pass an act repealing all the naturalization laws—and thereafter no one of foreign birth, not naturalized at the time of the passage of the act, can become an American citizen, and none but American citizens can constitutionally have a voice in selecting an American President, or an American Congress. A State can not pass an act of naturalization.

Perhaps a comparison of the articles of confederation upon this subject with the provisions of the federal constitution, and a reference to the cotemporaneous exposition of the latter, given by the ablest men of that day or of any day, may elucidate this matter, and place it beyond cavil or dispute. The fourth of the articles of confederation provides as follows:

The better to secure and perpetuate mutual friendship and intercourse among the people of the different States in this

Union, the *free inhabitants* of each of these states, paupers, vagabonds and fugitives from justice excepted, shall be entitled to all privileges and immunities *of free citizens*, in the several states, and *the people* of each state shall have free ingress and egress to and from any other state, and shall enjoy therein all the privileges of trade and commerce, etc." The federal constitution, as we have already seen, gives to Congress "the power to establish a uniform rule of naturalization throughout the United States," and declares further that "the citizens of each state shall be entitled to all privileges and immunities of citizens in the several states." In commenting upon this power of "naturalization" in No. 42 of the Federalist, in the close of that paper, Mr. Madison uses the following language.

"The dissimilarity in the rules of naturalization has long been remarked as a fault in our system, and as laying a foundation for intricate and delicate questions." Mr. Madison after quoting the article above, proceeds:

"There is a confusion of language here which is remarkable. Why the terms free inhabitants are used in one part of the article, *free citizens* in another, and *people* in another, or what was meant by superadding to 'all privileges and immunities of free citizens' the words 'all the privileges of trade and commerce,' can not easily be determined. It seems to be a construction scarcely avoidable however, that those who come under the denomination of *free inhabitants* of a state although not citizens of such state, are entitled in every other state to all the privileges of *free citizens* of the latter; that is, to greater privileges than they may be entitled to in their own states, so that it may be in the power of a particular state, or rather every state is laid under a necessity not only to confer the rights of citizenship in other states upon any whom it may admit to such rights within itself, but upon any whom it may allow to become inhabitants within its jurisdiction. But were an exposition of the term '*inhabitants*' to be admitted which would confine the stipulated privileges to citizens alone, the difficulty is diminished only, not removed.

The very improper power would still be retained by each state, of naturalizing aliens in every other state. In one state, residence for a short term, confers all the rights of citizenship; in another, qualifications of greater importance are required. An alien therefore legally incapacitated for certain rights in the latter, may, by previous residence, only in the former, elude his incapacity; and thus the law of one state be preposterously rendered paramount to the law of another, within the jurisdiction of the other. We owe it to mere casualty, that very serious embarrassments on this subject have been hitherto escaped. By the laws of several states, certain descriptions of aliens, who had rendered themselves obnoxious, were laid under interdicts inconsistent, not only with the rights of citizenship, but with the privileges of residence. What would have been the consequence, if such persons, by residence or otherwise, had acquired the character of citizens under the laws of another state, and then asserted their right as such, both to residence and citizenship, within the state proscribing them? Whatever the legal consequences might have been, other consequences would probably have resulted of too serious a nature not to be provided against. The new constitution has, accordingly, with great propriety, made provision against them, and all others proceeding from the defect of the confederation on this head, by authorizing the general government to establish a uniform rule of "naturalization throughout the United States." Nothing can be clearer than this. Before the adoption of the present constitution of the United States, each state had the right under the first articles of confederation to pass their own naturalization laws, which, of course were variant in the different states—this, coupled with the provision that the inhabitants or citizens of each state had the right of citizens in other states, produced the confusion so admirably delineated by Madison. To remedy which the Federal constitution gave exclusive power over the subject to the general government. The doctrine Mr. M. was combating would bring back all the confusion the constitution designed to obviate. If Illinois or Michigan, for instance, should confer upon a free inhabitant, an alien born, and not naturalized by the laws of the United States, the right of citizenship in Illinois, if such an one should remove to Kentucky, what would become of the provision "That the citizens of each state shall be entitled to all privileges?" etc. There is a different rule in Kentucky. An alien born can have no right of citizenship here. The constitution would be broken up.

But in the thirty-second number of the Federalist, Alexander Hamilton wrote thus: "An entire consolidation of the states into one complete national sovereignty, would imply an entire subordination of the parts; and whatever power might remain in them would be altogether dependent on the general will. But as the plan of the convention aims only at a partial union or consolidation, the state governments will clearly retain all the rights of sovereignty which they before had, and which are not by that act (the Federal constitution) exclusively delegated to the Union. This exclusive delegation, or rather this alienation of sovereignty, will only exist in three cases: 1st. Where the constitution, in express terms, grants an exclusive authority to the Union. 2d. Where it grants, in one instance, an authority to the Union, and, in another, prohibits the states from exercising the like authority. 3d. Where it grants an authority to the Union, to which a similar authority in the states would be absolutely and totally contradictory and repugnant." After giving examples of the two first cases put, of exclusive authority granted to the Union, Mr. Hamilton proceeds: "The third will be found in that clause which declares that Congress shall have power to establish a uniform rule of naturalization throughout the United States. This must certainly be exclusive," he adds, "because, if each state had power to prescribe a distinct rule, there could be no uniform rule." In the eightieth number of the Federalist, it is observed: "It may be esteemed the basis of the Union, that the citizens of each state shall be entitled to all the privileges and immunities of the several states." From the reason of the thing, and from these highest of all authorities, it is evident that this power is exclusively vested in the Union, and that the rule of naturalization must be uniform throughout all the states, or the Union is broken up at the basis. Nor does this reasoning, conclusive as it is, at all conflict with the right of a state to fix the qualifications of electors or voters within its limits. The qualification, when ascertained, must apply equally to all citizens of the United States. No citizen of the United States, (and in this respect, nor indeed in any respect, is there any distinction between the native and the naturalized,) having the legal qualifications, can be proscribed on account of the place of his birth. Nor, on the other hand, can any power short of the Union, Americanize an alien. In this way, and in this way alone, can the constitution be observed, and a uniform rule be established or preserved. In the quotation made from Mr. Madison, the power is shown to have been a necessary one. Unless it had been exerted, the existing confusions could not have been remedied. It is just as necessary now. If it be abandoned—if the national laws be repealed—the state governments will, from the necessities of their situation, and the nature of their population, be compelled to take it up. When the general government abdicates, or fails to exercise necessary powers, usurpation upon the part of the states is the inevitable, the absolutely necessary consequence.

The Federal Constitution designed evidently that none but *American citizens* should rule America. Its purpose was equally clear not to confine the rights of citizenship to those born in the United States. The high power of converting an alien into a citizen, of Americanizing a stranger by birth, was conferred exclusively upon the general government. An act nationalizing an individual, investing him with rights which the Constitution compels, in express terms, every state to respect, must needs be performed by the *national* government. No state could bind all the others by any separate act of its own. I have shown sufficiently the confusion which would inevitably follow — the unavoidable breaches which would be made in other parts of the constitution, if the several states should set up separate and different rules of naturalization.

The effort of Illinois or Michigan to admit persons, alien by the laws of the United States, to the rights of citizenship, and that made by Mr. Davis in Kentucky, to exclude American citizens in Kentucky from franchises which they must needs carry with them every where, to obliterate, by a state act, the stamp of nationality impressed upon them by the laws of the Union, are kindred errors, alike at war with the language of the constitution, the construction given to it by its wisest interpreters, the whole genius of our system, and the true idea of American nationality.

The right of expatriation—the right of a human being to throw off the involuntary and oppressive obligations imposed by the accident of birth within a particular jurisdiction, to shift his residence from one part of the globe to another, and by the spontaneous act of a full grown man to choose his country, is one of those American ideas which our fathers meant to establish and make practical by the institutions which they founded. The right to shift your allegiance is denied by the common law of England. *Nemo potest exuere patriam*—no one can throw off his country—is a maxim of that jurisprudence. A subject of the crown is one born within the king's legiance. Once a subject, always a subject, is the principle of the British law. The doctrine of the American constitution is different. Descended from men, who themselves had fled from oppression, the men of '76 completed the act of expatriation, by a declaration of independence and a forcible revolution. They framed a government upon which they conferred the power to convert aliens born into citizens, and to impose upon them exclusive and absolute allegiance, with the correlative duty of protection upon the part of the government, the common law to the contrary notwithstanding. In possession of a vast extent of fertile and unsettled land, the American fathers did not intend to close their door against further immigration. In the relative circumstances of the old and the new world, as to population and territory, they had sense enough to know that nature would press with irresistible force against any bar that artificial policy might attempt to raise. They sought not, therefore, to separate themselves from the human race—to surround themselves with an ocean of fire—to throw an impassable gulf between a republic so situated and the enslaved and suffering population of other countries. Considering such a policy to be as impossible in execution as it was merciless in design, they flung wide their gates. The influx of population from abroad was a fact impossible to prevent. How to deal with it was a practical question which they had to settle in their fundamental policy —*and they did* settle it by the fearless application of those principles which, in their declaration, they had proclaimed to be the birthright of mankind.

They believed with a deep and living faith in those principles. They had trusted their cause to them, they had founded their institutions upon them.

That political government among men derives its just powers from the consent of the governed was one of their *axioms.* They did not condescend to prove it by logic—they announced it as a truth self-evident to human reason, an essential element of human right, an indisputable postulate of freedom. From this they deduced their principle of representation in its largest sense.

The power claimed by the British parliament to tax the colonies was, as every one knows, the question which brought on the war of the revolution. The ground upon which the colonies denied the power was, that they were not represented in that parliament. They asserted the principle retrospectively, and contended that the colonies had always been independent of the British legislature, and such was the historical fact. In its grand extension, it embraces and distinctly recognizes the eternal truth, the basis of all liberty, that no legislation can justly bind, unless the subject of it consent to the law by himself or his representative. The principle is cardinal; it is absolutely inseparable from the American idea of civil liberty. Tear it away, and the idea and the fact—the principle and the liberty are gone.

From a profound policy, then, as well as an enlarged benevolence, (things which the truly wise have ever held to be identical,) they thought it safer, as well as more humane, to impart to the stranger all the blessings of freedom which they themselves enjoyed. An alien by birth, they determined to make him a citizen by adoption, and to bind him to the country of his choice by the strong cords of gratitude and affection, as well as interest. They did not think it either wise or safe to have a large number of foreigners always foreigners, in the bosom of a republic, always in full view of the most perfect civil liberty, yet deprived of its enjoyment; for liberty is an enjoyment as well as a right. To them it would be no republic. Excluded from office and from honor, with no voice in the councils, no power to hold real estate, no representation in the legislature of such rights as might remain to them, in what do persons thus situated differ from the subjects of an absolute despotism? They do differ in one, and that a most material circumstance.

Under the absolute government of a single person, whose will is the sole law, all below him are at least equal. It is some comfort to a man, if he be a slave, at least to feel and know that it is the common lot. The subjects of a single master are peers in servitude. Of all the forms of oppression, the most unbearable to human thought, yet the most irresponsible, insolent and irresistible, is the tyranny of an exclusively privileged class. Reason and experience, fact and theory, speculation and practice, agree in this, that the tyranny of caste over caste is the most corrupting to those above, the most crushing and intolerable to the heart and soul of those below, of any of the corrupting and crushing forms of tyranny heretofore known among men.

Our ancestors, therefore, did not mean to divide *American* society into horizontal strata, by a boundary line of religion and of blood, with those who had happened to be born in another part of the earth, and those of the Catholic religion, no matter where born, (these being of a faith so accursed that not even American birth and education could purify the taint,) safely stowed away below, while the favorites of heaven, the Protestants elect, securely seated on top, booted, spurred and mounted on the backs of the degraded class, might rule and ride a dominant and regnant party, armed with the exclusive rights of office and of suffrage—in other words, with power absolute and irresistible, save by arms.

They believed that a republic, founded upon the most perfect equality of rights among those subjected to its laws and government, was not only the most just and free, the most productive of happiness and improvement, the best calculated to develop the faculties, intellectual and moral, the most favorable to science and to virtue, but also that it was the most permanent and secure, whether from external force or from internal disorder. They believed in liberty sincerely, devoutly, without hypocrisy or doubt, as the fountain of all good things, as that which gives to the individual dignity and courage, to the state strength and grandeur, safety and permanence. Without it, in their judgment, there could be no patriotism, no love of country.

A state which reposes in the honest love of its citizens, a love founded in the private interest which each individual has in its preservation, is safer without revenue or arms, surrounded by a rampart of hearts, than an oppressive, unjust and unequal government, with all the guards and garrisons, the bayonets and fortresses which money, wrung by force from an unwilling and enslaved people, can build or buy.

Make the foreigner a citizen, and he enters upon the practical enjoyment of all the rights of other men. He is incorporated with the state, and feels himself a part of it. He loves it as his country in peace, he defends it with honor in war. Keep him a foreigner, and he hates you, as all those of a degraded caste loathe what is above them. He is a domestic enemy, ripe for revolution. If your enemy be his former master, and he fights for you in war, he fights with a halter round his neck. Captivity dooms him to the death of a felon. Your flag is not his flag, it does not cover him. In a land of liberty, he is a slave; in the home of his choice, he is a stranger; in peace, he has no civil rights; in war, no hopes of honor.

Without representation, our ancestors believed that there could be no civil liberty without an entire, total and permanent separation of the ecclesiastical state from the political, of the church from the civil government, of religion from the temporal power of the priest, no matter of what faith, and his dogmas, from the laws and the magistracy, there could be no religious liberty.

Our ancestors were not heathen or infidels. Devoted and Christian men, they believed that in founding a state without a religion, and in establishing perfect toleration, they were in fact establishing Christianity, and providing for the purity of the church and the extension of the gospel, according to its own free genius and the precepts of its founder. "My kingdom is not of this world," He said; and again, when speaking of the Jewish laws against adultery, he said, "Whoso looketh upon a woman to lust after her hath already committed adultery in his heart." It is to the heart and will that Christianity addresses itself, and seeks to reform human nature and purify human action by cleansing it at the fountain. When the church, in violation of the commands of its master, sought "to lift its mitered front" among the princes of the earth, and becoming a political establishment, aimed to extend and enforce the faith by compulsory regulation, the Almighty averted his face and his support far from it.

Never yet has Christianity leaned upon the arm of human government and force for support, that it has not been tainted and defiled by the alliance. Engaged in the struggle for wealth and power, embroiled in the passions and turmoil of earthly strife and mundane politics, the church abdicating her office, abandons her trust, and finally quits the conflict, with her holy vestments stained and polluted, her divine lineaments erased, and her just and appropriate influence overthrown.

The political weakness of the church constitutes its moral strength and grandeur.

Seeking no participation in the temporal power, coveting not the treasures of this world, she comes with a more commanding voice to soothe the passions in which she does not share, to arbitrate in the strifes to which she is no party.

When our constitutions bar the ministers of the gospel from political power, they do not seek so much to preserve the liberty of the state, as the proper dignity and purity of the church.

I perceive, gentlemen, that I am in the midst of the order of "Know-Nothings." You call yourselves the American Party." You have built a platform which you are pleased to call national. There is nothing national in it, nothing peculiar, nothing which distinguishes you from other parties or other persons, but the two principles of religious persecution, and the denial of the right of expatriation. These ideas are revolutionary and *anti-American.* You seek the overthrow of toleration, naturalization, and political equality among citizens, to tear away the threads which run like a fine tissue of gold through the whole web of our system, strings which are twisted with the very heart and life of our republic.

You say that you do not mean to interfere with the rights of conscience or any man's religious liberty, yet you make out a case against the Catholic which declares him necessarily an enemy of the state, the sworn subject of a foreign prince, a domestic traitor whose oath of allegiance to the state is a perjury, whose real master is the enemy of all human freedom, who is flooding this country with whole armies of priests and Jesuits, who wait but his orders and the coming hour of strength to overthrow the republic. You do not mean to persecute the Catholic, yet you charge him with designs and crimes against the state, springing necessarily from the nature of his religion, which would justify any extremity of violence, which would render his expulsion or extermination a wise, humane and necessary policy. There has been a time when the cry of popery and "popish plots" would lash the Anglo-Saxon mind to murder and to madness. Those days are long gone by even in England. The British government has expunged in the nineteenth century, her persecuting statutes. She has passed her Catholic emancipation act. The United States will not, rest assured she will not, clothe her young and buoyant limbs with the cast-off vestments of which even monarchy has grown ashamed. Every well-informed man knows that the tie between the Catholic laity or priesthood, and the Pope as spiritual head of the church, is not political. Every well informed man knows, that outside of the papal states in Italy, no Catholic owes any allegiance to the Pope as a temporal prince or potentate. He is at this time held on his throne by a foreign hand. He is protected against his own subjects by 8000 French bayonets.

No body in America is afraid of the Pope.

You say that the Catholics and the citizens of foreign birth are necessarily abolitionists. The history of parties will not bear out the assertion. Is the legislature of Massachusetts composed of men of foreign birth? Are the sixty-three preachers, members of that assembly, Catholic priests? Natives and Protestants every dog of them. Yet they have *nullified* the fugitive slave law. They are Know-Nothings also. They wish to proscribe the Catholic and the foreigner. With these men, the abolition of slavery is "the great idea" of the nineteenth century. They believe that to be the institution, which chiefly endangers "our nationality, our Protestant civilization, our Federal Union." How happens it that they should proscribe the Catholic and the naturalized citizen, if that class are with them in their great and paramount object? The fact is otherwise, and the history of parties proves it to be otherwise.

The whig party, under that name, exists no longer. The world, however, will see, rest assured they will, in "young Sam" nothing but a renewal of the old struggle for power, under a new name, and with new and dangerous principles. The true crime of the Catholics and the naturalized citizens is not that they seek to bring over to this country either the forms or the substance of despotism, either civil or religious. It is that they are too democratic. It is that they have defeated the whigs in their reiterated efforts to make a President and to control the government. Let the truth be told though the sky should fall. That party threw overboard such men as Webster and Fillmore. It was said that General Scott inclined to the Catholic religion. It was said that he had educated his daughters in a convent, that he had made an American army in Mexico kneel before a procession of priests, at the elevation of the host. He was nominated by a whig convention. The whig papers hurled their anathemas at General Pierce and New Hampshire, because that State had proscribed Catholics by law. General Scott was beaten. The overthrow was terrible. Curse the Catholics, they would not vote for a quasi Catholic candidate, when you offered him, and henceforth they should not be allowed to vote at all. It is the democratic party, not the Pope, which you hate and dread. The Constitution and the laws of the republic, heretofore deemed fundamental, do not work to please a defeated party, and they, following the beaten path of baffled factions, seek to change them.

Your new organization, gentlemen, seems to be strong, and to contain many elements of popular strength. Its novelty, the charm of secrecy, so well calculated to attract young and thoughtless men; the name of "American party," the cry of "Americans shall rule America," so gratifying to native pride, the promise of a dominant caste, so alluring to the tyrannic love of dominion, which, say what we will, forms at last an essential element of human nature; the invitation to all the Protestant sects, to unite in a crusade against a church, feeble and defenseless here, and odious, justly odious, to the Protestant—all these things seem ominous of success. The cry of abolitionism, too, against the wretched foreigner invited here by the generosity of our exsisting laws, is a word of fire in the South. The party sings a different tune in the North. There it is abolitionist, but still denounces the Catholic and the foreigner. They remember Polk, they remember that accursed acquisition of all the slave territory which lies south of the compromise line of 36° 30′, the annexation of

Texas, for which although rent from a Catholic power, the accursed papist and the foreigner still voted. They remember the Mexican war, in which, though waged against the same Catholic power from which Texas had been ravished, these accursed Catholics, the temporal subjects of the Pope, against their allegiance and the will and the interest of their real master, rushed by thousands to aid a *Protestant Republic* in conquering and ravaging a thoroughly Catholic State. The party North remembers the protective tariff so important to their gains, so dear to their avarice, and that these same Catholics and foreigners, aided to their utmost, the hateful slave states and the democrats to put it down. They adapt their music skillfully to the different tastes of their various audiences, but it is still the dirge to Catholics and foreigners. Although the worst and most powerful passions of the human mind are appealed to with tremendous emphasis, mark my words, it will not at all do. Many of their sworn soldiers will fall off from them. They may muster from the Protestant churches a small, a very small corps of ignorant fanatics, really frightened with the ghost of the Papacy, and a few bloody bigots anxious for the game of persecution, but the enlightened Christian clergy, understanding well the history of the church, and deeply imbued with the spirit of their master, will scorn the aid of the temporal power, and refuse to lean upon the secular arm for support to religion. The Bible and liberty, a free press and a free pulpit, are all they ask for the diffusion of the gospel. If this organization succeed, however, which may Heaven avert, they will convert the Catholic, native as well as foreigner, into a deadly and dangerous enemy of the republic, planted in the very bowels of the state. I mean not to threaten; God forbid; but men have been known to fight long and hard, and against desperate odds for their religion and their franchises. It is in vain for them to say that they mean not to disturb the vested rights conferred by naturalization, or to interfere forcibly with the Catholic mode of worship or their dogmas. The Catholics and the present naturalized foreigners know very well that it is hatred, deadly hatred of them, which has caused the new political organization. They see a political platform, in which there is no politics. War, commerce, negotiation, every thing that has been heretofore considered as appertaining to policy, either foreign or domestic, pretermitted. Hatred to them seems the only principle of the new party. Men, I say, have been known to fight for their religion and their franchises. John Huss was an obscure professor in a German University. The Emperor Sigismund when he burnt him at Constance, little dreamed that from the ashes of the friendless martyr there would rise the flames of a war in Bohemia which would shake the Austrian power and desolate Germany through long years of suffering and of blood. If the persecuting temper of the sixteenth century is to be renewed here, if American Protestantism so far forgets its genius and its mission, as to aid in rekindling the religious wars of that terrible period in quest of vengeance for the gone centuries of wrong, religion will suffer most. True christianity will vail her face and seek the shade, till better times. Men will be divided between a sullen and sordid fanaticism on the one side, and a scoffing infidelity on the other. Our national characteristics will be lost. American civilization will have changed its character. Our Federal Union will have sacrificed its distinctive traits, and we shall have exhibited a failure in the principles with which our government commenced its career, at which hell itself might exult in triumph.

THE END.

DR. ADAM CLARKE'S COMPLETE COMMENTARY ON THE OLD AND NEW TESTAMENTS.

With a portrait of the author, engraved expressly for this edition, accompanied with Maps, &c. Sheep, spring back, marble edge. The Commentary of Dr. Clarke is most deservedly popular, being not only a truly scientific and elaborately learned work, but it is also well adapted to family reading. Liberal in his views, benevolent in his character, Christian in his deportment, and deeply learned in Scripture lore, and all the science of the ancients as well as moderns, Dr. Clarke produced a work every way adapted to the wants of Bible students, preachers, and families. This work, although the largest published west of the mountains, is yet afforded at a price within the reach of all.

From the Nashville and Louisville Christian Advocate.

It would be difficult to find any contribution to Sacred Literature that has attained to a higher rank than the Commentaries of Dr. Adam Clarke. Whether regarded as a prodigy of human learning, or as a monument of what perseverance and industry, within the compass of a single lifetime, can accomplish, it will long continue to challenge the admiration of men as a work of unrivalled merit. It is a treasury of knowledge, in the accumulation of which, the author seems to have had no purpose in view but the apprehension of truth; not to sustain a particular creed, but the apprehension of truth for truth's own sake, restrained in the noble pursuits of no party tenets by no ardor for favorite dogmas. It is difficult to conceive of a complete library without this valuable work, and yet alone of itself, it affords to its possessor no mean variety of entertainment. Besides forming a moderate, but clear elucidation of the true meaning of the Sacred Word, it abounds with illustrations in science, the literature of all ages, and the history of all times and all countries; and as a lexicon for the exposition of abstruse phrases, of difficult terms, and the true genealogy of words of doubtful import, it immeasurably surpasses all similar works of the age.

"Of the merits of this work we need not speak, as its fame is as wide as the world of language in which it is written, and as imperishable as the name of its author; but of this edition we may say a word: It consists of four super-royal octavo volumes, two of the Old, and two of the New Testament. The type is clear, printed upon a beautiful white paper, of superior texture, bound in a strong and substantial manner, with marbled edges. The first volume of the Old Testament contains a superior steel engraving of the author. The last volume contains the usual copious alphabetical index, while the entire work is embellished with the usual number of tables and maps. Upon the whole, this is an excellent and cheap edition of this great work of this great man."

DR. ADAM CLARKE'S COMMENTARY ON THE NEW TESTAMENT.

2 vols. super-royal 8vo. Sheep, spring back, marble edge.

The increasing demand for Dr. Clarke's Commentary on the *New* Testament, has induced us to issue an edition on superior paper, large clear type, handsomely and substantially bound, containing 1978 pages, with a portrait of the author.

Of all "Defenders of the Faith," Dr. Adam Clarke is one of the most forcible in his arguments, clear in his elucidations, and pungent in his exhortations, as well as thoroughly accurate in scientific and historical researches, that have written on the Sacred Records.

THE COMPLETE WORKS OF THOMAS DICK, LL. D.

11 vols. in 2, containing An Essay on the Improvement of Society; The Philosophy of a Future State; The Philosophy of Religion; The Mental Illumination and Moral Improvement of Mankind; An Essay on the Sin and Evils of Covetousness; The Christian Philosopher, or Science and Religion; Celestial Scenery, illustrated; Siderial Heavens, Planets, &c.; The Practical Astronomer; The Solar System, its Wonders; The Atmosphere and Atmospherical Phenomena, &c. Illustrated with numerous engravings and a portrait. 2 vols. royal 8vo. Sheep, spring back and marble edge.

This edition is printed from entirely new plates, containing the recent revisions of the author, and is the only COMPLETE *edition published in the United States.*

The works of Dr. Dick are so well known and appreciated, (being such as should be in the possession of every family and made the daily study of its members, old and young,) that the attempt to praise them would be like gilding fine gold.

It has been the endeavor of the publishers to get up this edition in a style worthy of their merit; and they flatter themselves that they have succeeded in so doing, as to paper, typography, and binding of the work, neither of which can be surpassed at the East or West.

From the Presbyterian Review, Edinburg.

DICK'S WORKS.—Those who read at all, know both the name of Dr. Dick and the work itself, now reprinted. It has long found acceptance with the public.

From the Wesleyan Associated Magazine, London.

We hail this remarkably cheap and greatly improved edition of Dr. Dick's admirable and highly popular Works. It is a real love to the millions to be able to purchase such an excellent work for so inconsiderable a cost. We earnestly recommend this work to all our readers, and especially to all who desire to store their minds with general information.

From the Presbyterian of the West.

Eleven different works are embraced in these volumes, making it an edition full and complete. The range of subjects embraced in these several essays and scientific treatises, is varied, are all highly important and of practical utility to mankind generally. These characteristics of Dr. Dick's writings, while they render them permanently valuable, insure for them also a wide circulation among all classes of readers.

From the Cincinnati Gazette.

The best recommendation which can be given of Dr. Dick's Works, is the great popularity they have enjoyed, and the numerous editions of them, collected and separate, which have been published in England and America. Messrs. Applegate & Co. are deserving of much praise for the tasteful and handsome style in which they have issued the work, and at such a price as to be within the reach of all.

From the Central Watchman.

Dr. Dick's works have filled a place occupied by no others, and have presented the great facts of nature and the scientific movements and discoveries of the present age, in a manner at once both pleasing and instructive. They should have a place in every family library, and be read by all.

THE SPECTATOR.

With Biographical Notices of its Contributors. 1 vol., royal 8vo., 750 pages, with a portrait of Addison. Sheep, spring back, marble edge.

There is no work in the English language that has been more generally read, approved, and appreciated than THE SPECTATOR. It is a work that can be perused by persons of all classes and conditions of society with equal pleasure and profit. Of all the writings of Addison, the Spectator is the most suited to general reading; in the style of its composition and purity of dictum it is unsurpassed, and it has ever stood in the first rank among the English classics. Beside general notings of the state of English society in all its phases, at the time and anterior to that of writing, it inculcates sage maxims, morals, and advice, applicable at all times. It is bound in library style, corresponding with our Dick, Rollin, &c.

From the Central Christian Herald.

One hundred and forty years ago, when there were no daily newspapers nor periodicals, nor cheap fictions for the people, the Spectator had a daily circulation in England. It was witty, pithy, tasteful, and at times vigorous, and lashed the vices and follies of the age, and inculcated many useful lessons which would have been disregarded from more serious sources. It was widely popular. It contains some very excellent writing, not in the spasmodic, moon-struck style of the fine writing of the present day, but in a free, graceful, and flowing manner. It used to be considered essential to a good style and a knowledge of Belles-Lettres to have studied the Spectator, and we are certain our age is not wise in the selection of some of the substitutes which are used in its stead. It should yet be a parlor volume, which should be read with great profit.

But we do not design to criticise the book, but have prefixed these few facts, for the information of our readers, to a notice of a new edition of the work by Messrs. Applegate & Co. It is entirely of Cincinnati manufacture, and is in a style very creditable to the enterprising house which has brought it out.

From the Cincinnati Commercial.

Applegate & Co., 43 Main street, have just published, in a handsome octavo volume of 750 pages, one of the very best classics in our language. It would be superfluous at this day to write a line in commendation of this work. The writings of Addison are imperishable and will continue to charm youth and age while language lasts.

From the Cincinnati Gazette.

It is a source of general satisfaction to hear of the republication of a work of such standard merit as the Spectator. In these days, when the press teems with the issue of ephemeral publications, to subserve the purpose of an hour, to enlist momentary attention, and leave no improvement on the mind, or impression on the heart—it is a cause of congratulation to see, now and then, coming from the press such works as this; to last as it should, so long as a pure taste is cultivated or esteemed.

From the Cincinnati Daily Times.

Criticism upon the literary merits of the Spectator would be rather late and superfluous at the present time. Steele, Addison, and Swift are above criticism. This edition is gotten up in style and form that will make it peculiarly acceptable to the admirers of English literature. It is bound in one volume, with copious notes of the contributors prefixed. The type is clear and elegant, the paper good, and the binding excellently suitable for the library.

PLUTARCH'S LIVES.

With Historical and Critical Notes, and a LIFE OF PLUTARCH. Illustrated with a portrait. 1 vol., 8vo. Sheep, spring back, marbled edge.

This edition has been carefully revised and corrected, and is printed upon entirely new plates, stereotyped by ourselves, to correspond with our library edition of Dick's Works, &c.

From the Nashville and Louisville Christian Advocate.

PLUTARCH'S LIVES.—This great work, to which has long since been awarded the first honors of literature, is now published complete in one volume by Messrs Applegate & Co., of Cincinnati, and offered at so low a price as to place it within the reach of all. This is a desideratum, especially in this age of "many books." Next in importance to a thorough knowledge of history, and in many respects fully equal to it, is the study of well authenticated biography. For this valuable purpose, we know of no work extant superior to the fifty lives of Plutarch. It is a rare magazine of literary and biographical knowledge. The eminent men whose lives compose this work, constitute almost the entire of that galaxy of greatness and brightness, which stretches across the horizon of the distant past, and casts upon the present time a mild and steady luster. Many of them are among the most illustrious of the earth.

From the Ladies' Repository.

No words of criticism, or of eulogy, need be spent on Plutarch's Lives. Every body knows it to be the most popular book of biographies now extant in any known language. It has been more read, by the youth of all nations, for the last four or five centuries in particular, than any ever written. It has done more good, in its way, and has been the means of forming more sublime resolutions, and even more sublime characters, than any other work with which we are acquainted, except the Bible. It is a better piece of property for a young man to own, than an eighty acre lot in the Mississippi Valley, or many hundred dollars in current money. We would rather leave it as a legacy to a son, had we to make the choice, than any moderate amount of property, if we were certain he would read it. There are probably but few really great men now living, that have not been largely indebted to it for their early aspirations, in consequence of which they have achieved their greatness. It is a magnificent octavo, on solid and clear paper, well bound, and, in every way, neatly and substantially executed. Most sincerely do we commend it, again and again, to the reading public.

From Cist's Advertiser.

A beautiful edition of Plutarch's Lives, published by Applegate & Co., has been laid on our table. Who has not read Plutarch? and what individual of any force of character has not made the "Lives" his study? It was one of Napoleon's favorite books, and doubtless had its full share in forming his character, and fitting him for that splendid career of his, which has had no precedent heretofore, as it will hardly find a parallel hereafter. This volume is handsomely gotten up, and in every respect creditable to the good taste and enterprise of this firm.

From the Indiana State Sentinel.

Of the literary merit of this work, it is unnecessary to speak. Every school boy knows "Plutarch's Lives" is essential in every well-informed man's library. In the language of the translator of the present edition, "if the merits of a work may be estimated from the universality of its reception, Plutarch's Lives have a claim to the first honors of literature. No book has been more generally sought after, or read with greater avidity."

ROLLIN'S ANCIENT HISTORY.

The Ancient History of the Carthagenians, Assyrians, Babylonians, Medes and Persians, Grecians and Macedonians, including a History of the Arts and Sciences of the Ancients, with a Life of the Author. 2 vols., royal 8vo. Sheep, spring back, marble edge.

One of the most complete and impartial works ever published. It takes us back to early days, and makes us live and think with the men of by-gone centuries. It spreads out to us in a pleasant and interesting style, not only the events which characterized the early ages, but the inner world of thought and feeling, as it swayed the leading minds of the times. No library is complete without Rollin's Ancient History.

From the Western Recorder.

A new edition of Rollin's Ancient History has just been issued by Applegate & Co. The value and importance of this work are universally acknowledged. Every private library is deficient without it; and it is now furnished at so cheap a rate, that every family should have it. It should be placed in the hands of all our youth, as infinitely more instructive and useful than the thousand and one trashy publications with which the country is deluged, and which are so apt to vitiate the taste, and ruin the minds of young readers. One more word in behalf of this new edition of Rollin: It may not be generally known, that in previous English editions a large and interesting portion of the work has been suppressed. The deficiencies are here supplied and restored from the French editions, giving the copy of Messrs. Applegate & Co. a superiority over previous English editions.

From the Springfield Republic.

A superb edition of this indispensable text and reference book is published by Messrs. Applegate & Co. The work in this form has been for some years before the public, and is the best and most complete edition published. The work is comprised in two volumes of about 600 pages each, containing the prefaces of Rollin and the "History of the Arts and Sciences of the Ancients," which have been omitted in most American editions.

From the Western Christian Advocate.

The work is too well known, and has too long been a favorite to require any commendation from us. Though in some matters more recent investigations have led to conclusions different from those of the Author, yet his general accuracy is unquestionable

---

From the Methodist Protestant, Baltimore.

This work is too well known as standard—as necessary to the completion of every gentleman's library—that any extended notice of it would be folly on our part. We have named it for the purpose of calling the attention of our readers to the beautiful edition issued by the enterprising house of Messrs. Applegate & Co. Those who have seen their edition of Dick's Works, Plutarch's Lives, Spectator, &c., &c., may form a correct idea of the style. We call it a beautiful library edition. The paper is good, the type clear, the binding substantial, and the whole getting up just such as becomes standard works of this class.

MOSHEIM'S CHURCH HISTORY,

Ancient and Modern, from the birth of Christ to the Eighteenth Century, in which the Rise, Progress, and Variations of Church Power are considered in their connection with the state of Learning and Philosophy; and the Political History of Europe during that period, continued up to the present time, by CHARLES COOTE, LL. D. 806 pages, 1 vol., quarto, spring back, marbled edge.

From the Gospel Herald.

This edition forms the most splendid volume of Church History ever issued from the American press; is printed with large type, on elegant paper, and altogether forms the most accessible and imposing history of the Church that is before the public. The former editions of Mosheim have ever been objectionable in consequence of the amount of matter crowded into a single page. To do this, very small type were necessarily used, and the lines were so crowded, that the close and continued perusal of the work was very injurious to the eyes. This edition avoids all these evils, and we most heartily recommend it.

From the Masonic Review.

This great standard history of the Church from the birth of Christ, has just been issued in a new dress by the extensive publishing house of Applegate & Co. Nothing need be said by us in relation to the merits or reliability of Mosheim's History: it has long borne the approving seal of the Protestant world. It has become a standard work, and no public or private library is complete without it; nor can an individual be well posted in the history of the Christian Church for eighteen hundred years, without having carefully studied Mosheim. We wish, however, particularly to recommend the present edition. The pages are in large double columns; the type is large and very distinct, and the printing is admirable, on fine white paper. It is really a pleasure to read such print, and we recommend our friends to purchase this edition of this indispensable work.

From the Telescope, Dayton, O.

This work has been placed upon our table by the gentlemanly and enterprising publishers, and we are glad of an opportunity to introduce so beautiful an edition of this standard Church history to our readers. The work is printed on beautiful white paper, clear large type, and is bound in one handsome volume. No man ever sat down to read Mosheim in so pleasing a dress. What a treat is such an edition to one who has been studying this elegant work in small close print of other editions. Any one who has not an ecclesiastical history should secure a copy of this edition.

It is not necessary for us to say anything in relation to the merits of Mosheim's Church History. For judgment, taste, candor, moderation, simplicity, learning, accuracy, order, and comprehensiveness, it is unequaled. The author spared no pains to examine the original authors and "genuine sources of sacred history," and to scrutinize all the facts presented by the light of the "pure lamps of antiquity."

From Professor Wrightson.

Whatever book has a tendency to add to our knowledge of God, or the character or conduct of his true worshipers, or that points out the errors and mistakes of former generations, must have an elevating, expanding, and purifying influence on the human mind. Fully as important, however, is it that all the facts and phases of events should be exhibited with truthfulness, perspicuity, and vigor. To the Christian world, next to the golden Bible itself, in value, is an accurate, faithful, and life-like delineation of the rise and progress, the development and decline of the Christian Church in all its varieties of sects and denominations, their tenets, doctrines, manners, customs, and government. Such a work is Mosheim's Ecclesiastical History. Like "Rollin's History of the Ancients," it is the standard, and is too well known to need a word of comment.

GATHERED TREASURES FROM THE MINES OF LITERATURE.

Containing Tales, Sketches, Anecdotes, and Gems of Thought, Literary, Moral, Pleasing and Instructive. Illustrated with steel plates. 1 vol. octavo. Embossed.

To furnish a volume of miscellaneous literature both pleasing and instructive, has been the object of the editor in compiling this work, as well as to supply, to some extent, at least, the place that is now occupied by publications which few will deny are of a questionable moral tendency.

It has been the intention to make this volume a suitable traveling and fireside companion, profitably engaging the leisure moments of the former, and adding an additional charm to the cheerful glow of the latter; to blend amusement with instruction, pleasure with profit, and to present an extensive garden of vigorous and useful plants, and beautiful and fragrant flowers, among which, perchance, there may be a few of inferior worth, though none of utter inutility. While it is not exclusively a religious work, yet it contains no article that may not be read by the most devoted Christian.

From the Intelligencer.

This may emphatically be termed a reading age. Knowledge is increasing in a wonderful ratio. The night of ignorance is fast receding, and the dawn of a better and brighter day is before the world. The demand for literature is almost universal. The people will read and investigate for themselves. How important, then, to place within their reach such books that will instruct the mind, cheer the heart, and improve the understanding—books that are rich in the three grand departments of human knowledge—literature, morals, and religion. Such a book is "Gathered Treasures." We can cheerfully recommend it to all.

From the Cincinnati Daily Times.

This is certainly a book of rare merit, and well calculated for a rapid and general circulation. Its contents present an extensive variety of subjects, and these not only carefully but judiciously selected, and arranged in appropriate departments. Its contents have been highly spoken of by men of distinguished literary acumen, both editors and ministers of various Christian denominations. We cheerfully recommend it.

From the Cincinnati Temperance Organ.

A book of general merit, diversified, yet truly rich and valuable in its interests; thrilling in many of its incidents; instructive in principle, and strictly moral in its tendency. It is well calculated for a family book, one that a father need not be afraid to place in the hands of his children. We hope it will meet with an extensive sale.

GATHERED TREASURES FROM THE MINES OF LITERATURE.—"One of the most interesting everyday books ever published. Like the Spectator, it may be perused again and again, and yet afford something to interest and amuse the reader. Its varied and choice selections of whatever is beautiful or witty, startling or amusing, can not fail to afford rich enjoyment to minds of every character, and a pleasant relaxation from more severe and vigorous reading.'

GATHERED TREASURES.—"A choice collection of short and interesting articles, comprising selections from the ablest authors. Unlike voluminous works, its varied selections afford amusement for a leisure moment, or entertainment for a winter evening. It is alike a companion for the railroad car, the library and parlor, and never fails to interest its reader."

NOTES ON THE TWENTY-FIVE ARTICLES OF RELIGION,

As received and taught by Methodists in the United States,

In which the doctrines are carefully considered and supported by the testimony of the Holy Scriptures. By Rev. A. A. JIMESON, M. D. 12mo, embossed cloth.

This book contains a clear exposition of the doctrines of the Articles, and of the errors against which the Articles were directed, written in a popular style, and divided into sections, for the purpose of presenting each doctrine and its opposite error in the most prominent manner.

From Rev. John Miller.

It is a book for the Methodist and for the age—a religious *multum in parvo*—combining sound theology with practical religion. It should be found in every Methodist family.

From the Western Christian Advocate.

The author intended this volume for the benefit of the "three great divisions of American Methodism, the Methodist Episcopal Church, the Methodist Protestant Church, and the Methodist Episcopal Church South." The articles are taken up one by one, and their contents analyzed, explained, and defended with much ability. The style is clear and forcible; the illustrations are just, the arguments sound. The author has performed a good and useful work for all the Methodist bodies in the world; as his book will furnish a very satisfactory exposition of the leading doctrines of Methodism. We cordially recommend Mr. Jimeson's volume to the perusal of our readers, as well as to all Christian people, whether ministers or laymen.

DICK'S THEOLOGY.

Lectures on Theology. By the late Rev. JOHN DICK, D. D., Minister of the United Associate Congregation, Grayfrier, Glasgow, and Professor of Theology to the United Session Church. Published under the superintendence of his Son. With a Biographical Introduction. By an American Editor. With a Steel Portrait of Dr. Dick.

1 vol. Imperial Octavo, sheep, marble edge, spring back................
Do do do do do embossed do ....
Do do do do half antique do ....
Do do do do Imt. Turkey full gilt do ....
Do do do do Super. Turkey, beveled sides, full gilt.......

From the Christian Instructor.

"These Lectures were read by their Author in the discharge of his professional functions: they embody the substance of his Essay on Inspiration, and the peculiar views on Church Government, which he advanced in his Lectures on the Acts.

"The Lectures throughout, display an extensive and most accurate knowledge of the great variety of important topics which come before him. His system has all the advantages of fair proportion; there is nothing neglected, and nothing overloaded. His taste is correct and pure, even to severity; nothing is admitted either in language or in matter, that can not establish the most indisputable right to be so."

From the Christian Journal.

"We recommend this work in the very strongest terms to the Biblical student. It is, as a whole, superior to any other system of theology in our language. As an elementary book, especially fitted for those who are commencing the study of divinity, it is unrivaled."

From Professor Wrightson.

"This is a handsome octavo work of 600 pages, published in uniform style with the other valuable standard works of Applegate & Co. It contains a thorough and enlightened view of Christian Theology, in which the author presents in beautiful, simple, and forcible style, the evidences of authenticity of the sacred text, the existence and attributes of the Deity, the one only and unchangeable God. The fall of man, and its consequences, and the restoration of the fallen through intercession of the Crucified. It is one of the most simple and yet elevated of works devoted to sacred subjects."

METHODISM EXPLAINED AND DEFENDED.

By Rev. John S. Inskip. 12mo., embossed cloth.

From the Herald and Journal.

We have read this book with no ordinary interest, and, on the whole, rejoice in its appearance for several reasons—*First,* It is a concise and powerful defense of every essential feature of Methodism, now-a-days so much assailed by press and pulpit. *Second,* The general plan and character of the work are such, that it will be read and appreciated by the great masses of our people who are not familiar with more extended and elaborate works. *Third,* It is highly conservative and practical in its tendencies, and will eminently tend to create liberal views and mutual concession between the ministry and laity for the *good of the whole*—a feature in our economy never to be overlooked. *Fourth,* This work is not written to advocate some local or neighborhood prejudice; neither to confute some particular heresy or assault; but its views are peculiarly denominational and comprehensive, indicating the careful and wide observation of the author—free from bigotry and narrow prejudice.

From the Springfield Republic.

We have read this new work of Rev. J. S. Inskip with great pleasure and profit. It in very truth explains and defends Methodism, and, as the introduction (written by another,) says, "its pages cover nearly the whole field of controversy in regard to the polity of the Methodist Church, and present a clear and candid exposition of Methodism in a clear and systematic form, and highly argumentative style. It is a book for the times, and should be read by all who desire to become more intimately acquainted with the Methodist economy. It excels all other works of its class in the arrangement and judicious treatment of its subject." It has evidently been written with great prudence and care in reference to the facts and evidences on which the arguments are predicated. This book will doubtless be of general service to the Church, and an instrument of great good.

CHRISTIANITY,

As Exemplified in the Conduct of its Sincere Professors.

By Rev. W. Secker. This is a book of rare merit, full of thought-exciting topics, and is particularly valuable as an aid to Christian devotion. 12mo., embossed cloth.

From the Madison Courier.

This is a reprint of a quaint old English book, entitled "The None-Such Professor in his Meridian Splendor." It abounds in pithy sentences and suggestive expressions, and should be read by such as wish to put a spur to thought.

From Rev. N. Summerbell.

This work can be best understood by presenting an outline of its contents:

Part First, answers why Christians should do more than others.

Part Second, considers what Christians do more than others.

Part Third, shows that the Scriptures require of Christians singular principles, or to do more than others.

Part Fourth, imparts instruction to those who wish to do more than others.

This work is peculiarly free from sectarianism, and breathes out, in short but balanced sentences, the most Heavenly devotion and Christian piety, while probing the religious character with the most searching scrutiny.

SACRED LITERATURE OF THE LORD'S PRAYER.

In which the terms are defined, and the text carefully considered. 12mo., cloth.

"This is a volume of rare excellence, written in the author's usual style of great beauty and elegance. It sparkles with gems of elevated thought, and abounds in the most happy illustrations of the great philosophical bearings of the several petitions of the Lord's Prayer on the general system of Revealed Religion, while their philosophy is very forcibly applied to the various duties of practical Christianity.

"The introductory chapter is a learned and patient research into the real origin and history of the use of this prayer, while the succeeding chapters can not fail both to instruct the head and improve the heart. We have not read a more interesting book for many years, and can most cordially recommend it to every lover of chaste theological literature. It is a 12mo., gotten up in the best style of the art."

RELIGIOUS COURTSHIP;

Or, Marriage on Christian Principles.

By DANIEL DEFOE, Author of "Robinson Crusoe."

"Who has not read Robinson Crusoe? It has fascinated every boy, and stimulated his first taste for reading. Defoe has been equally happy in this present work, in interesting those of riper years, at an age (Shakspeare's age of the lover) when the mind is peculiarly susceptible of impressions. Although but few copies of this work have ever been circulated in America, yet it has a popularity in England coëxtensive with his unparalleled 'Crusoe.'"

From the Masonic Review.

Applegate & Co., have just issued, in their usual good style, a new edition of this old and valuable work by Defoe. It treats of marriage on Christian principles, and is designed as a guide in the selection of a partner for life. Young persons should by all means read it, and with particular attention, for it furnishes important directions relative to the most important act of life.

Home for the Million; or Gravel Wall Buildings.—This is one of the most desirable book published, for all who contemplate erecting dwellings or outhouses, as the cost is not over one-third that of brick or frame, and quite as durable. Illustrated with numerous plans, and a cut of the author's residence, with full directions, that every man may be his own builder.

The Camp Meeting and Sabbath School Chorister—A neat Sunday School Hymn Book.

Sacred Melodeon.—A Collection of Revival Hymns. By Rev. R. M. DALBY.

Nightingale; or Normal School Singer.—Designed for Schools, Home Circle, and Private Practice. On a Mathematically constructed System of Notation. By A. D. FILLMORE, author of Universal Musician, Christian Psalmist, etc.

Lectures and Sermons. By Rev. F. G. BLACK, of the Cumberland Presbyterian Church. 12mo., embossed cloth.

Western Adventure. By MCCLUNG. Illustrated.

American Church Harp.—A Choice Selection of Hymns and Tunes adapted to all Christian Churches, Singing Schools, and Private Families. By Rev. W. RHINEHART. 12mo., half morocco,

FARMER'S HAND-BOOK.

By JOSIAH T. MARSHALL, author of "Emigrant's True Guide." 12mo., cloth, 500 pages.

The publishers are gratified that they are enabled to satisfy the universal demand for a volume which comprises a mass of superior material, derived from the most authentic sources and protracted research.

The contents of the "Farmer's Hand-Book" can be accurately known and duly estimated only by a recurrence to the Index of Subjects, which occupies *twenty-four* columns, comprising about *fifteen hundred* different points of information respecting the management of a Farm, from the first purchase and clearing of the land, to all its extensive details and departments. The necessary conveniences, the household economy, the care of the animals, the preservation of domestic health, the cultivation of fruits with the science and taste of the arborist, and the production of the most advantageous articles for sale, are all displayed in a plain, instructive, and most satisfactory manner, adapted peculiarly to the classes of citizens for whose use and benefit the work is specially designed. Besides a general outline of the Constitution, with the Naturalization and Pre-emption Laws of the United States, there is appended a Miscellany of 120 pages, including a rich variety of advice, hints, and rules, the study and knowledge of which will unspeakably promote both the comfort and welfare of all who adopt and practice them.

The publishers are assured that the commendations which the "Farmer's Hand-book" has received, are fully merited; and they respectfully submit the work to Agriculturists, in the full conviction that the Farmer or the Emigrant, in any part of the country, will derive numberless blessings and improvements from his acquaintance with Mr. Marshall's manual.

LORENZO DOW'S COMPLETE WORKS.

THE dealings of GOD, MAN, AND THE DEVIL, as exemplified in the LIFE, EXPERIENCE, AND TRAVELS of **LORENZO DOW**, in a period of over half a century, together with his POLEMIC AND MISCELLANEOUS WRITINGS COMPLETE.

To which is added—

The Vicissitudes of Life,—By PEGGY DOW.

With an Introductory Essay,—By JOHN DOWLING, D. D., of New York. Making the best and only complete edition published. 1 vol, octavo, Library binding. Do., do., Embossed. Spring back, marble edge.

FAMILY TREASURY,

Of Western Literature, Science, and Art. Illustrated with Steel Plates. 8vo., cloth, gilt sides and back.

This work most happily blends valuable information and sound morality, with the gratification of a literary and imaginative taste. Its pages abound in sketches of history, illustrations of local interest, vivid portraitures of virtuous life, and occasional disquisitions and reviews.

WEBB'S FREEMASON'S MONITOR!

By Thomas Smith Webb, Past Grand Master, etc.

A New Edition, printed on fine paper, large and clear type, beautifully and symbolically illustrated, containing all the Degrees, from Entered Apprentice to Knights of Malta, together with a sketch of the Origin of Masonry, Government of the Fraternity, Ceremony of Opening and Closing the Lodge, with full directions for Instituting and Installing all Masonic bodies, to which is added—

A Monitor of the Ancient and Accepted Rite,

Containing ample Illustrations of all the Grades, from Secret Master to Sovereign Grand Inspector-General, including the series of Eleven Grades, known as the **INEFFABLE DEGREES**, arranged according to the work practiced under the jurisdiction of the SUPREME COUNCIL OF THE 33d DEGREE. By E. T. CARSON, Sov. G. Com. Ohio G. Consistory of P. R. S. 32°. 1 vol., 12mo., cloth, 420 pages. $1.00.

A Voice from all the Masonic bodies in Cincinnati.

CINCINNATI, June 1st, 1858.

GENTLEMEN:—Having carefully examined your new edition of "Webb's Freemason's Monitor," we find it to correspond with the System of work as now adopted in all the Masonic bodies in the United States, and we take great pleasure in recommending it to the Craft throughout the country, as being the most useful and well-arranged practical Manual of Freemasonry that we have yet seen.

D. H. MEARS, W. M. of N. C. Harmony Lodge, No. 2.
WILLIAM SEE, W. M. of Miami Lodge, No. 46.
J. M. PARKS, W. M. of Lafayette Lodge, No. 81.
HOWARD MATTHEWS, W. M. of Cincinnati Lodge, No. 133.
C. MOORE, W. M. of McMillan Lodge, No. 141.
E. T. CARSON, W. M. of Cynthia Lodge, No. 155.
ANDREW PFIRRMANN, W. M. of Hanselmann Lodge, No. 208.
WM. C. MIDDLETON, H. P. of Cincinnati R. A. Chapter, No. 2.
CHAS. BROWN, H. P. of McMillan R. A. Chapter, No. 19.
C. F. HANSELMANN, G. C. of Cincinnati Encampment, No. 3.

MESSRS. APPLEGATE & CO.

From the Grand Master of Ohio.

* * * The admirable arrangement of the emblems of Masonry in your edition of Webb's Freemason's Monitor makes the work complete, and I am much pleased to say it meets my entire approval. Accept my thanks for the beautiful copy sent me, which I assure you I prize highly. HORACE M. STOKES, Grand Master of Ohio.

GRAND LODGE OF INDIANA, May 24, 1858.

GENTLEMEN:—I have examined with care your late edition of "Webb's Masonic Monitor," and freely pronounce it to be the best book of the kind extant. The language, charges, &c., I have used in all my Masonic work, and would not change under any circumstances. I freely recommend the "Monitor" to be adopted and used in my jurisdiction.
SOLOMON P. BAYLESS, Grand Master of Masons in Indiana.

* * * I most cheerfully award to it my testimony, as being the best hand-book for the Masonic student now extant, and invaluable to the officers of the Lodge. JOHN M. PARKS, Grand Puissant of the Grand Council of Select Masters of the State of Ohio.

From Distinguished Officers of 32°.

* * * It is really the only complete MONITOR of the Rite in existence. As presiding officer of the Lodge of Perfection and Chapter of Rose Croix, in this City [Cincinnati], I have long been in need, for practical use, of just this work, and I thank Brother Carson, most heartily, for the valuable service he has rendered us of the Scotch Rite, in preparing it. The work is arranged according to the system adopted in the Northern Jurisdiction of the United States, and the directions are so full and complete, as to leave nothing to be desired. Yours truly,
GEO. HOADLEY, 32°.

* * * The work must prove an acceptable offering to the Fraternity, as well from the superior excellence of its mechanical execution, as from the intrinsic merits of its contents; and every Mason should possess himself of a copy.
I am, with respect, yours truly, CALEB B. SMITH, Past Grand Master of Indiana, and Grand P. of Cincinnati Council of Royal and Select Masters

---

METHODIST FAMILY MANUAL.

By Rev. C. S. LOVELL. 12mo., embossed cloth. Containing the Doctrines and Moral Government of the Methodist Church, with Scripture proofs; accompanied with appropriate questions, to which is added a systematic plan for studying the Bible, rules for the government of a Christian family, and a brief catechism upon experimental religion.

This work supplies a want which has long been felt among the members of the Methodist Church. As a family manual, and aid to the means of grace and practical duties of Christianity, it is certainly a valuable work. It also contains the Discipline of the Church, with Scriptural proofs, and appropriate questions to each chapter. It is certainly an excellent book for religious instruction and edification. We most heartily commend it to the Methodist public, and hope it may have a wide circulation and be made a blessing to all.

TEMPERANCE MUSICIAN.

A choice selection of original and selected *Temperance Music*, arranged for one, two, three, or four voices, with an extensive variety of *Popular Temperance Songs*. 32mo.

From the Summit, (O.,) Beacon.

This is a neat volume, well printed, and well bound, containing 256 pages. It is the best collection of temperance songs and music we have seen. Were a few copies secured in every town in Ohio, in the hands of the warm-hearted friends of the Maine Law, an element of power and interest would be added to temperance meetings, and a stronger impulse given to the onward march of the cold water army.

From the Temperance Chart.

This will certainly become one of the most popular temperance song books which has been published in the country. We think it is, so far as we have examined, the best collection of songs we have seen. Some of them are exceedingly beautiful and affecting.

From the Cleveland Commercial.

This is a popular Temperance Song Book, designed for the people, and should be in every family. We can recommend it to the patronage of all our temperance friends, as the best temperance songster, with music attached, we have seen. The music in this work is set according to Harrison's Numeral System, for two reasons: First, because it is so simple and scientific that all the people can easily learn it. Second, it is difficult to set music in a book of this size and shape, except in numerals.

UNIVERSAL MUSICIAN.

By A. D. Fillmore, Author of Christian Psalmist, &c., containing all Systems of Notation. New Edition, enlarged.

The title, "Universal Musician," is adopted because the work is designed for everybody. The style of expression is in common plain English, so that it may be adapted to the capacities of all, instead of simply pleasing the fancy of the few, who are already thoroughly versed in science and literature.

Most of the music is written in Harrison's Numeral System of Notation, because it is the most intelligible of all the different systems extant; and is therefore better adapted to the wants of community. Music would be far better understood and appreciated by the people generally, if it were all written in this way. For it is more easily written, occupies less space, is more quickly learned, more clearly understood, is less liable to be forgotten, and will answer all common purposes better than any other. But the world is full of music, written in various systems, and the learner should acquire a knowledge of all the principal varieties of notation, so as to be able to read all music. To afford this knowledge to all, is the object of the present effort.

Poetry, which is calculated to please as well as instruct, has been carefully selected from many volumes already published, and from original compositions furnished expressly for this work. Much of the music is original, which is willingly submitted to the ordeal of public opinion. Some of it certainly possesses some merit, if we may judge from the avidity with which it is pilfered and offered to the public by some, would-be, authors.

SPEECHES AND WRITINGS OF HON. THOMAS F. MARSHALL.

As a popular Orator of unrivaled powers and a writer of unsurpassed ability, Mr. Marshall stands foremost among the prominent men of his day. The great reputation he has acquired both as a speaker and writer, his long and active identity with and complete knowledge of the political and social history of our country, have created a wide-spread desire to see his numerous speeches and writings, on various subjects, in a permanent form. We feel confident that any one who has heard Mr. Marshall speak or read his writings, will appreciate their power and admire their beauty.

To meet this desire and to add a valuable contribution to the standard literature of our own country, we have spared neither pains nor expense to prepare the work in the highest style of the art.

The work contains all of Mr. Marshall's finest efforts, since 1832. His able report on Banking and paper currency,—his speech against JOHN QUINCY ADAMS, in Congress,—his memorable Slavery Letters, the celebrated eulogy on RICHARD H. MENIFEE, the Louisville Journal letter, and his great TEMPERANCE SPEECH, will all be found in the work. Besides these, it contains his entire Old Guard articles, and many other productions of equal interest and ability.

1 vol. Octavo, with splendid Steel portrait of Mr. Marshall, Library binding.
do do do do do half Antique.

From the Frankfort (Ky.) Commonwealth.

It is not necessary to *puff* this work; it will be sought by every man of literary taste in the country. It will prove a valuable contribution to our standard literature, and the fame of the author will go down to posterity as the purest of our American classics.

From the Maysville (Ky.) Eagle.

The work contains all those famous creations of genius that have rendered Mr. Marshall so remarkable as an orator and a man of genius, and is decidedly one of the most interesting books that has ever been published.

From the Bowling Green (Ky.) Gazette.

The reputation which Mr. Marshall has acquired as an eloquent orator and forcible writer, render this volume the object of almost universal desire. As a popular orator he stands at the head of the class of American speakers, possessing great powers of elocution, ripe scholarship, and the highest order of intellect.

From the Louisville Journal.

We presume that very few persons will decline taking this work. It will be found exceedingly brilliant and powerful. It is the productien of one of the master minds of the nation. Remarkable as Mr. Marshall is with his humor and his wondrous flights of fancy, he is, we think, still more remarkable for his strong, deep sense and inexorable logic.

CHAIN OF SACRED WONDERS.

Or a connected view of Scripture Scenes and Incidents, from the Creation to the end of the last epoch. By Rev. S. A. LATTA, A. M., M. D. Illustrated with two steel plates, and a number of wood cuts. 1 vol. 8vo. cloth, marble edge.
do do do library style.
do do do embossed.
do do do half antique.

From the Cincinnati Daily Times.

The publishing house of Applegate & Co. is entitled to great praise for issuing so many good and really valuable books, and so little of what is aptly termed "literary trash." The largest work ever issued this side the Alleghanies, was from the press of Applegate & Co., Clark's Commentaries, in several massive volumes. Dick's works have also been issued in a large and handsome volume by the same publishers.

The volume mentioned above is a work full of good reading, by an accomplished and scholarly writer. It is well adapted to the Christian family circle, to Sabbath school and religious libraries. The various sketches are admirably conceived, and written in a style of simple purity which is very attractive. The design of the author is to attract the attention of youth to the Bible, and with that view he has endeavored to make his work an instrument of much good. It is, indeed, an excellent book.

www.ingramcontent.com/pod-product-compliance
Lightning Source LLC
LaVergne TN
LVHW020924110826
845150LV00004B/759

* 9 7 8 1 4 2 5 5 5 4 0 3 3 *